Trust, Risk and Uncertainty

Trust, Risk and Uncertainty

Edited by

Sean Watson
School of Sociology
University of the West of England

and

Anthony Moran
School of Social Sciences
La Trobe University

First published 2005 by
PALGRAVE MACMILLAN
Houndmills, Basingstoke, Hampshire RG21 6XS and
175 Fifth Avenue, New York, N. Y. 10010
Companies and representatives throughout the world

PALGRAVE MACMILLAN is the global academic imprint of the Palgrave Macmillan division of St. Martin's Press, LLC and of Palgrave Macmillan Ltd. Macmillan® is a registered trademark in the United States, United Kingdom and other countries. Palgrave is a registered trademark in the European Union and other countries.

ISBN-13: 978-1-4039-0699-1 hardback
ISBN-10: 1-4039-0699-8 hardback

This book is printed on paper suitable for recycling and made from fully managed and sustained forest sources.

A catalogue record for this book is available from the British Library.

Library of Congress Cataloging-in-Publication Data
Trust, risk, and uncertainly / edited by Sean Watson and Anthony Moran.
    p. cm.
  Includes bibliographical references and index.
  ISBN 1-4039-0699-8 (cloth)
    1. Social ethics. 2. Trust. 3. Risk. 4. Uncertainly. 5. Dilemma. 6. Ethics–Psychological aspects. I. Watson, Sean, 1962– II. Moran, Anthony.
HM665.T78 2005
302′.12–dc22   2004063291

10 9 8 7 6 5 4 3 2 1
14 13 12 11 10 09 08 07 06 05

Printed and bound in Great Britain by
Antony Rowe Ltd, Chippenham and Eastbourne

Contents

List of Tables and Figures

Acknowledgements

We would like to thank the two commissioning editors at Palgrave, initially Heather Gibson and later Briar Towers, who have overseen this book from its beginnings in 2002 to its final production. Many colleagues have helped in the production of this book. We would like to thank in particular Professor Anthony Elliott and the Centre for Critical Theory (CCT) at the University of the West of England, together with colleagues throughout the University who supported the activities of CCT. At different times, Alison Garrod, Liz Wood and Fiona Watt provided invaluable administrative support at CCT.

The Leverhulme Trust provided Anthony Moran with a research fellowship during 2001–2002 which enabled him to spend time at CCT and to begin initial work on the book. The Australian Research Council also provided a fellowship that enabled the work to be carried through. La Trobe University's School of Social Sciences, and in particular the Politics Program, has provided a generous and supportive intellectual environment during the last two years.

Notes on the Contributors

Stuart Allan is Reader in the School of Cultural Studies, University of the West of England. He is the author of *News Culture* (Open University Press, 1999; second edition, 2004) and *Media, Risk and Science* (Open University Press, 2002). Recent edited collections include *Environmental Risks and the Media* (Routledge, 2000), *Journalism After September 11* (Routledge, 2002), and *Reporting War: Journalism in Wartime* (Routledge, 2004).

Alison Anderson is Principal Lecturer in Sociology at the University of Plymouth. She is author of *Media, Culture and the Environment* (UCL Press, 1997) and co-editor of *The Changing Consumer* (Routledge, 2002). Recent articles on journalistic portrayals of environmental risks, genetics and war have appeared in *Science as Culture, Sociological Research Online, Knowledge, Technology and Society* and *New Genetics and Society*. She is currently conducting research on nanotechnology and news media production with Alan Petersen, Stuart Allan and Clare Wilkinson.

Alison Assiter is Professor of Feminist Theory and Assistant Vice Chancellor at the University of the West of England. She researches and teaches in feminist theory, social theory and political theory. She has written a number of books, including *Enlightened Women* (Routledge, 1996) and *Revisiting Universalism* (Palgrave, 2003).

Arthur Baxter is a Principal Lecturer in Sociology in the Faculty of Humanities, Languages and Social Sciences at the University of the West of England. His teaching and interests are in the sociology of education, and his research activities have recently focused on looking at the effects of a variety of Widening Participation initiatives on school students' plans in relation to the possibility of attending university, and on the impact of bursary schemes on students from low-income backgrounds. Recent publications have been in *Studies in Higher Education* and *Widening Participation and Lifelong Learning*.

Tony Bovaird is Professor of Strategy and Public Service Management at Bristol Business School, University of the West of England. He is chair of the Local and Regional Governance Research Network and directs the evaluation of the UK Local Government Modernisation Agenda on behalf of the Office of the Deputy Prime Minister. His most recent book is *Public Management and Governance* (Routledge, 2003), with Elke Loeffler.

Carolyn Britton is a Visiting Lecturer in the Faculty of Humanities, Languages and Social Sciences at the University of the West of England. Her research interests are in the area of gender and education. Her work has been published in journals such as *Gender and Education*, and *International Studies in Sociology of Education*, and she has co-edited two books, the most recent of which is *Millennial Visions: Feminisms into the C21* (Cardiff University Press, 2001).

Lita Crociani-Windland is a part-time lecturer and research student at the University of the West of England. She is also a director of the Group Relations Network West of England and member of the Centre for Critical Theory and Centre for Psychosocial Studies, UWE. Her research interests concern the sociology of affect, group relations and psychosocial studies, continental philosophy and comparative sociology. Her professional background includes Italian translation and Special Educational Needs education.

Harry Ferguson is Professor of Social Work at the University of the West of England. He previously held the Chair in Social Policy and Social Work at University College Dublin and also has worked at University College, Cork and Trinity College, Dublin. He has published widely in the areas of child abuse, protection, domestic violence, fatherhood and masculinities, and social work and social theory. His most recent book is *Protecting Children in Time: Child Abuse, Child Protection and the Consequences of Modernity* (Palgrave, 2004).

David Green is a Senior Lecturer in Sociology at the University of the West of England. He researches and teaches on contemporary magic and esotericism, comparative sociology, and poverty, social exclusion and inclusion. He has published widely in the fields of pagan and magic studies and social exclusion. He is currently engaged in research on Left Hand Path esotericism, relationships between modern magic and masculinity, and the sociology of Neo-Paganisms.

Paul Hoggett is Professor of Politics and Director of the Centre for Psycho-Social Studies at the University of the West of England. He is a psychoanalytic psychotherapist and co-edits the journal *Organisational and Social Dynamics*. His research focuses on the state/civil society relationship; his most recent book is *Emotional Life and the Politics of Welfare* (Macmillan, 2000).

Peter Jowers is a Senior Lecturer in Politics in the Faculty of Humanities, Languages and Social Sciences at the University of the West of England. He researches on critical theory, Derrida and development policy.

Elke Loeffler is Chief Executive of Governance International, a non-profit organisation working with local communities to improve the quality of governance processes and the local quality of life. She worked previously in the Public Management division of OECD and is currently a rapporteur for the EU Quality Conference 2004. Her most recent book is *Improving the Quality of East and West European Public Services* (Ashgate 2004), with Mirko Vintar).

Anthony Moran is an Australian Research Council research fellow in the Politics Programme, School of Social Sciences, La Trobe University, Australia. He researches and teaches on political culture, nationalism, settler/indigenous politics and the politics of race. His work has appeared in journals including *Ethnic and Racial Studies, Political Psychology* and *Free Associations*. His most recent book is *Australia: Nation, Belonging and Globalization* (Routledge, 2005).

Ajit Nayak is a Senior Lecturer in Strategy and International Business at the Bristol Business School, University of the West of England. His research and teaching revolves around three main areas. First, his interest focuses on creativity, innovation and change and its implications for businesses and managers. Second, his work examines ontological, epistemological and methodological issues in management. Third, his work explores issues of self and identity in the workplace.

Alan Petersen is Professor of Sociology of Health and Illness, School of Sociology, Politics and Law, University of Plymouth. His research spans the fields of the sociology of the new genetics, the study of sex/gender differences, sociology of the body, and sociology of risk. His recent publications include *The New Genetics and the Public's Health* (Routledge, 2002) (with Robin Bunton), and *Genetic Governance: Health, Risk and Ethics in the Biotech Era* (Routledge, 2004) (edited with Robin Bunton).

Simon Thompson is Senior Lecturer in Politics in the Faculty of Humanities, Languages and Social Sciences at the University of the West of England. He teaches on contemporary political theory and the history of political thought. His work has appeared in various journals including *Constellations, Contemporary Political Theory* and *Policy and Politics*. He is co-editor of *Richard Rorty: Critical Dialogues* (Polity, 2001) and his monograph *The Political Theory of Recognition* will be published by Polity in 2005.

Sean Watson is a Principal Lecturer and the Head of the School of Sociology in the Faculty of Humanities, Languages and Social Sciences at the University of the West of England. He researches on social theory, sociology of affect, complex systems, neurosociology and continental philosophy. His work has appeared in journals including *Body and Society*, *Radical Philosophy*, and *Social and Legal Studies*.

Leah Wild lived as a Traveller for ten years. She is currently completing her PhD on 'New Age' travelling cultures. She teaches sociology at the University of the West of England, and the University of Bath.

Introduction

Sean Watson and Anthony Moran

From the early 1990s onwards writers like Ulrich Beck and Anthony Giddens, among many others, have brought home to English-speaking audiences the new conditions of risk and uncertainty faced by everyone living in the contemporary world. Beck, with his pioneering *Risk Society* (1992), established the notion that risk is increasingly globalised and the unavoidable condition of late modern life. Giddens worked a nearby vein, emphasising in books such as *The Consequences of Modernity* (1990) the importance of risk and uncertainty as evermore pervasive aspects of the way that we live our lives, relying on expert systems and established levels of ontological security simply to get by. Writers like Zygmunt Bauman (1991) have emphasised the inevitability of, and the difficulties, dilemmas and resistances to, living with doubt, ambivalence and uncertainty (see also Beck, 1997).

More recently, related debates focusing not so much on risk and uncertainty, but more on the importance of trust, have emerged. These debates are concerned with the possible breakdown of forms of social capital and civil society which make trust possible, for example in the work of Robert Putnam (see Putnam 2001, 2002). Such breakdown, it is suggested, creates new conditions of uncertainty which have profound effects at the psychological, social, political and economic levels.

Most of the literature covering these related areas of trust, risk and uncertainty is highly theoretical in character. This makes it somewhat inaccessible for many readers. This book, while theoretically rigorous, explores these key debates through accounts of current empirical and theoretical applications. This is not a range of papers written by theorists speaking to one another at a high level of abstraction, but by active researchers, from a range of disciplines and specialisms, exploring the applicability of these theoretical speculations to their own areas of work. This grounded, multidisciplinary approach makes it possible for the reader to build up a picture of the dimensions and relevance of the themes of trust, risk and uncertainty in the late/postmodern world.

Trust, Risk and Uncertainty brings together scholars with established and developing international reputations, as well as several new writers, to focus on these 'risk society' debates. We combine theoretical sophistication with close-to-the-ground analysis and new research in the fields of philosophy, education, social policy, government, organisational studies, health and social care, sociology, and cultural and media studies. The empirically-grounded emphasis is, we believe, a real strength which should add to the book's appeal and accessibility, especially for graduate and undergraduate students. Included in the collection are contributions from a number of already distinguished academics and social commentators. Among these are: the feminist critic Alison Assiter, author of *Pornography, Feminism and the Individual* (1989), *Althusser and Feminism* (1990), *Enlightened Women* (1996) and *Revisiting Universalism* (2003); the sociologist Alan Petersen, author of many books on public health, the body and risk, including *The New Public Health* (1996) and *The New Genetics and the Public Health* (2002); the political theorist and psychotherapist Paul Hoggett, author of *Partisans in an Uncertain World* (1992) and *Emotional Life and the Politics of Welfare* (2000); the political philosopher Simon Thompson, author of *The Political Theory of Recognition: A Critical Introduction* (forthcoming), and co-editor of *Richard Rorty: Critial Dialogues* (2001); the cultural studies theorist Stuart Allan, author of *News Culture* (1999); the media studies expert, Alison Anderson, author of *Media, Culture and the Environment* (1997); the social work and social policy expert Harry Ferguson, author of *Protecting Children in Time* (2004); the public management and governance experts Tony Bovaird and Elke Loeffler, authors of *Public Management and Governance* (2003); and the political scientist Anthony Moran, author of *Australia: Nation, Belonging and Globalization* (2005).

The themes of 'trust', 'risk' and 'uncertainty' seem especially pertinent in the context of the current world crisis after September 11. We have encouraged our contributors to be liberal in their approach, however, not necessarily reflecting directly on the impact of September 11, but exploring the broader and longer-term implications of these themes as they arise and gain expression within diverse fields of intellectual inquiry. The book brings together contributions from a wide range of disciplines to the major themes of trust, risk and uncertainty. The remit given to our authors is to reflect on those themes and to write out of their own disciplines in a way that speaks to an audience of non-specialists. The rationale for the project is that the different disciplines have something unique to contribute to the 'risk society' debate, and that the themes resonate well beyond disciplinary boundaries.

The book is divided into three parts which deal more specifically with theoretical, philosophical and moral concerns and those concerned more directly with institutions, organisations, social policy and cultural issues. There are thirteen chapters, each by a different author or authors.

Part One: The theory and philosophy of trust, risk and uncertainty

This part comprises a range of theoretical and philosophical responses to the trust, risk and uncertainty debates in specific contexts. The first two chapters are particularly concerned with theoretical approaches to understanding the conditions of uncertainty in late/postmodernity. Chapters 3 and 4 are concerned with developing ethical responses to, and in the context of, such uncertainty.

In Chapter 1 Paul Hoggett deals with uncertainty. He begins from the recognition that there has been a renewed interest in human agency from both sides of the Atlantic. He deepens our understanding of the nature of such agency by developing a model that draws on the psychoanalytic work of Melanie Klein and Wilfred Bion, among other psychaoanalytic and philosophical thinkers. This approach takes account of the human agent as both subject and object, and as one who acts reflexively on some occasions and unreflexively on others. Hoggett develops this line by taking up Zygmunt Bauman's notion of ambivalence as the exemplification of postmodernity, and Bonnie Honig's view of society as radically plural; that is, as one where a babble of different voices constantly interrupt one another, 'one praising what the other condemns'. This, then, is a society where there are no obvious rules that the heteronomous self can simply follow. Following Honig, we can think of such a world as 'dilemmatic space', where certainties are increasingly difficult to sustain or justify.

It is within this reflective context that Hoggett introduces an exploration of the dilemmas of ordinary life. Drawing on his current research into 'regeneration workers' (what we used to call community development workers), the chapter relies on an original case study of a 'regeneration work' manager within local government negotiating his way through a series of public and private dilemmas as he attempts to implement a complex consultative process that is built around an apparently irresolvable contradiction between the values of fiscal restraint and of 'empowering' residents in a disadvantaged area.

Simon Thompson's chapter is concerned with both trust and risk, and draws out the relationship between them and different modes of identity. The intuition he follows is that 'there are interesting and important links between attitudes to risk, types of trust, and certain characteristic forms of political belief and action'. He explores what he calls 'risks with identity', which Giddens, and indeed other third way advocates, argue are necessary and appropriate for late modern risk society. Thompson engages closely with the work of Giddens and Bauman in order to think through the social conditions of trust in late modern society. In doing this, he offers a very clear and critical introduction to some of their important and influential ideas about ontological security, risk and the cosmopolitan self. Thompson argues that the risk-taking individual is more likely to come from a particular social location of relative privilege, where such attitudes, stances and behaviours are expected and valued. Others, who lack the confidence, or indeed the wherewithal, to take such risks, occupy a different social location, seeking security in the embrace of community. Thompson's chapter raises the important question of whether we are wrong to approach identity in a normative sense. Indeed, he suggests that those who do not risk their identities may have very good reasons for not pursuing 'pure relationships' and the sort of authenticity and autonomy described and, Thompson claims, is approved of by Giddens. Less concerned with ongoing personal revision, their identities are more embedded within community. Such *traditional selves*, Thompson argues, are just as legitimate as risk identities, even if social scientists tend to see them as out of step with the requirements of late modernity. In addition, Thompson relates these issues, themes and arguments to a broader engagement with the politics of recognition, which is his central research focus in political philosophy.

In the wake of postmodern critiques of the foundations of knowledge, postcolonial critiques of ethnocentric discourse, feminist critiques of patriarchal structures and diagnoses of global risk, uncertainty and de-traditionalisation (to name but a few), the search has been on for tenable grounds for a normative philosophy of some kind. Some believe they may have found it in the writings of Emmanuel Levinas. In Chapter 3 Peter Jowers provides a superb introduction to the work of this very complex thinker. He demonstrates Levinas's own deep suspicion of language, knowledge and, indeed, the conscious, intentional subject itself. He shows that, for Levinas, the only possible ground for normative judgement lies in the ethical instincts of the pre-social, and unconscious, 'creature'. Somewhere prior to language, subjectivity and judgements lies a raw 'incarnate' self whose very constitution is presupposed by an ethical moment of engagement with the other. This is *the* moment of supreme risk and uncertainty. The 'creature' has no knowledge, makes no judgement, has no intention – yet it is the very foundation of our being for the other, the moment at which the other shatters our self-enclosed, narcissistic core and constitutes us as an ethical human subject–far from self-reflexivity perhaps (or perhaps a radicalisation of self-reflexivity), but a profound reaching towards ethics in a very uncertain world nevertheless.

In Chapter 4 Alison Assiter outlines a quite different approach to practical philosophy. According to this account, normative uncertainty and fragmentation in late/postmodernity might be attributed to a kind of cultural mind/body dualism. In this context, moral judgements are made without sufficient reflection; rather, they occur as a consequence of reactive responses to moral questions, based on a free-floating emotivism. She claims further that contemporary readings of Descartes as a mind/body dualist are highly simplistic. Instead, she suggests a reading that emphasises the integration of mind and body, reason and emotion and claims that such a reading could provide more certain grounds for the re-establishment of the moral universalist project which was characteristic of many Enlightenment thinkers. Interestingly, then, both the Cartesian Assiter and the Levinasian Jowers seem to be attempting to counter moral fragmentation and uncertainty, with a grounded ethical/moral universalism. But while Levinas grounds his ethics in the pre-conceptual 'creature' and is deeply suspicious of 'rational' judgement and, indeed, 'knowledge' of any kind, Assiter grounds her universalism squarely in Enlightenment reason.

Part Two: Trust, risk and uncertainty in institutions and organisations

In Part Two the themes of trust, risk and uncertainty are explored through research based in a range of key organisational settings. In some cases the role of the organisation in the context of trust and risk management is explored (e.g. Ferguson); in other cases the issue of identity and self in the context of organisational risk and uncertainty is emphasised (e.g. Baxter and Britton).

In Chapter 5 Harry Ferguson outlines some of the central features of the risk society hypothesis, as developed by Beck and Giddens. He does so in the context of an exploration of the implications of his own research on child protection. He describes the discursive transformations which have occurred since the beginnings of child protection in the nineteenth century. He outlines a period of 'simple modernity' in which child protection expert systems successfully 'sequestered' the reality of their success (and failure) in dealing with child abuse, neglect and death. They did so by suppressing information, but they were able to do so because this was a period of public trust in the ability of expert systems to counter such social problems effectively. Since the 1970s, however, this trust has broken down. Such expert systems have themselves become the object of risk assessment. Risk now seems unavoidable and, therefore, endemic. Success is unattainable, yet, at the same time, accountability for each failure is demanded, together with constant reflection on the dimensions of organisational failure. A culture of scandal and blame has arisen in the face of public anxieties about such contingency and risk. Ferguson looks at the personal strategies engaged in by the experts involved to deal with the anxieties that arise as a consequence of this impossible intolerance of failure. He also emphasises the ambivalence of such developments. While being part of a blame culture, they have also made genuinely safer futures for many children possible.

In Chapter 6, Arthur Baxter and Carolyn Britton examine how mature university students experience and account for the changes that are brought about by education. This experience, which, in many ways, is empowering for students, also brings associated risks to the self which have to be managed. Two such forms of related risk are discussed: those stemming from challenges to established gender roles within the family, and those associated with moving away from a working-class habitus. In this study students had to manage being thought superior and at times feeling superior to family and friends due to changes in vocabulary and perceptions brought about through education. These findings are compared to other studies which, while dealing with similar issues of risk and identity change, focus on issues of guilt and shame. They argue that their findings are specific to the type of subjects these students were studying and to their being at a pivotal point in the transition from old to new identities.

In Chapter 7, Ajit Nayak examines the rise of 'enterprising management' in current management discourse and practice. Nayak argues that it is a basis for the management of uncertainty and creativity, which involves a total, and risky, construction of the self through the consumption of an 'enterprising' working life as a basis for identity. He points out, however, that such responses to uncertainty and risk as the basis for organisational creativity are evacuated of ethical or moral content. Nayak also shows that such responses have a strong tendency to colonise our private existence. What the author describes is a new 'technology of the self', known among management consultants as 'Me Plc'. In establishing his case, Nayak draws on his own research and interviews on the British entrepreneur and organisational guru, Alec Reed.

In Chapter 8, Tony Bovaird and Elke Loeffler argue that it has become conventional to locate the current crisis in the legitimacy of the state within 'Western liberal democracies' in the growing lack of trust felt by citizens in state-funded professional bureaucracies and the representational politics which is supposed to regulate them. At the local level, the withering away of 'social capital', as citizens become used to 'bowling alone', has been postulated by Putnam to have made it even more difficult for civil society to substitute for state action. The communitarian manifesto of Etzioni has contested this, but so far has produced only fragmentary evidence, not coherent counter-examples. This chapter examines ways in which these competing discourses can be systematised to make it possible to test their relevance as a basis for political action at the local level. It reports work currently being undertaken by the authors as part of the Study Group on Local Governance for the European Group of Public Administration.

Part Three: Cultures of risk: the uncertainties of trust

The final part of the book includes work which explores the themes of trust, risk and uncertainty through impressive research into a diverse range of cultural phenomena.

In Chapter 9, Stuart Allan, Alison Anderson and Alan Petersen are concerned with the ways in which expert knowledge and journalistic priorities interact in the presentation of risk to the public. They focus, for the purposes of their chapter, on developments in cloning techniques and attendant concerns regarding the possibilities for human cloning. They present the pro- and anti-cases for human cloning. The former relate mainly to the perceived medical benefits of such techniques, while the latter concern fears relating to both imagined possibilities for human exploitation and objections rooted in religious belief. They then proceed to analyse, in some detail, the rhetorical strategies at work in the presentation of one particular case. This enables them to begin to ask questions regarding the diverging interests of journalists and scientific experts. They conclude by suggesting a need to realign this relationship between experts, journalists and public concerns about risk.

In Chapter 10 Leah Wild examines issues concerned with risk perception and identity construction as they relate to 'New Age' Travellers. She first examines the cultural role of nomadic groups as objects of suspicion, hatred and deep anxiety throughout history. She examines the relationship between outsiderness, marginality, liminality and perceptions of risk in the wider society. The chapter then describes the specific form that this anxiety has taken in relation to 'New Age' Travellers. Perhaps most importantly, she challenges much of the contemporary literature in this area by arguing that her research suggests that we must be wary of simplistically casting such groups as victims of unwelcome fantasy, stereotyping and marginalisation. She effectively problematises aspects of the risk hypothesis by showing how Travellers themselves have actively elected this role, that they actively reinforce it and that the experience of outsiderness, transgression and risk is central to their identity and libidinal economy.

In Chapter 11, Lita Crociani-Windland focuses on the unique civic structure of Siena, in central Italy. This structure has evolved over centuries in connection with the horse race known as the *Palio*. Crociani-Windland's work on such festivals in northern Italy serves to problematise the risk society theses in a number of ways. First, challenging the notion of de-traditionalisation, she shows how these festivals survive, and indeed thrive, on the basis of centuries-old traditions – traditions which are very much alive to both young and old. She also shows the way in which highly ritualised risk forms the basis of a channelling of collective aggression into powerful and enduring forms of social solidarity/capital which are productive of trust – and which show no signs of weakening under the impact of modernity. There is no sign of the disintegration of trust and civil society anticipated by much of the theoretical literature in this field. This strength derives from adaptability – from the ability of the community to accept a degree of fluidity and change, while maintaining enough structure for the tradition to hold its charisma. The focus of research for this chapter, then, is the link between affective dynamics and the development of the present structure as a pivotal source of social capital. The overall picture is that of a community that has achieved a balance between being and becoming, where identity, intensity, risk and trust can coexist. The *Palio* is not just the race, but a way of life–in the words of the Siennese, *'nel Palio ci sta sempre tutto'* ('everything can always be contained in the Palio').

In Chapter 12 Anthony Moran considers the way that distrust and uncertainty have shaped relations between Australia's settler and indigenous communities in the past, and in contemporary Australian society. Moran argues that the colonial relationship between settler and indigene has continued into the present. This gives rise to a sense of suspicion about the intentions of the other community, from each side of the racial divide. As he shows, this suspicion is played out in the controversy over Aboriginal land rights and native title, and in recent debates about the 'stolen generations'. Indigenous peoples have, in addition, a sense of grievance about unresolved issues arising from the European invasion and colonisation. Moran argues that this sense of grievance and separation from mainstream Australian life is one factor in what he perceives as a low level of civic engagement between the two communities. Moran draws on his own large-scale interview project with 'ordinary Australians' in order to reflect on the dynamics of uncertainty, suspicion and distrust felt by settlers for Aboriginal communities and causes. Trust between settler and indigene is a difficult achievement and always threatened by larger historical forces. On the other hand, there have been efforts from both sides of the colonial divide to build trust and to improve relations. These efforts have been evident in the reconciliation movement of the 1990s, and even in the much criticised assimilation era from the 1950s to the 1970s.

Finally, Chapter 13 examines certain aspects of the Giddens/Beck hypothesis through David Green's work on pagan magic. The view he develops is that paganism can be accounted for as a response to late modern 'ontological uncertainty' – but one which, as with Wild's account of 'New Age' Travellers, emphasises the creative potential of such risk and uncertainty. He particularly emphasises the central role of embodiment in this response, and points out that this is a theme generally neglected by the risk theorists. As with Crociani-Windland's account of Italian festivals, he suggests that certain historical continuities in pagan practices and identity throw some doubt on the 'late modern' theorists' account of 'de-traditionalisation'. At the same time, Green's research does give added weight to the claim that identities and practices centring on 'reflexivity' are particularly common in 'late modernity'. Finally, Green shows how responses to ontological uncertainty such as this can produce their own environment of risk, leading to high levels of inner group cohesion and secrecy.

References

Allan, S. (1999), *News Culture*, Buckingham and Philadelphia: Open University Press.

Anderson, A. (1997), *Media, Culture and the Environment*, NewBrunswick, NJ: Rutgers University Press.

Assiter, A. (1989), *Pornography, Feminism and the Individual*, London: Pluto Press.

—— (1990), *Althusser and Feminism*, London: Pluto Press.

—— (1996), *Enlightened Women*, London: Routledge.

—— (2003), *Revisiting Universalism*, Basingstoke: Palgrave Macmillan.

Bauman, Z. (1991), *Modernity and Ambivalence*, Cambridge: Polity.

Beck, U. (1992), *Risk Society: Towards a New Modernity*, London: Sage.

—— (1997), *The Reinvention of Politics: Rethinking Modernity in the Global Social Order*, Cambridge: Polity Press.

Bovaird, T. and Loeffler, E. (eds) (2003), *Public Management and Governance*, London: Routledge.

Ferguson, H. (2004), *Protecting Children in Time: Child Abuse, Child Protection and the Consequences of Modernity*, Basingstoke: Palgrave Macmillan.

Giddens, A. (1990), *The Consequences of Modernity*, Cambridge: Polity.

Hoggett, P. (1992), *Partisans in an Uncertain World: the Psychoanalysis of Engagement*, London: Free Associations Books.

—— (2000), *Emotional Life and the Politics of Welfare*, Basingstoke: Macmillan.

Moran, A. (2005), *Australia: Nation, Belonging and Globalization*, New York: Routledge.

Petersen, A. and Bunton, R. (2002), *The New Genetics and the Public's Health*, London and New York: Routledge.

Petersen, A. and Lupton D. (1996) *The New Public Health: Health and Self in the Age of Risk*, St Leonards, NSW: Allen & Unwin.

Putnam, R. (2001), *Bowling Alone*, New York: Simon and Schuster.

—— (2002), *Democracies in Flux: The Evolution of Social Capital in Contemporary Society*, Oxford: Oxford University Press.

Thompson, S. (2005), *The Political Theory of Recognition: A Critical Introduction*, Cambridge: Polity (forthcoming).

Thompson, S. and Festenstein, M. (eds.) (2001), *Richard Rorty: Critical Dialogues*, Cambridge: Polity Press.

Part One

The Theory and Philosophy of Trust, Risk and Uncertainty

1
Radical Uncertainty: Human Emotion and Ethical Dilemmas

Paul Hoggett

Agency and rationality

In contrast to North America, where interest in the human actor as agent has been around longer, in Europe interest in human agency in the social sciences has been more recent, a consequence of the crisis and decline of structuralist and post-structuralist models of social action. However, both sides of the Atlantic appear to have in common a conception of agency which, to simplify slightly, stresses the conscious choices that unitary subjects make. In recent writings I have sought to question this model of agency and specifically the idea that agency is necessarily reflexive (Hoggett, 2000); that is, that we normally know why we do what we do at the time of doing it. Most recently I have attempted to develop a model of agency which could take account of the human agent as subject and object and as one which acted reflexively on some occasions and unreflexively on others (Hoggett, 2001).

One area where much of the complexity and subtlety of human agency becomes manifest is that of ethical conduct. The idea of the human agent calmly making reasoned choices between ethical alternatives has been subject to considerable challenge recently. A different perspective has emerged which emphasises the dilemmas that ethical actors face in conditions of late modernity where societies are characterised by radical pluralism, ambiguity and uncertainty. This is a perspective which gives emphasis to the more tragic dimensions of ethical life and the pain which so often accompanies moral conflict.

This chapter is based on the early stages of a research project[1] I am involved in which explores the way in which 'regeneration workers' in impoverished areas in the UK negotiate the ethical dilemmas of their job. Regeneration workers operate at the grass-roots interface between government and local communities. We have chosen regeneration workers because they are uniquely situated – caught as they are between conflicting communities in an increasingly plural civil society; and caught between a state which currently declares its benign intent to tackle social exclusion and a civil society which is often highly ambivalent about the motives and agenda of government. More so than for other street-level bureaucrats (Lipsky, 1980), these practitioners deliver programmes rather than services. It has become commonplace to talk in terms of 'capacity-building' and the development of 'social capital'. If social capital refers to the 'networks, norms and social trust that facilitate coordination and cooperation for mutual benefit' (Putnam, 1995: 67), then it has become the task of regeneration workers to deliver this. This is a far less tangible task than service delivery and, as a consequence, practitioners operate with a considerable amount of discretion, not the least because, as Hill (1983: 89) noted, discretion is also enhanced when 'policy makers are far from clear what they really want'.

Ambivalence and moral conflict

In calling for a radical rethinking of ethical action under conditions of postmodernity Bauman (1993) insists on the centrality of ambivalence. According to Bauman, ambivalence is both part of our constitution as subjects (we are torn by contradictory impulses) and a characteristic of a society in which the subject has become disembedded from the taken-for-granted schemata that accompanied tradition or totalising systems of thought of a religious or political nature. As a result, the subject faces her/his moral choices alone, where the values 'rule books' of the past no longer act as a guide, where there are no obvious rules to follow, indeed where there is a plethora of different voices insisting on different rules.

Bonnie Honig (1996) writes in a similar vein, from the context of a society which is radically plural, that is, one where a babble of different voices constantly interrupt one another, 'one praising what the other condemns' as Bauman puts it. Honig suggests that this is a world in which there is no place like home: home as a place free from conflict and difference, home as a place of unity or, rather, union, no longer exists. But this does not stop us from looking for it. Indeed, as Bauman would put it, the more we are condemned to freedom – to having to make our own decisions in the absence of clear rules or signposts on which we can depend – the more anxious we become to find a place like home.

Honig suggests that in radically plural worlds the individual agent no longer inhabits a place where clear choices can be made between contrasting alternatives. Rather, the individual finds herself living out the contradictions and conflicts of the complex, diverse society in which she is situated by being pulled this way and that through a succession of dilemmas. Indeed, Honig argues that the contemporary human agent inhabits a 'dilemmatic space'.

The dilemmas of regeneration work

Ethical dilemmas are central to regeneration work. In the past, regeneration work in the UK was referred to as community development, a practice which has had an ambivalent but distanced relation to successive governments since the late 1960s (Mayo and Craig, 1995). Now this kind of work is located much closer to the centre of strategic interventions, especially 'modernisation' and 'regeneration' (Social Exclusion Unit, 1998). Its methods are a vital contributor to 'modernised' governance, connecting public bodies to each other and to citizens, identifying local need and engaging in dialogue with diverse social groups to improve services. Yet for practitioners much anxiety remains over the potential for incorporation into an agenda whose communitarianism has a strong normative dimension and which offers only a limited acknowledgement of structural inequality (Temkin and Rohe, 1998; Byrne, 1999). There are anxieties too about growing professionalisation (Davies, 1998) and the diminution of the community sector's independent voice (Anastacio *et al.*, 2000).

Regeneration work has also become the object, as well as the agent, of modernisation. The emergent audit regimes have challenged its collaborative and developmental ethic. Often working to unrealistic targets and time-frames, practitioners can become engaged in impression management. Pressure for quick, tangible and measurable outputs appears to deny the realities of development activities, whose impacts are often long-term, subtle and complex in form. Practitioners find they must also convince sceptical local citizens of the value of successive government initiatives.

Undertaking regeneration work in socially and culturally heterogeneous communities is particularly challenging because of the way in which different interests and value systems compete for attention and because the empowerment of some may be experienced as exclusion by others (Harrison, Hoggett and Jeffers, 1995; Miller and Ahmad, 1997). Milder but no less destructive hostilities are often exchanged between neighbourhoods, networks and even other professionals as they compete for scarce resources. Regeneration workers need to be able to work with the feelings of both other individuals and of groups, whether managing cynicism, combating despair or dealing with conflict (Hoggett and Miller, 2000). Such 'emotion work' (Hochschild, 1983) directed at others' feelings is the flipside of the work that regeneration workers need to do on their own feelings when negotiating the dilemmas they face.

Ethical dilemmas and human agency

Practitioners must therefore operate in increasingly complex and ambivalent contexts in which ethical conduct is far from obvious (Bauman, 1993). This 'dilemmatic space' is where choices are no longer clear cut (if they ever were), but where they are ambiguous, indeterminate and conflictual. More-over we bring to such choices our own ambivalence, that is, our own inter-nal conflicts and contradictions. Powerful affects, particularly anxiety, are elicited within this space and this may well limit the capacity of individuals to act reflexively (Hoggett, 2001).

Honig develops her argument by using the work of the English moral philosopher Bernard Williams. Williams' account of moral thought is dis-tinctive for a number of reasons. He is keenly aware of the incommensu-rable nature of many human values such as liberty and equality. Things don't fit together in the way we would like them to; rather, values rub up against each other, pulling us in different directions. Nor are we dealing with conflicts which can somehow be transcended. Some conflicts are to all extents and purposes irresolvable and simply have to be lived with. For Williams most moral decisions assume the form of dilemmas. He argues that dilemmas assume two basic forms:

I ought to do A and I ought to do B but I cannot do both A and B.
I ought to do C and I ought not to do C.

Regarding the first type, consider, for example, the dilemma of the whistle-blowers described by Robert Jackall in *Moral Mazes: The World of Corporate Managers* (1988). Many of Jackall's whistleblowers found themselves torn between their sense of justice and their anger at the malpractices that they witnessed and, on the other hand, their sense of loyalty to colleagues. By blowing the whistle (choosing A) they often felt (and were made to feel) that they had betrayed their colleagues. (Remaining loyal to colleagues would be choice B.) Susan Mendus (2000) refers to Macintyre's (1985) analysis of the tragic where he notes that, in such situations, 'to choose does not exempt me from the authority of the claim I choose to go against' (Macintyre, 1985: 143). We might note in passing that this type of di-lemma exemplifies the conflict between two different kinds of ethic–an ethic of justice and an ethic of care.

The second type of dilemma often occurs as a result of the inability of the other to contain their own ambivalence. Feldman (1989) suggests that such situations are endemic to family life. Young children, for example, are often unable to contain the ambivalent feelings they have towards a parent and as a result they project their inner conflicts into the parent. He describes a young girl who excitedly sits on her father's lap. If he rejects her advances he becomes positioned as a cold and distant patriarch; if he accepts them he colludes with her fantasy of taking her mother's place: 'thus there is no way the father can behave that will not stimulate the child's aggressive and/or sexual phantasies' (Feldman, 1989: 105). In other words, the father finds himself in a 'damned if I do and damned if I don't' situation.

In social policy studies, Mendus (1993) has argued that the lives of many women are marked by a series of conflicting demands (pertaining to both kinds of dilemma) from which there is no escape. You have to disappoint someone, and this imposes real limits on the reflexive agency that women are able to assert. This brings us, according to Honig, to a second valuable element in Williams' thinking. Williams recognises that human emotions are central to moral thought and behaviour. In choosing A I will experience guilt and regret for not choosing B; in choosing C I am torn by doubt as to whether I am doing the right thing. Indeed Williams (1973: 172) argues that in dilemmatic space, 'there is no right thing to do', the best that we can do is 'act for the best'. Williams (1981: 173) speaks of lying awake at night not so much full of regret about what was not done, but tormented by what was done.

Honig adds to Williams a different way of thinking about the human subject. For Williams the subject was still unitary, the conflict and difference was all 'out there'. But Honig argues that the conflicts and disjunctures are not only out there, they are also a constitutive part of our being. There is no place like home inside us. In this way Honig adds a psychoanalytic view of the subject to Williams' uncompromising pluralism.

Now if we take on board this view of life lived through a dilemmatic space, then doubt, shame, guilt and remorse characterise moral agency. In other words, anxiety becomes agency's constant companion. In the work that I am developing I want to explore how people deal with the anxiety at the heart of moral behaviour in contemporary life. The equipment I intend to take with me includes the psychoanalytic thinking that has been inspired by the work of Melanie Klein, in which the impact of anxiety on our capacity for reflexive agency has been a central theme.

Although it may not be immediately obvious, questions of moral value lie at the heart of Klein's picture of the human subject. For Klein our experience of what is good and bad in the world is inextricably bound up with our capacity for love and hate. We find pleasure in our hatreds as well as our loves and we seek satisfying objects for these passions. Nothing gives us more pleasure than an object we can hate unreservedly, which is so full of badness that it can be denigrated and criticised with impunity. This is a primitive morality, one in which the world is split into the good and the bad, and never the two shall meet. In fact, it is probably truer to say that as a result of this splitting goodness and badness both lose their meaning; instead of goodness there is something perfect and flawless, and instead of badness there is something execrable without any redeeming features. Klein reminds us that in the natural as opposed to supernatural world something is good because of our knowledge of its inevitable flaws, it is good only because of our appreciation of the bad within it, which the good somehow manages to transcend.

Unlike rationalist understandings of morality Klein insists on the inseparability of moral thought and feeling. A sound ethical position is not one that is somehow divorced from passion, but one in which moral feelings (love and hate) are coupled creatively with moral thought. From this perspective, ethical behaviour is both passionate and thoughtful. We choose and act because we feel strongly about something and yet we do this knowing of the complexity of the world, and specifically its mixture of good and bad characteristics. In acting in this way we know we may be doing wrong and yet we have the capacity not to be undermined by this thought.

The problem facing the moral agent in dilemmatic space is that in choosing A and acting for what she hopes is the best, the individual has to cope with both her anxieties about what is bad in the chosen course of action A (the bad within the good) and her anxieties about what is good in the rejected alternative, B. Klein suggests that the weaker our capacity to contain anxiety the less our capacity to face reality with all its painful complexity. This is what defence mechanisms – denial, splitting, etc. – do; they impoverish our thinking. How do we do this? What individual and trans-individual defences are typically deployed in dilemmatic space? What resources does an individual call on in traversing this space? What kind of features typically characterise the relationship between the human agent, 'I', and her/his values?

At this point I want to provide a vignette drawn from one of my pilot interviews.

A case study of an ethical dilemma

X is a manager working in a small British city. Earlier in his career he was a senior community developmental practitioner in one of London's poorest and most ethnically diverse boroughs. In his current job he operates in a corporate role, close to the chief executive and one of the key conduits between the elected politicians and the council's officer caste. He manages a range of corporate projects to do with equalities, regeneration and political and administrative modernisation. X was asked by the council to develop an innovative piece of consultation work with residents on one of the poorest housing estates in the city. This was a new departure for the city, which had no track record of trying to engage in new ways with its local civil society.

X's brief was to ensure that the consultation process reached out to voices that were not normally heard. The consultation was to be open-ended, focusing on what local residents wanted to be done in the area how it was to be done; and how the residents wanted to be involved in the implementation of the proposals that came out of the consultation. From the beginning, some of the committed local councillors and X decided that the key method to be adopted would be to recruit local residents themselves to conduct the consultation. This was an innovative strategy (although not unique), even by the standards of progressive local authorities, let alone his own city. Very quickly X and a junior officer dedicated to the project were able to recruit nearly 20 residents, all working-class and highly representative of the age, gender and cultural mix of the local population.

An initial meeting with the local recruits and a small number of other local agencies was highly positive. Indeed, X described the response as amazing. The local recruits were passionate about the planned project. Their passion was based on an accumulated anger that their area had a bad and undeserved reputation, that it had been used as a dump by housing and other agencies, and that there was a burning wish to change the perception of the area held by those living inside and outside it. X therefore assumed the role of project manager, but the bulk of the groundwork was to be undertaken by one of his junior officers, Z, bright, young and politically committed. According to X, as soon as the initial meeting had taken place he found himself 'emotionally caught up in it'. In contrast to the rest of his work, this seemed so alive and vibrant. As he put it, 'Local residents took control of the agenda, they grasped it saying "this is ours".'

After the initial meeting X got down to the business of making it happen. One of the first tasks he had to confront concerned the method of paying the local recruits. He soon realised that this was a minefield. Nearly all of the recruits were either unemployed or earned such low wages that they were on income support. If they were paid a formal wage, then most of what they earned would be clawed back in state benefit reductions. After a bit of research X discovered that some voluntary organisations in other parts of the country got round this problem by paying recruits in various forms of 'undetectable payment'. X sought to implement the same tactic. However, X quickly realised that this would fall foul of the local authority's financial regulations, would contravene the spirit of partnership working with organisations such as the Benefits Agency (the agency responsible for delivering state benefits), and so on. It was a political hot potato, which, if it became public, would cause huge embarrassment to his employers.

Here then was X's dilemma. He was torn between a commitment to genuine empowerment of the poor and socially excluded on the one hand, and the culture of financial and managerial accountability on the other. At a more macro level, he had hit the poverty trap full on and the inconsistencies of a government agenda which talked about empowerment but which maintained a set of fiscal policies which condemned the poor to continued social exclusion. X informed Z of his dilemma and of his need to put a stop to the payment tactic that they had sought to adopt. Relations between X and Z became extremely fraught. X called a meeting of the local recruits to inform them of his intention to abandon the method of payment. There was a huge row; many of the local recruits 'went bananas' and threatened to withdraw from the project.

X describes the following period as one of the worst in his working life. The anguish he felt was so great that he actively considered resigning. The solution he eventually pursued was to bring in an outside mediator. As a result of mediation a new tactic was adopted whereby the mediator's own community organisation became the 'employer' of the local recruits – something made possible by the much looser financial regulations which are part of charity law. Nevertheless, almost half the local recruits withdrew. The consultation proceeded, but with a reduced number of local recruits.

Looking back on this episode X had a number of reflections. He felt strongly that he should have been able to anticipate the problems that he was going to get into. He knew the local authority world inside out and had a reputation for being a highly competent manager able to operate in difficult environments in a professionally competent manner. I suggested that perhaps he was colluding with an irrational but widespread belief that managers should be able to predict all possible eventualities, a myth that chance, accident and the unforeseeable could be expunged from organisational life. He disagreed. He recognised the prevalence of this myth, but insisted that with hindsight the trap that he had been heading for was so obvious that it was shocking to him that he had not foreseen it.

He had some further reflections on the conflictual meeting. He was struck by the fact that local residents, despite their anger, did not blame him for what had happened but 'displaced' their rage onto other agencies who they felt must be behind this. Despite his protestations that it was he and he alone who had got them into the mess, local residents persisted in responding in what seemed to be a quite paranoid fashion. His anguish was not lessened by the fact that local residents had refused to hold him responsible. He felt that he had let them down.

We explored a number of dimensions of this episode. Although he wasn't a particularly 'psychologically-minded' individual, he mentioned that after the event, while on holiday with a friend, he had read a book by Erik Erikson on stages in the life cycle. He was struck by the way Erikson described a mid-life stage of generativity giving way to a final stage of integration and reflection. The episode had connected very powerfully to a feeling he had, but that he had not been aware of: that his generative phase was not yet over. The 'aliveness' of the local residents had contrasted starkly with the routinised nature of much of his corporate and managerial work. Here was something creative, something which also connected to his more youthful experience working in inner London. So the work had put him back in touch with and reawakened his own creative impulses. Hence he described himself as being so quickly 'caught up' in the project.

Towards the end of the interview I described a dilemma to him as a situation in which you feel yourself torn between two powerful imperatives, and that if you satisfy one the feeling is that it will be at the expense of the other. According to X, 'It felt as if it wasn't conscious, it felt as if I blocked out the unacceptable side of the dilemma and as a result I have just not been able to account for this to Z and I literally was not as conscious as I normally am and which is very much a part of the way I do things ... it wasn't a conscious blocking out, I can't ever remember doing that before'. I added that this seemed to indicate the powerful nature of the feelings that the episode reawakened. X replied, 'Oh yes, it took over, it took over'. He referred to 'emotional drives which go very deeply and go back a very long time which have caught up with me in terms of what drives me in terms of life ... if I look back on this job for the last five years or so it has not felt like a living job ... something quite deadened'. Again, speaking of the project, X talked of 'the freedom I felt'.

The psychodynamics of ethical conduct

The case study provides us with a number of points of departure. The first point to note is that X does not see the dilemma coming: 'it felt as if it wasn't conscious, it felt as if I blocked out the unacceptable side of the dilemma'. X had blotted out that part of reality which represented constraint, the world of local government and its financial regulations. Because of the strength of the desire awakened in him by this group of socially excluded citizens, such constraints suddenly felt unacceptably painful and he dealt with these incipiently frustrating feelings by attacking his own capacity for thinking.

Wilfred Bion, a key figure in the Kleinian tradition, developed the Kleinian analysis of the relationship between thinking and feeling (Hoggett and Thompson, 2002). He provides a more phenomenological account of the Freudian unconscious. When X says that he simply wasn't conscious of the impending constraints, he is referring to an absence of thought where we might have expected thought to be. This is more than simply a forgetting. The conflict X is in is 'wished away'; reality cannot be faced. But what is attacked is not only reality but also X's capacity to think about it. Bion describes this as hatred of thinking, an anti-episteme. This is a common method of trying to deal with dilemmas – we don't think about them until it is too late. Right at the beginning of his work with the residents X might have said, 'I am afraid that I cannot pay you to act as consultants on this project because the financial regulations of local government just don't allow it. There may be some ways round this, which I will investigate, but there is no guarantee. Are you willing to be consultants on a voluntary basis?' We can speculate about what was in X's mind at this early point in the project. Perhaps he felt anger at the injustice of the situation where poor people were being asked to give up their time for nothing, as if their time counted for little. Whatever it was, X avoided facing what he may have imagined to be the residents' disappointment or criticism. In Sophocles' *Antigone*, the paradigmatic dramatisation of an agonising dilemma, both Creon's pride and the intensity of Antigone's identification with her dead parents, compounded the tragedy. As Macintyre (1985: 163) notes, the human flaws of both the main protagonists influence the form of the tragedy, the course that it takes, but they do not constitute the tragedy, which lies in the conflict between two ethics – a duty to the state and a duty to one's family or clan.

X's difficulty was also compounded by the strength of his identification with the residents, and this brings us to a second aspect of the inter-subjective dynamics taking place. As soon as X meets the local residents he finds himself 'emotionally caught up' in the situation. Just as the local authority represented constraint for X, so the residents represented emancipation. But we are not just talking about external political values here (i.e. freedom and constraint); we are also talking about aspects of X's internal world. To say that our emotional lives and ethical lives are implicated in one another is to say that our private and public lives are engaged in constant interaction. The values that X held dearly, about ordinary poor people taking the power over their lives, were linked with his internal, creative impulse and the generative form that it takes in adult life (to create or procreate). His initial enthusiasm for the project, which drew on his consciously held values, became a passionate involvement once his initial encounter with local residents reawakened his own generative impulses, which had been suppressed as his career had taken him into the more bureaucratic aspects of his work. To describe it fully, the socially excluded residents came to represent something inside him that had also been excluded – his creativity.

The example graphically illustrates the criticism that Honig (1996) develops of Williams (1973). Williams' moral philosophy was a huge advance on prevailing rationalist perspectives because of his ability to understand the dilemmatic nature of choices typically involved in ethical behaviour. Williams can see that in this dilemmatic space there is never a right answer in which one can be free from moral anguish, from bad feelings of one form or another. For Williams the problem lies in external reality, which is far more messy, complex and tragic than rationalist moral philosophy allows for. Honig adds that the problems arise not just from the radically plural and endemically conflictual cultures in which we all now live. They also arise because of our inner conflicts, specifically the conflictual impulses and feelings which are a necessary part of being human. For X, powerful impulses were reawakened, which pushed against both internal and external constraints – so much so that the phantasy of freedom that took over X was one in which the idea of limit or constraint had been completely expunged, split off from his consciousness.

But if X's behaviour illustrates some of the magical ways in which we sometimes attempt to deal with dilemmas, it also illustrates great subtlety and humanity. One way of 'resolving' a dilemma is to deal with the ambivalent feelings we have by splitting. In deciding for A and against B, all that is right and good then becomes located in A and all that is wrong and bad becomes located in B. In *Antigone* Creon deals with the conflict of loyalty in this way. As his son Haemon says to him:

> 'Now don't, please, be quite so single-minded, self-involved, or assume the world is wrong and you are right. Whoever thinks that he alone possesses intelligence, the gift of eloquence, he and no one else, and character too ... such men, I tell you, spread them open – you will find them empty.'

In contrast, X had the capacity to contain his own ambivalence. For example, despite the row with the local residents X steadfastly refused to project any bad feelings on to them or onto his uncomprehending junior, Z. Instead, the bad feelings were directed inwards upon himself, partly destructively (he felt so bad he almost resigned) but partly constructively (leading to reflection, insight and changed behaviour). Indeed, X talked about the most vociferous of the local residents who had been the most argumentative. This was a difficult man, not easy to like, but someone whom X recognised was able to act as an effective conduit for the feelings of local residents. Two months after the row an incident occurred on the estate in which X and this man were able to work together very effectively to resolve a conflictual situation on the estate. To be able to say 'I may not like Y but that doesn't stop me from being able to work effectively with him and seeing some of his positive attributes' demonstrates a sophisticated capacity to act on the world despite one's ambivalent feelings.

Dilemmas are painful. Specifically, they elicit two kinds of painful feelings: guilt and shame. Guilt, because in negotiating a dilemma we cannot but hurt or damage some person or party. X was torn between betraying the trust of local residents or damaging the reputation of the local authority with which he identified. There was no right choice; all that X could do was act for the best, but in doing so X inevitably felt that he had failed. Speaking of tragic conflict, something which I feel lies at the heart of such dilemmas, Mendus (2000) notes that we are in the terrain not just of pluralism but also of the impossibility of harmonious reconciliation. As she puts it, such situations are characterised by 'pluralism, plus conflict, plus loss' (Mendus, 2000: 117). It is loss, which is experienced as failure. It is as if we internalise the flaws and faults of reality and make them our own, as if we must be responsible for what is irreconcilable in our world. From the tragic point of view, therefore, success is not possible, there is no resolution to the conflict; what we can aim for is, in Samuel Beckett's immortal words, 'to fail better'.

But I make a distinction between this sense of guilt and shame. The point I am making is that even if X had not tried to blot out one dimension of the conflict he was in, he would still have felt that he had failed. What compounded this sense of failure for X, however, was his feeling that, in the early stages at least, he had acted incompetently. Shame is linked to feelings of inadequacy rather than to anxiety about damage done to others.

Subjecting others to my claims

In radically undecidable situations one option, and a tempting one at that, is not to decide, not to act. But the problem is that inaction is itself a form of action. Indeed, by putting off a decision one very often makes things worse, maximising the degree of hurt that one party will feel when the fateful day can no longer be put off. But in acting one has, to some extent, to be one-eyed. In making one's choice one engages in an act of cruelty. As Meltzer (1975: 241) once put it:

> but it is also perhaps true that splitting processes are necessary for the kind of decisions that make action in the outside world possible. Every decision involves the setting in motion of a single plan from amongst its alternatives; it is experimental, involves risk, a certain ruthlessness towards self and others.

Meltzer's thoughts are particularly relevant to moral leadership. This chapter has focused on what is sometimes referred to as the 'passive voice', where self is *subject to* rival and incompatible claims. This tends to be the subject of moral philosophy rather than self's active voice, where we subject others to the authority of our moral claims. Moral philosophy is often strangely silent about leadership, that is, moral leadership. For if the dilemmas facing the self's passive voice demand sophisticated psychological resources, how much more so when the self seeks to lead others. What kinds of capacities are required of leadership which can combine passion and thoughtfulness? We only have to ask the question and Yeats' words spring to mind,

> The best lack all conviction, while the worst
> Are full of passionate intensity.

Note

1   'Negotiating Ethical Dilemmas in Contested Communities' a project funded by the Economic and Social Research Council (ref. RES-000-23-0127).

References

Anastacio, J. *et al.* (2000), *Reflecting Realities: Participants' Perspectives on Integrated Communities and Sustainable Development*. Bristol: Policy Press.

Bauman, Z. (1993), *Postmodern Ethics*, London: Polity Press.

Byrne, D. (1999), *Social Exclusion*, Buckingham: Open University Press.

Davies, C. (1998), 'Care and the Transformation of Professionalism', in T. Knijn and S. Sevenhuisjsen (eds.), *Care, Citizenship and Social Cohesion: Towards a Gender Perspective*, Utrecht: Netherlands School for Social and Economic Policy Research.

Feldman, M. (1989), 'The Oedipal Complex: Manifestations in the Inner World and the Therapeutic Situation', in R. Britton, M. Feldman and E. O'Shaugnessy (eds.), *The Oedipal Complex Today*, London: Karnac Books.

Harrison, L., Hoggett, P. and Jeffers, S. (1995), 'Race, Ethnicity and Community Development', *Community Development Journal*, 30(2): 144–57.

Hill, M. (1983), *Understanding Social Policy*. Oxford: Basil Blackwell.

Hochschild, A. (1983), *The Managed Heart: The Commercialisation of Human Feeling*, Berkeley, CA: University of California Press.

Hoggett, P. (2000), *Emotinal Life and the Politics of Welfare*, Basingstoke: Macmillan.

—— (2001), 'Agency, Rationality and Social Policy', *Journal of Social Policy,* 30(1): 37–56.

Hoggett, P. and Miller, C. (2000), 'Working with Emotions in Community Organisations', *Community Development Journal*, 35(4): 352–64.

Hoggett, P. and Thompson, S. (2002), 'Towards a Democracy of the Emotions', *Constellations,* 9(1): 106–26.

Honig, B. (1996), 'Difference, Dilemmas and the Politics of Home', in S. Benhabib (ed.), *Democracy and Difference: Contesting the Boundaries of the Political*, Princeton, NJ: Princeton University Press.

Jackall, R. (1988) *Moral Mazes: The World of Corporate Managers.* New York: Oxford University Press.

Lipsky, M. (1980), *Street-level Bureaucracy: Dilemmas of the Individual in Public Service*, California: Russell Sage Foundation.

MacIntyre, A. (1985), *After Virtue* (second edition), London: Duckworth.

Mayo, M. and Craig, G. (1995), 'Community Participation and Empowerment: the Human Face of Structural Adjustment or Tools for Democratic Transformation?', in G. Craig and M. Mayo (eds.), *Community Empowerment*, London: Zed Books.

Meltzer, D., Bremner, J., Hoxter, S., Weddell, D. and Wittenberg, I. (1975), *Explorations in Autism: A Psycho-Analytical Study*, Strathray, Perthshire: Clunie Press.

Mendus, S. (1993), 'Different Voices, Still Lives: Problems in the Ethics of Care', *Journal of Applied Philosophy*, 10(1): 17–27.

—— (2000) *Feminism and Emotion*, Basingstoke: Macmillan.

Miller, C. and Ahmad, Y. (1997), 'Community Development at the Crossroads: a Way Forward?' *Policy and Politics*, 25(3): 269–84.

Putnam, R. (1995), 'Bowling Alone: America's Declining Social Capital', *Journal of Democracy* 6(1): 65–78.

Social Exclusion Unit (1998), *Bringing Britain Together: A National Strategy for Neighbourhood Renewal*, London: SEU.

Temkin, K. and Rohe, W. (1998), 'Social Capital and Neighbourhood Stability: an Empirical Investigation', *Housing Policy Debate,* 9: 1.

Williams, B. (1973), *Problems of the Self*, Cambridge: Cambridge University Press.

—— (1981) *Moral Luck*, Cambridge: Cambridge University Press.

2
Trust, Risk and Identity

Simon Thompson

Introduction

When do people feel confident enough to take risks? When, by contrast, do they seek security instead? Of course, no one can avoid all risks all of the time. On the contrary: Ulrich Beck's (1992) idea of a 'risk society' suggests that the encounter with risk, and in particular the reflexive evaluation of that risk, are unavoidable in contemporary society. Choosing to travel by car rather than by train, to eat a high-protein diet rather than a high-fibre diet, to work in an office rather than in a factory, are decisions in which risk must be considered and confronted. But while it may not be possible to avoid risk *tout court*, it is nevertheless possible to embrace certain sorts of risk with more or less enthusiasm. Here I am particularly interested in a sub-set of risks that I shall call 'risks with identity' or 'identity-risks'. These are risks that people may take with the course and style of their life as a whole, risks that are closely bound up with their sense of identity. In this chapter I shall focus on the argument that different attitudes to risk can be correlated with different attitudes to identity. According to this argument, those happy to take risks are also those who value autonomy, wanting to live their lives in the manner of their own choosing. By contrast, those who wish to avoid risk will seek the security of community, wanting to identify themselves with a greater whole and to follow unreflectively its rules and norms.

The plausibility of these claims about risk and identity will form the central focus of this chapter. In order to explore these issues, I shall be concerned with three sets of questions. The first set concerns the differences between people's attitudes to identity-risks. Why are some people risk-takers and autonomy-choosers while others are risk-avoiders and community-seekers?[1] And what is the best explanation of the difference between these groups? How useful, for instance, is the idea of trust as an explanandum here? The second set of questions concerns the characteristic political forms that may be associated with these two groups. What sort of political demands does each group make? And what sort of political practices and institutions do they favour? Might we find, for instance, that underlying recent debates in political theory between liberals and communitarians is a significant difference in attitudes to risk?[2] If the first two sets of questions concern diagnosis, the third and final set focuses on prescription. If we think that one attitude to identity-risks (and its characteristic political mode of expression) is preferable to another, can we act in a way that promotes this attitude and discourages its rival? If, for instance, we want people to take risks and live autonomous lives, how could we encourage them to do so? If, on the contrary, we think that people should avoid risks and seek the protection of community, how could we help them to act in this way?

In order to explore these questions, I shall focus initially on Anthony Giddens' analysis of the idea of basic trust. However, since I believe that this account has a number of deficiencies and limitations, I shall turn to certain ideas found in Zygmunt Bauman's work in order to supplement and modify Giddens' account. Following a number of critical comments on Bauman, I shall turn to other thinkers, especially Nancy Fraser, in order to develop my argument further. The intuition that I shall follow is that there are interesting and important links between attitudes to risk, types of trust and certain characteristic forms of political belief and action. The existence of risk leads to the need to trust, and this affects different groups – and specifically their attitude to autonomy and identity – in different ways. As the argument develops, I shall pay particular attention to the sorts of demand for recognition that these groups make. To put this in terms that I shall explain later, while some demand recognition of authenticity, others hope to be granted recognition for identity. Finally, I shall draw the threads of my argument together by offering some thoughts on the conditions in which different sorts of political demands – and specifically demands for recognition – may be made.

Reflexive selves and traditional selves

Giddens' idea of basic trust, and the way that he relates this to relationships between individuals, provides a useful starting point for my investigations. This idea needs to be placed in the context of his social theory as a whole. Giddens believes that basic trust takes on a particular significance in the age of what he calls 'high' or 'late' modernity (1991: 3). Late modern societies have a number of important distinguishing characteristics, three of which are of particular importance. First, Giddens follows Beck's argument that these are 'risk societies'. They are, that is to say, social orders in which we must have 'a calculative attitude to the open possibilities of action, positive and negative, with which, as individuals and globally, we are confronted in a continuous way in our contemporary social existence'

(1991: 28; and see 1990: 124–5). Risk society is not simply one in which there are more and different risks to face than before. Rather it is a society in which ordinary individuals reflexively use knowledge about risks (and opportunities) in order continuously to plan their actions. Second, such societies are also 'post-traditional' in the sense that no single definitive tradition exists which is capable of providing an authoritative guide for our actions (1991: 2–3, 20; and see 194–5).[3] Third, late modern societies are characterised by 'institutional reflexivity'. In these societies our life-plans are organised on the basis of knowledge and information which, if (or when) revised, would lead us fundamentally to change those plans (1990: 38; 1991: 20). These three features – risk, absence of tradition, reflexivity – are linked closely together. Since we face a range of unavoidable risks and lack an authoritative guide to tell us what to do, we are compelled to be reflexive – consciously to calculate risks and then to choose between them.

From these characteristics of late modernity, a number of consequences follow for individuals and for their relationships with others. Let us begin with individuals themselves. As we have seen, in late modern societies it is necessary for individuals consciously to assess the risks that they face as best they can and, having made this assessment, they must take risky action (1991: 129).[4] In these circumstances, Giddens argues, the self becomes a *'reflexive project'* (1990: 124; 1991: 32). Each and every day individuals must take conscious decisions about how to live in the widely diverse contexts in which they exist. As he puts it, 'individuals have no choice but to make choices' (1994: 126). Given this, self-identity cannot be regarded as a stable and complete entity, composed of a set of fixed traits that is invariant over time. It must be seen to lie rather in the capacity to continue a narrative (1991: 54). Self-identity is continuously created by subjects who make up the story of their lives as they go along. In short, the individuals of late modernity think of themselves as what I shall sometimes simply call *reflexive selves*.

If we turn now to the relationships between subjects, we can see that individuals in late modern societies have a distinctive mode of association. To be specific, Giddens argues that in these circumstances, 'pure relationships' become possible (or unavoidable?). Such relationships are pure in the sense that they exist for their own sake; in particular, they are not founded on 'external conditions of social or economic life' (1991: 89). Consequently, they depend crucially on the mutual commitment of the parties involved, who remain in the relationship only for as long as they choose to (1991: 92–4). It follows that, since they depend on commitment rather than on external anchors, such relationships can exist only if there is 'mutual trust between partners' (1991: 96; and see 6, 186). Acting in a trustworthy way, and allowing oneself to trust the other, are both vital if the relationship is to be sustained.

Such trust underpins a number of other features of pure relationships. First, it is mutual trust that makes intimacy and mutual disclosure possible

(1991: 94–5, 186). As Giddens says, '[t]rust on a personal level becomes a project, to be "worked at" by the parties involved, and demands the *opening out of the individual to the other*' (1990: 121). Trusting each other, each party can open themselves up to the other, honestly revealing themselves as well as they can. Second, the existence of mutual trust and intimacy makes it possible for the parties in the relationship to work together on the co-creation of shared life-stories. That is to say, rather than revealing pre-existing identities to each other, the parties in a pure relationship work out who they are together; such a relationship is a voyage of mutually negotiated self-exploration (1991: 97). Giddens concludes that the pure relationship 'is morally mobilised only through "authenticity"' (1991: 186; and see 9). In other words, the only moral imperative that exists in such relationships is to come to know ourselves as best we can and then to reveal ourselves to the other as honestly as we are able. In such relationships, then, we are animated by a desire for recognition of our authentic selves – for what, in short, I shall call *recognition of authenticity*.[5]

In summary, Giddens regards the subjects of late modernity as reflexive risk-takers who are connected to one another in pure relationships based on mutual trust. At the same time, however, he is aware that there are some individuals who try to ignore risk and to avoid risky behaviour, including those risks involved in pure relationships. To be specific, such people seek to evade reflexivity by resorting to tradition, and they seek to avoid exercising their 'critical judgement' by submitting to a dominant authority. As Giddens says, some individuals 'find that the freedom to choose is a burden and they seek solace in more overarching systems of authority' (1991: 196). For such individuals, self-identity is not regarded as a reflexive project, one freely chosen or freely fashioned; instead it is seen as a fully formed and complete entity, one that is defined by fixed patterns of rules and values laid down by tradition. Even in the conditions of late modernity, then, there are individuals who think of themselves as what I shall simply call *traditional selves*.

Individuals who try to avoid risk may also try to avoid pure relationships. Such relationships are inevitably risky: since they demand the ongoing commitment of all parties, it follows that they can be terminated at will: 'the relationship can be voluntarily broken, and is acknowledged by both parties to be only "good until further notice"' (1991: 187).[6] But how can would-be risk-avoiders also steer clear of pure relationships? While Giddens is not explicit about this, I think that we can make some inferences from what he says. In what I shall simply call *non-pure relationships*, risk-averse individuals will associate with each other on the basis of 'external conditions' (1991: 89). That is to say, the parties to the relationship will allow the wider systems in which they are located to determine the character of this relationship. In particular, they will be happy to have this relationship shaped and controlled by the authority to which they submit, according to the traditions with which that authority is associated. I may choose to marry only someone chosen for me by my family; I may associate only with my co-religionists in the way that my religion prescribes.

It follows that non-pure relationships are correlated with a conception of self-identity rather different from that associated with pure relationships. In this case, self-identity is not regarded as the outcome of an ongoing process of mutual exploration and negotiation (1991: 97) in which the aim is for appropriate acknowledgement of the authentic self. The parties in the non-pure relationship instead demand recognition for an already existing and fully formed identity. Here, in violation of Giddens' own injunction, the individual *does* 'simply "recognise the other" and in the responses of that other find his self-identity affirmed' (1991: 97; and see 54). In contrast to the acknowledgement of authenticity, this is a case of what I shall call the *recognition of identity*. In this case, it is intended that recognition follows automatically from an acknowledgement of certain facts about an individual's identity.

Basic trust and pure relationships

Before attempting to assess the plausibility of the explanation Giddens offers for the correlation of reflexive selves with pure relationships and traditional selves with non-pure relationships, I want to offer some comments about its status. In particular, I want to argue that this is a strongly ideological account and not just a neutral description. By this I mean that Giddens' analysis is underpinned by a set of values which lead him to approve of some ways of living and to condemn others. To be specific, he favours lives of individual autonomy, mutual intimacy and a search for authenticity, and disapproves of lives of subordination to authority, identity-recognition and reliance on tradition. This may seem to some to be rather a facile claim. Surely, they may object, Giddens is simply reporting on the character of late modernity, and specifically on the values – including those of autonomy and authenticity – which he finds there. In my defence, I would point out that it is quite possible to offer a report on the condition of modernity, but then to condemn that condition. Critics of modernity such as Alisdair Macintyre and Leo Strauss do just this. Giddens, by contrast, tends to elide the distinction between reporting and exhorting. He says: this is how things are, and this is how we must live. I contend that in this position we find at least an implicit endorsement of the values of late modernity.

To support this claim, consider how Giddens describes those who seek to opt out of pure relationships and to refuse to see their lives as the projects of reflexive selves. Here he implies, or so I contend, that such individuals are trying to live inauthentic lives – to live in *mauvaise foi*, as the existentialists would put it. These risk-averse individuals know that risk exists and that wishful thinking cannot make it go away. 'A person may take refuge in a traditional or pre-established style of life as a means of cutting back on the anxieties that might otherwise beset her.' However, as Giddens immediately remarks, 'the security such a strategy offers is likely to be limited, because the individual cannot but be conscious that any such option is only one among plural possibilities' (1991: 182). In other words, this individual is trying to fool herself. She chooses one option as if it were the only one, while knowing perfectly well that many equally plausible options exist. Giddens' general point, so I would contend, is that the conditions of late modernity compel us to evaluate risk and choose between risky alternatives without an authoritative guide to show us what to do, and that to pretend otherwise is to ignore the moral burden that these conditions impose.

To return to the main thread of the argument, I want to focus on the way in which Giddens seeks to explain the relationship between particular types of person and choices of risk-strategy by reference to factors of *individual psychology*. By this I do not mean to imply that Giddens' theory is strongly individualistic, as would be a theory which sought to explain the formation of the individual identity without reference to anyone beyond that individual. Rather it is an individual account since it explains the ability to take risks by reference to the circumstances of particular individuals' life-histories. To be specific, Giddens' account is founded on an idea of 'basic trust' (or 'ontological security') which is regarded as the feeling of confidence that the individual has in the reliability of other people and the environment (1990: 92; 1991: 129). Such trust, founded on the 'loving attentions of early caretakers' (1991: 38), leads the infant to put faith in those caretakers. This trust forms the core of the adult's ability to filter out 'many of the dangers which in principle threaten the integrity of the self' (1991: 54). Someone with basic trust believes that the people with whom they interact, and the environment through which they move, will not let them down. If they ask for directions, it does not occur to them that strangers might lie to them. If they go to sit on a chair, they do not fear that it might collapse beneath them. In this way, basic trust forms a 'protective cocoon' which enables individuals to keep their lives going, believing that the world around them will continue uneventfully (1991: 54, 129).[7]

For my present purposes, the important thing to understand about basic trust is that Giddens uses it to explain the difference between reflexive selves in pure relationships and traditional selves in non-pure relationships. His fundamental claim is that basic trust makes risk-taking behaviour possible: if you have basic trust, you can consciously take risks; if by contrast you lack it, you will seek to deny the existence of risks and avoid taking them whenever possible.[8] This will also be true of those risks associated with the creation and maintenance of pure relationships. Since such relationships are inherently risky, the same logic should apply: people who enjoy basic trust are able to risk pure relationships, while those who lack such trust seek non-pure relationships. To push this a little further, I would suggest that this same contrast can also be put in more directly political terms. Those with basic trust, who reflexively take part in pure relationships, can be said to have chosen a life of autonomy. Such people want to keep their options open – to stay in a particular relationship as long as it suits them, but to retain the right to move on whenever they wish. By contrast, those without such trust, who resort to tradition and defer to authority in non-pure relationships, can be said to be seeking safety in community. They want to be part of a greater whole which provides them with direction in their lives. They are prepared to abandon autonomy for the comforts of security that membership in a community brings.

In the rest of this chapter I shall be concerned with assessing the plausibility of this thesis. For the moment, let me point out one important implication. Since an individual's fundamental attitude to risk is formed by the time they reach adulthood, it does not seem likely that much can be done to alter that disposition. As Giddens says, the bonds 'established with early caretakers ... leave resonances affecting all close social relations formed in adult life' (1991: 64). Of course, a lot will hang on how powerful these resonances are. But we can say that the stronger they are, the less it will be possible to alter basic trust and to affect all the things which depend upon it. The limits of individuals' willingness to be reflexive, to enter pure relationships and to choose autonomy will be set by the circumstances of their care in early infancy. Once the self is formed, its core of basic trust (or lack of such trust) is fundamentally unchangeable. In fact, one long-term strategy for change does suggest itself. This would be to restructure the conditions in which infants are raised in order to increase the likelihood that they would be able to develop basic trust. Of course, this would necessarily be a long-term project. Some might feel, furthermore, that such a strategy represents a distasteful form of social engineering. To this, the only sensible reply is to point out that all child-care regimes are necessarily the result of some degree of such engineering in the sense that they are the product of particular political policies, legal decisions and social practices which are based on cultural understandings, economic circumstances, and so on.

Pride and shame

Before turning to alternative sources of inspiration for an explanation of the relations between trust, risk and identity, I should say that Giddens' account of the condition of late modernity does include other resources that can be used as part of a better explanation. In contrast to the individual psychology of basic trust, he also develops a *social psychological* account of pride and shame. Both the individual psychology of basic trust and the social psychology of pride are inter-subjective in the sense that they understand trust and pride to depend crucially on the relationship of self to other. However, while the account of basic trust is individual in the sense that it refers to the circumstances of specific individuals' life-histories, the account of pride is social since pride is an affective state that can be experienced by a group as a group (rather than as a set of discrete individuals). My argument will be that this latter account can be used to supplement the explanation of attitudes to identity-risks which is rooted in individual psychology.

Giddens argues that pride and shame form an important axis in the construction of self-identity. Pride – or self-esteem – is a feeling of 'confidence in the integrity and value of the narrative of self-identity' (1991: 66). People with pride are able to narrate a coherent life-story, confident that this story has value. They feel that their life is worth living, that the things they do, and the relationships they form, are meaningful and worthwhile. Shame, the opposite of pride, 'consists of repressed fears that the narrative of self-identity cannot withstand engulfing pressures on its coherence or social acceptability' (1991: 65). People who feel shame are not able to construct a consistent story about their self-identity, and they believe that the story they do tell shows their life to be of little value. As Giddens says, shame 'is fundamentally anxiety about the adequacy of the narrative by means of which the individual sustains a coherent biography' (1991: 65). People who feel shame fear that the choices they make, and associations they forge with others, are without meaning. While pride keeps meaninglessness at bay, shame leads to the danger of being engulfed by meaninglessness.

The significance of this analysis of pride and shame for my principal thesis will become clear as this chapter unfolds. For the moment, I offer a number of remarks about this analysis which I shall pick up on later. First, it is worth emphasising that pride and shame are closely connected to self-identity. As Giddens says of shame, it 'bears directly on self-identity' (1991: 65). Pride enables the individual to engage successfully in the reflexive project of the self, while shame can fatally undermine this project. Second, pride and shame are fundamentally inter-subjective qualities. Giddens comments that, 'founded on the social bond, pride is continually vulnerable to the reactions of others' (1991: 66). If I am treated with appropriate respect or loving concern by others, my pride is sustained. But if I am slighted or neglected, my pride may be severely damaged. In just the same way, shame is a function of my relations with others. I feel shame when I have certain traits exposed to others which I feel are inadequate. More generally, I feel shame when I believe that, in my relationship with a respected or loved other, I am judged to be wanting (1991: 67). Thus, while basic trust is the result of a one-off *'emotional inoculation'* (1991: 39) given (or withheld) in infancy, pride (and shame) can constantly fluctuate according to the way in which I am treated by those around me.

Third, pride and shame are closely related to trust. With reference to the latter emotion, Giddens puts it like this: 'Shame and trust are very closely bound up with one another, since an experience of shame may threaten or destroy trust' (1991: 66). How can my feeling of shame destroy my trust in others? In explaining this link, Giddens says that, if I think the other's response to me shows that my understanding of the other's view of me is false, then trust between us will be undermined (1991: 66). I think that we can best understand this remark by going back to the relationship between intimacy and trust mentioned earlier. Here it was asserted that, if the partners in a relationship disclose themselves to each other, they can develop trust in each other. But what if I reveal something of myself to the other, only to find that the other reacts negatively to this revelation? To take a trivial example, I may confess that I am arachnophobic, only to have the other mock me for this fear. In a more serious case, I could reveal that I had in the past acted ignobly, only to find that the other cannot understand and will not forgive my behaviour. In either case, I am likely to feel shame about that part of me which I had exposed, and as a consequence the trust between me and the other is to some degree undermined.

Other consequences follow from this connection of pride and trust. To begin with, if I feel (or just fear feeling) shame, then I cannot open myself up to the other as I would in a pure relationship. Thus I cannot achieve the intimacy that can be found in such relationships, and I cannot engage in a journey of mutual exploration in order to find my authentic self. Guarded in my relationships, I may connect only on a superficial level, shunning intimacy and avoiding commitment. In extreme cases, I may develop what R. D. Laing, following Donald Winnicott, calls a 'false self' (Giddens, 1991: 59). Furthermore, I may have no desire to search for authenticity. Since I lack pride, my narrative of self-identity will seem to me to be without worth. My choices will seem pointless, my options without value. Thus even if I had the opportunity to be autonomous, I may lack the motivation to use this opportunity. Why bother to make of myself something unique, when such uniqueness is merely trivial variation? Finally, shame may also undermine my willingness, not just to risk trusting others, but to take risks of any kind. Without pride, I lack confidence in the value of my self-identity, and thus I am less likely to take any kind of risks which put that identity on the line. In particular, I may fail to live an autonomous life. I leave this thread of the argument hanging here. Before weaving it back into my main narrative, I want to explore a perspective on trust, risk and identity which is very different from that found in Giddens' work.

Cosmopolitans and communitarians

Zygmunt Bauman offers a perspective of trust, risk and identity which throws interesting light on Giddens' position. On the one hand, these two thinkers share a number of ideas. First, Bauman's characterisation of the present as an age of 'liquid' modernity (2001: 74; and see 2000) is not dissimilar in detail from Giddens' account of 'late' modernity. Second, from this characterisation of the age, he draws very similar implications about self-identity. To be specific, he also follows Beck's argument that, since no certainty exists, it is necessary to choose one's identity (2001: 60–1). Finally, once more like Giddens, Bauman makes a distinction between two groups of people. There are those who are, as it were, true to the conditions of liquid modernity; these are the risk-takers and autonomy-choosers. However, there are also those who would seek to ignore or escape these conditions; these are the risk-avoiders and safety-seekers. On the other hand, there is a number of significant differences between these two thinkers' positions. Of particular interest to me here, Bauman's explanation of different attitudes to the risks of identity brings economic factors much more to the fore than they are in Giddens' individual psychological account. It is this aspect of Bauman's argument which is the focus of my concern in this chapter.

Before considering Bauman's explanation though, we must look at the distinction on which this is intended to cast light. On one side of this distinction is the group he describes as a new 'global elite' (2001: 62). These are the people who have benefited from the processes of globalisation rampant in the age of liquid modernity. Thus Bauman characterises them as the 'exterritorials' who are 'not defined by any locality' (2001: 54) but rather by their mobility across the globe's surface. For this elite few, the modernist promise has been fulfilled: for them, freedom of choice really is the freedom to choose. That is to say, this group finds that the formal right to make decisions about how to run their lives – including the choice of identity – is matched by a substantive ability to make use of that right in practice. Since this is so, this elite values 'self-creation' and 'self-assertion' (2001: 64). They do not want to be tied to any particular identity because they want to be free to exercise and enjoy the freedom to choose their identity, to be one sort of person today and another tomorrow. Perhaps one could go so far as to say that this elite has a horror of fixed identities: for them, the greatest failure would be to be stuck with one identity, with one unchanging sense of self. Drawing on Jonathan Friedman's analysis, Bauman suggests that this elite's experience is one of 'modernity without modernism' (2001: 75). They enjoy the possibility of transgression, but this transgression is not informed by the idea that there is a final destination which guides and gives purpose to it. For this elite, one might say, transgression is for transgression's sake. With particular reference to the idea of exterritoriality, I shall refer to this conception of self-identity as one of *cosmopolitanism* (2001: 60).

This idea of the cosmopolitan self can be associated with a particular conception of the relationship between selves. At first blush, one might think that this sort of individual would be strongly opposed to any identification with a community. Membership of such a collectivity, especially if this is regarded as a community of obligation, would hamper individuals' project of self-creation and threaten to render their identity inflexible. In fact, Bauman suggests, members of the global elite do hanker after community, since, to put it slightly paradoxically, they feel the absence of a sense of belonging – and an authority of numbers – that membership of such a community would bring them (2001: 63). However, in contrast to a community of obligation, members of the global elite want a strongly voluntary community, one that is no more than what Bauman calls 'an assembly of revocable conventions' (2001: 61). Such a community is based on purely voluntary commitment and will last only for as long as its members want it to last (2001: 64–5). Given this degree of voluntariness, the source of unity for such a community cannot be shared and entwined moral duties. Instead, it is unified only because its members make the same subjective judgements about how to live (2001: 65). It is for this reason that Bauman refers to it as an 'aesthetic community' (2001: 72). To employ Paul Hirst's (1994) phrase, this elite regards the associations they form as communities of 'choice' rather than of 'fate'.

On the other side of the distinction that Bauman makes are those individuals who wish to avoid autonomy and seek safety instead. In stark contrast to the cosmopolitan elite is the multitude who are adversely affected by globalisation. Compared to the elite, this group are relatively unprivileged, poorly resourced and hence not self-reliant (2001: 99–100). For this group, 'the right to a free choice of identity' was 'an illusion all along' (2001: 100). The formal freedom of choice offered to them does not convert in practice to actual freedom to choose. Although individuals *de jure*, they cannot translate this into individuality *de facto* (2001: 58).[9] As a result of their position, members of the multitude do not value self-creation and self-assertion. Without sufficient resources, they cannot choose who to be. Instead, Bauman contends, they seek security in community, safety in belonging (2001: 100). They want to identify with a greater whole and to let this identification determine their identity. With reference to its attachment to community, I shall refer to this idea of self-identity as the *communitarian self*.

Once more, this idea of self-identity can be correlated with a particular conception of the relationship between selves. Communitarians yearn for precisely the sort of community that cosmopolitans despise. Rather than a voluntarily joined and aesthetically bonded community, they desire an 'ethical community' formed by ongoing and interlaced obligations and rights (2001: 72). To be a member of such a community is to have deep moral commitments to other members, just as they have such commitments to you. The reason that communitarian selves want such a community is because they believe that it will provide them with certainty, security and safety. In particular, it will provide them with what Bauman calls 'communal insurance against the errors and misadventures which are the risks inseparable from individual life' (2001: 72). In other words, membership provides collective protection against risk. In order for it to be able to do all this, such a community cannot be based on voluntary membership. Members must regard it as a collectivity that they have no choice but to be a part of. Thus such a community has a 'death do us part' logic (2001: 75), which is very different from that of the 'good while it lasts' logic of aesthetic community. Once more drawing on Hirst's analysis, members of the unprivileged multitude regard the collectivities in which they are located as communities of 'fate' rather than of 'choice' (1994).

I want to conclude my comparison of these two groups by exploring the political demands which each of them characteristically makes. I have argued that Giddens draws a contrast between those who seek recognition for authenticity and those who seek it for identity. It might appear at first blush as if Bauman would make the same distinction. Since the elite engages in perpetual self-creation, one might imagine that their goal is to secure appropriate acknowledgement for the authentic selves that they create. Indeed, Bauman does appear to make an argument like this. Forging for themselves a distinctive mode of being, cosmopolitan individuals want credit for this achievement: 'Identity appears to be but a matter of choice and resolution, and choices are to be respected and resolution is to be rewarded' (2001: 61). By contrast, since communitarian selves reject individual self-creation for the safety of collective identities fixed by communal membership, one might imagine that they would seek automatic recognition for that identity. There is certainly some validity to this hypothesis about Bauman's position. In other ways, however, it is rather misleading. What in fact he argues is that both types of community make the same sort of political demands, but that they do so for very different reasons. Both elite and non-elite communities demand recognition for their distinctive differences. They want appropriate acknowledgement for a collective identity which they believe to be unique to them. But the logic underlying this demand is very different for the two different types of communities. As we shall see later, moreover, this is a difference which makes a difference: it explains other important distinctions between the politics of these two types of group.

Let me explain. First recall that the aesthetic communities formed by members of the elite are voluntary. Bauman argues that precisely because they are voluntary, these communities tend to fanaticism. Inability to close ranks leads to an intense focus on the distinctive qualities of that community (2001: 65–6). If membership cannot be controlled, then doctrine can. It is this logic which motivates the demand of an aesthetic community for the recognition of its collectively created distinctiveness. Up to now I have implied that membership of the ethical communities formed by members of the multitude is also voluntary. I have suggested that the disadvantaged react to their situation by forming communities regarded as mutual aid organisations. But I must admit that this simplifies Bauman's account of ethical community. In fact, he argues – rightly in my opinion – that the reason why some people are disadvantaged in the first place is that they have been forced into communities by powerful others – that is, members of the elite (2001: 89). First, then, such communities are formed by a process of external enclosure. People are denied the right to assimilate (2001: 95–6), deprived of the ability to choose an identity (2001: 100), ghettoised and separated from others as alien elements (2001: 103). Only then do such communities engage in the process of self-enclosure. They construct a strong ethos of loyalty to the community (2001: 96–7) and attempt to recoup their pride by, for instance, asserting that 'black is beautiful' (2001: 89–90). Thus Bauman argues that in the case of ethical communities there is enclosure 'from both directions' (2001: 103). Members are initially forced into their community, and only after this do they 'choose' – or perhaps it would be better to say 'choose to identify with' – that community. Given this, it is clear that when ethical communities demand recognition of their distinctive identities, they do so for reasons rather different from those of aesthetic communities. They demand appropriate acknowledgement of their identities since they hope that, as a consequence, this will protect them against certain hazards which would otherwise threaten them (and they also hope that this will be a way of boosting their collective self-esteem).[10]

Resources and risks

Earlier, I argued that Giddens uses an individual psychological theory, based on the idea of basic trust, in order to explain people's attitudes to the risks of identity. It is important to note that he also hints at a material dimension to this explanation. Thus he suggests that attitudes to risk can be shaped in particular by systems of welfare. What he calls 'positive welfare' places emphasis 'on the mobilizing of life-political measures, aimed once more at connecting autonomy with personal and collective responsibilities' (1994: 18). In other words, such a welfare-system is designed to enable individuals to act autonomously – that is, to take risks – while also remaining aware of their responsibilities to others. I now want to suggest that Bauman offers an interesting twist on such a material explanation. As I have already intimated, he focuses on economic factors in order to account for different attitudes to risk. Instead of attempting a psychological explanation for a failure of nerve by some individuals to live a life of freedom, he propounds instead an explanation in which material resources play a key role. To put it in the briefest possible terms, this explanation suggests that those who have resources can take risks and choose individual autonomy, while those who do not have the resources cannot take risks and choose safety in community instead. Once we connect this proposition to the distinction drawn between the new global elite and multitude, we can see how Bauman's explanation is intended to work.

As we have seen, the new global elite is able and willing to take risks. Of particular interest here, they value autonomy over identity in order to retain the possibility of constantly transforming their sense of selves. In stark contrast, the new global multitude is not able and willing to take risks. Instead, they value identity over autonomy and seek the security of a stable sense of self rooted in community. As far as I can see, Bauman's explanation for this correlation of the elite with risk-taking and the multitude with risk-avoidance is relatively straightforward. Members of the elite are willing to take risks because they are well resourced and hence self-reliant. Their resources provide them with the security they need in order to be able to take risks.[11] If a particular choice of identity has unforeseen and disagreeable consequences, then they can draw on their resources and choose again. By contrast, lacking the resources necessary to make them self-reliant, members of the multitude do not value the possibility of self-assertion and self-creation. For them, the consequences of a wrong choice of life-style would be catastrophic. Lacking the resources to undo this decision and choose again, they would be stuck in a situation with highly detrimental consequences for their welfare. As a consequence, without resources, they are not willing to risk the choice of identity.

Thus we can see that Bauman's resource-based explanation of attitudes to identity-risks is quite different from the trust-based explanation offered by Giddens. In what remains of this chapter, I shall argue nevertheless that these two explanations are not incompatible. Indeed, my suggestion will be that they can be brought together to the benefit of the greater whole. In order to lay some of the groundwork for this proposed synthesis, I need to point out one important implication of Bauman's position. While a purely psychological perspective may not be able to suggest a political solution to the problem of risk-aversion, Bauman's economic explanation of different attitudes to risk-taking does suggest such a solution. If risk-aversion is a function of the ownership of resources, then something can be done to alter this attitude to risk. It is possible to devise a political strategy capable of affecting this attitude.

Here Bauman follows Nancy Fraser's (2003) analysis of what she calls 'social justice in the age of identity politics'. Fraser's thesis is that in our present times a conception of justice as the fair distribution of resources has been wrongly eclipsed by a rival conception that sees justice purely in terms of the recognition of identity. Bauman is attracted to this analysis because he agrees with its emphasis on the need to bring issues of resource distribution back into the picture. Going further, I would argue that he has at least an implicit commitment to the idea that there is a need to redistribute resources from the elite to the non-elite.[12] To support this claim, I would point to a couple of claims which Bauman does explicitly make. First, he reports with approval Bruno Latour's view that the 'good society' is one which provides all its members with a chance of living a decent life (2001: 79). Second, he notes with regret the passing of an idea of community 'as a site of the equal sharing of jointly attained welfare; as a kind of togetherness which presumes the responsibilities of the rich and gives substance to the hopes of the poor that such responsibilities will be taken up' (2001: 62). Here, I think, Bauman gets very close to an explicit expression of the principle of resource redistribution which I am attributing to him. If this attribution is accepted, and if Bauman's explanation of different attitudes to risk is right, then it follows that such redistribution will have a significant impact on attitudes to risk. To be specific, it will increase the numbers of those prepared to take risks, including those involved in living an autonomous life since, *ex hypothesi*, they will have the resources needed to protect them against such risks.

A synthesised account

My principal aim in this chapter has been to consider different explanations of attitudes to the risks of identity. I have argued that in Giddens' analysis of late modernity we find a distinction between what I have called reflexive and traditional selves, in which the former are risk-takers and the latter are risk-avoiders. On my reading, Giddens' explanation of their different attitudes to identity-risks rests heavily on what I have characterised as an individual psychology of basic trust. With such trust, one is prepared to take risks about how to live; without it, one will try to avoid such risks at all costs. I then turned to Bauman's analysis of liquid modernity in order to consider the rival account to be found there. This time a distinction is made between what I have called cosmopolitans and communitarians, such that the former sense of self-identity is associated with risk-taking and autonomy-choosing, and the latter with risk-avoidance and safety-seeking. I have argued that, for Bauman, these different attitudes to the risks of identity can best be explained by reference to an economic analysis of resource distribution. With enough resources, one is prepared to take on the risks of identity; but without such resources, one will be very chary about doing so.

What I want to argue now is that these are not incompatible analyses. Indeed, I believe that, if Giddens' psychological theory is supplemented and modified by Bauman's economic analysis, the result will be a more defensible account of the relations between trust, risk and identity. I then want to go further and argue that two more dimensions should be added to this synthesised account. First, I shall contend that Bauman neglects the cultural side to Fraser's theory of social justice, one that focuses on the wrongs of misrecognition. Then I shall return to Giddens' analysis of pride and shame in order to show how this can add a social psychological element to the final synthesis. In particular, it can provide a vital link between the economic and the psychological dimensions of the account. I now offer a number of comments about each of these four dimensions in turn.

I believe that Giddens' analysis of basic trust can play a vital role in a complete account of attitudes to the risks of identity. It provides the aspect of that account which explains the role played by purely individual factors, those that concern specific individuals' life-histories. There seems no doubt that the early experiences of infants with their caretakers have a profound effect on their subsequent relationships with other subjects. To think of this effect in terms of basic trust seems both plausible and insightful. At the same time, it is important to note that Giddens regards trust more generally as an ongoing aspect of all relationships. We have seen, for instance, how he argues that the development of trust is closely bound up with the achievement of intimacy in pure relationships. Thus, while basic trust may be to all intents and purposes a fixed element of an individual's psychological disposition, trust between particular subjects can vary according to a number of different factors. Finally, with regard to this part of the argument, it is worth recalling how Giddens correlates trust with pride and shame. He argues that, while shame undermines trust, pride underpins it. For an individual to feel shame in front of others erodes the possibility of them trusting each other. By contrast, if an individual feels approval or love from others, then their consequent pride makes it easier for them to trust those others. I shall return to this idea very shortly.

I also believe that Bauman's economic analysis of resource distribution can play an important part in this synthesised account of identity-risks. This analysis supplies the aspect of that account which identifies the role that economic factors play in determining whether individuals will take risks with their identity. While I think the claim that concern about recognition has wholly eclipsed concern about redistribution is somewhat hyperbolic, it is nevertheless true that the politics of identity loom much larger in the minds of certain cultural and political commentators than what was called the politics of class. There is no doubt that this balance needs to be redressed. Individuals' location in the economic structure of society, and in particular the control that this location gives them over the resources which can render them self-reliant, profoundly affects the risks they are prepared to take, including those risks involved in relationships with other individuals. To reiterate the point made earlier, economic self-reliance is likely to reduce risk-aversion, while economic dependency is likely to increase it. Finally, on this aspect of the problem, it should perhaps be pointed out that *in sensu stricto* self-reliance reduces risk itself rather than reducing the reluctance to take risks. Nevertheless, I do not think that this has a profound effect on the argument here. It remains true to say that those who possess sufficient economic resources can take decisions about their lives which are risky since deeply uncertain, while admitting that the harmful consequences (risks) of those decisions going badly is reduced.

A third element of my proposed synthesis is what I shall refer to as the cultural analysis of recognition. This analysis can help us to identify the role that cultural factors may play in shaping individuals' attitudes to the risks of identity. As we have seen, Bauman is explicit about his debt to Fraser's account of social justice, and in particular its dual focus on redistribution and recognition. He recommends, for instance, a 'blend' of distributive justice and the politics of recognition (2001: 78). Yet I want to argue that Bauman fails to pay sufficient attention to the second part of this blend. Let me refer you to a couple of passages from his book on *Community* in support of this claim. At one point, he reports with approval Richard Rorty's view that material deprivation, rather than 'intolerance to cultural otherness', is 'the deepest source of all inequality and injustice' (2001: 106). At another point, he argues that, with the focus on a 'culturalist' right to recognition, 'the unfulfilled task of the human right to well-being and a life lived in dignity falls by the board' (2001: 88). While Bauman echoes Fraser's call to undo the unwarranted displacement of redistribution by recognition, at some points his proposed rehabilitation of redistribution goes too far, threatening in its turn wholly to displace recognition.

I think that Fraser herself is right to insist that these two moments of justice must be held in balance. Although she concedes that all injustices have an economic and a cultural component, some injustices are much more cultural than economic. Her own example of homophobia would be a case in point since the injustices suffered by gay men and lesbians are predominantly cultural in character. As Fraser says, 'the social division between heterosexuals and homosexuals is not grounded in the political economy ... The division is rooted, rather, in the status order of society, as institutionalized patterns of cultural value construct heterosexuality as natural and normative, homosexuality as perverse and despised' (2003: 18). The point here is that certain injustices are predominantly and irreducibly cultural in character. Overcoming such injustices, therefore, requires above all a change in patterns of cultural recognition rather than a redistribution of resources. For my present purposes, it is important to understand the consequences of such injustices for the risks of identity. Even if individuals control sufficient resources to make them economically self-reliant, they will not risk certain choices of identity if those identities are vilified by prevailing 'patterns of cultural value'.

Even with these three elements in place, I want to argue that this account is still incomplete. A fourth and final element is supplied by what I shall call the social psychological analysis of pride and shame. This analysis provides a way of identifying the part that psychological factors affecting whole groups play in determining how individuals face up to the risks of identity. In order to see how it can play this role, recall some of the key features of Giddens' analysis. First, while pride is a feeling of confidence in the value of one's self-identity, shame is the lack of such confidence. Second, both of these affective states are connected to trust: if I have pride, I am more likely to trust others, whereas if I feel shame, I am less likely to trust them. Third, both of these affective states also have effects on attitudes to risk. There is both a direct and an indirect link here. The former suggests that, if I would not be proud of the identity I am intending to choose, I may not feel that this choice is worth the risk. The latter, indirect link goes back to the previous point about the connection of pride and trust: if lack of pride means that I cannot trust others, then as a result of that mistrust I may not take risks with my identity.

I want to argue that pride and shame, understood in this way, are affective states that can be experienced by groups, and that such experiences have significant effects on the attitudes of their members to trust, risk and identity. They are not simply emotions felt by particular individuals as a result of their interaction with other particular individuals. Rather, pride and shame can be experienced by all members of a group as a result of changes in that group's environment. To be specific, I contend that these group effects operate through the economic and cultural processes I have just identified. That is to say, if a group enjoys sufficient resources and positive acknowledgement of its collective identity, then it will feel pride as a group. If, by contrast, a group lacks adequate resources and its collective identity is disparaged, then it will experience shame. In this context, it is worth considering Bauman's comment that, as a consequence of their inability to translate their existence as individuals *de jure* into individuality *de facto*, the under-resourced multitude suffers humiliation (2001: 100). If we then bring Giddens' analysis back into the picture, we can see how an environmental change can affect a group's pride or shame, and that this will have direct consequences on the ability of members of the group to trust others and to take risks with their identity. For instance, the withdrawal of a welfare benefit aimed at single mothers will of course have significant impacts on their economic position. According to my hypothesis, as a consequence of the reduction in their economic self-reliance, their pride will also suffer, and hence so will their ability to trust others and their willingness to take risks.[13] By contrast, consider the case of the UK's Local Government Act 1988. The notorious section 28 of this Act prohibits local authorities from 'promoting homosexuality by teaching or by publishing material'.[14] Were this to be repealed, it could have a significant effect on reducing the stigma presently suffered by gay men and lesbians. Once more, according to my hypothesis, as a consequence of this reduction in stigma, the pride of members of this group will improve, and hence so will their capacity for trust and risk-taking.[15]

Finally, I should perhaps observe that my proposal to add a psychological element to justice as recognition is one that Fraser herself would reject since she is determined to keep her account independent of any form of what she calls 'psychologism'. She distances herself from the claim that the problem with misrecognition is that it causes psychological harm, in the sense that individuals who are not adequately recognised will as a consequence lack self-esteem or a sense of self-worth. While she acknowledges that misrecognition can cause such psychological harm, Fraser denies that this is why it is unjust. Rather its injustice lies in its role as a barrier to parity of participation. In defence of my position here, I would point out that those offering psychological accounts of recognition contend that the psychological harm caused by misrecognition is not a side-effect but a direct obstacle to parity of participation. This argument suggests that misrecognition prevents the development of pride, and this in turn is the necessary precondition for the effective exercise of autonomy. If I do not feel myself to be of worth, I am not likely to make the most of the opportunities available to me to live a fully self-actualising life. I want to argue, then, that since the psychological harm of misrecognition directly undermines parity of participation, then the cause of that harm can rightly be considered an injustice.

Conclusion

In this chapter I have explored two rather different ways of explaining different attitudes to the risks of identity. In Giddens' account, basic trust plays a fundamental role in explaining why some individuals are prepared to take risks and others are not. For Bauman, economic resources are the key to understanding why some people are happy to choose lives of autonomy, while others look for security in community. I have argued that these two explanations can both play their particular part in a greater whole. But I have also suggested that other sorts of explanation need to be brought into the picture. To be specific, Giddens' account of pride, and Fraser's account of cultural recognition, also have their part to play. While I have not had the space here fully to defend my proposed synthesis, I hope that I have at least done enough to indicate how it would work.

It may be worth making one final remark about the character and status of this combined account. I said at the start of this chapter that I would begin by asking diagnostic questions, before moving on to questions about prescription. In other words, I wanted to know first how to explain different attitudes to identity-risks, and then I wanted to consider what could be done to affect those attitudes. In the course of the chapter, I would suggest, there has been such a gradual shift from diagnosis to prescription, from description to recommendation. This shift has occurred since I have focused increasingly on Bauman's and then Fraser's theories

of social justice. Both offer accounts of the just society which I believe
have important implications for the risks of identity. To put this rather
crudely, they imply that a just society would be arranged in such a way
that individuals would be happy to exercise their autonomy and regard
their lives as ones of self-creation. The wish to avoid autonomy and the
flight to community are then explained as reactions to remaining injustices. If this reading of the argument is right, it prompts at least two
important questions. Does this account of social justice express a strongly
modernist perspective in that it assumes that progress will bring increasing
desire for freedom? And does this account amount to an exercise in utopianism, based as it is on the belief that in a just world, individuals will be
autonomous self-creators? Although I think that these are interesting
questions, they will have to wait for another day.

Notes

1 In the course of the chapter I shall attempt to justify this correlation of risk-taking
with autonomy-choosing, and risk-avoiding with community-seeking.
2 For a useful overview of the debate between liberals and communitarians, see
Mulhall and Swift (1996).
3 Note that such societies are not post-traditional in the sense that no tradition
exists. Rather, since a 'plurality' of traditions exists, no one tradition can guide
us (1991: 196).
4 In extreme cases, there is an active courting of risk – for example, smoking
(1991: 124–6).
5 See Taylor (1992) for an insightful discussion of the 'ethics of authenticity'.
6 As we shall see, such relationships are also risky since to disclose oneself to the
other may be to court humiliation and shame.
7 Note that Misztal's reading makes Giddens' account more complex, with a
distinction being found between 'basic trust' and 'elementary trust' (1996: 90–1).
8 Giddens believes that basic trust may also be able to explain creativity (1991:
41).
9 As a result of this inability, furthermore, such individuals are likely to experience
humiliation (2001: 100). This point will become of importance later in this
chapter.
10 Bauman offers further reflections on the fate of the new global poor in his
Globalization (1998).
11 In a later section of this chapter, I shall ask whether these really are risks given
the fact that *ex hypothesi* the elite's resources protect them against the possible
harmful effects of risky action.
12 Perhaps a somewhat less provocative way of putting this would be to say that it
is necessary to guarantee all citizens a minimum level of resources.
13 Such a policy change is also likely to add directly to the social stigma which the
targeted group already suffers from.
14 Details of this section of the Act can be found at www.hmso.gov.uk/acts/
acts1988/Ukpga_19880009_en_5.htm.
15 The repeal of this legislation may also have a minor positive effect on the
economic position of this group.

References

Bauman, Z. (1998), *Globalization: The Human Consequences*, Cambridge: Polity Press.
—— (2000), *Liquid Modernity*, Cambridge: Polity Press.
—— (2001), *Community: Seeking Safety in an Insecure World*, Cambridge: Polity Press.
Beck, U. (1992), *Risk Society*, London: Sage.
Fraser, N. (2003) 'Social Justice in the Age of Identity Politics', in N. Fraser and A. Honneth, *Redistribution or Recognition?: A Philosophical Exchange*, London: Verso.
Giddens, A. (1990), *Consequences of Modernity*, Cambridge: Polity Press.
—— (1991), *Modernity and Self-identity*, Cambridge: Polity Press.
—— (1994), *Beyond Left and Right: the Future of Radical Politics*, Cambridge: Polity Press.
Hirst, P. (1993), *Associative Democracy*, Cambridge: Polity Press.
Misztal, B. A. (1996), *Trust in Modern Societies*, Cambridge: Polity Press.
Mulhall, S. and Swift, A. (1996), *Liberals and Communitarians*, London: Blackwell.
Taylor, C. (1992), *The Ethics of Authenticity*, Cambridge, MA: Harvard University Press.
—— (1995), 'The Politics of Recognition', in his *Philosophical Writings*, Cambridge, MA: Harvard University Press.

3
Risk, Sensibility, Ethics and Justice in the later Levinas

Peter Jowers

Introduction

During the Rwandan massacres of 1997, Paul Rusesabagina, manager of the Hôtel des Mille Collines in Kigali, repeatedly used a fax line which the Hutu leaders had forgotten to cut, vainly attempting to alert the White House, the Ministry of Foreign Affairs in France and others to the horrors of the genocide there, knowing that if caught, he faced instant death. 'He would stay up until four in the morning – sending faxes, calling, ringing the whole world.' The church of Sainte Famille was just down the hill from the hotel. Later, Paul exclaimed, 'But you know, Sainte Famille also had a working phone line, and that priest Father Wenceslas, never used it. My goodness!' Asked why, he answered, 'That's a mystery ... Everyone could have done it.' Challenged during the period as to the incongruity of carrying a gun, Father Wenceslas replied, 'They've already killed fifty-nine priests; I don't want to be the sixtieth' (Gourevitch, 1998: 132–6).

Anton Schmidt was a German soldier whose name came up in the course of the Adolf Eichmann trial. He helped Jewish partisans by supplying them with forged papers and trucks until apprehended and executed by the Germans. Hannah Arendt, noting the silence which descended on the court on hearing this tale, remarks, 'How utterly different everything would be today in this courtroom, in Israel, in Germany, in all of Europe, and perhaps in all countries of the world, if only more such stories could have been told' (Arendt, cited in Bernstein, 2002: 259).

Under these extreme conditions, of maximum uncertainty risking almost certain death, why did two men act on behalf of others rather than themselves? Why are we not prepared to risk hospitality in the form of asylum when we know that she whom we turn away risks death? Why do we not trust our instinct to help her?

I examine Emmanuel Levinas's contribution to these pressing questions and his contention that to act ethically is to be willing to go to the point of substituting one's life for others, for strangers. Jacques Derrida's discussions of the aporias which proliferate around conditional and unconditional hospitality circle this point (Derrida, 1999, 2001, 2002b; Derrida and Dufourmantelle, 2000). We generally do not act so because a 'violence' inherent within cognition overrides sensibility. Concern with knowledge, conceived either theoretically or practically, within a totalising, substantialist ontology, outweighs our care for each other.

The parameters of Levinas's critique of totality, usually abbreviated as 'ontology', are well known. Totality as he conceives it includes the idea that 'the entirety of philosophy is conceived on the basis of its Greek source', thus 'the founding concepts of philosophy are primarily Greek and that we cannot think outside this medium which has now become global' (Derrida, 1978: 81). Different interpretations of this heritage are possible but are mere differences within a common metaphysical structure or 'domination of the same'. Even as we try to escape from or revitalise this tradition we are caught within it. Philosophies in this tradition, perhaps best exemplified by G. W. F. Hegel, are philosophies of 'security'. They reduce anything heterological, singular and unique which lies beyond knowledge and submit them to its truth. Anything outside is 'captured' and systematised within the predetermined circuits of potential knowledge. This is the reduction of radical alterity to the same. Otherness is subsumed as a 'this or that', within an already determined horizon, capable of incorporation as knowledge within language (Levinas, 1998b: 110).

Levinas notes that:

> Being is manifested with a theme. Perhaps from this comes intellectualism's ever-renascent power, and the pretension to absoluteness of speech, which is capable of embracing everything, relating everything, thematising everything, even its own failures, even its own relativity. (1998b: 109)

Even intuition cannot escape this imperialism of thought.

Space precludes any serious discussion of the complexities surrounding Levinas's conception of totality. Minimally, it is important to understand that he linked it to war and violence. The ethical relation is subsumed within abstraction. We are not open to the uniqueness of other persons in their singularity because we are already always seduced by the priority of thought, categorising them. A fetishised violence and paganism of place, nations, borders, inclusion and exclusions, customs and controls on migration, etc. follow from this move. Levinas's eloquence concerning the violence of totality is renowned. 'Individuals are reduced to being bearers of forces that command them unbeknownst to themselves. The meaning of individuals ... is derived from totality (*TI*: 22).[1] Totality has been the basis on which we have sought to institutionalise justice in the search for the good life lived within just institutions. Our repeated failure has been all too evident.

Thinking necessarily takes place within language; the most sophisticated thought derives from Greek philosophy. We cannot escape the inherent violence of the link between thought and language which permeates our institutions. This is the classic criticism of Levinas. He cannot but write in a language which, if he is determined to think philosophically, must necessarily be a language permeated with Greek derived conceptuality against which he rails. The substance of the charges Derrida outlined so magnificently in his essay 'Violence and Metaphysics' in *Totality and Infinity* argues that while Levinas had wanted to articulate the primacy of the 'ethical' encounter between self and Other, which comes prior to any ontological concerns, his very attempt was betrayed by its necessary capture within the circuits of Greek thought. His emphasis on the primacy of speech and the impossibility of separating thought and language intensify his dilemma (Derrida, 1978).

The substance of my account here links to the idea that *Otherwise than Being* was a sustained attempt to respond to these charges. This is well known. Levinas has, if he is to persuade his interlocutors of the primacy of ethics, to write of such human encounters in a language which resists as far as possible that of ontology while simultaneously knowing he will succumb to it.

Levinas circles around a black hole towards which all his arguments relate, the encounter which is ethical but which resists conceptualisation and language. He tries repeatedly, because of the demands for justice – a discussion with which this paper ends – to bring to language an ethical dimension which is beyond it. Always, he seeks to avoid reducing that enigmatic encounter to tired ontological forms of expression. It is an almost impossible task he sets himself, acknowledging that betrayal is inevitable! I offer an exploration of the motif in Levinas's work of how the ethical encounter is born from incarnate sensibility. This motif is to be found in *Otherwise than Being*, and should be understood as a response to Derrida's critique and as deepening Levinas's ethical saying.

Bernstein notes that whatever specific motif we follow through Levinas's work, we arrive at the same point (Bernstein, 2002: 252). He argues that 'Levinas's entire philosophic project can best be understood as an *ethical* response to evil' and to the problem of evil which we must confront after the end of theodicy (Bernstein, 2002: 252–3). The encounter – it takes several names – is Levinas's response.

Theodicy traditionally attempts to reconcile the problem of evil as unnecessary suffering with faith in a beneficent God. Derrida often remarks on its specifically Abrahamic provenance, his term for our intertwined Judaic, Christian and Islamic traditions of the Book (Derrida, 2002a: 42–101). Theodicy is a temptation. It either denies God's culpability, saves morality in the name of faith or, worst of all, makes suffering bearable (Bernstein, 2002: 255). Theodicy persists in watered-down, secular progressivism. Appeals to the vindication of history still taint public discourse. Levinas and Derrida recognise that theodicy is over and that the problems of suffering and evil have to be confronted now. This accounts for the urgency of their opening towards the ethical and examination of quite how it underpins demands for justice.

Any simple definition of the ethical would fall prey to ontological thought. Levinas 'summons us to a dislocation', a departure from the familiar 'Greek site, and perhaps ... every site in general' (Derrida, 1978: 82). Discussion of his work adds another disseminatory strand; it follows his conversational model of philosophical practice (*OB*: 20).

One must not confuse Levinas's discussion with conceptions of ethical and moral decisions traditionally linked to consciousness. Our ethical sensibility 'prefigures' all conscious decisions and acts entwined or woven within them as an inescapable affective undertow which, if denied, haunts us if we are not attentive to its fluxions. To be ethical is to be responsible to and for the Other, and even for what s(he) does.[2] The beginnings of a response to our current evils rest on a realisation of the limits of knowledge and an attentiveness to sensibility. There we may find the inspiration to act differently when faced with extreme risk, because through our singular experiences as incarnate, we sense other's vulnerability.

Levinas's non-genetic argument

Levinas's argument does not seek to explain the emergence of ethical sensibility let alone consciousness as the entry of the subject into the law(s) of society. He eschews attempts to 'explain away' ethical responsibility by reducing it to something acquired and transmitted by conscious adults to the as yet unconscious child, such that any specific person's ethical sensibility would be a hit-or-miss affair of socialisation. He returned to a core presumption within Husserlian phenomenology, its antagonism towards psychologism. 'Our analyses claim to be in the spirit of Husserlian phenomenology' (*OB*: 183). However, with Heidegger, he resists Husserl's intellectualised conception of the transcendental ego. Levinas's 'reduction' of *doxa* or the taken-for-granted, the prototypical phenomenological move which enables its practitioners to bring to attention the unnoticed facets of everyday life, seeks to move beyond findings derived from conscious intentionality to those linked to sensibility as animate bodies, the emergence of incarnate 'identities' and their interaction (*OB*: 53 and 71).

For Levinas, to be human is to be ethical. 'Ethics' and 'morality' are often used interchangeably in philosophy and merely stipulative definitions given of them. Levinas was utterly opposed to any link between ethics and 'ethos'; the mores, customs and morals of distinct 'ethnos' or people, yet simultaneously wanted to distinguish his argument from any rationally grounded moral system such as that advocated by Kant. Ethics is an encounter between two people as sensate creatures before it is anything else.

Ethics is not to be linked to philosophies or therapies of consciousness where moral error is conceived as resulting from a potentially knowable, but as yet sequestered part of our minds which, if drawn to consciousness, might be altered. Grounded in incarnate sensibility, the ethical is out of time, literally 'anarchic', incapable of being recuperated fully by consciousness. It is 'the good beyond being'. It leaves merely enigmas and traces which, if tracked, begin to make sense of core facets of interpersonal experience.

Ethics entwined within consciousness: temporal and spatial metaphors

Levinas insisted that 'Responsibility for the other ... is human fraternity itself' (*OB*: 116). The ethical relation occurs where and whenever two people meet, but does not include human–animal ones. I cannot explore this dubious limiting of the ethical to specifically intra-human encounters nor the problematic conceptions of fraternity and it basis within masculine virility here (Derrida, 1992: 280–2; 1997; Critchley, 1992; Sandford, 2002).

Sensibility and the ethical relationships it determines occur simultaneously with consciousness, running 'parallel', in tandem, and entwined with or alongside all human encounters. We often choose to treat conscious encounters coolly as merely distanced communication of information. Justice demands this mode. Nevertheless, communicative encounters are always more, even if we choose to treat our interlocutor with civil indifference or hostility. Levinas uses temporal[3] and spatial terminology to get at this intersection of sensibility, ethics and consciousness though skewing traditional conceptions repeatedly. For example,

> Immemorial, unrepresentable, invisible, the past that bypasses the present, the pluperfect past, falls into a past that is a gratuitous lapse. It cannot be recuperated by reminiscence not because of its remoteness, but because of its incommensurability with the present. (*OB*: 11)

Elsewhere, when he writes 'in the "prehistory" of the ego posited for itself, speaks a responsibility', his unease with the terms he is forced to mobilise is explicitly flagged (*OB*: 117). Examples abound. The 'self is ... older than the ego' (*OB*: 117); it is 'anarchic' (*OB*: 121). Levinas has an almost inexhaustible lexicon of terms to write of non-recuperable time insisting on a range of experience permanently recalcitrant to consciousness. It will never be capable of being remembered, retold, subject to reminiscence, recollection, historicity or thematisation. It cannot be used for science, religion or eschatology, and defies myth. Yet, enigmatically, it haunts consciousness.

A simple, 'ontological' way of conceiving this sensibility would be to think of a mind being permanently impacted on at all times by flows of material connections it enters into within its environment, but of which only a minimal part could ever be brought safely to consciousness.

We shall see that Levinas offers a quasi-transcendental account of ethical sensibility implying its applicability to all human beings. It contrasts, however, to rationally grounded moral, legal and political forms of justification which, to his mind, have merely led to endless war and have lost all legitimacy.

Levinas cannot escape spatial metaphors either when tracking ethical responsibility. These are as deceptively ontological as temporal ones. He is profoundly aware that any substantialist ontology commits one to certain, essentially Kantian, conceptions of spatiality.

> But for Kant, space remains the condition for the representation of an entity, and thus implies subjectivity. ... Essence carries on as presence, exhibition, phenomenality or appearing, and as such requires a subject in the form of consciousness and invests it as devoted to representation. (*OB*: 179)

Any substantialist ontology implies commitment to *conscious* subjectivity. Hegel's speculative idealism took this simple observation to its limits where individual subjects become necessary 'moments' or playthings of an essence or Being unfolding itself through concretion and time only to return to itself. Phenomenology continued the link between subjectivity and spatiality, merely deepening and making reflective awareness of spatiality more subtle by emphasising the dynamics of kinaesthetic perception.

> The whole of the subjective is, according to Brentano's formula, which was taken up by Husserl, either representation or founded upon representation; every thesis is convertible into a doxic thesis, a positing or recognition of entities, a welcome of presence. (*OB*: 179)

Levinas's quarry was a self lying on the hither side of being; it 'is the underside of a fabric woven where there is consciousness' (*OB*: 103). The performative problem Levinas knew he faced consists of the attempt to write of processes having effects on consciousness 'whose active source does not in any way, occur in consciousness' (*OB*: 102).

Saying and the said

In Levinas's vocabulary, *Saying* is a sensate, expressive experience founded on incarnation. It is the human encounter prior to and beneath ordinary language which operates as its very condition of possibility. Levinas characterises the latter as *the said*. Adhering to this distinction, he partly succeeds in escaping Derrida's critique by enabling a much sharper distinction to be drawn between ethics which better 'escapes' the violence of categories taken from ontological totality and justice, which necessarily uses them.

Through its very incarnate expressivity, *Saying* 'signifies'.[4] Signification, as used by Levinas, denotes any expressivity sensed when a self encounters another. Such signification is non-intentional, not to be confused with any Saussurean usage. 'The plot of proximity and communication is not a modality of cognition' (*OB*: 48). It occurs prior to any thematisation, conceptualisation, information or sociality. *Saying* may take place 'by way of' the sensed epiphany of another's face, or even their whole body but is not equivalent to them. They belong to cognition. *Saying* is not occurring if we notice the colour of another's eyes. This small example points to the gulf between a sensed proximity of the Other and a cognitive relation, however minimal or intuitive, to the Other which emerges when we use ordinary language. *Saying* runs within human communication, but is constantly dissimulated as we are mesmerised by the content of what is being communicated and the substantiality of the Other, rather than the fact that we, as humans, are communicating.

'*Saying*' is characterised in endlessly shifting ways. It is as if Levinas were chasing a butterfly which constantly evades capture because he does not want it entrammelled within ontological categories. He emphasises its involuntary, passive quality. *Saying* happens when egotistical identity breaks up, is exposed, loses its inward complacency (self-love) and made vulnerable by the Other's approach, responds. *Saying* is explicitly contrasted to conscious intentionality. It is not a consciousness coinciding with itself, going out and returning, consolidating itself by reducing otherness to similarity. *Saying* breaks up the 'ego', it exiles it from itself and it turns it inside out. The subject of *Saying* does not give signs but responds to them, is called through them, by and to the Other. Levinas insists that response takes priority before any comprehension of what is expressed thus resisting the primacy of intentionality and interest. Response is disinterested.[5] *Saying* is an extreme vulnerability and exposure to, and denuding by, the Other. One risks insults, wounding and the fission of one's very punctuality or centredness. One's unity and very form is torn up.

Saying is, then, interwoven with the said, 'it imprints its trace on the thematisation itself' (*OB*: 46–7). Our everyday sociality and communication stand within this primary experience of the encounters with the Other. Llewelyn notes that 'Prior to my being possessed by language ... is my possession by the human being who speaks to me'. Sociality stems from an initial being possessed by and obsessed with the Other. Obsessions control us; we do not choose them and are passive with regard to them. Levinas sought to describe what Llewelyn names deep Saying, 'deep *dire*', an expressivity which is anterior to, but informs all substance-inflected actual language (Llewelyn, 2002).

Towards enjoyment, suffering and the self

Like classical utilitarianism, Levinas established a contrast between enjoyment and suffering, satisfaction and pain. Unlike them he does so at a level of 'passive' sensation. Putnam claims he is an ethical intuitionist who 'does not appeal to abstract arguments to ground ethics' (Putnam, 2002: 54). We do not comprehend others' states and rationally respond; we feel. Derrida noted the immense interest in this issue of sensations and passivity within French philosophical circles in the 1950s and 1960s (Derrida, 1992). Dreyfus has pinpointed this as the weak point in Husserlian phenomenology specifically with regard to debates concerning the precise sense of *noema* (Dreyfus, 1982). Levinas's ethics is not grounded in an individual's self-conscious calculus of self-interest. Entirely opposed to such thought, Levinas sought to 'avoid the schema of an intentional subject which is will, inwardness in being and (self) interest' (*OB*: 178). He opposed this with a dislocated subject 'on the hither side of the dark designs of inwardness', which he called 'the-one-for-the-other' (*OB*: 179–80) or disinterestedness. Levinas's thought is part of a questioning of all the essential predicates which cluster around the concept of the subject. As Derrida puts it, these are numerous and diverse, ordered around presence to self, which implies 'a certain interpretation of temporality; identity to self, positionality, property, personality, ego, consciousness, will, intentionality, freedom, humanity etc.' (Derrida, 1992: 274). Levinas's discussion of sensate creatures and sensibility systematically refuses and challenges such predicates.

Creatures and creation

Levinas traces the emergence of the self from sensibility explicitly using the terms *creature* and *creation* on numerous occasions. Resisting Husserl, Levinas cannot use terms such as 'world' and 'consciousness' freely. Ego and its links to transcendental ego are particularly problematic. He could not use 'earth'; Heidegger had appropriated that term in his later work on the 'fourfold' (Young, 2002) and Levinas's ever-deepening antipathy to his thought is well known. *Creation* is Levinas's surrogate term. It connotes something of the opening onto the divine without doing so explicitly, and it is formless enough to avoid the charge of being overly 'ontological' and determinate. Levinas shows a particular fondness for a vocabulary that escapes definition. Holiness with its etymological roots in scintillation, shining or shimmering is a typical example.

He notes that 'Western philosophy ... remains faithful to the order of things and does not know the absolute passivity, beneath the level of activity and passivity which is contributed by the idea of *creation*' (*OB*: 110; my emphasis). He partly distances himself from its theological connotations for 'the word *creation* designates a signification older than the context woven about this name. ... It is refractory to reassembling into a present and a representation' (*OB*: 113; my emphasis).

Creatures are not self-conscious, but they may be minimally conscious. For example, they may be attached to an object of desire they cannot escape, thus being obsessional. *Creatures* are on the hither side of self-conscious egotism. In many characterisations of the ethical, the approach of the Other, as an experience of radical alterity, singularity and uniqueness has cause to instigate a traumatic journey from the 'safety' and home of the complacent ego towards the sensible incarnate creatures we are simultaneously. Such ideas are a key to understanding Derrida's recent work on hospitality. The stranger dislocates us into an exile within our 'home'. The journey as one of loss, wounding, exile, becoming stranger or dissolution, and so on, are the very conditions from which our capacity to respond to those in need derives. Levinas loves to play on the difference between Odysseus, who returns 'home' to Ithaca, and Abraham, always in exile but 'father of us all'. The very violence of Levinas's language is a response to the urgency he senses of those in need. It is as if he wants to combat the coldness of the ego's self-assurance with the heat of his imagery, despite arguing for 'weakness' and 'a relaxation of virility without cowardice' derived from 'the little humanity which adorns the earth', which is so urgently needed (*OB*: 185).

The ego

The ego 'is consciousness reflecting upon itself ... a recuperation of the self'. This enables it to protect itself from the proximity of others and their look. There are shades of Sartre here. Able to look at itself 'from all points of view' by 'detaching itself to look at itself', the ego remains 'an un-attackable subject' (*OB*: 92). Sovereign self-consciousness and its link to distance via sight, with a consequent drive to conceptual abstraction, theory and thematisation, constitute one of Levinas's most enduring thematic clusters against which the ethical self is measured. Sovereignty issues in ontologically reified distancing from other humans (Jay, 1993). Distance is different from a necessary separation that the self undergoes when encountering the Other. It subsumes singularity, within mere difference; the individual becomes merely the exemplification of the abstraction, the moment in a larger pattern or totality. Brutality is not far from this scene. As Levinas noted much earlier:

> The visage of being that shows itself in war is fixed in the concept of totality, which dominates Western philosophy. Individuals are reduced to being bearers of forces that command them unbeknown to themselves. The meaning of individuals (invisible outside of this totality) is derived from the totality. (*TI*: 21–3)

Perhaps philosophical totality is merely the secularisation of older, mythic Greek themes of mortals as merely the playthings of the gods. The sovereign ego protects itself. Enclosure, property, borders, lines become suffocating. The ego entombs itself unless open to sensibility, the new, the Other and, above all, the risk of proximity.

While Levinas most often uses 'ego' negatively, there are times when his terminology is extremely lax. He is notorious for his lack of consistency in these matters. Context usually determines which sense he intends. I use *creature* when discussing sensibility and sensation, and *self* when this creature has stabilised enough to become responsible because responsive, though not yet a fully self-conscious creature. I think this is as close as one gets to Levinas's intentions. *Ego* ought to be used to describe self-conscious selves open to the traces and enigmas entwined within themselves because incarnate, but often Levinas elided it with the sense of self just noted.

Sensibility

Sensibility is described in two ways by Levinas. One might be characterised as a subtractive or negative conception which moves from the conscious ego towards the self. The other constructive conception builds from a discussion of sensible bodies and, by way of a discussion of enjoyment and suffering, ends at a point where a stabilised sensibility becomes a self capable of responding to another person. In both instances the ethical encounter supervenes on the body as materiality and sensibility. Levinas distinguishes between sensibility as a general condition and sensations which are discrete, differentiated and logically 'later', linked to the self's emergence from being creature. The self emerges as a learnt capacity to differentiate within general otherness and as such connects at a minimum to displeasure and the need for foresight, and, at the worst, to suffering as fortuitous pain.

Levinas offers a series of examples which later will be used analogically around his varied treatments of the ethical encounter. Sensibility is not fulfilment (*OB*: 72). The latter implies a cognised hunger as intentionality. Lack implies some troubling flicker of 'sensation now become knowing'. Food as sensation satisfies hunger, not the thought of hunger. There is a fusing of the sensing and the sensed. 'The emptiness of hunger is emptier than all curiosity.' Eating, driven by emptiness, seeks satiation. Savour as sensation is not the same as taste which discerns difference between food objects. We taste bread, a cultural object. Savour links to survival; it satisfies the creature's hunger or quenches thirst. Un-cognised objects are ground into 'prime matter'. Matter does its job of filling emptiness prior to any cognition. Matter 'materialises' in satisfaction. A direct sensate link between exterior and interior beyond any intentional relationship of cognition or possession emerges. Levinas gnomically states, 'satisfaction satisfies itself with satisfaction' (*OB*: 73). Put differently, 'life enjoys life'. Enjoyment is mindless and occurs 'before any reflection' on the part of a creature. Imperceptibly, via emergent taste as differentiation, a sensate proto-subject tentatively emerges and becomes incarnate in the sense that it begins to take on – though not consciously – a sense of its bodily volume and extension. Thus, via eating, volumetric spatiality emerges. The repetition of biting, not thought, 'becomes the identification called me'.

Thus boundaries and *One*, or a nascent self, emerge from the restless life-force in the 'process of satisfaction'. The creature now differentiating volume or spatiality via orality impatiently pursues satisfaction, contentment and the enjoyment of its own appetite. This is not cognitive or visual but visceral. Enjoyment is 'the singularization of an ego coiling back upon itself' (*OB*: 73). Levinas uses 'ego' loosely here. This movement of sensory egotism is likened to the winding of a skein. I take this to mean that hunger and its satisfaction are an endless back and forth movement which, as repetition, pleases the creature. 'It has to be able to be complacent in itself' to a point where it fully exhausts the essence of sensibility. Identity as self, as a concentrated sensory point, emerges from repetition. Thus, from sensibility, via increasingly discrete sensations, a singular sensibility emerges. Levinas uses the Husserlian notion of *eidos*, signalling a sense of completion. It is as if a creature seeking satisfaction repeats itself into a singularity as structured sensibility. Repetition marks out spatiality as an emergent, passive, non-conscious but structured dimension of creation which includes extended body. Repetition is not all. Sensibility is passive and vulnerable to the slings and arrows of its 'exposedness to the other' (*OB*: 74). Suffering just happens; it is for nothing.

Pain

This sensibility's drive to enjoyment can be thwarted, its nascent 'inwardness' affected by pain. Levinas notes that 'the corporeality of the subject is the pain of effort' which arises from fatigue linked to the effort of foresight, the necessity for movement and labour (*OB*: 54). If that were all, then the passivity of the subject faced with its own reproductive needs would remain self-absorbed and its trajectory would take it towards capture by the complacent ego with its repressions and narcissism (*OB*: 55).

Instead, the Other intervenes at the sensate level of the self which – is it yet who? – becomes 'obsessed with responsibility for the oppressed who is other than my self' (*OB*: 55). This intervention by the Other, in the space of necessity, fatigue, labour and pain, hurls the self from full self-absorption, towards its ethical capacity. 'Due to it, the struggle remains human', but it 'does not simulate essence' because the self's response to the Other cannot be chosen voluntarily. The obsession, the lack of choice in having to respond to the Other, is a new form of wounding pain. The real pain is the inability of the self to close in on itself in enjoyment as solitary self-satisfaction and become self-absorbed as a subject which 'does not "join up" at two ends' (*OB*: 55). This new pain 'assembled in corporeality' is thus sensible, felt, affective. It links to fatigue, ageing, outrage, sickness and wounding. Pain is always immanent, about to happen, as the Other intervenes within complacent enjoyment. 'Imminence as pain arises in sensibility lived as well-being and enjoyment.' It is even more painful than anything arising from the effects of ageing, etc. for the unavoidable being for-another 'arises in the enjoyment in which the ego is affirmed, is complacent, and posits itself' (*OB*: 55). Again, ego is used loosely here. Perhaps the pain of having to respond to the Other is that of being torn from complacency as proto-intentionality that has emerged from sensibility, such that the knot that is the self in enjoyment moving towards ego, finds that trajectory thwarted.

The negative conception of creatures

Negatively, the *creature* is nearly all that the ego is not:

> Must we call *creature* status his 'hither side', which a being retains no trace of, this hither side older than the plot of egotism woven in the *conatus* of being? (*OB*: 92)

Conatus, taken from Spinoza, is nearly always used negatively by Levinas. It symbolises mere life-force, a competitive struggle of one life-form against another, the very antithesis of the ethical. The *conatus* is linked to self-interest, which 'takes dramatic form in egoisms struggling with one another, each against all' in a 'multiplicity of allergic egoisms which are at war with one another' (*OB*: 4–5I).

Negatively conceived, the ethical encounter strips away egotism when Levinas follows an opposing trajectory from ego towards self. The impact of the encounter on the ego transforms it. Levinas drives from the ego, towards the limits of the self as point, or repetitive self as almost creature. An ego following this trajectory is described as a stranger, its identity hunted and contested where even one's poverty would be like 'a skin still enclosing a self', still trying to set itself up in an 'inwardness as a substance'. To be almost creature is to 'empty oneself anew of oneself' a giving up of oneself comparable to 'a haemophiliac's haemorrhage'. It is as if one were almost at the hither side of one's own 'nuclear unity', on the other side of any ego still identifiable and protected. Levinas often uses metaphors linked to nuclear fission and explosion to drive at what happens to the self when approached by another.

At its limits, even the self becomes *almost* totally emptied of the quasi-formal identity of being someone. The ego is disturbed to the point of no longer having any intention. It is to be exposed over and beyond any act of self-exposure. The self arrives at an end point of almost pure expressivity. Levinas sometimes calls this state '*The One*'. It is un-declinable. It cannot be I, thou, (s)he or it. Such differentiation comes out of stable identity. Here, the *One* is profound 'passivity in passivity'. Levinas writes of the One 'speaking'. This is speaking in the sense of *Saying* as almost pure expressivity, a body in proximity to another body, one creature exposed to another, but organised residually and sufficiently enough, to recognise the Other. This is the limit to which this negative 'reduction' of the ego is pushed. At this point, Levinas writes of the 'passivity to which the ego is reduced in proximity' as 'sincerity or veracity' (*OB*: 92) introducing the ethical moment again. He circles around the same point of profound passivity, where the self, or One in this case, is taken hostage, captured by its obsessional responsibility for the other in this almost totally sensible condition.

Proximity

We cannot refuse responsibility to the Other in this sensible dimension. Levinas never ceases to hammer this point home. It is not an issue of conscious choice. For the moment let us imagine that he means that in proximity, one creature as minimal self necessarily *responds* to another. True to his phenomenological leanings, Levinas is concerned with first-person experience. Proximity is conceived as the self's experience as 'mine'. I am called into question. My enjoyment is traumatically blown apart. I alone am responsible. As only a little more than sensate creature, I am passive, my responsibility is affective not cognitive, I have no choice in the matter and do not seek reciprocity, exchange or return care. The space between creatures is asymmetrical, curved. The Other, my 'neighbour' or the stranger, and so forth, is 'higher', and as my ethical master as teacher, is inspirational and holy in the sense that as infinite, unknowable, non reducible, she opens out onto the infinite beyond totality, beyond or otherwise than any cognised being (*OB*: 63).[6]

Levinas is driving at a form of encounter between human beings prior to consciousness which, through proximity, 'is the implication of approaching one in fraternity'. Response to the Other's subjectivity as self, is 'prior to consciousness, but via sensibility one is caught up with him in fraternity [*sic*]' (*OB*: 82–3). Proximity arises neither from the 'the troubled tranquillity' of a sovereign ego which wants to be left alone, nor is it merely an intersection of random affective flows, nor 'the makeshift of an impossible confusion'. The once ego now become self and now 'almost' creature is exposed. This is the minimal point at which proximity, the opening of one to the Other, occurs. Here, or then, the self is open, vulnerable, restless, decentred and metaphorically naked, without defence. Not all the metaphors are negative. Proximity might be regarded as 'better than all the rest' or other moments, it might be 'the plenitude of an instant arrested' (*OB*: 92).

The self and materiality

Levinas repeatedly uses both, the reality of and metaphors drawn from, the acts of respiration, palpation or feeling and gustation to convey the impossibility of cutting ourselves from the world and *analogically* to explore ethics. Exploration of the link between being and respiration unfortunately cannot be carried out here (Derrida, 1978; 1989). The illusion of an isolated ego is Levinas's target. Incarnation, sensibility and ethics belong together.

'The sensible experience of the body is ... from the start incarnate' (Levinas, *OB*: 76). Sensibility he links to maternity, vulnerability and fear. 'The sensible – maternity, vulnerability, apprehension – binds the node of incarnation into a plot larger than the apperception of self' (*OB*: 76). I cannot discuss maternity here; suffice to say that it is perhaps the clearest example of being-for-another there is, and of a strange passivity where one goes into labour, endures labour, thus subverting the active sense of this term. Also it is a condition where to be too conscious, to 'work' at delivery is often counter-productive (Derrida and Ferraris, 2002: 359–60).

Levinas uses the term *plot* in opposition to theme as it implies a dialogic pattern of unpredictability, of the subject being caught up in events he cannot control. Sensibility surrounds the self from two directions. The self cannot consciously account or bring to any kind of consciousness those material flows which impinge on it and make it age, suffer illness, and so on. Nor can it 'fix' the Other in her proximity which it senses, is responsible for, but cannot fully comprehend. Sensibility implies networks, flows, loose centres, nodes, the *One*, 'me', poised between an indeterminate sensibility and emerging self-consciousness.

Emphasis on these sensory links to creation challenges the primacy of the distanced 'visual' dominance linking theory, abstraction, distance, the eye, egotism and truth within the Western philosophical tradition. Respiration, palpation, gustation and other tropes linked to sound and voice deepen Levinas's emphasis on the sensory. Bodies palpate, feel and are felt. Nature caresses or violates them. The following is but one long peon to sensibility. It is worth noting the relief sensory connectivity brings to consciousness locked in a prison of its own making when facing commentators who castigate Levinas's masochism:

> Freedom is animation itself, breath, the breathing of outside air where inwardness frees from itself, and is exposed to all the winds. ... That the emptiness of space would be filled with invisible air, hidden from perception, save in the caress of the wind or the threat of storms, non-perceived but penetrating me even in the retreats of my inwardness, that

this invisibility or this emptiness would be breathable or horrible, that this invisibility is non-indifferent and obsesses me before all thematisation, that the simple ambiance is imposed as an atmosphere to which the subject gives himself and exposes himself in his lungs, without intentions and aims, that the subject could be a lung at the bottom of its substance – all this signifies a subjectivity that suffers and offers itself before taking a foothold in being. It is a passivity, wholly a supporting. (*OB*: 180)

Such examples could easily be multiplied. What is so interesting is that Levinas then consciously draws on such material processes in order to convey the core of his discussion of the ethical in yet another way. Just as breath gives life unbeknown to she who breathes, so, analogically, the encounter with the Other gives another kind of life, that of the psyche.

Psyche and pneuma

Levinas does not use the *psyche* in any of the standard senses, though he is fully aware of them (*OB*: 69). Psyche always signals a point where a minimal self crosses over into being human by way of its sensate proximity with the Other, thus founding ethical responsibility for another. Levinas repeatedly plays on the connection between psyche and breath – the Greek *pneuma* – and a panoply of motifs around inspiration, exhalation and respiration. The psyche is a strange condition between form and non- form of the self. It is a 'de-phasing', a 'loosening' or 'unclamping' of identity where the same – the *One* – is prevented from coinciding with itself (*OB*: 68). It is where egotistical identity is lost. The ego is sloughed off like the skin of a snake, enabling another identity to emerge. As a node, beyond being, 'I' am more a link or filament or an entwining of myself and the Other. My sense of self oscillates between responsibility for the Other and the gift that very responsibility grants 'me' by calling me to an ethical existence. The gift is my humanity or purpose, as being-for-the-other. The gift is received only by shattering emerging complacency and certainty.

Levinas is at his most opaque here. The idea of the 'psyche in the soul' is introduced at this point. Soul can be taken in a non-religious sense to imply a larger whole, which includes sensibility, the One as minimal self, and now psyche, the 'one-for-the-other', all operative at 'levels' prior to the conscious ego but which inform and deform any complacency consciousness may pretend to.

The psyche in the soul 'is the other in me' (*OB*: 69). This could be conceived materially. The past, utterly recalcitrant to memory or recall as neuronal patterning, lies embedded, striated as neuronal pathways within the self. Many others 'live on' within and unbeknown to me, a past prior to any consciousness, but which in turn, as trace, affect any ego pursuing self-interested ends. For Levinas, it is a responsibility for the other that lives within 'me' as my psyche. I am other, almost. The psyche is but a complex node lived as 'one-for-the-other'. The psyche oscillates around a sense of self which has to be forsaken for the other, but which, returning, results in a sense of a deeper impossibility of acting responsibly for the other, which can never be assuaged. He calls this condition both a 'malady of identity' and the only possibility of freedom. It is malady because it is both unavoidable and cannot be fulfilled. Shockingly, traumatically, the Other, because she Signifies, is unlike any other sensation and has to be responded to.

The call

The psyche senses a 'call' from outside, stemming from the proximate expressivity of the Other. The psyche as incarnation senses another body in proximity; the Other as expressive subjectivity. She, neighbour, makes demands on me, or in Levinasian terms – derived and profoundly reordered from Heidegger – 'calls' me, placing me under an *injunction* or command. The Other 'solicits', 'institutes', 'accuses' or 'elects' me to cite some of the terms Levinas uses in this connection. I am incarnate, I feel and, above all, am both an enjoying and suffering sensate creature who involuntarily responds to and for the Other who suffers and, at this very root or on this ground, can do no other but passively place myself at their service, in their 'hour of need'. There is no choice. I am not a slave. In this involuntary response to the Other, I found my human self in responsibility. Levinas repeatedly cites the phrase 'Yes, I am here' as the psyche's *response* to the Other prior to any cognition as the founding moment of sociality which is always laced within the said.[7]

The psyche, as being-for-the-other, needs incarnation and proximity. The self involuntarily responds to the Other's vulnerability via sensibility, prior to any conscious sense of compassion, sympathy or empathy. I do not place myself consciously in another's 'shoes' by first imagining my way into their suffering.[8] I respond affectively. The Other takes me hostage in the sense that I, as minimal sensate self, cannot bear them suffering. I involuntarily respond to suffering because pain has happened to me and their worse pain must be alleviated. My capacity for pain meets the vulnerability of being for the other. Such affective 'truth' underpins our capacity for compassion. Otherwise we would remain coldly distance, dispassionate and uninvolved in the fate of the Other. Levinas writes:

> It is through the condition of being hostage that there can be in the world, pity, compassion, pardon, proximity ... Being hostage is ... the condition for all solidarity. (*OB*: 117)

Taking responsibility for the outrages suffered by the Other 'is the source of all compassion' (*OB*: 116).

The psyche is the point at which the minimal sensate self and Other interlink to the point of substitution, and the sense of being taken hostage occurs. Responsibility is placed on us. It informs our consciousness. Its flickering traces haunt us as guilt, conscience, remorse, expiation, atonement. Is this capacity for guilt universal or merely linked to the sacrificial structures of Abrahamic lineage (Derrida, 1992; 1995: 108–15)? Levinas writes:

> The animation, the very pneuma of the psyche, alterity in identity, is the identity of the body exposed to the other, becoming 'for the other', the possibility of giving. (*OB*: 69)

This pneuma, or breath, is literally and spiritually *inspiration*. It is a different type of 'breathing in', as involuntary as the air the lungs take in. Just as air facilitates life prior to any intentionality, so too the approach of the other gives the self ethical meaning, makes us human, takes us from the pure fatality and meaningless of a merely material universe where the conscious ego locked up in its self-absorption merely finds monotony, the horror of the monochrome materiality that Levinas always characterised as the 'there is' or '*il y a*' and which always emerges from ontology and is assuaged by ethics. The Other in proximity as node brings out this new identity, but is one 'at the service of the other'. Strangely, the Other brings a certain type of contradictory stabilisation to the self always in danger of slipping back towards mere responsiveness to stimuli signalling either enjoyment or danger. *Response* becomes responsibility.

Singularity or uniqueness

Another important part of Levinas's plot is that of *singularity* or human uniqueness. My response to the Other is to uniqueness. She is sensed, but unknowable, uncategorisable and excessive. Infinite, in that she always exceeds anything I can imagine of her, she is always more than any idea I would pigeonhole her within. She escapes, exceeding my 'grasp' and any possibility of thematisation. Levinas's and Derrida's endless play with the complex etymological roots linking the entire semantic complex around 'holding', grasping and 'tension' (stemming from the Latin words *tenere*, *tendere* and the Greek *teinô*) are complex and fascinating. Sadly, I cannot trace them here (e.g. Derrida, 2002b: 360). Infinity, which appears in proximity, punches a hole in being as totality. As William Burroughs would put it, 'the tapes are burnt'. She is absolutely other. If thematised, violence against her singularity has been committed, a possibility the demand for justice always brings. She has been subsumed instrumentally within my projects, reified and degraded by being 'written off' as the same, identified as 'this or that'. Violence lurks close to such egoism (*TI*: 33–40).

Levinas repeatedly refers to diachrony when discussing proximity. A neighbour, subject to the non-time of the sensate creature and a lived temporality as emergent self, is utterly different from that of mine; hence diachrony.

> Proximity is a difference, a non-coinciding, an arrhythmia in time, a diachrony refractory to thematisation, refractory to the reminiscences that synchronise the phases of a past. (*OB*: 166)

The psyche as opening to the Other's mysterious uniqueness and singularity cannot be seen as 'a conditioning or principle'. Such origins as *arche* always lead to metaphysical closure and totality. Rather, it has to be conceived of as an opening to risky and utterly unpredictable possibilities beyond thematisation. Each new approach brings this possibility.

Sensory entanglement with the incarnate, singular, particular, unique, immediacy of the Other determines the emergence of a specifically human ethical subjectivity. Otherwise the self-organised creature would remain either animal and inhuman, or violent egotism. Levinas's philosophical targets here are: the universalising reduction of the singularity of each person to mere 'moments' of universal history as within Hegel, the imperial ego in its intellectualised, hyper-cognitive Husserlian form, and Heidegger's affective but self-absorbed attesting self. By founding the ethical in sensibility opening the one for the Other, some hope of non-belligerent relations between humans linked to just institutions can be retained.

Levinas's wager, his *kerygma* or proclamation, is that we are constituted relationally, in care for others not self. 'The psyche or animation', he writes 'is the way a relationship between uneven terms, without any common time, arrives at relationships' (*OB*: 70). Psyche signals non-indifference and this relationship of the one for the other needs incarnation. 'An animate body or an incarnate identity is the signifyingness of this non-indifference' (*OB*: 71). The psyche is founded in proximity or the coming into relation as encounter of two particular sensate bodies which Signify. True to phenomenology, the link or relation is experienced asymmetrical. The Other approaches 'me'. My affective response singles me out. Only I can respond, torn from my place, exiled from enjoyment and my complacency. Signification occurs because the Other's expressivity strikes my sensibility, my body uprooting me. 'Signification is not an ordinary formal relation, but the whole gravity of the body extirpated from its *conatus*' (*OB*: 72).

Thus, incarnation sustains ethics; hence his discussion of sensibility. 'Only in enjoyment does the I crystallise' (*TI*: 144). Levinas insists that 'the corporeality of one's own body signifies as sensibility itself, a knot or a denouement of being' (*OB*: 77). Elsewhere, Levinas argued that 'the incarnation of human subjectivity guarantees its spirituality' (Levinas, 1985: 97). Levinas's originality is to conceive of these knots – elsewhere he writes of nodes – in Being as first sensibilities and as such only tentative organised nuclei always capable of fission, explosion, substitution by new forms, as occurring in open relations to otherness and Others.

Some responses to Levinas

Critchley (1992: 107–44) makes much of the need to interrupt, to engage with Levinas and not faithfully reiterate his ideas. Many have taken up this challenge. Levinas's language of hostage, substitution, trauma, wounding has caused outrage and spilt much ink. Flurries of outrage accusing him of using masochistic language fundamentally misunderstand his attempts to link sensibility to ethics. Kearney writes that 'his hyperbolic language borders at times on masochism and paranoia' (2003: 71). Critchley elsewhere calls him 'a master of the literature of horror' (1997: 80). These are themselves hyperbolic and one-sided readings, which overemphasise *Otherwise than Being*, not taking into account the implied background of *Totality and Infinity* where another more joyous tone celebrates enjoyment, intimacy, fecundity and parenthood. Levinas's earlier treatment of enjoyment resonates with themes lifted from Bataille. 'To enjoy without utility, in pure loss, gratuitously ... in pure expenditure – this is the human' (*TI*: 133). The darker tropes of the latter deliberately contrast with the former. The immersion in sensibility making enjoyment so glorious where 'the I is thus at home with itself' (*TI*: 132) intensifies the impact of the dislocating wrench of the Other's call, which so traumatically shatters self-absorption forging the ethical subject from the sensible self.

Levinas, in his determination to drive home the centrality of the ethical, underplays a necessary moment of narcissistic enjoyment and self-love founded on sensory intentionality towards material, not human, otherness. Perhaps this explains his complex and suspicious relation to the aesthetic in general, with the exception of poetry and prophetic writing. Was there a residual resistance to the graven image? An intensification of aesthetic sensibility as it entwines with the injunction from the Other might render a more balanced relation to ecological creation on which our joint humanity rests. Heidegger has much to offer here if tempered by the prior Levinasian injunction of the Other. The limits of ethics to the human Other might then be transcended.

Ricoeur insists that the self which is subject to injunction, or 'called' in proximity, has to be fuller than an emergent sensible creature or traumatised, obsessed and dislocated ego, and that Heidegger's self-absorbed moment of attestation as response to an inner voice of conscience, of self-worth, has to link to the external call the Other places on us. Ricoeur pursues a third way:

> To Heidegger, I objected that attestation is primordially injunction, or attestation risks losing all ethical or moral significance. To Levinas, I shall object that the injunction is primordially attestation, or the injunction risks not being heard and the self not being affected in the mode of being-enjoined. (1992: 355)

I am not sure. Would not this attesting self colonise the immediate, affectively sensed presence of the Other? Would its 'discernment' be a rush to judgement? What is the balance between the two modes of self and Other? Levinas argues that the ethical is the transition from sensory absorption to subjectivity as responsibility and Ricoeur that the transition in some sense has already had to have been made for me to respond to the Other. Levinas allows in his discussions of the need for foresight, suffering and pain, enough to enable the One, or self, to respond at the sensory level to the tribulations it senses the Other is undergoing. As noted earlier, the very movement of 'egotism' Levinas likened to the winding of a skein where repetitive coiling of sensibility on itself by way of enjoyment generates a rudimentary sense of self. Consequently, he writes: 'Without egoism, complacent in itself, suffering would not have any sense.' Without suffering the self would have no possibility of signifying 'for the other by unwinding its coils' (*OB*: 73). It is in having suffered, not in self-attestation, that we respond to the Other.

Kearney, following Ricoeur, argues that Levinas and others address the ontology of sameness to 'arrive at more ethical appreciation of otherness'. They remind us that the human stranger escapes our 'egological schemas and defies our attempts to treat him or her as a scapegoated alien, or, at best an alter ego'. Kearney asks how we should act if we cannot fully know the Other. On this reading Kearney claims we are left with the problem of discernment. He asks (2003: 66–7), 'How can we tell the difference between benign and malign others'? Kearney seeks techniques on which to base ethical decisions in the real world where, while not being overhasty and exclusionary, we might simultaneously discriminate between benign strangers and malign aliens. He is bothered by the lack of knowledge. This is to miss the core of Levinas's argument.

Levinas never denies the need for justice and, with it, moral systems, law, institutions, politics and decisions and discernment, as we shall see. He seeks to draw them back 'down' as it were, to the sensory basis from whence flows the psyche's openness to the Other and the ethical relation upon which, and for which, ontology, cognition and the edifices of sociality are subsequently forged. Entwined within the decisions and calculations of conditional hospitality lies the pull or undertow of a radical impossibility of judging the Other, or discerning whether they are a dangerous alien or needy stranger. We never 'know' at first! At the moment we start 'discerning', we leave the immediacy of proximity for the violence of cognitive distance. Levinas insists on this risk of not knowing as the very possibility of even making such discrimination, of the very possibility for judgement and in the face of injustice, its endless revision. Decisions concerning strangers will always leave a bad taste. Condemned the moment we discern, yet we must. The chance that the Other we have turned away or interned offers us will never come again; the new is forsworn, and the risk has not been taken! We have not picked up the cards she has dealt. We hazard either imprisonment in the poisoned suit of egocentricity – or suffering from her malignancy. In the imbrication of incarnate bodies meeting in proximity where the knot or entanglement both is and is not, individuated and where the field of sensory flows leap and flow asymmetrically, we find the origins of justice.

Justice

Thus far, discussion has been restricted to Levinas's repeated attempt to characterise the ethical relation between the self and Other as face to face. In this respect he is true to phenomenology, which wished to ground ideality in the apodictic certainty of first-person experience. On that basis only, Husserl argued, science might be founded. Analogically, the ethical encounter affirms justice. The sensate encounter beyond cognitive 'experience' serves as its always singular ground. It cannot be generalised cognitively, but must be. The immediacy of the face to face seems attenuated these days. Is it unrealistic within our media saturated epoch (Stiegler, 1998, 2001; Derrida and Stiegler, 2002)? Levinas's discussion of justice enables us to understand his insistence on the ethical and how it points towards a necessary move from 'proximity' of unique individuals to more abstract, institutional relations of social and political realities within which we find ourselves as citizens which must be endlessly rebuilt as they fail to provide the justice we desire (Levinas, 1998a: 196). Levinas insists on the absolute primacy of the ethical over ontology. The immediate nexus of intertwined sensibility must inform philosophically grounded knowledge when forging the good life, lived within just institutions. The contrary attempt to found or justify existing institutions on the basis of either some rational deduction based on axiomatic assumptions concerning self-interested subjects or the inner working-out of some theodicy, however secularised, is doomed not only to failure but to the perpetuation of injustice and war.

The ethical is 'always' before the law, always ahead of it, entwined within it and yet is its opaque measure. Levinas, unlike Hegel, makes no attempt to flesh out procedural and institutional forms of political life. His self-imposed task is to assert that their legitimacy always rests on the immediacy of the ethical bond of human sociality. He accepts the necessary but inevitably fallible concretion of the ethical within institutions in the drive towards justice. Derrida calls this messianism without messiahs, 'democracy to come' or simply the open, unprogrammed future, the 'to come' (Derrida, 1990, 1994, 2002a, 2002b; Caputo, 1997). We will never arrive at heaven on earth, but we have a measure to call evil, as unnecessary suffering, to account.

Levinas's discussion of justice rests on a reworking of certain Husserlian assumptions. The latter understood philosophy as the attempt to realise the *idea*, understood in the Kantian regulative sense as an enterprise in which humanity collectively seeks genuine science as universal knowledge. This *idea*, towards which knowledge progresses but never fully attains, would be both *total*, an integrated conceptual system of knowledge and accepted as binding by any rational person only if 'grounded in, and developed through, *absolute insight*, and hence ... *absolutely justified*' (Smith, 2003: 4; see also Derrida, 1989). For Husserl, that certainty derives from reflection on the active constitutive role of the inner and logical workings of the transcendental ego. To achieve this, our everyday 'natural attitude' (*doxa*) has to be held in abeyance. For Levinas, sensibly grounded being-for-the-other, derived not from introspection but from the passive experience of a self taken hostage, plays a similar role. It can never be absolutely justified as intellectual and abstract knowledge. The radical alterity of the Other, the rip in the texture of being the infinity of the Other announces, shatters the possibility of totality. It cannot stabilise as knowledge. It alters anew in each event of proximity. The ethical is an event, not a moment or part of a totality. It is 'beyond being' understood as a linked horizon of 'beings' constituted within the *idea*.

Levinas, using phenomenological method, mostly holds the practical issues of human sociability and justice in abeyance, bracketing them in an *epoche*. He poses the obvious retort bluntly. 'Why know? Why is there a problem? Why philosophy?' (*OB*: 157)? Why, if ontology is so flawed, does he continue to use it while seeking to dislocate it? The answer is the demand for justice.

The third party

Justice stems from the entry of the third party. All questioning and consciousness, and hence philosophy, stems from the incipient realisation in any proximity there is, implied, in another. Paying attention, being taken hostage by the Other, excludes the possibility of the same relation with another at the same time. Her suffering might be more urgent! We do her an injustice, but to turn from our neighbour, from the immediacy of the present encounter, would also be to commit a crime. We are trapped in debt we have not chosen, but which we have incurred. The responsibility to the Other is an immediacy 'antecedent to questions', but it is troubled, becomes a problem 'when a third party enters'. The entry of another on the scene perturbs the one-way relation from the self to the Other; my responsibility to you. It introduces an experiential contradiction in the 'Saying'. Whom should we respond to? Why? At this point 'the limit of responsibility' is reached. The question is born. Levinas notes:

> Justice is necessary, that is, comparison, coexistence, contemporaneousness, assembling, order, thematisation, the visibility of faces, and thus intentionality and the intellect, and in intentionality and the intellect, the intelligibility of a system and thence also a co presence on an equal footing as before a court of justice. (*OB*: 157)

If the entry of the third party triggers the emergence of consciousness, it is one founded in proximity. Without proximity would be mere enjoyment and suffering, utterly egotistical and hence pointless, fatal, lonely and inhuman. The reversal of the ethical and ontological is to be found in these simple lines.

Levinas is careful to specify that the entry of the third is not necessarily empirically present, the 'other is from the first, the brother [*sic*] of all other men' (*OB*: 157). Sensibility prior to cognition must contain an inherent movement beyond itself, in the direction of consciousness, as transition towards proto-abstractive abilities if that thesis can be sustained. Levinas's logic at this point is extremely opaque when he argues that 'weighing, thought, objectification' depends on a decree which betrays the *Illeity* of the Other (*OB*: 158). Illeity understood in one way is the sheer sensed presence, the 'himness' [*sic*] of the Other's presence, prior to any demanding of shibboleths, identification as one of mine or theirs, before all questions, before language as the said, before any discernment as benign stranger or malevolent alien. The absurdity of traumatised asylum-seekers having to register their request within a few hours in a language and bureaucratic system they cannot understand sustains the more general point (Derrida, 2002a). I cannot discuss here the 'gratingly patriarchal' (Sandford, 2002: 147) tone of Levinas's treatment, exclusion and subordination of the feminine nor the full complexities surrounding 'Illeity'.

The emergence of justice betrays Illeity, it is a violence perpetrated on the one-for-another relationship of proximity, but simultaneously it opens a different relation to 'her', that of justice. I am now responsible to her, still not as understood as abstraction, but simultaneously as a member of society and as citizen. The betrayal has 'cooled' the immediacy of proximity, but still informs it with its 'warmth'. The movement to abstraction, to questioning informed by the demand for justice, signals the origins (*arche*) of society, legally secured rights and specified responsibilities or duties. The scales of justice as comparative weighing up of competing claims demand representation; the *Saying* becomes and must be fixed in the *said* as book, law and science. Philosophy's time has come.

Derrida's beautiful *Archive Fever* is a profound meditation on this necessity and the dangers of ethical betrayal on the part of those with the authority (*archons*) who control access to and interpretation of the book as written law (Derrida, 1996). This 'violent' betrayal of ethical proximity necessarily persists. Ethics is entwined 'before' the law emerges. Betrayal occurs because, as conscious subjects, we become concerned with justice. As citizens we have become subject to, or always potentially capable of, being hauled 'before' the law. These themes are developed in Derrida's seminal essay 'Force of Law: The "Mystical Foundation of Authority"' (1990).

Justice is given meaning because it is always entwined with and can draw breath from proximity. 'The one for the other of proximity is not a deforming abstraction. In it justice is shown from the first ... it is born from ... the one-for-the-other, signification' (*OB*: 159). Proximity is the 'centre of gravitation' around which the edifice of being, the state, politics and techniques revolve. It is important that 'society' for Levinas does not mean our ethnos, our nation, 'us'. The state is always 'on the verge of integrating into a we, which congeals both me and my neighbour' (*OB*: 161). Thus, 'Justice remains justice only in a society where there is no distinction between those close and those far off, but in which there also remains the impossibility of passing by the closest' (*OB*: 159). There the guest has no responsibility. I only have it for and to her. Our hospitable laws should welcome her.

Conclusion

The motif of the ethical encounter in Levinas's late work has been explored. Its dependence on materiality and sensibility has been established. The creature as sensibility was distinguished from self and ego. An examination of saying, proximity, pain, worked towards understanding Levinas's conception of the psyche, singular responsibility and being for others. The source and point of justice were traced. The ethical encounter is one of almost absolute risk. Few take it consciously. Is Levinas convincing when arguing that it happens to us all as sensate creatures? Was Levinas whistling in the wind, merely offering hope when facing the appalling horrors of the age? Paul and Anton showed that some act both responsibly and consciously!

Notes

1   I use *TI* for *Totality and Infinity*, and *OB*, for *Otherwise than Being* in what follows.
2   It is standard practice to translate *autrui*, the personal other, by 'Other' and *autre*, impersonal objects by 'other': see the translator's footnote in *Totality and Infinity*,

p. 24. Levinas is notoriously inconsistent in following his own rule and never more so than in *Otherwise than Being*.
3   Levinas, following Heidegger, uses the term 'temporal' with its experiential connotations of worldly and earthly existence to distance himself from more usual 'ontological' treatments of 'time' derived from Aristotle.
4   Levinas is inconsistent in his capitalisation of 'Saying'.
5   In *OB* this is often written dis-inter-ested-ness, to emphasise response as relation.
6   Levinas oscillates between writing in the first and third person, between 'I' or 'me' and 'the self'. I shall too.
7   Unfortunately, themes linked to responsibility and Levinas's reworking of guilt, the inner call, conscience, and so on in Heidegger cannot be explored here. Nor can his reworking of Husserl's account of inter-subjectivity as explored in the fifth of the latter's *Cartesian Meditations* be considered.
8   That was Husserl's route.

References

Bernstein, R. (2002), 'Evil and the Temptation of Theodicy', in S. Critchley and R. Bernasconi, *The Cambridge Companion to Levinas*, Cambridge: Cambridge University Press, pp. 252–67.

Caputo, J. D. (1997), *The Prayers and Tears of Jacques Derrida: Religion without Religion*, Bloomington: Indiana University Press.

Critchley, S. (1992), *The Ethics of Deconstruction*, Oxford: Blackwell.

—— (1997) *Very Little … Almost Nothing*, London: Routledge.

Derrida, J. (1978), 'Violence and Metaphysics: an Essay on the Thought of Emmanuel Levinas', in *Writing and Difference*, translated by Alan Bass, London, Routledge & Kegan Paul, pp. 79–153.

—— (1989), *Of Spirit: Heidegger and the Question*, Chicago: University of Chicago Press.

—— (1990), 'Force of Law: The "Mystical Foundation of Authority"', reprinted in *Acts of Religion*, London, Routledge, pp. 230–300.

—— (1992), 'Eating Well', translated by P. Connell and A. Rondel, in E. Weber (ed.), *Points … Interviews, 1974–1994*, Stanford: Stanford University Press, pp. 255–87.

—— (1994), *Spectres of Marx*, translated by P. Kamuf, London: Verso.

—— (1995), *The Gift of Death* (*GD*), translated by David Wills, Chicago: University of Chicago Press.

—— (1996), *Archive Fever: A Freudian Impression*, Chicago: University of Chicago Press.

—— (1997), *The Politics of Friendship*, translated by G. Collins, London: Verso.

—— (1999), *Adieu to Emmanuel Levinas*, translated by P-A. Brault and M. Naas, Stanford: Stanford University Press.

—— (2000), *Without Alibi*, edited and translated by Peggy Kamuf, Stanford: Stanford University Press.

—— (2001), *On Cosmopolitanism and Forgiveness* (*CF*), translated by M. Dooley and M. Hughes, London: Routledge.

—— (2002a), *Acts of Religion*, London: Routledge.

—— (2002b), 'Hospitality', in his *Acts of Religion*, London: Routledge, pp. 358–420.

Derrida, J. and Dufourmantelle, A. (2000), *Of Hospitality*, translated by R. Bowlby, Stanford: Stanford University Press.

Derrida, J. and Ferraris, M. (2002), *A Taste for the Secret*, Cambridge: Polity.

Derrida, J. and Stiegler, B. (2002), *Echographies of Television*, Cambridge: Polity.

Dreyfus, H. L. (ed.) (1982), *Husserl, Intentionality and Cognitive Science*, Cambridge, MA: MIT Press.

Gourevitch, P. (1998), *We Wish to Inform You That Tomorrow We Will Be Killed with Our Families: Stories From Rwanda*, London: Picador.

Jay, M. (1993), *Downcast Eyes: The Denigration of Vision in Twentieth Century French Thought*, Berkeley: University of California Press.

Kearney, Richard (2003), *Strangers, Gods and Monsters*, London: Routledge.

Levinas, E. (1985), *Ethics and Infinity: Conversations with Philippe Nemo*, translated by R. Cohen, Pittsburgh: Duquesne University Press.

—— (1998a), *Entre Nous: on Thinking-of-the-Other*, translated by M. B. Smith and B. Harshav, London: Athlone.

—— (1998b), *Collected Philosophical Papers* translated by A. Lingis, Pittsburg: Dusquene University Press.

Llewelyn, J. (2002), 'Levinas and Language', in S. Critchely and R. Bernasconi, *The Cambridge Companion to Levinas*, Cambridge: Cambridge University Press, pp. 119–38.

Putnam, H. (2002), 'Levinas and Judaism', in S. Critchley and R. Bernasconi, *The Cambridge Companion to Levinas*, Cambridge: Cambridge University Press, pp. 33–62.

Ricoeur, P. (1992), *Oneself as Another*, Chicago: University of Chicago Press.

Sandford, S. (2002), 'Levinas, Feminism and the Feminine', in S. Critchley and R. Bernasconi, *The Cambridge Companion to Levinas*, Cambridge: Cambridge University Press, pp. 139–60.

Smith, A. D. (2003), *Husserl and the Cartesian Meditations*, London: Routledge.

Stiegler, B. (1998), *Technics and Time, Volume 1: The Fault of Epimetheus*, Stanford: Stanford University Press.

—— (2001), 'Fidelity at the Limits of Deconstruction', in T. Cohen (ed.), *Jacques Derrida and the Humanities: a Critical Reader*, Cambridge: Cambridge University Press.

Young, J. (2002), *Heidegger's Later Philosophy*, Cambridge: Cambridge University Press.

4
Moral Uncertainty, Feminism and Descartes' Demon

Alison Assiter

In this chapter the theme of moral uncertainty in the modern world is addressed through a discussion of Descartes' mind/body dualism. I suggest that such uncertainty may, to some degree, be attributed to a kind of cultural mind/body dualism which makes reasoned moral judgement virtually impossible. I suggest, further, that a more careful reading of Descartes may help overcome such cultural dualism and establish firmer grounds for practical philosophy.

Descartes is sometimes described as the 'father' of modern philosophy (see, for example, Scruton, 1984; Sorrell, 1984). Descartes pioneered the idea that through the power of human reason, knowledge claims can be scrutinised. By clarifying the conditions under which certain knowledge is possible, he set modern philosophy on its current course. Part of this chapter argues that there is at least one area of Descartes' thinking that has been misrepresented by his critics, analytic and 'continental' alike. I will suggest a revision of a fairly common reading of Cartesian reason and more specifically of dualism. I believe this revision to be particularly significant for women and other groupings that have been traditionally subjugated.

Descartes is often derided for holding what is taken to be an absurd view of the nature of the human subject. This subject is supposed to be a purely rational thinking thing that is separated from its body, from nature and from bodily emotions. I will suggest that there is a range of areas of contemporary culture which have, despite themselves, taken on this much derided Cartesian view. I will suggest some areas of contemporary culture where it appears that a purely bodily, non-rational view of emotion is implicitly taken for granted.

Cartesian critics

The commonplace interpretation of Cartesian dualism concentrates on the distinction between the subject, which is essentially a thinking or rational thing, and the body, seen as a kind of machine or a portion of extended matter. From this version of dualism is said to follow a whole gamut of errors, including a general philosophical method, which places the 'rational' subject at its core, an improbable search for secure foundations for knowledge and a particular conception of the modern subject.

The dualistic account of the human being has received extensive criticism partly on the grounds that Descartes provides only an insufficient explanation of the causal relationship between the thinking self and extended substance. Ryle, for example, effectively satirises the idea of 'ghostly' mental entities that play a causal role in relation to physical movement and are conceived as thinking things accessible only by private introspection. He says of the doctrine that (he) shall often speak of it, with deliberate abusiveness, as the 'dogma of the Ghost in the machine' (Ryle, 1949: 15–16). Moira Gatens, comparing Descartes' account of the mechanistic body unfavourably with Spinoza's account in the *Ethics*, notes how substance dualism leads to a conception of the human as a strange hybrid; mind and mechanistic lifeless body (Gatens, 1996: 109).

Apart from these philosophical problems of interactionism, Gatens also suggests that Descartes' dualistic conception of mind and body was essential to Western modernity as it validated the idea that the mind, by an act of will, could alienate the body's labouring capacities in return for a wage (Gatens, 1996: 55). Val Plumwood moreover attributes to Descartes the responsibility for introducing a dualism of a genuine human self, without the qualities of animal or nature, and a mechanical nature, bereft of the qualities now identified with the human. In this instrumental, technical view, nature became a market resource without significant moral or social constraint (Plumwood, 1993: 111). In Plumwood's view, the real self for Descartes is 'alien to the body and nature', independent from its devalued body. For similar reasons, Rosi Braidotti begins her critique of philosophical modernity with the claim that 'anti-Cartesianism has been put on the agenda of modernity: it raises questions concerning the structure of subjectivity in such a way as to challenge dualism, of which the Cartesian body-and-soul dichotomy is the paradigm, and in so doing to change the very definition of the function of philosophy' (1991: 1).

Descartes and paranoia

Picking up a thread of criticism similar to that suggested by Richard Rorty (1980: 50–1), Naomi Scheman compares Descartes with Freud's and Lacan's analyses of Judge Schreber. Schreber's paranoia manifests itself as the belief that hostile, male forces are about to transform him into a woman. Scheman proposes a parallel reading of Cartesian method, whereby the self is supposed to constitute itself as a knowing subject through a process of symptomatic inversion. By detaching itself from various objects in the world, the ego purges itself of frightening desires and passions, but these desires return to haunt the ego in the form of a world that is hostile to it. The self of Descartes is thus the remnant of a psychological drama, purged of desire, unwarranted assumptions, views of others one might describe as common-sensical and now controlling the influence of the body. An example of para-noia or not, Genevieve Lloyd (1984: 38–49) considers Descartes' method in relation to emerging scientific disciplines and accentuates his insistence on a single and unified scientific method, premised on the rational exercise of the 'purged' mind.

Lloyd clarifies this connection between rational method and masculinity, a connection that is not intuitively obvious, as Descartes was himself at pains to point out the accessibility of the method. Indeed, in the *First Discourse*, he writes that his mind is in no way out of the ordinary and that reason or good sense is complete and entire in each one of us (Descartes, 1968: 27). Yet, as Lloyd notes, the development of the Cartesian method depends on certain conditions which are elaborated by Descartes at the beginning of his meditations: 'my mind is free from all cares and that I have obtained for myself assured leisure in peaceful solitude in order to apply myself seriously to the destruction of all my former opinions' (ibid.: 97). In response to this, his correspondent, Princess Elizabeth, replies:

> The life I am constrained to lead does not allow me enough free time to acquire a habit of meditation in accordance with your rules. Sometimes the interests of my household, which I must not neglect, sometimes conversation I cannot eschew, so thoroughly deject this weak mind with annoyances or boredom that it remains, for a long time afterward, useless for anything. (quoted in Lloyd, 1984: 49)

It was not just the 'dailiness of life' that suggests a connection between exclusivity and Cartesian dualism. I have noted above the hierarchical relationship putatively holding between mind and body, and it could be argued that by separating reason from emotion, ensouled mind from mech-anistic nature, the contemplative life from the quotidian, Descartes endorsed existing values also associated with gender.

Reason?

I will argue in a later section that this is a misreading of the real Descartes. It is interesting and significant, however, that this perspective is one which, it seems to me, is reflected in current cultural thinking in various ways. The perspective assumes a particular and a somewhat implausible notion of reason, on the one hand, and of emotion, on the other. Reason, on the assumed outlook, is the property of a disembodied mind. This mental entity is detached from any kind of context. Liberal rationalists, whether it is in the sphere of epistemic thinking or in relation to moral claims, are said to abstract away all qualitative differentiating features of human beings and consider them all as alike in respect of the possession of a rational nature. This outlook is associated not only with Descartes, but also with Plato and Aristotle. Humans are differentiated from other animals by means of the possession of reason. The absence or purported relative deficiency of this capacity is then used to justify the ill-treatment of slaves, women or any other grouping who may, according to the protagonist, be regarded as being lacking in the relevant respect.

The perspective attributed to Descartes was viewed by Kant (1933) as leading to conflicts and contradictions. Without the mediation of the understanding and of perception, according to Kant, reason is led into antinomies that are irresoluble. In relation to themes like the question of whether or not the world has a beginning in time and limits in space, Kant argues that equally compelling reasons can be given for each side of the argument. Reason is inevitably led, in the absence of the constraints of the understanding, into such conflicts. Derrida (1976), more recently, picked up this theme with his claim that every form of discourse can, in the end, be seen to contain the elements of its own undoing.

I do not for a moment deny that these forms of thinking are proper for philosophers. They cannot be resolved merely by suggesting that the activities of reason should be curbed by introducing the body, the emotions or the understanding as moderating influences. However, if reason is allowed to wander in general unfettered by the understanding, then, ultimately, and taken to its logical extreme, one is led to the claim that there is no truth, that one cannot determine, with respect to any individual claim, whether or not it is true. This claim, while it is a familiar one in recent postmodern thought, is palpably not true. As Kant recognised, when the understanding is brought to bear on the pure operations of reason, one is able to distinguish true from false claims. One would not, indeed, even be able to make the claim attributed above to Derrida unless it were possible to distinguish true from false claims.

Emotion

Alongside this outlook on the mental subject and on reason goes a certain perspective on the nature of emotion. Emotion, on the view that has it separate from reason, becomes 'pure experience' along the lines of sense data. Where Hume can be regarded as supporting such a view, he has emotion reduced merely to physiological sensations. For example, I could be said to be experiencing anger when my pulse races or my muscles tense. This view of the nature of emotion has been characterised by Fricker (1991) as 'positivist'.

But just as the view described above of the purely rational subject may be said to offer an implausible outlook on the nature of the subject and on the character of rationality, so too is this perspective implausible about emotion. In fact, emotion may be present without physiological sensations, and vice versa. In most cases, it is not until reason interprets an emotion that the emotion is registered.

Cultural manifestations of this conception: free-floating emotion

Despite the implausibility of the outlook, or perhaps even because of its implausibility, it seems that the view ascribed to Descartes manifests itself in a number of cultural phenomena in the present day. Something that has been notable recently is the cult of the public display of emotion; the cult of turning private emotional distress into a public phenomenon. There is the rise of self-disclosure television – for example, Oprah Winfrey or Michael Jackson as revealed by Martin Bashir. There is the cult of Princess Diana. When she lived she exposed her private emotions to the public, and, in death, thousands 'mourned' her and cried for an image they believed they engaged with. Here the emotion manifested appears to have scant or no connection with the event about which the emotion is apparently occurring. In the case, for example, of someone who cries or who despairs because they have lost a loved one, the emotions are causally connected with the loss. In the case of the thousands who mourned for Diana, by contrast, the emotions were simply physiological sensations, apparently unrelated to any real event linked to the person that could have caused them. There are indeed 'real' emotions that constitute pure physiological sensations, but only where there is a connection with the cause, as in the case of someone who cries out because they are in pain. But this emotion, as we will see in the discussion of Descartes that follows in the next section, ensues from the connected mind/body. The display of apparent despair following Diana's death, however, is not connected to anything in any of the agents' experience that could have caused the emotion. One might argue that it is emotion disconnected from conscious reflection – free-floating emotion. It seems to be a cultural manifestation of the disconnectedness attributed to Descartes.

A related, though different, manifestation of the same phenomenon is the reaction to figures like Ian Huntley (the British school caretaker convicted of murdering two schoolgirls) or Saddam Hussein. Figures who can be represented as 'evil' and as therefore deserving of public opprobrium exonerate the rest of us from having to deal with the difficult matter of carefully working out what constitutes morality and of what is a reasonable and an unreasonable moral feeling or sensibility. A character like Huntley is clearly depicted as behaving in an immoral fashion; he can be characterised quite simply as evil. Evil in the context is not a matter that needs careful consideration. We do not need to consider moral or ethical questions carefully. We – the rest of humanity – are set up as clearly rational beings, whilst those who are depicted as evil lie at the other extreme of the polarity and are set up as behaving in a non-rational, purely emotional manner.

In fact, it is probably the case that individuals such as Huntley or Saddam Hussein are supremely rational. However, the media representation of them allows them to be depicted as pure evil and it therefore allows others to be represented, by exception, as moral and rational beings. In effect, then, these cases are upholding the much derided view of emotion that has been attributed to Descartes: the representation of Huntley as pure evil depicts him as pure emotion; as non-reflective and non-rational. Such a depiction is itself an emotional reaction to his behaviour that is unconsidered; unreflective. The purely emotional reaction appears to exonerate the rest of us from considering what real moral behaviour ought to be like. It is an irresponsible reaction to evil because it is an unconsidered one. In various ways, then, these cultural phenomena seem to embody the disconnection of reason and emotion, mind and body, actually attributed to Descartes.

Warfare

I would now like to examine briefly what is I think a much more extreme exemplification of the same sort of phenomenon – the second Iraq war and some of its ramifications.

There is a commonplace conception of warfare, which is not borne out in the literature on just wars, which sees it as irrational, outside the scope of morality, outside the scope of right and wrong. As Walzer puts it, 'some among [those who talk about war] have insisted that war lies beyond (or beneath) moral judgement. War, on this outlook, is a world apart where life itself is at stake, where human nature is reduced to its elemental forms, where self interest and necessity prevail' (Walzer, 1977: 3). War strips away civilisation and reveals our nakedness. Hobbes and Thucydides are described by Walzer as offering two of the most compelling versions of this kind of argument. In his *History of the Peloponnesian War*, Thucydides describes a dialogue between two Athenian generals in which they reject the need for justice. Instead, they speak of the imperative to defer to what is feasible and necessary. This, they say, is what war is really like. The generals argue that if they allow the Spartan colony of Melos to stay as it is, or to remain neutral, that would be a weakness and might inspire rebellion in other areas. If the Athenians do not attack, they claim, that would be a revelation of weakness and would invite attack on they themselves. Note here the uncanny parallel with the war in Iraq (of March 2003) and with the reasoning given by Bush and Blair. In the latter case, one of the arguments for going to war was that not to do so would be to invite attack on the forces of reason and good. The Melians, for their part, believed that they must stand firm 'for they had the gods on their side'. Again, there is notable parallel with the stance on Saddam Hussein. The Athenians, it must be said, went further than the Western allies in the case of Iraq. The former 'slew all the men of military age, made slaves of the women and children and inhabited the place with a colony sent hither afterwards of 500 men of their own' (Thucydides, *The Histories*, Book 7). Thucydides does recognise that this stage of the wars was not fought by the Athenians when they were at the height of their powers and when their commitment to freedom and humanity was at its greatest. Rather, this war was fought at a stage in the course of the Athenian city state where it 'embodied', in Walzer's words, ' a certain loss of ethical balance, of restraint and moderation' (1977: 7). At the time of these wars, the city state was beginning to decay and lose its way. I will leave the reader's imagination to draw any parallels with the present day.

However, Walzer also makes the point that the Athenian war, as well as representing the decline of certain of the values of the city state, also represented toughness and an ability to see an action through. This is how, according to Walzer, Hobbes read Thucydides. It is also possible to read Tony Blair in this way when he says, in the face of all the evidence that intelligence was flawed, that there were no weapons of mass destruction, that the legal case for war was at best doubtful, that 'the threat is there and demands our attention'. The 'threat' had to be 'dealt with'. Blair's speech, at this stage, no longer specifies what this 'threat' consists of. Rather, it demands that the United Nations be reformed, so that it 'represents the 21st century reality' (Tony Blair, speech, 5 March 2004).

This conception of warfare is arguably one where force forms a realm of its own, with laws of its own, distinct from the moral realm. The destruction of the Melians was thought to be necessary for the preservation of the Athenian empire. But, as Walzer puts it, there is no asking of the prior question: was the preservation of the empire itself necessary? The preservation of the empire becomes its own end. There were Athenian generals who doubted the wisdom of continuing the empire. Secondly, as Walzer puts it, it exaggerates the knowledge of the generals. They do not say with certainty that Athens will fall unless Melos is destroyed. They do not say with certainty that the destruction of Melos will reduce the risks to Athens. Again, I shall not state any parallels here with the present day, although they are palpably present.

One point of all of this, again put this way by Walzer, is that if people act in accordance with their own interests, driven by fears of another, then consideration of justice is ignored. On the Hobbesian perspective, in the state of war there is no morality, because there is no sovereign who has created the possibility of civil society. The state of warfare, so conceived, lies outside the domain of morality, outside reason. It is effectively the expression of pure, non-rational emotion: of fear of 'the Other', of a desire for preservation of self. Once again, we see the much derided Cartesian view in evidence. War becomes the expression of non-rational emotion. Such a view clearly increases the uncertainty faced by all of us.

This sort of approach to warfare and its aftermath may also have governed the recent treatment of the prisoners in Guantanamo Bay. These prisoners were imprisoned without trial, without access to lawyers and on the basis of only circumstantial evidence.

Fearfulness in the face of the Other is a common feature of the developed world at the present time. Michael Moore, in his film 'Bowling for Columbine', effectively documented the nature and extent of such fear in contemporary USA. Fear, in this context, in Moore's view, is not rational. There are no more guns per head of the population in Canada than there are in the USA, yet the level of security and the fear of being gunned down is significantly greater in the USA than in Canada.

One might argue, then, that the paranoid dividing of mind and body which Scheman attributes to Descartes is in fact characteristic of contemporary culture more generally. A disconnection between emotion and reason is associated with free-floating emotional responses, together with a fragmented and uncertain moral universe. But might a more careful reading of Descartes ironically provide clues for the re-establishment of more firmly grounded practical philosophy? I believe that it can.

An initial response

In the next section of this chapter I argue that the account of Cartesian dualism described in the first section offers a misleading reading of the actual Descartes. My aim is not to prove that Descartes is not a dualist, but to suggest that three aspects of the presentation of the problem are questionable. In my view Descartes did *not* deny that human beings are embodied agents and he did *not* believe that there are obscure ghostly things in the mind that somehow cause bodily movements. Furthermore, Descartes did not hold precisely the view of nature attributed to him.

To begin with it is important to understand that when Descartes described human and non-human behaviour as mechanical, he was principally indicating its regularity and predictability, although there were different implications for human and non-human animals. He believed that machines could perform many actions just as well as human beings, for the simple reason that machines are more accurate. 'A clock, consisting only of wheels and springs, can count hours and measure time more accurately than humans can in all our wisdom' (Adam and Tannery [AT], 1897–1910, VI 59). In the seventeenth century, 'mechanic' applied to almost anything that manifestly worked on mechanical principles, and covered pulleys, wedges, inclined planes, screws and levers. Further, as Baker and Morris (1996) point out, machines, like clocks, were objects of wonder and awe; they were miraculous. Pulling together these two notions, we have the idea that bodies work according to specific principles and are objects of awe and wonder. Part of Descartes' aim in calling behaviours 'mechanical' was to obviate the need for Aristotelian vegetative and sensitive souls.

Embodiment and Descartes

Even if it is accepted that Descartes' notion of the 'body as machine' is less austere than initially supposed, most commentators – for example, Gatens – presume that all that exists does so as one or other of the distinct substances. If this were indeed the case, then regardless of any revision of Descartes' idea of the body, a whole range of problems would still follow from the dualism. But I will argue that the dualist account omits a third Cartesian notion: the unified mind/body. Surprisingly, desire, for Descartes, is embodied and dependent. The key to the idea of embodiment can be found in his work on the passions. In *Meditation VI*, Descartes remarks:

> When we need to drink, the throat becomes dry in such a way as to move the nerves, and thus the inner parts of the brain. That movement produces the feeling of thirst in the mind because on such an occasion nothing would serve us better than to know that we need to drink in order to preserve our health. (Descartes, 1968: 166–7)

The indication that a more than intimate connection exists between the body and mind is further supported by his description of the ego as being in 'quasi permixtum' with its own body, in conjunction with it. If we concentrate on the former description, then we can revise the traditional understanding of the mind being lodged in the body as a pilot in a ship, for although Descartes certainly does say that, he continues by referring to this relationship as close conjunction or 'intermingling' (ibid.: 159).

No one would deny that Descartes describes the mind as a 'thinking thing', whose whole essence is to think (ibid.: 54). However, the mind not only doubts, understands, affirms, denies, is unwilling and willing, but also imagines and has sensory perceptions (ibid.: 28). Indeed, Descartes defines 'thought' broadly to include sensory awareness. This is clarified in the account he offers of sense perception.

Bodies have sensations and these give rise to sensory perceptions. The sensation of pain occurring in the foot, for example, stimulates the mind to try to rid itself of the cause of the pain. Then we find that a 'sadness of the mind' follows from the feeling of a pain (ibid.: 154). Descartes describes such perceptions as confused for two reasons: first, the word 'confused' distinguishes them from perceptions that are 'clear and distinct', for example, judgements in mathematical physics; and second, to suggest that such a perception may contain one or more thoughts. 'I feel thirst' actually expresses two thoughts: one is the thought 'my throat feels dry'; the other is the thought 'I want to drink'. The only plausible interpretation is that the perceptions can be 'intrinsically confused' because it is not in the interests of the individual to separate them out. The idea of a third thing, a unity of body and mind, as the condition for such confused perceptions is supported by Descartes' general account of the passions. These passions are concerned with the well-being of the human being, not with the longevity of body as machine but with the benefit provided to a 'minded body'. Indeed, Descartes refers to the union of mind and body as 'our nature', and the pattern of correlations between thoughts and bodily movements are 'our nature' (AT, VI, 76). So, it could be argued that human beings have confused perceptions for a particular purpose – to make them aware of what is beneficial and harmful to them – and the suggestion seems to be that the soul has a nature that it would not have were it not united with the body.

Without such a unity it would not be possible to make sense of the Cartesian account of 'higher' passions. These include pride, esteem, self-satisfaction and generosity. Respect for others is grounded in self-esteem because esteem is an inclination the soul has to represent to itself the thing esteemed. Commenting on how esteem may be directed towards the self, Descartes writes, 'I observe but a single thing in us which could give us just cause to esteem ourselves, namely the use of our free will and the dominion we have over our volitions' (1985: 103). Self-esteem concentrates attention on other, 'lower' passions, allowing us to redirect disturbing and inappropriate passions. The relationship between 'lower' and 'higher' passions can be described as first- and second-order desires. According to Frankfurt (1971), I have second-order desires when 'I may desperately want a cigarette, but I may also not want to get cancer'. The consideration that there might be a cognitive element in the desires or passions is given weight by Descartes' description of the 'higher' passion of generosity, which is a passion that dissuades the individual from 'scorning' others. Thus passions can encourage some patterns of behaviour and discourage others.

There are thus two facts about the soul: that it thinks and that, being united with its body, it can act and be acted upon (Baker and Morris, 1996: 169). Only a revision of Cartesian dualism, accounting for a unity of body and mind, could provide a sensible interpretation of 'confused' perceptions. Indeed, such a reading gains further textual support: 'My nature teaches me, by these sensations of pain, hunger, thirst, that I am closely joined, and, as it were, intermingled with my body' (ibid.: 169). Without such a unity it would not be possible to make sense of the Cartesian account of emotions. In a letter to Princess Elizabeth, Descartes comments: 'whoever possess the form and the perfect resolve always to use his reasoning powers correctly, as far as he can, and to carry out what he knows to be best, is truly wise, so far as his nature permits' (1968: 191). Far from arguing, as many commentators have claimed, that true knowledge proceeds from reason alone, Descartes is asserting that the highest form of wisdom originates from a unity, an effective combination of reason and will that leads to appropriate action. For contemporary feminists, keen to develop an account of emotion that shows it to be something more than physiological sensations, 'pure experience' along the lines of sense data, Descartes is on the side of the angels. Fricker (1991) has argued, for example, that when sensation is bound up with an emotion, it is not until reason interprets the sensation that the sensation is registered. Emotions, she has argued, are constructed by rational thought processes. Descartes should not be seen as an opponent of this notion. There may be in addition unconscious desires that form the residue of partly satisfied needs and desires. However, Fricker's account here distinguishes emotions from pure physiological reactions. Descartes' preliminary account of emotion, offered here, is not antithetical to this.

How might we reconcile this emergent idea of unity with the definition of the self that is, in essence, a thinking thing? The latter definition is the consequence of an argument based on the claim that although he can doubt the existence of the body, he cannot doubt the existence of his mind and that he knows without doubt that he exists through an intellectual perception of any current mental state. The 'I that is certain that he is' is only the 'I' in a narrow sense. The thicker conception of the self described here includes sensations and passions. A revised reading of *Meditation II* would suggest not that the self is identical to a thinking substance, but rather that it is possible to be certain of the existence of an I that thinks without making any assumptions about the existence of the body. *The Meditations* are really an expedition into epistemology in order to secure various grounds for our beliefs. However, before justification is assured all beliefs have to be open to doubt.

The purpose of revisionism

The contemporary dismissal of Cartesianism resonates with a rejection of universalism more generally. Even some of those sympathetic to universalism, like Gideon Calder, consider that 'human universality, as an idea or as an ideal, seem(s) like an overweening Enlightenment conceit' (Calder, 1998: 140). In this final section, I will argue that Cartesian philosophy offers us something vital and relevant because it can help us find a way through the deep uncertainties, and consequent mistrust, which are linked closely to moral pluralism and relativism.

It is common currency in ethics and epistemology, and postcolonial, feminist and communitarian theories, that value and other types of pluralism are both factually inevitable and normatively desirable. Plurality is considered to reflect the diversity of human reality and to rescue ethics from endorsing interested codes of behaviour that are often disguised as moral principles. The plurality of values appears to be normatively desirable because it coincides with social and political assertions of difference. But I would like to question this assumption and ask whether or not the 'cultural imaginary' is necessarily or only contingently plural. To put this slightly differently, are values plural only in today's 'post-/late modern', 'detraditionalised', 'reflexive', 'risk' society, or is pluralism characteristic of all possible worlds?

It is possible to articulate the belief that our moral universe is irreducibly plural only from a perspective that allows or acknowledges a conversation between those holding different values. If a conversation is possible, then we can infer that commonalties hold across the plural values. It was to this end that Aristotle outlined an account of the Good and linked it to an idea of practical wisdom, which can be applied to each and every individual, regardless of location.

Even if the reader does not wish to accept this specific view, it seems to be significant that there is evidence of the much-derided perspective attributed to Descartes gaining currency in the contemporary cultural context. Rather than Descartes himself holding the derided view, I am arguing that he held something very different. He suggested, rather, that emotions should not simply be allowed free rein, as in the case of the popular condemnation of popular hate figures. Instead, these emotions should be reflected on, analysed, called to account. Morality on this view would not be equivalent to the unfettered expression of unreflective moral sentiment; rather moral judgements would be made with careful cognisance of different courses of action. This is not to offer a full description of the nature of moral reasoning or of appropriate moral principles to follow in any given case, but it is to suggest that morality cannot merely involve unreflective condemnation of another as 'evil' or outside its scope. It must involve more engagement and reflection than that. Descartes, I am suggesting, recognised that it is only a unified body/mind that is capable of acting morally. Indeed, he recognises that true knowledge proceeds not from reason alone.

Descartes has become a convenient target held responsible for a whole gamut of philosophical errors. Unwittingly, it seems that intellectuals may, by expressing the derided view so readily, have given it currency. I believe that a process of reasoned reflection on moral emotions/feelings should lead one to recognise a cognitive account of morality which is grounded, with some degree of certainty, in human nature.

Conclusion

In this chapter I have presented the commonplace view attributed to Descartes, and I have suggested that this outlook is reflected in certain cultural phenomena today. I have, for example, argued that certain ways of reading the war in Iraq show resonances of the oft-derided view of the separation of reason and emotion that is attributed to Descartes. I offered a revised account of Descartes' dualism with the intention of drawing out a 'third thing', a unity of body and mind. From this I established that the Cartesian concept of the subject is a much richer idea than that usually identified as the *cogito*. The epistemic method, which brings into question all beliefs, is one that everyone, given the right circumstances, can follow, and the principles within reason, which enable the individual to assent to various beliefs, are to be found in every individual. To this I have added that when understood as a unity, the self can discern more certain grounds for practical reason, based in human nature. If there are aspects of this nature that are common to all individuals, then a minimal universalism emerges.

In response, critics of universalism such as Iris Young would argue that any universalising perspective must exclude a number of individuals. Her argument is that all universal accounts identify what is common across individuals, because identification is made through concepts, and every concept has an opposite, it is therefore necessarily the case that some individuals will be excluded. But it is not at all clear why, just because each concept has an opposite, that reasoning itself cannot be a universal process. Similarly, to characterise what might be true of human beings in a minimal sense does not mean reducing an individual to that and nothing but that. If this seventeenth-century philosophical method can be revised, then we might discover the grounds for a moral respect due to each and every individual.

Acknowledgements

I am indebted to Gillian Howie for some very useful editorial suggestions on an earlier version of this.

References

Adam, C. and Tannery, P. [AT] (1897–1910), *Oeuvres de Descartes*, 12 vols., Paris: Leopold Cerf.
Ariew, R. and Grene, M. (1995), *Descartes and his Contemporaries, Meditations, Objections and Replies*, Chicago and London: The University of Chicago Press.
Assiter, A. (1996), *Enlightened Women*, London: Routledge.
Baker, G. and Morris, K. (1996), *Descartes' Dualism*, London and New York: Routledge.
Blair, T. (2004), Speech, in *The Guardian*, 5 March.
Braidotti, R. (1991), *Patterns of Dissonance*, Cambridge: Polity Press.
Calder, G. (1998), 'Liberalism without Universalism', in Brecher, B., Halliday, J. and Kolinska, K. (eds) *Nationalism and Racism in the Liberal Order*, Avebury Series in Philosophy, Aldershot: Ashgate.
Cornford, F. M. (1907), *Thucydides Mythistoricus*, London: Duckworth.
Derrida, J. (1976), *Of Grammatology*, Baltimore and London: Johns Hopkins University Press.
Descartes, R. (1968), *Discourse on Method and Other Writings*, London: Penguin.

Descartes, R. (1985), *The Philosophical Writing of Descartes*, 2 vols., trans. J. Cottingham, R. Stoothhoff and D. Murdoch, Cambridge: Cambridge University Press.

Frankfurt, H. (1971), 'Freedom of the Will and the Concept of a Person', *Journal of Philosophy*, 68.

Fricker, M. (1991), 'Reason and Emotion', *Radical Philosophy*, no. 57, Spring Issue, Oxford: Blackwell.

Gatens, M. (1996), *Imaginary Bodies, Ethics, Power and Corporeality*, London and New York: Routledge.

Gilroy, P. (1993), *The Black Atlantic, Modernity and Double Consciousness*, London: Verso.

Kant, I. (1933), *Critique of Pure Reason*, trans. Norman Kemp-Smith, London: Macmillan.

Lloyd, G. (1984), *The Man of Reason, 'Male' and 'Female' in Western Philosophy*, London: Methuen.

Lyotard, J. F. (1979), *The Postmodern Condition*, Manchester: Manchester University Press.

O'Neill, O. (1996), *Towards Justice and Virtue*, Cambridge: Cambridge University Press.

Parekh, B. (2000), *Rethinking Multiculturalism: Cultural Diversity and Political Theory*, Basingstoke: Macmillan.

Plumwood, V. (1993), *Feminism and the Mastery of Nature*, London: Routledge.

Rorty, A. (1986), *Essays on Descartes' Meditations*, Berkeley and Los Angeles: University of California Press.

Rorty, R. (1980), *Philosophy and the Mirror of Nature*, Oxford: Blackwell.

Russell, B. (1946), *History of Western Philosophy*, London: Allen and Unwin.

Ryle, G. (1949), *The Concept of Mind*, London: Hutchinson.

Scheman, N. (1993), 'Though This be Method, yet there is Madness in it', in Scheman, N. (ed.), *Engenderings, Constructions of Knowledge, Authority, and Privilege*, London: Routledge.

Sorrell, T. (1994), 'Descartes' Modernity', in J. Cottingham (ed.), *Reason, Will and Sensation*, Oxford: Blackwell.

Scruton, R. (1984), *A Short History of Modern Philosophy*, London: Routledge.

Walzer, M. (1977), *Just and Unjust Wars*, Harmondsworth: Penguin.

Young, I. M. (1990), *Justice and the Politics of Difference*, Princeton, NJ: Princeton University Press.

Part Two

Trust, Risk and Uncertainty in Institutions and Organisations

5
Trust, Risk and Expert Systems: Child Protection, Modernity and the (Changing) Management of Life and Death

Harry Ferguson

The dynamics of trust and risk take different forms in relation to different social issues and sites of social life. A striking feature of this is that children have become key subjects around whom contemporary obsessions with risk are focused (Jackson and Scott, 1999). From the predatory paedophile to the 'cruel' parent who abuses and kills their child, child abuse and risk now have a compelling hold on the popular imagination and public policy. A vital feature of this situation is that the focus is not simply on the tragedy of child abuse and death itself, but the relationship between trust and risk and the experts and professional systems that work with the problem.

Trust in the expert systems of child protection appears especially vulnerable and weakened given that since the 1970s there has been a number of high-profile cases involving serious system failures by professionals where children have died despite the attentions of social workers and other professionals. For three decades now across the Western world the issue of the deaths of children in child protection cases has hung like a dark shadow over the professions that work with child abuse, and especially social work. Media, academic and front-line professional interest in such child protection failures is truly international as the dead children form a litany to which we constantly return (Stanley and Goddard, 2002).

This is typified by the social reaction to the murder of eight-year-old Victoria Climbié in London in 2000, who died a horrific death despite the attentions of social services, health professionals and the police. Victoria died with 128 separate injuries to her body after suffering months of torture and abuse by her great-aunt, Marie-Thérèse Kouao, and Kouao's boyfriend, Carl Manning, who are now serving life sentences for her murder. Victoria was brought to London by Kouao from the Ivory Coast less than a year before she died. Her parents hoped this would give her the opportunity of a better education and life, yet Kouao failed to enrol

Victoria in a school. She was starved, beaten, scalded, burned with ciga-
rettes and left in a freezing bathroom trussed up in a bin bag strapped into
a bath. A public inquiry into Victoria's death, chaired by Lord Herbert
Laming, was initiated by the government and illustrates how such scandals
and the investigations that are central to them are now extraordinary cultural phenomena in their own right. The inquiry's website (www.victoria-
climbie-inquiry.org.uk) received around three million hits in the period
30 September 2001 to 30 September 2002 and the average visitor session
lasted 20 minutes (compared to an internet average of three minutes),
which shows that people were reading the material rather than merely
surfing (Laming, 2003: 21). The 400-page inquiry report argues that a mass-
ive system failure occurred, with an estimated 12 bungled occasions when
Victoria could have been rescued. As a result, new legislation and other
major reforms are under way as part of the 'biggest re-organisation of child
protection services in 30 years' (*Guardian*, 10 September 2003).

The appalling violence and suffering perpetrated on children in such
extreme cases is an obvious feature of the scandalous quality such events
and public disclosures contain. A number of mechanisms have been developed by nation states to manage such child protection 'failures' (on the UK,
see Reder, Duncan and Gray, 1993; Reder and Duncan 1999; on Australia,
The New South Wales Child Death Review Team Report, 1997; on the USA,
the report of the *US Advisory Board on Child Abuse and Neglect*, USABCAN,
1995). What all countries have in common is the construction of child protection in terms of 'scandal politics', which refers to the pattern of increased stress on public disclosures of welfare failures and revelations in news
media that are shaming for public figures and services (Lull and Hinerman,
1997; Chaney, 2002: 116). In what follows I use the general notion of
'scandal' to refer to this process of aggressive media reporting of child protection case 'failures' and increasing demands that the state be held
accountable for preventing them recurring.

The effectiveness of entire child welfare systems has come to be viewed
through scandal politics and the prism of child deaths, despite their being
only a very small minority of all investigated cases. In the process, in
conditions of late modernity, the environment of trust and risk in child
protection has been transformed. My aim in this chapter is to provide a
sociological analysis of this change and to draw out some key theoretical
implications that it contains for our understandings of trust and risk, as
well as some of its implications for children, families and professionals.

Risk, child protection and simple modernity

Developments in child protection over the past century or so fit remarkably
closely with the sociological analysis of modernity provided by Giddens
and Beck, although in some important respects I seek here to develop their

work on the nuances of trust and risk. Recent events and the (changing) meanings of social work and child protection are best seen in the context of a shift to 'reflexive modernization' (Beck *et al.*, 1994) and radicalised conceptions of security and danger that have emerged in what Beck (1992) calls 'risk society'. To follow Beck in claiming that we live in a risk society does not mean that life is necessarily more risky today than ever before. There is nothing new about children being 'at risk'. Life today is *not* inherently riskier for children. The emergence of a new kind of risk anxiety surrounding children has arisen from major changes in the source and meaning of risk, resulting in notions of children at 'high risk' and risk assessment becoming central to child protection (DHSS, 1988b; Parton, 1991).

The notion that professionals fail children at risk is in fact historically quite recent. For much of the twentieth century child death was a routine experience for child protection workers. From the beginnings of the child protection movement in 1889 through to 1914 in the UK and Ireland, a staggering 13,613 children died in child protection cases investigated by the lead agency, the National Society for the Prevention of Cruelty to Children (NSPCC). These children had by no means all been killed by their parents. They reflect how such work intersected with broader and very serious social problems of poverty and infant mortality. Thus in many NSPCC cases children were probably *dying anyway* from a variety of causes and became caught up in the new powers and classifications of child protection. A key dynamic of the child protection movement was an emphasis on growth and development and the desire to spread its practices across geographical boundaries. The existence of child death was actually viewed as a sign that child protection was working *well* and highly publicised on those terms because it meant that increasing numbers of vulnerable children were being reached by professionals. The NSPCC used to publish statistics on these deaths to show the value of its work and how successfully it was reaching children: 'that it is certain that the Society is telling on the life of children' (NSPCC *Annual Report*, 1897: 38). Deaths were largely explained in terms of concepts of sin and moral decay rather than blame and accountability. Deaths were always regretted, but were handled with a relative absence of existential *angst*, while professional careers were never threatened despite the failures (Ferguson, 2004).

Public disclosure of deaths continued through to the 1930s. By now, however, fewer child protection cases were ending in death (NSPCC *Annual Report*, 1936: 34–5). This was due not only to effective child protection interventions, but crucially because children were generally healthier thanks to a better diet, public health reforms and child welfare services. Child protection had come to surround children who were, by and large, *living anyway*. By the late 1930s information about deaths in child protection cases ceased to be made public and had gone out of view. This did not happen because the problem was 'solved', but arose rather from a process of sequestration which involves the institutional repression of troublesome information concerning death and other signs of organisational 'failure' (Giddens, 1991). Agency failures to protect were sequestered by the 1930s because disclosure of such hazards threatened the authority, optimism and trustworthiness of the expert system. The management of child life and death had been transformed by a series of interconnected developments, which constituted modern child protection in terms of a powerful professional belief in the transformative capacity of social intervention to promote child welfare and an ideology that held that children not only could, but *should*, be protected in time.

A key influence was the profound transformation that occurred in the social value of children through the twentieth century. Zelizer (1985) describes how this arose from the introduction of child labour laws and compulsory schooling, which transformed the wage-earning 'non-child' of the nineteenth-century labouring poor into the category of the economically worthless child scholar. By the 1930s children had gained a new sentimental value – while they were now economically 'useless', they were emotionally 'priceless'. The defining characteristics of 'the child' today – parental dependence, economic and sexual inactivity, and absence of legal and political rights – were largely born here. Professionals contributed to, and drew from, the 'sacralization' of childhood, which lowered thresholds of tolerance of child death in society generally. In the process, 'the death of all children – rich and poor – emerged as an intolerable social loss' and was 'transformed into a public campaign for the preservation of child life' (Zelizer, 1985: 27). Avoidable child death became publicly unacceptable and helped constitute the ideology that children should be prevented from dying through child protection interventions. This occurred in a context where death in general had become a problem within modernity, a point I return to later in the chapter.

Following Beck and Giddens, the period from the 1920s through to the early 1970s can be characterised in terms of 'simple modernisation'. In those social conditions it was typical of child protection professionals and agencies to make powerful scientific claims to knowledge, enlightenment and progress. Child protection discourse was spared the application of scientific scepticism to itself (cf. Beck, 1992: 155). A strong demarcation was fostered between experts and lay people. Traditionally, lay people certainly demonstrated a critical awareness of child welfare practices as evidenced by the huge levels of individual and communal resistance to child protection (Ferguson, 1992). Such reflection was, however, part of a context in which expertise remained largely uninterrogated at a public level. Right through to the 1960s, science remained a 'tradition' as expertise was approached as though it were akin to 'traditional authority' (Giddens, 1994b: 128). This enabled experts to fudge over knowledge about agency failures and any scepticism they had about the real limits to protecting children in time, while at the same time advancing the application of their results to the lay public in a hugely optimistic, authoritarian fashion. The sequestration of child protection by the 1930s meant that when professional errors and 'failure' to protect did occur, knowledge about them was institutionally repressed and problems such as death hidden from public view. Thus, it was not that error did not occur in child protection. Rather, the lack of public attention to issues such as child death was a reflection of how the treatment of mistakes and risks was socially organised in that phase (cf. Beck, 1992: 159).

On the rare occasions when 'failures' were publicly disclosed prior to the 1970s, errors served to expand the power bloc of child care experts within the welfare state. The plausibility of experts was, at worst, only superficially undermined by accidents (Beck, 1995: 67). This was evidenced by the tragic case of Denis O'Neill, whose death at the hands of his foster parents had such a profound impact on postwar legislation and the development of child care services in the UK (Monckton, 1945; Packman, 1981). Social work and child care experts could face a public sphere whose doubts they could sweep aside by claims of their success and with promises of further liberation from constraints not yet understood (cf. Beck, 1992: 154–5).

Child protection, risk and reflexive modernisation

The sequestration of child protection reflected how a new concept of risk had entered social policy, one that was no longer derived externally from nature and concepts of sin, but from the internal codes of expertise and science. A form of 'manufactured risk' (Giddens, 1994a), it is based on the use of reflexively organised knowledge and the competence and decision-making skills of expert systems (Beck, 1992). The conditions of possibility had been laid for science and expertise to expand the concept of 'child abuse' and for exhaustive inquiries into apparent system failures in child protection, all of which began in the 1970s. It was then that social workers and other professionals became the subjects of detailed inquiries into the circumstances surrounding the deaths of children in cases in which they had known the children to be at risk. At the same time, child abuse was being 'rediscovered' through the pioneering work of medical practitioners such as Henry Kempe, who deliberately coined the emotive phrase the 'battered child syndrome' to draw attention to how children were seriously harmed and killed by their parents (Kempe *et al.*, 1962). It was at this time too that child sexual abuse began to undergo a significant process of discovery in the wake of the activist work of the women's movement (Finkelhor, 1984; Driver and Droisen, 1989). While there were continuities, acknowledgement that serious harm is perpetrated against vulnerable children by 'dangerous' parents and other carers involved a distinct shift in recognition compared to the order of meanings of simple modernity. Indeed, the very term 'child abuse' as a generic term to cover physical, sexual, emotional abuse and neglect entered the vernacular of child protection in the 1970s and 1980s.

At one and the same time, professionals and organisations were confronted with new knowledge of risks to children and with shocking public disclosures which showed that child protection systems were failing to protect children from serious abuse and death. These were shocking in their own right because of the extent of trauma and violence perpetrated against children, as each scandal revealed a similar pattern of starved, neglected, physically and sometimes sexually violated children, who had suffered multiple injuries from the physical abuse inflicted on them. They were also shocking in the sense that they appeared to be completely new and to reflect a real decline in professional standards. This misguided sense of newness had its roots in the sequestration of child death that I have showed occurred from the 1930s. Ironically, at a time when further improvements in practice meant that deaths in child protection work had become a rare event, managing the risk of system failure rather than celebrating success became the defining approach. The paradox of contemporary risk anxiety about children and childhood is that it has arisen at a time when children have never been safer, when child protection systems have never been more elaborate and technically competent. This does not mean that they are good enough, only that in general they have never been so effective.

This paradox can be explained by changes in the source and meaning of risk. In the reflexive social order that has emerged since the 1970s, the 'traditional' assumptions and forms of social organisation of simple modernity have broken down. Child protection exemplifies how if, under simple modernity, expertise was spared the application of scientific scepticism to itself, in reflexive modernity the sciences are confronted with their own products, defects and secondary problems (Beck, 1992: 154). Problems of risk management in child protection now include hazards brought about by the development of the expert system itself.

What have become visible are the dangers, the 'bads', produced by modernity from which we all feel threatened – child protection failures, along with pollution, family breakdown, unemployment, and so on. The central institutions of late modernity – government, industry and science – are the main producers of risk. This manifests in how expert systems routinely socially construct the universe of events surrounding 'cases' within an historically specific ideology of 'child protection'. 'Child abuse' is a product of a labelling process based on clinical evidence with respect to the presenting condition of the child and social evidence built around moral judgements about the character of parents (Dingwall *et al.*, 1983; Thorpe, 1994). What is coming to light today is significantly a product of the development of ever more elaborate expert systems and a shift in social perception, which has brought long-repressed crimes like child sexual abuse into view, rendering them classifiable in social practice (Corby, 2000).

Reflexivity means something more than 'reflection', which people have always had a capacity for. An important dimension of reflexivity is about 'reflex' – a response to the 'bads', the dangers produced by modernity itself. Unlike reflection, reflexivity is not just individualistic, conscious or intentional, but occurs on an institutional level. Reflexive modernisation is, in important respects, about the reflex response of institutions to disclosures of the side-effects produced within an earlier 'simple' modernity (cf. Lash, 1994: 200). Modernisation can thus be said to be becoming reflexive when it becomes its own theme (Beck, 1992: 19). The reflex response of institutions produces new contexts for reflection by individuals, whose responses in turn reflexively shape the institutional practices to which they are reacting. The concept of risk society provides a term for this relationship of reflex and reflection (Beck, 1994).

The manner in which modernisation risks surrounding the deaths of children in child protection cases are 'side-effects' produced by modernity itself is implicit in the child death inquiries where the difficulties revealed are conceptualised as *system* failures and defined in terms not of an undersupply of practice, but of the multitude of (uncoordinated) work that went into the cases (Reder *et al.*, 1993). The same is true of instances where professionals have been criticised for overreacting to child sexual abuse suspicions and allegedly wrongly taking children into care (Butler-Sloss, 1988). The reflex response of institutions to disclosures of these 'bads' resulted in the decision-making party concealed in such errors becoming visible (cf. Beck, 1992: 175). In terms of *institutional reflexivity* the child protection system is a classic form of advanced modern institutionalised risk system which has at its core the kind of reflexive monitoring of risk that is intrinsic to modernity; the 'risk profiling' that is based on analysis of what, in the current state of knowledge and current conditions, is the distribution of risks in acting on behalf of children in a myriad of possible ways (Giddens, 1991: 119). Fundamentally, risk concerns future happenings as related to present knowledge and practices. While the future has always been intrinsically unknowable, in late modernity the future becomes a new terrain lending itself to colonial invasion through risk calculation. Risk is about the 'colonization of the future' (ibid.: 111). The central importance that 'risk assessment' has taken on in child protection today concerns attempts to render the future under control and safer for children identified as 'at risk' of future harm (DHSS, 1988b).

In such circumstances, expertise is demystified and loses its traditional authority. As a consequence, authority is pervasively questioned; every decision is risk-laden and potentially open to public scrutiny. Professionals like social workers are painfully aware of such risk anxiety. As one interviewee from my own research (Ferguson, 2004) exemplified it:

> I think social workers are much more aware that every decision you take can now be judged, so obviously you're conscious of that in your work and it does naturally bring a level of anxiety and pressure to the job.

Expertise is targeted not only as a source of solutions to problems, but also as a *cause of problems*. At the core of risk society is an awareness of risk *as risk*. This involves knowing that 'knowledge gaps' exist in terms of risks which cannot now be converted into 'certainties' by religious or magical knowledge (Giddens, 1990: 125). Concomitantly, there is an awareness of the limitations of expertise: knowledge that 'no expert system can be wholly expert in terms of the consequences of the adoption of expert principles' (ibid.). As Giddens (ibid.: 111) elaborates, 'Where risk is *known* to be risk, it is experienced differently from circumstances in which notions of *fortuna* prevail. To recognize the existence of a risk or set of risks is to accept not just the possibility that things might go wrong, but that this possibility cannot be eliminated.' Modes of generating confidence in hazardous actions are by definition unavailable. Child protection is constituted as a form of *manufactured uncertainty*.

One disturbing consequence of these processes has been the emergence of a powerful blame culture, both within organisations and in how professionals are routinely pilloried by the general public, public representatives and the media for failing to protect children. As Beck (1992: 75) observes, 'risk society contains an inherent tendency to become a *scapegoat society;* suddenly it is not the hazards, but those who point them out that provoke general uneasiness'. A 'blaming-system' emerges (Parton, 1996a) where stirred-up public fears and insecurities come to surround new perceptions of risks and danger and these are diverted onto those professionals who become 'receptacles for public anger' (Ruddick, 1991).

The work of Mary Douglas is instructive here. For her, risk is seen as having largely replaced older ideas about the cause of misfortune, concepts such as sin. These are now discredited and have been replaced by the 'modern sanitized discourse of risk' (Lupton, 1999: 46). Douglas sees risk as acting mainly as a locus of blame, in which 'risky' groups or individuals are singled out as dangerous (ibid.: 3). A 'risky' Other may pose a threat to the integrity of one's own body or the community in which one lives, to symbolic order. What is striking today is the way in which this sense of threat to the community extends beyond the paedophile or parent who neglects or kills their child and has become focused on expert systems, especially social work. Risk acts as a 'forensic resource' in providing explanations for things that have gone wrong. Large institutions are singled out as responsible and 'to blame' for risks. Every death, every accident and every misfortune is 'chargeable to someone's account'; someone must be found to be blamed. As Douglas (1992: 16) writes:

> Whose fault? is the first question. Then, what action? Which means, what damages? What compensation? What restitution? And the preventive action is to improve the coding of risk in the domain which has turned out to be inadequately covered. Under the banner of risk reduction, a new blaming system has replaced the former combination of moralistic condemning of the victim's incompetence.

The outcome has been precisely attempts to 'improve the coding of risk' through proceduralisation and imposing greater accountability. Because of its closeness to and structurally ambiguous relationship with those dangerous Others who abuse children, social work itself represents a threat to ontological security and becomes a focus of the blaming system. Now, it is not only 'abusing' families but social workers (and, much less frequently, other professionals caught in the eye of the storm) who are subjected to purity and pollution rituals by the community, by being publicly exposed in the media, humiliated and dismissed from their jobs. Reflexive modernisation has given birth to new parameters of professional experience which must be mapped out in terms of the phenomenology of having to manage trust and risk as risk in a context where traditional psychological supports are no longer meaningful and new dangers and opportunities have opened up in child protection in risk society.

Sequestration, body projects and death in late modern child protection

I have been examining a structural transformation that has occurred within expert systems and between them and lay people which has radicalised experiences of trust and risk in the construction of late modern child protection. I now want to show how the kinds of institutional reflexivity and individual reflection that are so central to contemporary risk anxiety in child protection were constituted in the context of changing meanings and experience of death in modernity. The phenomenological *angst* that is at the core of modern risk anxiety in child protection is rooted in personal and professional engagement with existentially troublesome information concerning death, around which it has become increasingly apparent that knowledge gaps and manufactured uncertainties exist.

Professionals such as social workers are faced with the challenge of finding ways of trying to transform pervasive risk anxiety into feelings of relative security. Some – my research suggests a minority (Ferguson, 2004) – continue to rely on traditional resources such as superstitions. One social worker in my study, for instance, had a lucky shirt he wore to court;

another carried crystals. These remain half-hearted superstitions, however, rather than truly effective psychological supports. In the workplace most adopt more rational approaches, which revolved around getting advice and support for tricky cases. The presence of close, supportive peer relationships was seen as crucial to survival, as was good supervision, which dealt with feelings and personal development as well as administrative and clinical issues, and effective workload management.

A powerful strategy for living with risk anxiety was what, after Shilling (1993), can be called 'body projects'. Social workers spoke of getting massages to help them relax, of the importance of 'spiritual' things, transcendental meditation, and going swimming, to aerobics and doing various other sports to help them cope with stress and bring balance into their lives. Exercise, as one put it, is 'very therapeutic', while for another, it 'gets the old aggression out'. Effectively, then, for child care professionals working with risk anxiety is a lifestyle issue. Managing it (well) is incorporated within individualised life planning and strategies for living a life of one's own (Beck and Beck-Gernshiem, 2002). This needs to be fully understood not only in terms of organisational responses and institutional reflexivity, but at the level of *self*-identity. In late modernity, identity is no longer something that is shaped by tradition, external controls (such as religion) and the class and gender roles ascribed at birth, but by individuals through reflexive engagements with expert knowledge. The self becomes 'a reflexive project' (Giddens, 1991). In social conditions where expertise is routinely opened out to public scrutiny, people have to constantly use available knowledge to reflexively shape their own lives and, by extension, deaths. This inherently threatens our sense of ontological security, representing a huge existential challenge to us all.

Death, as Giddens observes (1991: 50), is associated in human consciousness 'with anxieties of an utterly fundamental sort'. In order that citizens can maintain an ontologically secure sense of self, death in late modernity continues to be sequestered. It is not possible to present statistics for the post-1970 period on child protection 'cases ending in death' as I have done for 1884–1936, because that information was institutionally repressed by child welfare agencies. What we know about deaths in child protection work since the 1970s is represented in the child abuse scandal cases. Scandals like child abuse inquiries constituted a new way of managing and selectively disclosing information about deaths in child protection cases within an overall sequestration of experience. This has been able to happen in a cultural context in which changes are occurring in discourses around death and a resurgence of activity concerned with making the phenomenon of death a subject for wider public debate. The development of the hospice movement and debates around euthanasia are examples of this, as are the profound implications of the emergence of HIV/AIDS (Walter, 1994). The increased visibility of death in child protection discourse has occurred in the general context of healthy attempts to make death a subject for wider public debate: as part of a partial 'return of the repressed' (Giddens, 1991: 202).

On the other hand, I want to suggest that death has become a subject of child protection discourse because of an intensification of the tendency for death to be constructed within modernity as a particular problem (Ariès, 1974; Bauman, 1992). Although never explicitly recognised or openly discussed in the, by now, huge literature, much of the discourse around advanced modern child protection represents an increased discomfort with death and a furthering of the process of sequestration (see Smith, 2002). Whether or not such deaths are made public in the first place is a highly selective process. Far from resulting from a more open attitude within welfare organisations, those cases that do become public tend to do so through the media and politicians following up on disclosures made at criminal trials of abusing parents.

Within a sequestered realm of experience it is not death in some simple sense which is the source of concern. Attention is focused on the expert systems which seek to prevent death and manage life. This reflects the fact that outside religious discourse, discussion of death has become largely a preoccupation with sickness. 'Death is only a "problem" when it is premature death – when a person has not lived out whatever, given certain risks, a table of life expectancy might suggest' (Giddens, 1991: 204). In this sense, there are few more disturbing phenomena in advanced modern society than the archetypal premature deaths of highly socially valued children who were *known* to be at high risk of such a fate: the deaths of children in child abuse cases.

As recently as the turn of the twentieth century the sight of the dead was relatively common. However, the extension of the average life-span across the twentieth century has made death far more remote today than it used to be from living people in general. People can grow up without ever having seen a dead body (Elias, 1985: 85). Death is no longer part of normal life. Moreover, death is increasingly taboo in a modern consumerist culture which routinely glamourises and celebrates youth. The slim body, the healthy body, the normal body is a youthful body. The tendency is to defer death by engaging in 'body projects' of dietary, health and fitness regimes which promote a prolonged life and, at worst, to deny death altogether (Shilling, 1993). All signs of the dying and the dead are still heavily sequestered, pushed further than ever out of sight of the living and behind the scenes, expunged from the home and placed in the domain of medical experts in hospitals, hospices and funeral parlours (Elias, 1985: 85).

In reality, by the 1970s the actual experience of dealing with child abuse deaths among practitioners was rare and, thankfully, to this day the vast majority of professionals never encounter dead children in their work. The return of the repressed has meant that it is the *discussion* of death which occupies a form of public space, while actual bodily evidence and direct experience of death remains sequestered away from the public gaze (Mellor and Shilling, 1993). Nevertheless, the fear of confronting death remains no less great for all that. Scholars of child protection have attributed professional fears in child protection to the risks of being publicly held to account and humiliated as part of a high-profile inquiry into the death of a child on one's caseload (Hill, 1990; Parton, 1991). Inquiries, as I have shown, do represent new dangers and fears for professionals. But such interpretations have neglected and under-theorised the extent of the profound *existential* crisis that has developed for professionals. What has been left out is the fears professionals have of being responsible for children's prolonged suffering. Feelings among the social workers in my study (Ferguson, 2004) that they had let children down were common, the consequences of which weigh heavily:

> I let this child down, that comes into it, there's a huge amount of things come into it really, well, like, if a child is being abused. In a case where I was involved with a teenager ... after two and a half years she disclosed about CSA [child sexual abuse], and I felt I should have known this. I was involved, you know, but it never came out; I didn't do enough, I should have picked up more, I should have, I suppose you are constantly questioning yourself.

Such 'constant questioning' is at the core of risk anxiety in late modern child protection and is symptomatic of professionals' experience of risk as risk with respect to profoundly troublesome existential matters and knowledge that those risks cannot be eliminated – and least of all with respect to death, the greatest post-traditional crisis of all. This kind of risk anxiety manifests itself in complex ways, and not in any simple terms as a professional obsession with death. It translates rather into an inherent concern with the riskiness of promoting child life in the context of uncertain futures.

Social workers and other child care professionals are arguably no less likely to deny and defer death than anyone else. As members of the 'new middle classes' they occupy a social space which has a central concern with 'lifestyle' and body projects, including healthy eating regimes and walking holidays (Bourdieu, 1986). The greater visibility of death and the reflexivity of late modernity confronts people with the prospect of dying in a manner which can radically disrupt their lifestyle and body regimes (Mellor, 1993). 'The more investment we make in body projects, the more difficult and disturbing it will be to come to terms with their end' (Shilling, 1993: 187). Bauman (1992) argues that strategies of 'self-care' surrounding issues of health and the body now fill the gap left vacant by the relative absence of survival strategies derived from religion. The return of the repressed in child protection has therefore meant that social workers have had to confront an existential crisis, not just with respect to the implications of 'professional' risks of serious abuse and death to their child clients, but the meaning that such engagement holds in relation to *their own* lives and deaths. As Shilling (1993: 189–90) argues, 'Unable to confront the reality of the demise and death of their own bodies, the self-identities of individuals are often made insecure by the presence of death in other people's bodies.'

These processes of reflexivity and individualisation have both created the social conditions that make it more possible for children to gain more protection and for public outcry when they do not. It is the uniquely individualised child who lives or dies, who has acquired not only a right to life, but a right to a biography, a life of their own. In the faces of Victoria Climbié and others we glimpse the vulnerability of our own children and ourselves as carers. Individualisation, living a 'life of one's own', has had the effect of imbuing life with a hunger for life, adventurousness and a combination of ebullience and mortal distress. The specialness and precariousness of what can be made in a life thus renders dying and death unthinkable. As Beck and Beck-Gernsheim (2002: 154) observe, 'If I suddenly cease to be there, others are no longer able to keep the end of the end under control.' This is especially true of the deaths of children. What happens in the end is not that they die but that child protection stops working.

The complexities of trust, risk and expert systems in late modernity

The effect is that today public disclosures of avoidable child deaths and suffering have become more intolerable than ever, with far greater accountability (and blame) demanded when protection does appear to fail. Yet the impact on trust and risk has been contradictory. The more acute risk anxiety has become among the public and professionals, the more the importance of trust to the effective operation of expert systems has increased (Smith, 2001). In a post-traditional order, trust in expertise is based on the assumption of technical competence. It is *revisable* and can, in principle, be withdrawn at a moment's notice (Giddens, 1994a: 89). On the one hand, public disclosures of agency failures have indeed reduced trust in child protection professionals and created a defensive, over-anxious fear of blame among workers, whose practice is now over-regulated and managed. Creativity and more intuitive, soulful forms of work with children and families are being suppressed. What is required are forms and styles of organisational life which 'contain' or 'hold' workers in their anxiety (Ward, 1995; Froggett, 2002) in ways that promote their ontological security and capacities to develop meaningful relationships with service users while understanding and accepting the risks inherent to child protection.

On the other hand, however, scandal politics has created new opportunities for trust to evolve and boosted the risks that lay people are prepared to take to gain protection. Almost despite itself, the media in all its blaming and negativity has created a live and critical public domain which has produced genuinely progressive possibilities for greater protection. Child abuse – how to stop it, how to survive it – and risks to children are staples of media reporting and perhaps the most heavily discussed social issue of our time (Jackson and Scott, 1999). In engaging with this new kind of information, the reflexive individual as consumer and citizen comes to possess a good deal of 'expert' information. The much more reflexive, critical nature of today's society means that people are a good deal more concerned about how they are governed than in the pre-1970s period of simple modernisation. In a world of 'clever people' (Giddens, 1994b: 94), most people most of the time know a great deal of what social workers, other professionals, administrators and politicians know. This does not mean that they are intellectually superior and 'cleverer' in the academic sense, but that they have to be able to cope with so many more (multiple) choices and so much information, much of it contradictory (Beck and Beck-Gernshiem, 2002).

Thus, the paradox is that while child protection scandals have prompted a severe dislocation of trust in the expert system, the public disclosures they have facilitated have provided vital information and enabled other victims/survivors of child abuse to decide to take risks and make disclosures. By far the most significant referral source in child protection cases today is mothers, while children themselves are actively involved in significant numbers of cases coming to light (Ferguson and O'Reilly, 2001). This shows how reflexive citizens are now actively engaged in a new kind of 'intimate citizenship' (Plummer, 1995), appropriating the new public knowledge of abuse and protection systems in the course of constructing their own biographies and are bringing forward more and more cases of child abuse. Individuals can here be seen to be seeking to colonise the future for themselves as an intrinsic part of their life planning, a form of mastery or control which parallels the overall orientation of modern institutions towards colonising the future (Giddens, 1991: 125).

This does not mean that children, mothers and the fewer men survivors who disclose always get the service they want (Hooper, 1992; Dempster, 1993; Farmer and Owen, 1995). Of equal concern is the fact that it is clear from prevalence studies that significant numbers of abused children do not even make it into child protection systems in the first place. The numbers of adult survivors and children disclosing abuse in research studies considerably outnumber the rates of children coming to the attention of protection services (Cawson *et al.*, 2000; McGee *et al.*, 2002). One of the biggest challenges facing child protection is how to develop forms of 'active trust' (Giddens, 1994a) in services which will lead to disclosures, reports and protection for all of the abused children who need it.

What is equally clear, however, is that in late modernity 'risk' is not just a negative, blame-ridden, dangerous phenomenon and child protection procedures and interventions must not only be seen as constraining, but viewed also in a positive light as enabling, creating new opportunities for protection from violent acts that were traditionally repressed and for reflexively organised life planning. Similar processes of empowerment are evident at a social and political level in the significant role that adult survivors of abuse have played in the radicalising of child protection through demanding accountability and explanations for system failures. The growth in self-help initiatives also demonstrates that the state does not have a monopoly on promoting empowerment, healing and defining what 'child protection' and risk society actually are.

References

Ariès, P. (1974), *Western Attitudes toward Death: From the Middle Ages to the Present*, Baltimore: Johns Hopkins University Press.

Bauman, Z. (1992), *Mortality, Immortality and Other Life Strategies*, Cambridge: Polity Press.

Beck, U. (1992), *Risk Society: Towards a New Modernity*, London: Sage.

—— (1994), 'The Reinvention of Politics: Towards a Theory of Reflexive Modernization', in U. Beck, A. Giddens and S. Lash (eds.), *Reflexive Modernization*, Cambridge: Polity Press.

—— (1995), *Ecological Politics in an Age of Risk*, Cambridge: Polity Press.

Beck, U. and Beck-Gernsheim, E. (2002), *Individualization*, London: Sage.

Beck, U., Giddens, A. and Lash, S. (1994), *Reflexive Modernization: Politics, Tradition and Aesthetics in the Modern Social Order*, Cambridge: Polity Press.

Bourdieu, P. (1986), *Distinction: a Social Critique of the Judgement of Taste*, London: Routledge.

Butler-Sloss, Lord Justice, E. (1988), *Report of the Inquiry Into Child Abuse in Cleveland 1987*, London: HMSO.

Cawson, P., Wattam, C., Brooker, S. and Kelly, G. (2000), *Child Maltreatment in the United Kingdom*, NSPCC: London.

Chaney, D. (2002), *Cultural Change and Everyday Life*, Basingstoke: Palgrave Macmillan.

Corby, B. (2000), *Child Abuse: Towards a Knowledge Base*, Milton Keynes: Open University Press.

Dempster, H. (1993), 'The Aftermath of Child Sexual Abuse: Women's Perspectives', in L. Waterhouse (ed.), *Child Abuse and Child Abusers, Protection and Prevention*, London: Jessica Kingsley.

Department of Health and Social Security (1988a), *Working Together: A Guide to Inter-Agency Co-operation for the Protection of Children from Abuse*, London: HMSO.

—— (1988b), *Protecting Children: A Guide for Social Workers Conducting a Comprehensive Assessment*, London: HMSO.

Dingwall, R., Eekelaar, J. and Murray, T. (1983), *The Protection of Children: State Intervention and Family Life*, Oxford: Blackwell.

Douglas. M. (1992), *Risk and Blame: Essays in Cultural Theory*, London: Routledge.

Driver, E. and Droisen, A. (1989), *Child Sexual Abuse: Feminist Perspectives*, London: Macmillan.

Elias, N. (1985), *The Loneliness of Dying*, Oxford: Basil Blackwell.

Farmer, E. and Owen, M. (1995), *Child Protection Practice: Private Risks and Public Remedies*, London: HMSO.

Ferguson, H. (1990), 'Rethinking Child Protection Practices: A Case for History', in *Taking Child Abuse Seriously* (The Violence against Children Study Group), London: Routledge.

—— (1992), 'Cleveland in History: The Abused Child and Child Protection, 1880–1914', in R. Cooter (ed.), *In the Name of the Child: Health and Welfare, 1880–1950*, London: Routledge.

—— (1996), 'The Protection of Children in Time: Child Protection and the Lives and Deaths of Children in Child Abuse Cases in Socio-historical Perspective', *Child and Family Social Work*, 1, 205–17.

—— (2004), *Protecting Children in Time: Child Abuse, Child Protection and the Consequences of Modernity*, Basingstoke: Palgrave.

Ferguson, H. and O'Reilly, M. (2001), *Keeping Children Safe: Child Abuse, Child Protection and the Promotion of Welfare*, Dublin: A. & A. Farmar.

Finkelhor, D. (1984), *Child Sexual Abuse: New Theory and Research*, New York: Free Press.

Froggett, L. (2002), *Love, Hate and Welfare: Psychosocial Approaches to Policy and Practice*, Bristol: Policy Press.

Giddens, A. (1990), *The Consequences of Modernity*, Cambridge: Polity Press.

—— (1991), *Modernity and Self-Identity: Self and Society in the Late Modern Age*, Cambridge: Polity Press.

—— (1994a), *Beyond Left and Right: The Future of Radical Politics*, Cambridge: Polity Press.

—— (1994b), 'Living in a Post-traditional Society', in U. Beck, A. Giddens and S. Lash (eds.), *Reflexive Modernization*, Cambridge: Polity Press.

Hill, M. (1990), 'The Manifest and Latent Lessons of Child Abuse Inquiries', *British Journal of Social Work*, 20: 197–213.

Hooper, C. A. (1992), *Mothers Surviving Child Sexual Abuse*, London: Routledge.

Howe, D. (1992), 'Child Abuse and the Bureaucratisation of Social Work', *Sociological Review*, 40: 491–508.

Jackson, S. and Scott, S. (1999), 'Risk Anxiety and the Social Construction of Childhood', in D. Lupton (ed.), *Risk and Sociocultural Theory: New Directions and Perspectives*, Cambridge: Cambridge University Press.

Kempe, C. H., F. N. Silverman, B. F. Steele, W. Droegmuller and H. K. Silver (1962), 'The Battered Child Syndrome', *Journal of the American Medical Association*, 181: 17–22.

Kirkwood, A. (1993), *The Leicester Inquiry 1992*, Leicester: Leicestershire County Council.

Laming, H. (2003), *The Victoria Climbié Inquiry*, London: Stationery Office.

Lash, S. (1994), 'Reflexivity and its Doubles: Structure, Aesthetics, Community', in U. Beck, A. Giddens and S. Lash, *Reflexive Modernization*, Cambridge: Polity.

Lull, J. and Hinerman, S. (1997), 'The Search for Scandal', in J. Lull and S. Hinerman, (eds.), *Media Scandals: Morality and Desire in the Popular Culture Marketplace*, Cambridge: Polity.

Lupton, D. (1999), *Risk*, London: Routledge.

McGee, H., Garavan, R., de Barra, M., Byrne, J. and Conroy, R. (2002), *The SAVI Report: Sexual Abuse and Violence in Ireland*, Dublin: Liffey Press.

Mellor, P. and Shilling, C. (1993), 'Modernity, Self-identity and the Sequestration of Death', *Sociology,* 27: 411–32.

Monckton, Sir Walter (1945), *Report on the Circumstances which Led to the Boarding-out of Denis and Terence O'Neill at Bank Farm, Minsterly and the Steps Taken to Supervise Their Welfare*, Cmd. 6636, London: HMSO.

New South Wales Child Death Review Team Report (1997), *Annual Report, 1996–1997*, Sydney.

Packman, J. (1981), *The Child's Generation*, London: Blackwell and Robertson.

Parton, N. (1991), *Governing The Family: Child Care, Child Protection and The State*, London: Macmillan.

—— (1994), 'Problematics of Government: (Post)modernity and Social Work', *British Journal of Social Work,* 24: 9–32.

—— (1996a), 'Social Work, Risk and "the Blaming System"', in N. Parton (ed.), *Social Theory, Social Change and Social Work*, London: Routledge.

Plummer, K. (1995), *Telling Sexual Stories: Power, Change and Social Worlds*, London: Routledge.

Reder, P., Duncan, S. and Gray, M. (1993), *Beyond Blame: Child Abuse Tragedies Revisited*, London: Routledge.

Reder, P. and Duncan, S. (1999), *Lost Innocents: A Follow-up Study of Fatal Child Abuse*, London: Routledge.

Ruddick, M. (1991), 'A Receptacle for Public Anger', in B. Franklin and N. Parton (eds.), *Social Work, the Media and Public Relations*, London: Routledge.

Shilling, C. (1993), *The Body and Social Theory*, London: Sage.

Smith, C. (2001), 'Trust and Confidence: Possibilities for Social Work in "High Modernity"', *British Journal of Social Work,* 31: 287–307.

—— (2002), 'The Sequestration of Experience: Rights Talk and Moral Thinking in "Late Modernity"', *Sociology,* 36(1): 43–66.

Stanley, J. and Goddard, C. (2002), *In the Firing Line: Power and Violence in Child protection Work*, London: Wiley.

Thorpe, D. (1994), *Evaluating Child Protection*, Buckingham: Open University Press.

USABCAN (United States Advisory Board on Child Abuse and Neglect) (1995), *A Nation's Shame: Fatal Child Abuse and Neglect in the United States*, Washington, DC: Department of Health and Human Services.

Walter, T. (1994), *The Revival of Death*, London: Routledge.

Ward, A. (1995), 'The "Matching Principle": Exploring Connections between Practice and Training in Therapeutic Child Care: Part 1 – Therapeutic Child Care and the Holding Environment', *Journal of Social Work Practice,* 9(2): 177–89.

Zelizer, V. (1985), *Pricing the Priceless Child: The Changing Social Value of Children*, New York: Basic Books.

6
'They kind of think that I'm better than they are': Risk, Identity and Change in the Lives of Mature Students in Higher Education

Arthur Baxter and Carolyn Britton

Introduction

Widening participation has become a central plank of the British government's education agenda, with the target of increasing participation in higher education to 50 per cent of the age group by 2010. While the main thrust of this policy is directed at excluded groups such as young people from working-class and minority ethnic backgrounds, mature students are also perceived as potential beneficiaries of an expanding higher education system. The argument for widening participation is couched not only in terms of economic and human capital needs, but also in terms of individual development, and is linked with another key idea of the *Dearing Report* (National Committee of Inquiry into Higher Education, 1997): lifelong learning. Education is thus seen as empowering, in that it enhances employability and is a vehicle for personal development. The view that education is empowering is one that informs many studies of mature students. In these studies empowerment is variously defined as helping students to break out of domesticity; increasing opportunities for paid work; gaining independence from traditional family structures; providing opportunities for forging new domestic roles and identities; or providing a route to independence following family breakdown (Edwards, 1993; Pascall and Cox, 1993; Maynard and Pearsall, 1994; Leonard, 1996; Merrill, 1999).

There is also recognition in some of the literature that this empowerment may not be unproblematic, that the personal changes which higher education brings may have negative as well as positive effects; in other words, that risks may accompany opportunities. But in most studies, one or other of these discourses, empowerment or risk, is the dominant discourse, and the trend has been towards a greater focus on risk as this concept has become increasingly central to social theory.

The concept of risk is central to the contemporary theories of modernity (Giddens, 1991; Beck, 1992; Lash and Urry, 1994). Beck, for example, in his thesis of reflexive modernisation and risk society, argues that it is the very successes of modern society which lie at the root of the risks associated with late modernity:

> Sources of danger are no longer ignorance but knowledge; not a deficient but a perfected mastery over nature; not that which eludes the human grasp but the system of norms and objective constraints established with the industrial epoch. (Beck, 1992: 181)

A key feature of reflexive modernisation is the developing process of individualisation. Individualisation is not a new phenomenon of the late twentieth century, but the form that it takes in advanced modernity is different from previous epochs. It is a contradictory process in that:

> The individual is indeed removed from traditional commitments and support relationships, but exchanges them for the constraints of existence in the labour market and as a consumer ... The place of *traditional* ties and social forms (social class, nuclear family) is taken by *secondary* agencies and institutions, which stamp the biography of the individual and make that person dependent upon fashions, social policy, economic cycles and markets, contrary to the image of individual control which establishes itself in consciousness. (ibid.: 131)

Thus late modernity is characterised by the continued collapse of fixed signposts such as community, social class and gender. This means that biographies do not simply unfold according to custom and tradition, and identities are not simply ascribed but have to be forged out of a range of possibilities and worked on over time (Giddens, 1991).

> The normal biography thus becomes the 'elective biography', the 'reflexive biography', the 'do it yourself biography'. This does not necessarily happen by choice, nor does it necessarily succeed. The do it yourself biography is always a 'risk biography', indeed a 'tightrope biography', a state of permanent (partly overt, partly concealed) endangerment. (Beck and Beck-Gernsheim, in Elliott, 1999: 157)

Mature students are, by definition, a group of people who are attempting to use education to shape their own biographies and identities in a reflexive way; they have self-consciously made decisions about themselves and the future course of their lives. Often, these decisions involve a major change from or break with their past lives and identities.

Risk in the study of mature students: reviewing the literature

Wakeford's (1994) work was an early attempt to use a concept of risk to analyse mature students' experience. She uses a concept of social risk, derived from the work of Douglas (1986). The main lesson Wakeford draws from her discussion of Douglas's work is that risk is defined subjectively, in contrast to the idea that risk can be objectively assessed. She also discusses the issue of where risks reside, arguing that Douglas is using a concept of risk 'which emphasises the social and relational aspects of identity' (Wakeford, 1994: 246). In making explicit her own definition of risk, Wakeford says:

> In this research the theoretical idea of social risk is based on my identification of the expressed dangers to social relationships within the talk of the interviewees. Thus it is based on the subjective constructions of the students and of my identifications, rather than attempting to measure any 'objective' risks of becoming a mature student.

Thus risk is defined as a social construction, of students' perceived risks to their relationships and self-identities.

Later work has also defined risk in terms of whatever acts as a barrier or is seen as a cost by participants or researchers. Archer and Hutchins (2000), in an article much quoted by other researchers, use concepts of risk and cost interchangeably. They talk of a variety of risks, the major one being that of failure. They refer explicitly to Beck only in their conclusion, when introducing Beck's idea of the uneven distribution of risk, which works to reproduce inequality:

> The inherently riskier position occupied by poor working class respondents means that they cannot make choices regarding participation in the same way as relatively 'protected' middle class students. (ibid.: 569)

The problem with these approaches is that risk is defined in terms of what actors see as problems in achieving their particular projects. We have pointed out earlier, however, that Beck's use of the term is more specific. It refers to risks associated with biography in a context where fixed signposts that made biography relatively unproblematic have now been removed. It is this lack of fixed markers or constraints which generate risk in the construction of biography.

We would argue, however, that this view of risk, while pointing to some of the problems actors face in constructing their biographies, does not fit with mature students' accounts and perceptions of their experience. Some recent work on mature students has begun to challenge the idea of the elective biography. For example, recent work on the process of choosing universities has emphasised the material constraints operating here, in particular those arising from gender and class, the markers that Beck argues are now of limited force in our lives (Reay *et al.*, 2002).

Diane Reay (2002) argues that mature students try to hold on to the class aspects of their identity that education may remove from them. She describes students as 'holding on to a cohesive self that retained an anchor in what had gone before'. She argues for a modification in the view that identity construction is free-floating, and talks of 'the complexities and contradictions of reflexive modernization in which projects of the self can be aligned with a strong sense of community commitment and a desire to "give back"' (ibid.: 403).

This point has been developed by Ball *et al.* (2002), who also criticise Beck's view of reflexive modernity. After outlining some of the class-based differences in choice, they argue that the evidence cannot be interpreted simply as a story of reflexive modernity. Quoting from Cohen and Hey (2000: 5), they argue that 'The "transgenerational family scripts" of the middle class and private school students remain embedded within deeply normalized grammars of aspiration that "exert a prospective and regulative influence on actual life chances and choices"' (Ball *et al.*, 2002: 69).

In our own work, Bourdieu's concept of habitus has proved the most useful for thinking about class-based constraints, particularly in relation to the ways in which class penetrates subjectivities. This, of course, invokes a view of the world where such constraints still have a force which actors have to deal with in a variety of ways (Bourdieu *et al.*, 1999). In the next section we explore the perceived risks associated with higher education among one group of mature students. Drawing on some of the theoretical literature on risk, we analyse their accounts of how their lives and identities have changed during their time in higher education. We look at the generation of risk in two contexts; first, the context of family and intimate relationships where the risks are mainly perceived to be to established gender roles and relationships; and second, the context of friendship and other social relationships where the gap between 'old' and 'new' (educated) identities is perceived as undermining class identity. While we highlight gender identity in the first context and class identity in the second, we do not mean to suggest that these are separate in reality. Rather, masculinity and femininity are classed, and class-based identities are also gendered.

The study

The data we discuss in this chapter are derived from a longitudinal study of mature students in a social science faculty of a 'new' university in the UK. These students entered higher education in 1992 and graduated in 1995. In the present chapter we draw on data collected from the same group of students in their final year of study, when they were asked to reflect on some of the changes they had experienced over the course of their degree.

Of the 59 mature students who entered the social science programme, we chose 21 for in-depth study, selecting only those who were aged over 25 or who had had a significant break from education before entering university. While the original interview sample included 21 students, there was some attenuation in the sample due to dropout, and the data discussed below draw on interview material with five male and nine female students. The four men with partners and primary school age children were all in their late twenties or thirties, of whom three (Tim, Mike and Stan) were living with their partners at the time of interview whilst the other (Terry), lived in a student house during the week and travelled to see his partner and her child at weekends. Maurice, the eldest of the men, is divorced and lived with his parents. They all have in common that they left school with few qualifications and returned to education largely through access courses.

The nine women differ in their ages and family situations. While, like the men, four (Helen, Jennifer, Katie, Wanda) have young school age children, two (Tracey, Lesley) have teenage children and one (Tessa) adult children who had left home. One student (Deborah) was married with no children and one (Mona) was single. These students vary in terms of their own class background and that of their partners. The issues raised in this chapter are more pronounced for those with working-class origins and/or with working-class partners. These students are therefore more often represented in the data.

The next section analyses how the students talk about their domestic relationships and their perceptions of the risks of becoming a mature student. These risks are seen to centre primarily on the challenges posed to established gender roles and relationships. However, while these are overtly stories about changing gender relations, they are simultaneously narratives of class and social mobility. The risks of class mobility and its effects on self-identity are explored in the following section.

Families at risk?

> *'He just thinks that once the degree's over I'll be back to normal.'*
> (Katie, talking about her relationship with her husband)

In the accounts that follow, it was clear that being a mature student was perceived as a threat to the security of family life, in particular, a threat to the previously taken-for-granted gender division of labour and responsibilities. These risks to family life are, however, not uniform, but gendered and classed. The dynamics and consequences of change are different for male and female students, and social class interacts with gender to produce different outcomes.

Predictably, perhaps, women's accounts suggest that the risks to their family relationships posed by their becoming a mature student are higher than for male students. While men's accounts also describe tensions in family relationships, the resolutions of these tensions appear to be more favourable.

Tim's and Stan's stories illustrate some of these points. Stan's partner was initially very resistant to the changes which his decision to become a student entailed. Their relationship became strained because of their different expectations. She still expected him to be a 'provider', to adhere to a traditional form of working-class masculinity, while he resented the fact that she did not take paid employment to help out because she did not see it as part of her role. Their relationship became so fraught that for a time he left her and their child:

> Stan: *We come from a very very ... we come from South Wales, working class. Her mother was like that, my mother was like that, it was the sort of situation, the man provided.*
> Interviewer: *Yes. And are these ideas changed at all?*
> Stan: *For me?*
> Interviewer: *For your partner.*
> Stan: *Yes. We have discussions now, um, we're thinking about expanding our family in the near future, and the discussions centre round, perhaps, both of us keeping part-time work going, and sharing the load as regards child rearing.*

In his account, therefore, Stan's actions challenge class-based conceptions of masculinity associated with his particular class habitus. After an initial impasse which threatened to break up the relationship, their relationship changed in unanticipated ways. He feels that his partner has gained a lot of confidence since he became a student and this has helped to break down the traditional division of labour which their shared class background had led them to adopt.

Tim left the police force to become a student, with the support of his wife. She moved from part-time to full-time work as a physiotherapist to facilitate this change and Tim took over the bulk of the childcare. Initially, therefore, because of Tim's former occupation and that of his wife, becoming a student involved only minor modification of his habitus and imposed little strain on their relationship. It did, however, bring unanticipated changes in the longer term. The arrangement was meant to last for four years, but, when interviewed in his third year, Tim described how his wife had changed her mind:

> *She doesn't want to stop working now ... Judy's particularly at the moment, she's only been doing it for twelve months, got a job where she has her own department and she's reorganising it and doing all sorts of things with it and thoroughly enjoying herself. So she doesn't want to stop work at the moment.*

In both these cases, therefore, it could be argued that the partners of these male students have adjusted, but in ways that were empowering to them. Tensions within their relationships seem to have been resolved by the women becoming more self-reliant.

From the women students' accounts, however, it seems that when they become mature students, it is they, not their partners, who adjust to the new situation. They do not expect to receive, nor do they get, the kind of support which would significantly shift the burden of family responsibility onto their male partners. There is little change, therefore, in notions of appropriate masculinity and femininity within the home.

The women's accounts are similar in that they dwell on the difficulties of combining higher education with domestic responsibilities, which echoes other literature on this topic (Edwards, 1993; Blaxter and Tight, 1994). This has involved them in devising strategies for managing/juggling their different responsibilities, to ensure that their new role/identity as a student does not infringe too much on established relationships within the family. Even when describing their partners as supportive, there is some awareness of subtle (and sometimes not so subtle!) changes in the relationship. Accounts of 'the supportive husband' rest not on practical support, but 'support' defined negatively – as not opposing their decision to enter higher education, rather than positively as facilitating their time as a student.

Katie, when asked about the effects on relationships in her household, says:

> *Well, it's my husband ... he thinks I'm under a lot more stress than he's ever been, and I have, he thinks I can ... flip a lot quicker than I used to ... just before the exams last year, I threw him out of the house! He was in his slippers and shirt and I just threw him out! ... he got in the car and sat on the Downs for two hours until he felt it was safe to come home, and he said, 'I've never known you like this', he said, 'You've never been like this' .. . And he said 'I'll be glad when this is over', he said 'I can't cope with this, I want you, you know' and he's been very good in that sense ... he just thinks that once the degree's over, I'll be back to normal.*

Wanda, who also describes her husband as 'very supportive', highlights the implicit assumptions that changes in relationships will only be temporary:

> Interviewer: *Would you say that it's imposing strains on your relationship?*
> Wanda: *Um, no, I don't think so, I think it's er, we're very much give and take, um, it hasn't been easy but it's something that's just going to take a specific length of time and then things hopefully will move back to some sort of normality.*

For Tessa, a middle-class woman in her forties, the main strain on family life appears to have been her relationship with her daughter, who went to university at the same time. Tessa now says that she should have waited to do her degree until after her daughter, thus putting her own needs on old until her family's were met.

For these women, becoming a mature student challenges taken-for-granted assumptions about domestic roles. Changes brought about by education impact not only on roles, however, but also on identities. In the next section we analyse how students perceive and negotiate their changing identities, particularly in relation to language.

Inhabiting different worlds: the implications of acquiring a new language

> *'"You're not at university now", he says sometimes, but the thing is, you change.'*
>
>   (Tracey, talking about her relationship with her husband)

When talking about how education has changed them, the students in the study identify two key themes. The first is 'becoming more assertive and confident', while the second, related theme is 'taking on a new language of academia'. This can be conceptualised sociologically as a process of acquiring new forms of cultural capital through education, which has significant effects on their sense of self, as well as on relations with friends and colleagues who still inhabit the 'old' world. Katie illustrates this well:

> *'I listen to the news and they sort of come up with some terminologies and I understand it, it's almost as if I'm speaking another language basically, in a sense.'*

It is the relationship between the new and old perception of the world that challenges relationships and poses threats to identity. Tracey describes the gap between the language of academia, at which she has become proficient, and the language of ordinary conversation in her social milieu.

> *'My language has changed. You figure words now, and know what they mean. I'm not quite sure about spelling them mind, but, um, I've got a wider perspective on things you see, um, understand things more, like when things come on the TV or radio about politics, you can understand it or – even knowing economics in the first year – still that basic understanding there at things and that. I understand a lot more things, and why things are how they are.'*

Tim describes how his family, whose business he works in, has commented on changes in him.

> *'I had a comment last week ... my brother was writing something and I was actually processing it ... and he noticed that I'd changed words as I have done a lot lately. He said other people had commented to him that I was suddenly using quote "big words".'*

Education changes people, therefore, by giving them a new language, which reflects their different understanding of the world that surrounds them. In this sense they experience themselves as having become different sorts of people, of having developed aspects of themselves in different ways. In this process they risk losing parts of themselves and their former lives as they struggle to manage the different worlds. Many of our respondents simultaneously inhabit different and conflicting worlds; the world of student life as compared with domesticity, the world of working-class life as compared with the newly developing educated world associated with the middle class. They therefore have to adopt strategies to manage these relationships.

Wakeford (1994), in her study of Access students, argues that, to minimise risk, students treat the identity of student 'as if it were a distinct segment of themselves, another 'hat' which they had to wear,' and speak as if their 'identities were divided into parts which were complex and/or contradictory' (Wakeford, 1994: 224). Edwards (1993) also describes how students separate family and education to preserve their relationship with their partner. These risk management strategies are clearly evident in many of our sample, such as Stan and Tracey.

Stan, married with child, and a former wood turner, describes himself as follows:

> *My situation, I have to be a Jekyll and Hyde really, no one has a clue (I live on a council estate) about what I speak of ... in general my friends don't understand or don't want to understand, so I find myself very stilted conversation. In ... some respects I really have to drop my level of conversation. Sometimes it's a bore, it really is a bore. I can't cope with it. My friends will call round, um, friends of long standing will call round, and I find it difficult to keep conversation going.*

In using the imagery of Jekyll and Hyde, Stan is implying a strong discontinuity between different aspects of his personality, between his new educated self and his former self known to his old friends.

Tracey, married with children, has an equally strong sense of being divided. However, she expresses this most strongly in relation to her family:

'You change, you get in the car, I get in the car at W——, I'm a housewife and mum, I get out here I'm a student, get in here a student, I get home, I'm a housewife and mum when I get out the car.'

In her account, different selves are separated geographically by a car ride. Like Stan, therefore, she describes her experience of a split between herself and her old friends, manifested in the language she uses. For them, the new identity of student clashes with their former selves, yet they have to maintain relationships with people who still know them in their old identities. This involves them in the quite stressful strategy of concealing aspects of their new selves in certain situations.

Maurice, in his forties, lives with and cares for his parents. He continues to maintain contact with people who have known him for some time, largely through work. While not describing this as a difficult issue, he does adopt strategies to manage the likely negative effect of him outwardly demonstrating this new educated identity.

'I think it's easy to, to sometimes to betray what you've been up to by the type of language you slip into, and I'm very mindful of that, you know moving in different spheres, and so I put different hats on. You know, since I've been here there are sort of key thinkers that I've enjoyed reading round … but I would never mention his name in the workplace, um, yeah.'

Mike's situation is different in that many of his old friends are themselves becoming students and he has relatives who have been successful in education. Education seems to have added a gloss to a personality that was already interested in issues and argument. In his first interview he referred to himself (when working as a chef) as 'the social conscience of the kitchen'. The cultural capital he has gained at university seems to be a continuation of his previous orientation to the world. Nevertheless, he is aware of the issue:

'If you go down the pub, I mean er, I don't like to raise sort of say political issues or social issues, but if some one else raises it I'll chat about it.'

The continuing salience of class and gender?

We argued in the introduction that Beck's concept of the 'risk biography' has a specific meaning, that the basis of risk today stems from the lack of fixed signposts such as community, class and gender which used to structure lives. The implication of this is that people have much more agency in shaping their lives unhindered by the constraints of gender and class. While there is evidence of this in students' accounts, what emerges in the above accounts more strongly is the continuing force of traditional structures in shaping their lives.

This theme of the continuing salience of class and gender has been taken up by a number of studies, drawing on the work of Bourdieu, which have sought to renew interest in social class as it affects subjectivity (Phoenix and Tizard, 1996; Reay, 1996; Skeggs, 1997; Lawler, 1999):

> Categories of class operate not only as an ongoing principle which enable access to and limitations on social movement and interaction, but are also reproduced at the intimate level as a 'structure of feeling' in which doubt, anxiety and fear inform the production of subjectivity. (Skeggs, 1997: 6)

The risks our students describe can be conceptualised as stemming from the development of new forms of cultural capital associated with a change in class-based habitus (Bourdieu, 1976, 1986; Bourdieu *et al.*, 1994, 1999; James, 1995; Skeggs, 1997). Habitus refers not merely to the external markers of social position, such as occupation, education and material wealth, but also to embodied dispositions which generate thought and action (Bouveresse, 1999). A key aspect of this embodied habitus is language which, according to Bourdieu, 'provides us with a system of transposable mental dispositions' (Bourdieu *et al.*, 1994, quoted in Charlesworth, 2000: 120). Mature students can be seen to be developing new forms of embodied cultural capital, of which language is a key aspect. Taking on a new language of academia engages students in a project of social mobility which may involve a break from their former habitus; 'Becoming academic is simultaneously an erosion of working-classness' (Reay, 1996).

The process of moving between classes has very strong emotional and affective aspects which colour the lives of those who experience it. A classic account of this process is Jackson and Marsden's study of working-class children who gained 'A' levels in grammar school in Huddersfield between 1949 and 1952 (Jackson and Marsden, 1962). At grammar school many of these children reported a feeling of not belonging, which related to their mixing with a greater number of middle-class children as well as experiencing for the first time the distinctive ethos of the grammar school. The effect of this experience was to weaken the hold of neighbourhood ties on the children. This was fought over in areas such as dress codes, sport, leisure activities and clubs:

> Working-class children felt themselves being separated from their kind. The choice between school and neighbourhood was faced daily in small concrete incidents. For the teachers these incidents were merely part of the pattern of manners, part of the training in 'tone' which distinguished the grammar school from the general community ... for the child something much more central to his living was being locally but continually strained. (Jackson and Marsden, 1962: 127)

To be successful, therefore, meant developing a whole new set of ways of looking at the world, which for many involved the rejection and devaluation of one's background.

In many ways this study is historically specific, linked to the postwar baby boom, the working through of postwar equal opportunities policies, and the predominance of the institution of the grammar school with its particular cultural and social agenda. It may be surprising to some who wish to deny the salience of class today to issues of identity to find that contemporary studies of young people find similar problems (Phoenix and Tizard, 1996; Hird, 1998). Hird describes working-class pupils who want to go to university having to learn a new middle-class discourse which might change them in certain ways:

> Krista: *I'm sort of doing something different ... I want to stay in school and go to university.*
> MH: *Do you think it will affect you in any way?*
> Rose: *I doubt I'll have changed much. Probably a bit more of a snob ...*

Studies by Skeggs (1997) and Lawler (1999) demonstrate the continuing salience of class for working-class women. Skeggs, in her study of women on care courses, shows how the pursuit of respectability is a means by which women from some sections of the working classes can demonstrate their lack of identification with that class. It is recognising how they are positioned as working-class by others, and the negative evaluation this entails, which 'is essential to their processes of subjective construction' (Skeggs, 1997: 4). Lawler studied women who had become middle-class through educational achievement or through marriage. Rather than being experienced as stories of success and achievement, this experience was characterised by 'pain, the sense of displacement, and the shame which can accompany such a move' (Lawler, 1999: 7). It is these women's lack of history of being middle-class which made their new class identity so precarious. They felt a sense of cultural inadequacy and of shame. The hold of these women on middle-class habitus was still weak, so they were still aware of their own cultural inadequacies in relation to this.

These issues impinge on the lives of our mature students in a slightly different way. Rather than being concerned with disidentification (Skeggs, 1997) or expressing shame, the students in our study are constantly aware of being seen as superior by their old friends. It is this imputation of superiority which causes most anxiety for them. Superiority is the other side of the coin to shame, the former is experienced in relation to friends who shared a previous (working-class) habitus, the latter in relation to a middle-class habitus into which one is entering or becoming established.

Helen expresses this very clearly. She is a single parent from a working-class background having to maintain involvement in networks associated with the upbringing of her child. Helen recounts her experience of being thought 'superior' when she brings her opinions into her friendships.

> Helen: *Yes, they kind of think I think I'm better than they are. So they think I think too much and got too many opinions, sometimes. And they kind of, nobody really, they don't understand what higher education is, so they see it as grand, up in the air, you know, so they think I'm looking down at them. And sometimes I do. I must admit, I can't help it sometimes, I think their opinions are totally invalid you know.*
> Interviewer: *How do you manage that, do you tell them that, do you tell them so, or do you tell them?*
> Helen: *No. They'd never babysit for me!*

Maurice, who had risen up to a managerial position, still works part-time and has not told the people he meets there that he is in higher education. This is his explanation:

> '*I don't like to give people that are, that I used to mix with in the workplace, if you like, manual workers particularly, the impression that I'm somehow um, better than they are if you like. I try to use my increased knowledge and aware-ness that I may have gained to, um, to help in terms of communication. So when somebody says to me a particular thing, I might use any extra insight that I've got in that particular area, I may decode it and use it in a language that they can understand, because I see myself as identifying with that group more if you like.*'

These accounts are full of ambiguity. The students do not want to appear superior to their friends, but are ambivalent about whether they actually feel superior. Helen rather ashamedly admits that she does at times; Maurice does not, but the tone of his remarks seems to suggest superiority. Other students express this ambiguity by remarking that they have not actually changed at all, when at other times they are quite clear that education has brought about great changes in outlook.

Conclusion

This chapter has examined some of the risks associated with becoming a mature student, and the different ways in which students represent and manage these risks to their self-identities and social relationships. We have argued that higher education, through its culture and practices, is a key site for the construction of new identities, which may conflict with other/prior identities. While all the students in our sample experienced higher educa-tion as disruptive in some way, their accounts expressed this differently, depending on their gender and class locations. Changes in identity brought about by education were, unsurprisingly, more challenging to working-class students than to those from more middle-class backgrounds, and managing change in family relationships was more problematic for female than for male students. Female partners of male students appeared to respond more positively to changes in family life than male partners of female students, which probably reflects 'net gains' for women associated with new forms of masculinity (Wakeford, 1994) as well as the greater cultural acceptability of men pursuing their own self-interest (Britton and Baxter, 1999).

These are stories of a divided habitus where the experience of education leaves the students stranded between different worlds:

> Such experiences tend to produce a habitus divided against itself, in constant negotiation with itself and with its ambivalence, and therefore doomed to a kind of duplication, to a double perception of self, to successive allegiances and multiple identities. (Bourdieu *et al.*, 1999: 511)

The risks of education are higher for working-class students, whatever their gender. For them, returning to education sets them on a trajectory of class mobility, which is experienced as a painful dislocation between an old and newly developing habitus, which are ranked hierarchically and carry connotations of inferiority and superiority.

The cultural assumption of the superiority of their new (middle-class) habitus over their old (working-class) habitus produced anxiety and guilt, but not the sense of 'shame' which some studies have found. The women in Skeggs' study (1997) had returned to education via 'caring' courses, which could be said to reinforce traditional gender identities and to put less distance between them and their former lives than more academic courses. This may explain why this group of women returners had such an ambivalent attitude to their working-class roots. On the one hand, they disowned them (disidentification) and felt a sense of 'shame', but on the other, they defined themselves in opposition to the middle class that they aspired to join.

It might be expected that there would be less ambivalence around class identity among those who had 'made it' to the world of academia. However, in her study of academic women from working-class backgrounds, Reay (1997) found that despite the fact that they had 'made it', they still suffered a feeling of 'shame' or cultural inadequacy, a sense that they were only 'passing' as academics. They carried with them their sense of class inferiority in their relations with new (middle-class) friends and colleagues, highlighting the fragility of their new identities.

The students in our study did not express a sense of 'shame' or inferiority in relation to their old identity and habitus, but did express some anxiety around *being perceived by others as superior*. We would argue that their different response reflects the fact that they were at a pivotal stage in the process of transition between new and old identities. They could not yet achieve this physical and emotional separation, because they were still embedded in their old habitus, but this may be one of the strategies that some of them will use to resolve the problems of inhabiting different worlds in the future.

Of course, we cannot, on the basis of our limited sample, claim that the risks or the outcomes will be the same for all mature students. The nature of their social science courses, for example, may accentuate risk by working more directly on language and perception. What we hope we have brought is some insight into the processes of identity formation of a particular group of students whose experiences are similar to, but also different from, others.

Our work supports other recent work on mature students (Skeggs, 1997; Lawler, 1999) concerning the continued salience of social class as a basis for identity, despite the fairly widespread view that this is no longer the case. For our students, social class is experienced not simply as an abstract structure, but as a 'structure of feeling' (Williams, 1977) which impacts on their lived experience as they struggle to manage the tensions between old and new habitus.

We also show how, for these students, class and gender forces are interwoven in the development of individual biographies. Despite the opportunities presented by education, gender roles and identities, like class identities, are also experienced as constraints on action. The 'elective biography' of Beck's 'risk society' (Beck, 1992), which puts the individual at the centre of action, sometimes appears a little hollow in the context of working-class women, in particular, who feel and are constrained by the exigencies of family life. Beck argues that 'in order for one to survive, an ego-centred world view must be developed' (1992: 136). This assumes a model of selfhood which may be appropriate for men, but less so for women (Britton and Baxter, 1999).

References

Archer, L. and Hutchins, M. (2000), 'Bettering Yourself? Discourses of Risk, Cost and Benefit in Ethnically Diverse, Young Working Class Non Participants' Constructions of Higher Education', *British Journal of Sociology of Education* 21(4): 555–74.

Ball, S., Davies, J., David, M. and Reay, D. (2002), 'Classification and Judgement: Social Class and the "Cognitive Structures" of Choice of Higher Education', *British Journal of Sociology of Education* 23(1): 51–72.

Baron, S., Riddell, S. and Wilson, A. (1999), 'The Secret of Eternal Youth: Identity, Risk and Learning Difficulties', *British Journal of Sociology of Education* 20(4): 483–99.

Beck, U. (1992), *Risk Society: Towards a New Modernity*, London: Sage.

Beck, U. and Beck-Gernsheim, E. (1996), 'Individualization and "Precarious Freedoms": Perspectives and Controversies of a Subject-oriented Sociology', cited in A. Elliott (ed.) (1999), *The Blackwell Reader in Contemporary Social Theory*, Oxford: Blackwell, pp. 156–68.

Blaxter, L. and Tight, M (1994), 'Juggling with Time: How Adults Manage their Time for Lifelong Education', *Studies in the Education of Adults* 24(2): 162–79.

Bourdieu, P. (1976), 'The School as a Conservative Force, Scholastic and Cultural Inequalities', in R. Dale, G. Esland and M. Macdonald (eds.), *Schooling and Capitalism: A Sociological Reader*, London: Routledge & Kegan Paul.

—— (1986), *Distinction: A Social Critique of the Judgement of Taste*, London: Routledge.

Bourdieu, P., Passeron, J-C. and De Saint Martin, M. (1994), *Academic Discourse: Linguistic Misunderstanding and Professorial Power*, Cambridge: Polity.

Bourdieu, P. *et al*. (1999), *The Weight of the World: Social Suffering in Contemporary Society*, Cambridge: Polity.

Bouveresse, J. (1999), 'Rules, Dispositions, and the Habitus', in R. Shusterman (ed.), *Bourdieu: a Critical Reader*, Oxford: Blackwell.

Britton, C. and Baxter, A. (1999), 'Becoming a Mature Student: Gendered Narratives of the Self', *Gender and Education* 11(2): 179–93.

Charlesworth, S. J. (2000), *A Phenomenology of Working-Class Experience*, Cambridge: Cambridge University Press.

Cohen, P. and Hey, V. (2000), *Studies in Learning Regeneration: Consultation Document*, London: University of East London and Brunel University.

Culpitt, I. (1999), *Social Policy and Risk*, London: Sage.

Douglas, M. (1986), *Risk Acceptability According to the Social Sciences*, London: Routledge.

Edwards, R. (1993), *Mature Women Students: Separating or Connecting Family and Education*, London: Taylor and Francis.

Hall, S. (1996), 'Who Needs Identity?', in S. Hall and P. du Gay, *Questions of Cultural Identity*, London: Sage.

Hird, M. J. (1998), 'Theorising Student Identity as Fragmented: Some Implications for Feminist Critical Pedagogy', *British Journal of Sociology of Education* 19(4): 517–27.

Giddens, A. (1991) *Modernity and Self Identity*, Cambridge: Polity.

Jackson, B. and Marsden, D. (1962), *Education and the Working Class*, Harmondsworth: Penguin.

James, D. (1995), 'Mature Studentship in Higher Education: Beyond a "Species" Approach', *British Journal of the Sociology of Education* 16(4): 451–66.

Lash, S. and Urry, J. (1994), *Economies of Signs and Space*, London: Sage.

Lawler, S. (1999), 'Getting Out and Getting Away', *Feminist Review*, 63: 3–24.

Leonard, M. (1996), 'Transforming the Household: Mature Women Students and Access to Higher Education', in S. Davies, C. Lubelska, and J. Quinn, *Changing the Subject: Women in Higher Education*, London: Taylor and Francis.

Maynard, E. M. and Pearsall, S. J. (1994), 'What about Male Mature Students? A Comparison of the Experiences of Men and Women Students', *Journal of Access Studies* 9: 229–40.

Merrill, B. (1999), *Gender, Change and Identity: Mature Women Students in Universities*, Aldershot: Ashgate Publishing Group.

National Committee of Inquiry into Higher Education (1997), *Higher Education in the Learning Society*: *Report of the National Committee* (Chairman Ron Dearing), Norwich: HMSO.

Pascall, G. and Cox, R. (1993), *Women Returning to Higher Education*, Buckingham: The Society for Research into Higher Education and the Open University.

Phoenix, A. and Tizard, B. (1996), 'Thinking Through Class: The Place of Social Class in the Lives of Young Londoners', *Feminism and Psychology* 6(3): 427–42.

Reay, D. (2002), 'Class, Authenticity and the Transition to Higher Education for Mature Students', *Sociological Review* 50(3): 398–418.

—— (1996), 'Dealing with Difficult Differences: Reflexivity and Social Class in Feminist Research', *Feminism and Psychology*, 6(3): 442–56.

Reay, D., Ball, S. and David, M. (2002), '"It's Taking Me a Long Time but I'll Get There in the End"': Mature Students on Access Courses and Higher Education Choice', *British Educational Research Journal* 28(1): 5–19.

Skeggs, B. (1997), *Formations of Class and Gender*, London: Sage.

Wakeford, N. (1994), 'Becoming a Mature Student: The Social Risks of Identification', *Journal of Access Studies* 9, Autumn: 241–56.

Williams, R. (1977), *Marxism and Literature*, Oxford: Oxford University Press.

7
Managing Uncertainty and Subjectivity

Ajit Nayak

Introduction

The idea that organisations are facing uncertainty is not a new one. Three themes dominate the discussion in the current literature on organisations – environmental, structural and managerial uncertainty. First, the demise of a stable business environment due to globalisation and technological advances has signalled the uncertain competitive landscape facing organisations. Second, the demise of bureaucracy and hierarchy has signalled the rise of uncertainty in terms of organisation structure. Third, the loss of certainties in terms of knowledge has signalled the rise of uncertainty in terms of managerial decision-making. These themes have been articulated in the organisational literature since the 1960s (see Burns and Stalker, 1961). However, there has been an increasing emphasis in recent years on the implications of uncertainty for the subjectivity of organisational participants. Environmental, structural and managerial uncertainties are discussed not only in terms of their impact on organisations, but also in terms of the identity of organisational participants. These discussions suggest that organisational participants are engaged in 'managing' the uncertainty in terms of their subjectivity and identity (Grey, 1994; Townley, 1995; du Gay, 1996). While questions concerning work-based identities are not new, the current discussions argue that organisational participants have become 'enterprising managers' of themselves and their work lives. In this sense, subjectivities in organisations are framed in terms of participants actively 'consuming' their work lives. The 'enterprising manager' has to manage the consumption process and be responsible for the choices made. The manager is seen as an autonomous, enterprising and responsible individual, who actively engages in a project of the self through work. As Miller and Rose (1990: 27) state:

> [W]ork is no longer necessarily a constraint upon the freedom of the individual to fulfil his or her potential through strivings for autonomy,

creativity and responsibility. Work is an essential element in the path to self-realization ... work now passes through the psychological strivings of each and every individual for self-fulfilment.

The manager's subjectivity is articulated through the consumption of work life, and s/he is responsible and takes responsibility for the choices made in striving for self-fulfilment.

My aim in this chapter is to explore three issues. First, I explore the reconstruction of work life of organisational participants at Reed Executive Plc, a large recruitment company in the UK. I describe the structural and cultural reconstruction of the company in terms of enterprise, creativity and autonomy. The case study illustrates the way organisational participants are seen as managers and active consumers of their work lives. Second, I explore how the reconstruction as an enterprising manager is not restricted to work life. The case study illustrates how the 'enterprising manager' aims to colonise all arenas of life and not just work-based life. Third, I examine the implications of the colonisation. I argue that the moral worthiness of the 'enterprising manager' is eliminated by the colonisation and leads to equating managing uncertainty with the project of managing oneself in an enterprising manner.

Before illustrating the reconstruction of organisational life at Reed Executive Plc, I start with a brief introduction to the rise in uncertainty in organisations and the framing of organisational subjectivity in terms of enterprise, creativity and autonomy as the solution to the uncertainty.

Enterprise discourse

The framing of organisational participants as enterprising managers has been extensively articulated in the discourse of enterprise (Miller and Rose, 1990; du Gay and Salaman, 1992; du Gay, 1996; du Gay, Salaman and Rees, 1996). Enterprise discourse can be seen in terms of two interlinked elements. First, there is an organisational form argument which states that organisations need to restructure in terms of markets. The restructuring is posed as an opposition between bureaucratic and flexible forms of organisations:

> The notion of enterprise occupies an absolutely crucial position in contemporary discourses of organisational reform. It provides a critique of 'bureaucratic culture' and offers itself as a solution to the problems posed through delineating the principles of a new method of governing organisational and personal conduct. (du Gay *et al.*, 1996: 267–8)

Second, there is an identity argument that the above quote refers to. The enterprise discourse constructs work identities of individuals and groups as being enterprising and entrepreneurial. 'Enterprise refers here to the "kind of action, or project" that exhibits "enterprising" qualities or characteristics on the part of individuals or groups' (du Gay, 1996: 56). Thus, enterprise discourse encapsulates the change in organisational form from bureaucratic to entrepreneurial and a change in individual identities from a passive one to an enterprising one.

du Gay and Salaman (1992) identify the focus on the 'sovereign consumer' as the technique of the enterprise discourse. The reformulation of organisations and work identities is based on the need to be close to the consumer. The rise of the customer focus can be seen in conjunction with several other broad trends. Increases in competition, deregulation and new technologies have changed the markets that organisations operate in and put pressure on organisations to find new ways of developing competitive advantage. Techniques of 'knowing your customer' highlight the importance of various market segments, the need for strategic product differentiation and quality-conscious consumers. All these changes reconfigured organisations by replacing hierarchical management structures with 'market' structures and by creating semi-autonomous business units or profit centres that add value to the organisation. Business units related to one another along market lines and intended to be customer-focused.

The reconfiguring of organisational work forms, implied by the enterprise discourse, emphasised the need for a cultural reconstruction of the subjectivity and identity of the organisational participants as enterprising. This can be seen within the broader political attempts at redefining the self. Four distinct 'characters'[1] form the basis of the political redefinition of the self – enterprising self, sovereign consumer, active citizen and conservative self (Heelas, 1991). The enterprising self aims to reform the self as someone who takes risks and initiatives to create economic wealth. As Norman Fowler, the Minister for Education at the launch of the Enterprise in Higher Education Initiative, stated, the student is envisaged as 'generating and taking ideas and putting them to work, taking decisions and taking responsibility; taking considered risks; welcoming change and helping to shape it; and creating wealth ... [all should acquire] key managerial and business competencies' (*THES*, 1 July 1988, quoted in Heelas, 1991: 73). The sovereign consumer focuses on individual choice. The self is seen as someone with active desires and demands that need to be met, provided they are within the bounds of conventional wisdom. Rather than the 'culture of dependency' (for example, on the welfare state) and passively accepting the services provided, the sovereign consumer actively chooses the type of services s/he wants to consume. The active citizen aims to emphasise the notion of responsibility to the wider community in pursuing the goals of the enterprising self and the sovereign consumer. The active citizen pursues individual choice and freedom, but guards against *selfish* individualism.

As Douglas Hurd, a cabinet minister in the UK's former Conservative government stated, 'We've got to say to those people doing quite well, look, there's a community to which you also belong – be an active citizen within it' (*The Sunday Times*, 16 October 1989, quoted in Heelas, 1991: 75). The final character that defines the enterprise culture is the 'conservative self'. This represents a return to the Victorian virtues of fairness, integrity, honesty and courtesy. The aim is to provide a clear distinction between right and wrong. Emphasis is placed on the virtues of self-discipline in terms of spending money, hard work, patriotism, civic responsibility and family life.

Although the political definition articulated the 'active citizen' and the 'conservative self' as characters of the cultural reconstruction of the self, management discourse placed a greater emphasis on the 'enterprising self' and the 'sovereign consumer'. The 'enterprising manager', who demonstrates self-motivation, initiative, creativity and takes responsibility for his/her own actions, is seen as the solution to the uncertainties faced by organisations. The 'enterprising manager' is one who engages in actively consuming his life and is driven by optimising his/her potential, and in doing so, ensures the success of the organisation. The organisation becomes the means through which the manager achieves the objectives of managing his/her subjectivity. The project of managing one's own subjectivity becomes the route through which organisations remain competitive and succeed in the uncertain world.

In the next section I illustrate the cultural reconstruction of the subjectivity of organisational participants in terms of enterprise and the association of organisational success with the enterprising manager. The case study describes the practices and policies initiated by top management at one of the major recruitment companies in the UK.

Case study: Reed Executive Plc

This case study is based on Reed Executive Plc and associated companies. At the centre of the group of companies is the founder and chairman of Reed Executive Plc, Alec Reed, who exemplifies the culture of enterprise, creativity and autonomy. Alec Reed started his company at the age of 26 and Reed Executive opened its first recruitment agency in Hounslow in 1960. The idea for the business came to Reed when he was running a small accounting department at Gillette. Having left school at the age of 16, Reed had learnt accountancy at night school before joining Gillette. This provided him with his first insight into starting his own business:

Gillette's used agencies and I signed the cheques. One local one took a big ad at Christmas – they had 18 branches, that was a lot back then – and they put how much business they had done: how many jobs they had placed, how many temporaries they had. So I, being a bit of an accountant, divided it all by 18 and thought 'Bloody hell, I could manage on half that'. It wasn't a very good idea of theirs – they are not in business any more.[2]

However, the main drive for starting the business came from the frustration he faced at Gillette. Reed had several ideas he wanted to try out, but did not have the opportunity to do so. Being turned down for a graduate trainee scheme Reed felt that his potential was not being fulfilled: 'I just left Gillette on a Friday and I opened a shop on the Saturday morning. I brought with me from Gillette's about 20 jobs. It went like a bomb from the word go.'

The main reason for the instant success was the building of Heathrow Airport. This provided an active labour market for Reed to benefit from brokering:

> I didn't see it until about ten years later … They were building Heathrow. They were pinching all the labour from Hounslow and others were pinching it back, and sufficient were coming through our offices to make it successful. The first office was Hounslow and the second was Spelthorne which was also Heathrow. We then opened probably another ten offices and none of them made a profit!

As more offices were opened they weren't as profitable as the Hounslow and Spelthorne branches. But Reed maintained his operations by diversifying and innovating. The company was floated on the stock exchange in 1971, by which time it had grown to around 70 branches. Currently, there are reports that James Reed, Alec Reed's son, the current CEO, is planning to buy back the company from the stock market because the market is too restrictive. The turnover of Reed Executive Plc was £349.4 million in 2002 and it employs more than 2,000 people (Reed calls them co-members). At present Reed Executive Plc consists of Reed Accounting, Reed Connections, Reed in Partnership, Reed Insurance, Reed Learning, Reed Solutions and Reed Technologies. This was a result of 'an internal "starburst" restructuring of the company's operations' (Reed, 2003: 49) in 2000. 'The aim was to devolve greater power to our co-members and ensure that the company was as close as possible to its customers in the numerous markets in which we compete' (ibid.).

Culture of creativity and enterprise at Reed Executive

Reed Executive has pioneered several creative ideas that have maintained its position as the leading recruitment company. From its inception, Alec

Reed developed a culture of creativity and enterprise. Acknowledging the fortuitous start of the company with the building of Heathrow Airport, Reed states:

> I think another thing that was successful was that we had loads and loads of ideas and that we were refreshing the thing all the time. Lots of ideas have disappeared, but we have got this culture of ideas.

This culture is illustrated by his enthusiasm for ideas:

> There was this once, we realised that most of the shops make money on Saturday. And we closed ours ... so on Saturday we changed it to a record shop. We sold records on Saturday. We did this in Richmond. The boards that we had our advertising on, on Friday night the manager would change them around and they would have record covers on them, like Frank Sinatra, etc. And we would wheel out records on wheels ...

Thus, Reed was willing to experiment with several unconnected and tangential ideas in order to generate creativity and keep the enthusiasm for idea generation. In the first ten years of business Reed identifies two key ideas that contributed to its success. First, pricing more than the competitors, which provided the company with a financial cushion:

> I charged 25 per cent more than the competition ... I grew up in the area [Heathrow] and it was the hottest market around in the country, probably the world. And it was intuitive to charge 25 per cent more than anybody else ... It gave us tremendous power having 25 per cent more income. We had more money to spend on advertising and more business in turn. And then we had freshness about the place. We had very crude advertising, but it was fresh every week. And people know if you are fresh, have more polish, and they are attracted to you.

The second key idea was starting companies that would compete with Reed Executive:

> Initially, we opened new businesses and they didn't make a profit. We had two key branches and one of our competitors planned to move in two doors away from our best branch. So, what the hell do you do about that? We took the lease instead and dreamed up another four-letter word – King – and opened as our own competitor. We began a second chain of employment agencies. The rationale there was that you could place your branches in a list from top to bottom in terms of profitability. Whenever a branch in a town was above the average, we reckoned there

was still mileage in the market and we could take a further share by opening a King agency.

This creative strategic response to competition enabled Reed to survive with only a few stores making profit. Reed did not restrict itself to starting new businesses in the recruitment industry:

> The thinking was that the employment agencies were going off, so we could bring two agencies into one. But we couldn't get rid of the properties. So we opened them as travel agencies. So we had that, and that failed, and we got rid of it.

Reed also diversified into health products with Medicare. The same principle of generating ideas was followed in that company as well:

> One of the things in Medicare was that we were boring our customers to death. So we started doing some fun promotions. The first was a big foot sale. Anyway we covered all the windows and walls in feet all through the shop, and it was the big foot sale. And all it was doing was selling foot powder, deodorants and the like ... And then we had this idea and we created something called Medi-Bear. And so in each branch we had a Medi-Bear and then a Medi-Bear birthday party.

On a larger scale, the success of Reed Health Group (RHG) can be seen as an example of creativity and the philosophy of peoplism within the Reed Group. RHG started its life in the mid-1960s as Reed Nurse. It expanded through the 1970s and 1980s and launched Reed Paramedic (later renamed Reed Health Professionals) in 1984 and Reed Social Care in 1988. Reed Executive gave individuals within the organisation space to pursue these opportunities and develop them into successful businesses. The success of Reed Health Group led to a demerger with Reed Executive in 2001. Rather than see this as a loss of business and employees, Reed Executive saw this as a natural extension of 'peoplism'. As Alec Reed states:

> Surely a demerged venture represents the loss of the stars that we aim to retain? This is not the case; the key to successful venture peoplism is knowing when to let go. RHG made a good name for itself within the health-care market, benefiting Reed Executive through the extension of our brand ... The point of divergence is where common sense dictates that the intrapreneurial venture is ready to go it alone. A demerger such as ours, with no acrimony, and an agreed business relationship for the future is the ultimate peoplist success. The parent company gave the venture space to grow and did not let possessiveness over the origins of

RHG cloud the development of the best strategy for the company. (Reed, 2003: 121)

The demerger of RHG illustrates the emphasis placed on the talented people rather than the success of the company. Although the demerged company has become a separate legal entity, it still carries the Reed badge and has James Reed on its board of directors. Thus, the connection between the two companies is maintained.

Another example of creativity within Reed Executive was the move into online recruitment. Reed.co.uk was set up in 1995 and aimed to become the leading company in online recruitment. Its competitors online at that time were Stepstone, Monster and Guardian Jobs, which were e-businesses, and Michael Page, Hays and Adecco, which were high street recruitment agents. The main difference between the high street recruitment agencies online (including reed.co.uk) and the e-businesses was the business model they used to generate revenues. The e-business used an advertising revenue model. These businesses hosted the job advertisements from other recruitment companies and businesses for a fee, but mainly relied on the banners and advertising on the web pages and a strongly branded site name. The high street recruitment agencies used an independent model. These businesses used the website as an extension of their branch networks. Following the independent model, reed.co.uk was not able to establish itself as a leader in the online recruitment market because it did not attract visitors to its website. Compared to the e-businesses, which publicised their websites strongly (for example, Stepstone.co.uk sponsored Channel 4 sports), Reed.co.uk did not attract attention. What enabled reed.co.uk to become the largest online recruitment was the creativity of its employees:

> The key development in overcoming this obstacle came from an idea submitted through the company's employee suggestion scheme, 'ReedTHINK'. Although the idea could have been deemed to act against Reed's interests, the directors recognised its potential and the co-member who submitted it was awarded a £100,000 bonus. That idea was 'Freecruitment'. It involved inviting businesses including rival recruitment agencies to advertise as many jobs as they liked on reed.co.uk, for free. (Reed, 2003: 158)

'Freecruitment' allowed everyone to advertise their jobs on the reed.co.uk website free of charge. This ensured that the Reed website got a lot more traffic. 'For example, at the end of July 2002, reed.co.uk had over 92,000 jobs advertised. Typically, an advertising revenue model will host in the region of 20,000 jobs, with one example, "Workthing.co.uk", hosting 18,500 ... Independent models tend to have slightly fewer jobs, with

Michael Page website offering 15,100' (Reed, 2003: 159). Reed also provided additional information on industries and organisations to attract potential jobseekers. Everyone was allowed to register and upload the job information themselves which kept the cost to a minimum. In order to maximise the benefits of having all the advertisements on its website, Reed also developed software that enabled its branch network to search the online database for suitable matches. 'Reed online installed a process known as "autosift", which automatically exports the details of any candidates matching key criteria to the nearest appropriate branch' (ibid.: 160). Reed.co.uk have also added features such as 'Job Sleuth' tool, which automatically sends emails and text messages mobile phones and 'ANYJOB' which allows users to apply for and track any job around the world.

Along with the creativity at Reed Executive, Alec Reed has set up several charities that complement Reed Executive. These charities enable the boundary of the organisation to be permeable and focus on the peoplist individuals. The employees of the charities are management trainees from Reed Executive who want to learn something new by spending a year with one of the charities. For example:

> The chap who really made the breakthrough with Reed Training ... had been running Reed Charity ... He took the skills he had learned with Reed Charity, which had been struggling for years, and applied them to Reed Training.

In order to monitor the progress of organisations in a peoplist economy, Reed argues that new modes of accounting are required. Reed suggests that performance indicators and accountancy in general has not kept pace with the rise of peoplism. The current norm of valuing companies based on price-to-earnings ratios (P/Es) does not capture the nature of organisations within a peoplist economy. Reed thinks that a profit-to-enterprise ratio is needed to reflect the nature of a business performance. This ratio is designed to show the proportion of profits derived from new ideas and processes. Alec Reed explains how this works:

> Within Reed Group our total profit is generated by the branch network, some of which has been in place for over 40 years, by our website and by the success of relatively new recruitment specialisms such as Reed Education or Reed Marketing. The idea is to favour profit derived from recent innovations while discounting profits from cash cows. Therefore, profits from business processes that have been in existence for over ten years are divided by two, while profits from newer innovations are multiplied in acknowledgement of their potential, as well as current, value. Profits derived from processes in place between five and ten years remain neutral. (Reed, 2003: 140)

Reed argues that the profit-to-enterprise ratio is the key determinant of success for organisations.

Reed uses the p/e ratio to refocus the organisation on creative ideas and innovative solutions. Along with the 'ReedTHINK' scheme, the organisation sets targets for awarding money for innovative ideas:

> We deliberately give the money before ideas are proved or adopted, to show that if a co-member provides the idea, we will provide the award and adopt the risk of whether it works or not. This is important: divorcing the execution of the ideas from their creators reinforces the value of ideas and innovation in and of themselves, and encourages enterprising behaviour throughout the organization. (Reed, 2003: 44)

One of the key attributes that Reed emphasises is intuitive intelligence: 'Intuitive intelligence is the benchmark at Reed, and co-members must show they have it before they are rewarded with responsibility' (ibid.: 43). Reed draws on psychology research carried out by his colleague, Michael Eysenck, at Royal Holloway University. They outline four components that form the basis of intuitive intelligence. First, 'the ability to perform intellectual functions requiring little learning or formal instruction ... [second] the ability to think rapidly and decisively without needing to have recourse to logical modes of thinking ... [third] a clear preparedness to contemplate the unknown and to use unconventional approaches; to be independent and

---

Assume that a company makes a profit (excluding one off gains) of £1,000,000 in a year. This profit can be divided into:

- £500,000 from products or services in place for over 10 years
- £300,000 from products or services in place for 5–10 years
- £100,000 from products introduced between 3 an 5 years
- £100,000 from recent innovations that have been in place for less than 3 years

The Profit: Enterprice Ratio can be calculated by discounting older profits and multiplying newer profits as follows:

10 years +:   £500,000 is divided by 2, giving £250,000
5–10 years: £300,000 remains neutral
3–5 years: £100,000 is multiplied by 5, giving £500,000
0–3 years: £100,000 is multiplied by 6, giving £600,000

The profit: enterprise ratio is worked out by dividing the discounted and multiplied figure by the total profit of £1 000 000, giving a P/E ratio of 1.65.

(Adapted from Reed, 2003: 140–1)

Figure 7.1   Illustration of the Profit-to-Enterprise Ratio

original in one's thinking ... [and fourth] a high level of self-confidence, especially in the value of one's intuitive ideas' (ibid.: 107–8).

To support the intuitive intelligence of its co-members Reed provides them with the freedom to pursue their ideas. An example of this is:

> our foray into online temporary recruitment, in the form of TempJobs. Four of our co-members saw an opportunity to get the organisation into the online temp market more quickly than our competition could do it. We were happy to support the venture, in view of the benefit that it could potentially bring to the company. (ibid.: 118)

Another example of this is Reed's 'Who Wants to be a Millionaire' competition, which is run internally. The competition invites co-members to devise new business ideas that they can run and make a profit within two years. The competition was run for the second time in 2002. The winners of the first competition were given the resources to start the business:

> The winner of the first competition was Reed Property Appointments ... placing property and estate management professionals into employment ... we are committed to giving the two co-members involved a fair amount of time to make it a success. The commitment to seeing these ventures through, with a guarantee that the idea will not be dropped in panic if it is not an instant success, is an essential part of venture peoplist policy. (ibid.: 120)

Neither venture succeeded:

> TempJobs did not, in fact, work out as planned, and never really got off the ground. However, the factor that marks this venture out as a success for peoplism is the fact that all of those involved in TempJobs were welcomed back into Reed; not as failures, to be shunted into meaningless positions, but as successes who were still capable of attaining great things within Reed (ibid.: 119)

Similarly, Reed Property Appointments did not succeed. However, this has not deterred the company from retaining the employees and running the competition again.

Peoplism

The culture of enterprise and creativity at the Reed Group is underpinned by Reed's philosophy of peoplism. In his book *Capitalism is Dead: Peoplism Rules* Reed argues that there has been a radical shift in the way businesses and societies are organised. 'It has altered the criteria by which success in the Western world is determined' (Reed, 2003: 165). One of the defining features of the new economy is the 'naked individual':

> Peoplism strips individuals bare of much of the protective padding of the past as many traditional support structures, including the family and the community, lose the relevance they once held. There is a distinctive split between the peoplist rich, those with enterprise skills such as creativity, innovation, the ability to solve problems and create opportunities, and the peoplist poor, those without such skills. (ibid.: 1)

Reed argues that the enterprising individuals have become the key factor in determining how the wealth is distributed in a peoplist economy. These individuals are able to command the terms and conditions of their employment, leaving organisations with the challenge of attracting and retaining them.

Reed outlines five main challenges facing businesses in a peoplist economy. First, he argues that human resource management needs to refocus on talented and bright people within the organisation:

> Companies must support their commitment to co-members by having a peoplist director with strategic responsibilities in the controlling triumvirate. Human Resources (HR) departments need to refocus their approach into one of strategic holism, and embrace intuitive intelligence as their benchmark when attracting, recruiting and retaining talent. As ideas and creativity are the currency of success, companies must develop innovative idea deposit schemes and bonuses, with the ultimate goal being to set up a venture peoplist system. At best, companies can only hope to harness particular talent for a limited period. (ibid.: 165–6)

Second, he argues for a shift in accounting practices to measure and monitor the new drivers of success:

> Companies should adopt profit:enterprise ratios so that stakeholders are able to discern the levels of innovation and enterprise being driven through the organisation. Tighter, more relevant accounts should be produced at shorter time intervals over longer time periods. (ibid.: 166)

Third, companies need to understand the importance of corporate badging:

> Companies must have a responsive and responsible attitude to using technology to target consumers, whilst actively losing promiscuous clients and customers ... Developing a corporate badge and garnering excellent public relations is a key business priority, although these must not be pursued at the expense of living up to those goals. (ibid.: 167)

Fourth, companies need to restructure themselves in order to allow freedom for new ideas and talented people:

> Key talent must be given the freedom to transfer across departmental 'silos'. The era of the specialist is fading as the business environment changes too rapidly to indulge knowledge niches, encouraging a concomitant rise in 'enterprising specialists' who are able to have an impact in any part of the company. (ibid.: 167)

Fifth, Reed argues that companies should create an enterprising culture, which encourages creativity and innovation through reward and encouragement:

> Companies should create a process culture in which innovation and enterprise behaviours are encouraged, facilitated and rewarded ... Business strategy is the key intangible asset that will shape all other intangibles, including corporate culture, co-member commitment and your badge ... UPS [Unique Strategic Position] must be both flexible and progressive, since the business successes of the future will strategize on the run; confirming intuitive intelligence as the number one sought-after competency for co-members. (ibid.: 168).

A UPS is the organisational answer to the dominance of intuitive intelligence and enterprising individuals.

Discussion

The Reed case study illustrates how organisational life is reconstructed in terms of managing the enterprising self. The co-members are actively encouraged to take responsibility for their careers and use the organisation to fulfil their ambitions and talent. The organisation is structured in order to allow the co-members to express their creativity and be rewarded for it. Reed's philosophy of peoplism demonstrates the underlying basis of the work life at Reed Executive and its associated companies. However, this only emphasises the 'enterprising self' and 'sovereign consumer' part of the political redefinition of the self stated earlier. Recall that four characters – enterprising self, sovereign consumer, active citizen and conservative self – encapsulate the political redefinition. We can clearly see that the reconstruction at Reed Executive emphasises the enterprising self, who is engaged in optimising the project of the self, and the sovereign consumer, who has the freedom and responsibility to choose the means of leading a fulfilling life. But the reconstruction marginalises the 'active citizen', who refrains from selfish individualism, and the 'conservative self', who embodies the virtues of honesty, self-discipline and hard work, as important characters. The 'active citizen' and the 'conservative self' are implied in the relationship between optimising one's own life and economic growth, but there is no discussion of the virtues endorsed by the peoplist economy. The self does not engage in a discussion of the morality of the peoplist economy and the enterprising manager. This supports the character of the Manager described by MacIntyre (1985). MacIntyre argues that the Manager excludes moral discussion. The character of a Manager reframes all relationships in terms of manipulative rationality. For the Manager, the distinction between manipulative and non-manipulative relationship is dissolved. The goal of optimising one's own life is given and all lies outside the scope of discussion. MacIntyre asserts that the cultural and moral ideal that the Manager embodies is that of a morally neutral emphasis on the goal of optimising one's life. The Manager operates in the realm in which ends are taken to be given and are not open to discussion.

MacIntyre's Manager is the epitome of managerialism. The separation of facts and values, where the Manager takes the goal of becoming an enterprising manager as given and sees his task as achievement of goals, revisits the discussion in business ethics on the separation between personal and organisational morals. Early writing in business ethics separated out the personal morality of managers from their corporate actions. As Jackall (1988: 6) states:

> [W]ork causes people to bracket, while at work, the moralities that they might hold outside the workplace or that they might adhere to privately and to follow instead the prevailing morality of their particular organisational situation. As a former vice-president of a large firm says: 'What is right in the corporation is not what is right in a man's home or in his church. What is right in the corporation is what the guy above you wants from you. That's what morality is in the corporation.'

The ability to separate corporate acts as being free from personal morals and values is central to the debate on business ethics. Prompted by MacIntyre's character of the Manager, researchers on business ethics attempted to recognise the moral tensions faced by managers. For example, Watson (1998) argues that rather than characterise the Manager as someone devoid of morals, the interlinking of the corporate and private moral worlds needs closer attention. For Watson, managers do not bracket out personal morals, as Jackall stated. Watson (1998) illustrates how managers debate with themselves about the dilemmas raised by the tension between corporate and private morals. Watson's ethnographic study of boardroom discussion found that '[a]ttempts to draw out from managers the "theories" which they applied in their managerial work produced accounts which "typically constituted a highly integrated mixture of the principled and the pragmatic, the normative and the positive" (Watson,

1996: 332) ... These managers wanted – one might even say "needed" – to talk about these moral matters ... the moral debate in this boardroom is not only far from strained and artificial, it is sophisticated and heartfelt' (Watson, 1998: 259). Watson's argument recognises that managers debate the difficult task of acting morally with a great deal of sophistication.

Although Watson illustrates the uncertainty between corporate and personal morals facing managers, it ignores the colonisation of personal morality by corporations (Deetz, 1995). The discourse on the enterprising manager formulates the morality of the self in terms of corporate money, corporate goals and corporate stability. As the Reed case study demonstrates, the reframing of personal morals in terms of peoplism blurs the distinction between the private and the corporate. The project of the self articulated by peoplism and implemented at Reed colonises the personal morality in terms of the morality of enterprise.

Strong evaluation and the enterprising manager

The colonisation of the personal morals by organisational morals is best illustrated by Alec Reed's philosophy of peoplism. Peoplism does not restrict itself to a description of organisational life. Instead, it purports to be a philosophy that needs to be embraced by society in general. Reed argues that 'enterprise skills' should form the basis of education in schools. As Reed argues:

> With today's school population we could change the course and culture of our companies. We have to ensure that school leavers have the confidence, decision-making ability and pragmatism to run the most important business of all – Me Plc ... I would like to see enterprise adopted as a style of learning across all subjects and at all educational abilities.

In order to implement this philosophy, Reed, through his charity has sponsored the re-invention of Compton High School in North London as the Compton Enterprise and Sports Academy. The investment of £2 million by Alec Reed and £18 million by the UK government is designed to create an academy of excellence that promotes creativity, initiative and enterprise in all aspects of schooling. By incorporating 'enterprise' in all aspects of education from a young age, the aim is to create individuals who are engaged in managing Me Plc throughout their lives, rather than when they enter the world of paid employment.

The implication of the colonisation of personal morals through the incorporation of 'enterprise' in schools eradicates the scope for discussing the morality of enterprise. It takes away the possible voices that may object to legitimising the project of the self as morally acceptable. In order to reclaim the debate on the morality of the enterprising manager, we need to view responsibility in terms of 'strong evaluation' (Taylor, 1985, 1989). We have seen that peoplism as a philosophy sees the enterprising manager as being responsible for the choices s/he makes. However, this sees 'responsibility' in a narrow sense, as choice. People are responsible for the choices they make in fulfilling the project of the self. As we shall see, Taylor conceives responsibility in terms of evaluating the basis on which choices are made.

Taylor (1985, 1989) argues that a key feature of human agency is that it is constituted within frameworks of 'strong evaluation'. Whether traditional notions of the primacy of honour, Platonic accounts of the virtues of reason and self-mastery, or modern understandings of the expressive power of inner selves, strong evaluation is an essential part of human agency. It is the human agent's capacity for reflective self-evaluation and responsibility. Drawing on Frankfurt's (1971) distinction between first-order and second-order desires, Taylor argues that humans have the ability to evaluate their choices. Unlike animals, humans have the ability to choose which desires to fulfil. Taylor argues that we need to differentiate between two forms of evaluations that underpin the human ability to choose. Consider the example of an employee having to choose between her desire to leave office at 5.30 and the desire to stay for another hour to finish some minor paperwork. She may be able to resolve the two desires on the basis of which is more convenient – to leave at 5.30 and get stuck in traffic or use that time to finish the paperwork. Or she may decide on the basis of which would give her more satisfaction. Or she may decide on the basis of which desire she is more attracted to today (she may prefer the traffic to paperwork on some days). What the example lacks is a thorough evaluation of choices. Consider an example of a lecturer who works through the weekend. The motivation for choosing to work outside office hours is based on the notion of 'professionalism' that the lecturer considers of qualitative worth. He considers not being able to finish the work as unworthy of himself in a professional capacity. The difference between the two bases of evaluating is what Taylor labels 'weak' and 'strong' evaluation. There is a qualitative difference between deciding on the basis of convenience, satisfaction or attractiveness and deciding on the basis of 'worthy' motivations. The key difference is that with 'weak' evaluation we are concerned with outcomes, but with 'strong' evaluation we are concerned with the quality of our motivation. Strong evaluation makes a distinction between choosing on the basis of the 'qualitative *worth*' (Taylor, 1985: 16; emphasis original) of different choices.

Along with self-evaluation and the qualitative worth of the grounds of choosing, Taylor argues for the existence of responsibility in strong evaluation. The idea that humans are responsible in one sense is implicit in our ability to choose to defer action and evaluate them. Indeed, it is a necessary feature of distinguishing between good and bad choices. Thus, in this sense we are responsible for our actions. A stronger sense in which humans are responsible is conveyed in the use of 'valuation'. Not only are we responsible for our actions, we are also responsible for the basis of evaluations. Thus, we are responsible for endorsing the basis of evaluations. The basis of moral life is determined by this sense of responsibility.

It is important to recognise that Taylor is arguing that the categories and horizons of strong evaluations are not purely individual. They are socially produced and reproduced, and are *constitutive of human existence*. The various ways of being human and of being an individual are constituted within and partly by them. It is also important to recognise that 'strong evaluation' as reflective self-evaluation and responsibility does not imply that a person is able calmly to reflect and evaluate action. Ambivalence, contradiction and tension are inherently part of 'strong evaluation'. Taylor points to affectual and cognitive issues in 'strong evaluation'. Feelings of guilt, shame, pride, etc. are inherently part of evaluations. If one feels guilty about certain actions, this needs to be seen as an emotional expression of the basis of evaluation. Recognising the emotional expression raises questions about desirable choices for action, not just desired ones. There is a qualitative distinction between desired and desirable actions for Taylor, one that raises questions about how the 'desirable' is reflected and articulated. Taylor's answer to this question leads him to articulate the link between desirable values and self-identity and strong evaluation as the irreducible background of self-identity. For Taylor, it is not possible to preserve an identity without value orientation. Nor is it possible to maintain value orientation during identity crisis. Thus, being a human agent necessarily constitutes questions of desirable values and judgements about these values. These values and judgements are articulated and re-articulated in answering the question of managerial subjectivity.

By attempting to introduce enterprise in schools and reframe all spheres of life in terms of the project of the self, the aim is to eliminate the question of whether the goal of self-fulfilment through the consumption of work life is a worthy one. The link between uncertainty and the enterprising manager, and the reframing of all spheres of life in terms of enterprise does not leave any scope for strong evaluation of the morality of enterprise.

Conclusion

In this chapter I have argued that managing uncertainty is seen as being synonymous with becoming an enterprising manager. The reframing of organisational subjectivity in terms of the enterprising manager assigns autonomy and responsibility to the self. The self is seen as responsible for the choices s/he makes. There has been a rise in 'experts' who help the organisational self to make the choices in managing 'Me Plc'. We can see the range of 'how to' books that attempt to help the enterprising manager by reducing the anxieties associated with the uncertainties of the current 'fast-changing' pace of organisational life. These books 'give meaning to life in the face of meaninglessness, for example consumption, leisure, sex, family ... [and] work' (Garsten and Grey, 1997: 215). Along with these self-help books, experts such as therapists, fitness instructors, financial advisers, consultants, etc. play an important part in identifying choices, teaching the tools and techniques to achieve them, and optimising one's life. Underlying the notion of the enterprising manager alluded to in the self-help books and by 'experts' is the equating of choice and responsibility. They emphasise that people have a choice. People have the freedom and autonomy to choose their careers, life styles and the way they manage themselves. The freedom and autonomy imply that the person is responsible for the choices s/he makes. Within organisations the emphasis on the enterprising manager is abundant. The rise in organisational discourse on 'empowerment' and 'creativity' has firmly established the autonomy of the self as an enterprising consumer of work life. However, the discourse on active citizen and conservative self has been marginalised. Active participation in the organisational community is seen as antithetical to the competition between enterprising selves within the community. Career progression is at the expense of other participants in the community and irrespective of the community welfare. Notions of fairness, integrity, honesty and courtesy are also antithetical to the enterprising self. The examples of corporate fraud, mis-selling, misleading sales tactics and work victimisation point to the marginalisation of the virtues of the conservative self.

The Reed Executive case study illustrated Alec Reed's attempts to reframe organisational life in terms of enterprise. The cultural and structural reconstruction of Reed Executive and its associated companies highlights the philosophy of peoplism developed by Alec Reed. Peoplism, with its emphasis on individual autonomy and creativity, is seen as the new defining principle of work life. The implications for organisations are that they need to adapt to the new morality of the enterprising manager. However, the new morality is not restricted to work life. Reed argues that the whole society, including the education system, needs to embrace the enterprising manager: 'Enterprise education is just the tip of the iceberg of what is needed. A complete refocus is required by companies, educators and politicians. We must all learn a new game' (Reed, 2003: 175).

The colonisation of the private spheres of morality by the philosophy of enterprise, as described in the Reed's attempt to introduce 'enterprise' in schools, raises important questions about the possible resistance to the spread of managerial objectives and morality. The spread of organisational morals into all areas of life and the reframing of the self in terms of the project of fulfilling one's own life eradicates the space for discussing whether such a goal is worthy. The space to articulate other forms of subjectivities (for example, based on gender, ethnicity, professional practice, political ideology) is subsumed under the rationality of enterprise. The danger is that managing uncertainty becomes synonymous with managing 'Me Plc' in an enterprising manner and taking responsibility for the choices made in life.

Notes

1 'A *character* is an object of regard by the members of the culture generally or by some significant member of them. He furnishes them with a cultural and moral ideal. Hence the demand is that ... role and personality be fused. Social type and psychological type are required to coincide. The *character* morally legitimates a mode of social existence' (MacIntyre, 1985: 28).
2 Interview conducted by the author with Alec Reed, 2003. The author conducted two interviews with Alec Reed in 2003. Quotes from Reed not accompanied by a reference are drawn from these interviews.

References

Burns, T. and Stalker, G. (1961), *The Management of Innovation*, London: Tavistock.
Deetz, S. (1995), 'Character, Corporate Responsibility and the Dialogic in the Postmodern Context: A Commentary on Mangham', *Organisation*, 2(2): 217–25.
du Gay, P. (1996), *Consumption and Identity at Work*, London: Sage.
du Gay, P. and Salaman, G. (1992), 'The Cult[ure] of the Consumer', *Journal of Management Studies*, 29(5): 615–34.
du Gay, P., Salaman, G. and B. Rees (1996), 'The Conduct of Management and the Management of Conduct: Contemporary Managerial Discourse and the Constitution of the "Competent" Manager', *Journal of Management Studies*, 33(3): 263–82.
Frankfurt, H. (1971), 'Freedom of the Will and the Concept of a Person', *Journal of Philosophy*, 67(1): 5–20.
Garsten, C. and Grey, C. (1997), 'How to Become Oneself: Discourses of Subjectivity in Post-bureaucratic Organisations', *Organisation*, 4(2): 211–28.
Grey, C. (1994), 'Career as a Project of the Self and Labour Process Discipline', *Sociology*, 28(2): 479–97.
Heelas, P. (1991), 'Reforming the Self: Enterprise and the Characters of Thatcherism', in R. Keat and N. Abercrombie (eds), *Enterprise Culture*, London: Routledge, pp. 72–90.
Jackall, R. (1988), *Moral Mazes: The World of Corporate Managers*, New York: Oxford University Press.
MacIntyre, A. (1985), *After Virtue*, second edition, London: Duckworth.
Miller, P. and Rose, N. (1990), 'Governing Economic Life', *Economy and Society*, 22(2): 171–92.
Nash, L. L. (1995), 'Whose Character? A Response to Mangham's "MacIntyre and the Manager"', *Organisation*, 2(2): 226–32.
Reed, A. (2003), *Capitalism is Dead: Peoplism Rules*, London: McGraw Hill.
Taylor, C. (1985), *Human Agency and Language: Philosophical Papers*, Vol. 1, New York: Cambridge University Press.

—— (1989), *Sources of Self: The Making of the Modern Identity*, New York: Cambridge University Press.

Townley, B. (1995), 'Know Thyself: Self-awareness, Self-formation and Managing', *Organisation*, 2(2): 271–89.

Watson, T. (1996), 'How Do Managers Think? Morality and Pragmatism in Theory and Practice', *Management Learning*, 27(3): 323–41.

—— (1998), 'Ethical Codes and Moral Communities: The Gunlaw Temptation, the Simon Solution and the David Dilemma', in M. Parker (ed.), *Ethics and Organisations*, London: Sage, pp. 251–68.

8
Communities, Trust and Organisational Responses to Local Governance Failure

Tony Bovaird and Elke Loeffler

Introduction

Trust is a key element in all social relationships. In this chapter we look at how the level of trust affects the relationship between citizens, service users and the public sector, understood as both elected politicians and the professional bureaucracies which are engaged to carry out the wishes of dominant political groups.

The chapter argues that trust is a subtle relationship which is hard to engender and, once lost, even harder to rekindle. However, where this relationship is present, it makes it possible to achieve many social outcomes which would otherwise be beyond the reach of individual action and of government.

The chapter examines how public organisations, at both local and national government levels, react to failure in local governance systems, and maps out some of the conditions which are likely to determine which types of intervention are likely to have more chances of success.

The weakening of community government

The twentieth century saw an unprecedented growth in the role of government. This has widely been traced to two key causes, in addition to the effect of the two world wars in ratcheting up the level of public sector resource mobilisation in many parts of the world: the growing desire in society to achieve levels of social justice which were very different from those which would have been achieved by market forces alone – the argument from 'equity'; and the growing understanding that there are many complex human and social needs which are unlikely to be met by firms in the market sector – the argument from 'market failure'.

However, in the last quarter of the twentieth century, belief in government as a solution to social problems waned rather dramatically. In welfare states, although huge strides had been made in dealing with the traditional economic and social ills of unemployment, ill-health and poor housing, governments were seen as having created high levels of dependency in the most vulnerable groups in society – the very groups they claimed to be trying to help most (Shakespeare, 2000). In the old 'state socialist' economies, government was increasingly seen to be an inefficient – and even unfair – mechanism for achieving social ends. Furthermore, in both kinds of society there appeared to be a growing range of issues – what Rittel and Weber (1973) called 'wicked problems' – in the face of which the traditional mechanisms of government intervention appeared relatively powerless and unsuccessful.

Consequently, political movements across the ideological spectrum sought to redefine the role of government. The earliest signs of this came in the 1970s from the Eurocommunist parties of France, Italy and Spain, which sought to find a rationale for sharing power in the democratic process within their countries by recognising a larger potential role for the market within the welfare state than they had hitherto been prepared to accept, while still maintaining the paramount role of the public sector in regulating capitalism and providing social services. Very soon afterwards came the 'right-wing' backlash against the traditional welfare state in the shape of the Thatcher and Reagan administrations in the UK and US, respectively.

Thatcher and Reagan took very different stances on the role of local government. The Reagan administration tended to identify the greatest problems with 'big government', particularly at the Federal level, and therefore was keen to devolve many powers and decisions from Washington to the state and, even more, to the local level. Furthermore, Reagan tended to react to complaints about the efficiency and the conduct of local government with the riposte that it was up to local voters, not Federal government, to find the remedy for such ills. The Thatcher administration was much more active in trying to steer and control local government – it despised the 'loony left' which it believed ran much of British local government and acted quickly (though not, in the end, successfully) to emasculate it and by removing many services from it. Council housing, for example, was sold and funding for social housing was redirected to housing associations. Moreover, those services that remained within government's remit were increasingly subject to compulsory competitive tendering (CCT) or other forms of market testing, which were meant to ensure that far fewer public services were delivered by local government or by other public sector organisations.

However, the 'wicked problems' did not go away. Indeed, in the 1990s it became increasingly evident, not only in the UK and US but in many other European countries as well, that there was an incipient crisis in community governance. The key economic, social and environmental problems experienced at local level were largely common to most of these countries:

- a re-emergence in the early 1990s of the fiscal crisis which had appeared in the early 1970s and again early 1980s, but which had been made worse by the rapid relocation of employment away from old industrial centres, with consequent long-term damage to their local tax base;

- a realisation that the lack of capital expenditure in local authorities following the fiscal crises of the early 1970s meant that vital services were now less able to respond to local needs;
- a rapidly ageing population, with consequent demands on social care services and a simultaneous decrease in the proportion of the population in employment and hence paying taxes;
- an increasingly fragmented society, where it was now common for families to have only one parent, where elderly people lived separately and often far away from their children and grandchildren, and where young people sought economic and social independence at an early age;
- huge increases in drug abuse, particularly among the young, with major effects on their ability to complete their education, to get and keep jobs, and to keep out of trouble with the police and the courts;
- partly as a by-product of the above trends, a rapid rise in crime, particularly street violence and burglary, which often was perceived to be at such levels that it terrorised whole neighbourhoods and particular groups of people, especially elderly people, young people and minority ethnic groups;
- rising levels of racism in some urban areas, particularly where social and economic problems were high and ethnic groups had not been successfully integrated;
- polarisation of performance at school, with boys falling behind girls, and children from some ethnic groups doing much worse than those from the rest of the population, coupled with rising levels of truancy and exclusion from school, so that some groups were systematically failing to get the education they needed to have any chance of regular and decent employment;
- rising concern that environmental problems in modern economies were worsening and were only partly soluble by 'big government', leading to a growing conviction that the imaginative solutions required would have to be locally designed and implemented if they were to be appropriate to the problems.

Moreover, these problems exhibited dynamic interactions with each other. Their existence gave rise to – and was in turn exacerbated by – a growing concern with the levels of risk and uncertainty faced by citizens – though admittedly for some citizens more than others. The new climate of risk has been seen as including four mutually reinforcing factors (Taylor-Goodby, 2000: 10):

1. the risks that people face in everyday life are more marked than in the period of secure growth after the second world war, but they are concentrated in certain social groups;

2. many of the new risks are unpredictable but may well be more socially pervasive;
3. retreat of the welfare state means that one of the mechanisms for managing insecurity is no longer available;
4. changes in the way in which people think about their social world tend to undermine trust in the capacity of both private and state services to handle the consequences of uncertainty and this again increases the apprehension of risk.

These economic and social problems were matched by a series of political and professional problems which meant that solutions were no longer seen purely as administrative and technical in nature:

- professionals were no longer seen by politicians – and the public – simply as the representatives of a technically neutral knowledge base, but as advocates in the resource mobilisation and allocation process, keen to advantage themselves as well as their 'clients';
- managers were seen by politicians to be defensive of their own organisational bases, and not simply interested in improving the quality of life of citizens and service users;
- politicians were increasingly seen by professionals and managers – and by the public – as manipulative of public issues for electoral success, rather than as representatives of the 'public interest' or the 'public good' (and, in the academic world, public choice theory provided a conceptual basis for each of these first three tendencies);
- the public increasingly expects services to be provided quickly, but public sector organisations are still expected to conform to a series of governance principles which can slow them down;
- the public also increasingly expects its needs to be met holistically, but most organisations find it difficult to 'join up' services across organisational boundaries and data-sharing between organisations is significantly hindered by the operation of the Data Protection Act and similar requirements;
- politicians became aware that their own agencies had limited power to tackle the problems they faced, but were reluctant to yield power to other organisations, and least of all to amorphous 'partnerships' which neither they nor the public could easily hold accountable;
- politicians were also reluctant to see the emergence of bigger local government units, which might be more efficient in service delivery, but would be seen by the public as remote and unresponsive.

In consequence, the traditional means to deal with the emerging problems were widely seen as inadequate. The interest of both practitioners and academics began to focus increasingly on other ways by which these problems might be addressed.

Conceptualising organisational failure: moving the blame from staff to citizens?

As the crisis of community governance has deepened, the search for scapegoats has widened. While central and local government have continued their longstanding attempts to pin the blame for most problems on each other, both have also begun to accuse other stakeholders of playing inadequate roles in the new circumstances.

One of the first attempts to bring other stakeholders more fully into the community governance picture was the movement towards 'public/private partnerships' in the late 1970s and early 1980s (Bovaird, 1986). In many UK and US cities, the private sector was encouraged – even subsidised – to play a more active role, first in urban regeneration, then in the provision of many services previously provided 'in-house' in the public sector, and later in the sponsorship of many services, particularly cultural and sporting facilities and activities. Later, in the 1990s, the themes of citizen and service user participation were revisited, taking further some approaches which had been sporadically popular since the 1960s (Martin, 2003).

In the academic literature we can trace a similar attempt to widen the understanding of the underlying causes of the growing failure in community governance. We can characterise this as a trend from policy analysis, which was the 'new science' of the 1960s, to organisational analysis in the 1970s and 1980s, and then to 'holistic analysis' in the 1990s. The classic focus of public policy analysis in the 1960s was essentially on the pathology of service failure and how these failures might be tackled. As the focus moved in the 1970s to analysis of organisational failure, individual services became seen essentially as only contributory elements to organisational strategies. The New Public Management (NPM), from the early 1980s onwards, replaced this focus on single organisations with a critique of the overall service system in which public agencies found themselves. NPM was a step forward from the policy analysis of individual services which had dominated the 1960s, but it was simultaneously a step backwards from much of the organisational analysis of the 1970s, which had explicitly recognised that failure in the public sector had often extended to political institutions, not merely service provision. Finally, the 'holistic' analyses of the 1990s suggested that the system of public sector organisations and professional service providers was itself just a set of sub-systems within a much wider system of communities, and that failures of public services and of public organisations were a natural outcome of inadequate social capital and dysfunctional behaviour within communities.

Each of these perspectives on public sector failure had its chosen scapegoat. Classic policy analysis tended to blame politicians for not understanding the briefing they received from their policy analysts – particularly economists (Schultz, 1968). During the 1970s, the blame for organisational failure was laid variously at the feet of politicians, top managers, middle managers or front-line staff. NPM, from the early 1980s onwards, drawing heavily on public choice theory, replaced this personalisation of blame with a critique of the way in which all interest groups, but particularly producer groups, within the overall service system attempted to maintain and improve their position vis-à-vis each other (Newman, 2002). The public governance approach of the 1990s also took a multi-stakeholder approach, suggesting that all stakeholders shared the blame for not trying more actively to put new institutions in place which would encourage, and even reward, joined-up actions across networks and seamless services for each citizen (Perri 6 *et al.*, 2002).

In practice, these abstract formulations found explicit manifestations in the interactions and rhetoric of specific stakeholders. As far as local government is concerned, it has very often found it easy to argue that, where local governance failure appears to be occurring, the fault does not lie with the local authority in that area but rather with the poor functioning of the institutions of civil society in their area – whether that be the apathy of citizens, the narrowness of the local voluntary sector or the lack of imagination and corporate responsibility of businesses in the area. To paraphrase Brecht: the people have now lost the confidence of the government, which therefore has decided it needs to change them.

However, central government takes a different view. The current UK central government response, when it believes it has detected local governance failure, is essentially to blame the responsible organisation – which it always considers to be the local authority – and to change its management. The CCT regime was an especially punitive attempt to change internal management practices in local government, as well as externalising those managements which could not respond appropriately. For some time after New Labour came to power, it believed that its new Best Value regime could be more effective than CCT, essentially seeking the same outcomes but through a more voluntaristic process. However, the Best Value regime was quickly overlaid with a set of instruments based on a 'command and control' philosophy – national mandatory performance indicators, much more extensive inspection regimes, central government intervention and 'recovery support' for local authorities, which were seen to be failing to meet the targets and requirements imposed by these new instruments.

While central government since the mid-1980s may appear to have maintained a much more managerialist conception of organisation failure in local governance than did local authorities, the prescriptions of central government have not been markedly different from those of the local authority sector. In both cases, the future has been seen in terms of achieving more successful engagement of all local stakeholders. Local government tends to see this as the activation of stakeholders who have been reluctant and resistant in the past, while central government tends to see it as the mobilisation of forces which local government has systematically attempted to bypass and ignore in the past. However, the lesson is clear: local government is no longer sufficient to solve critically important local problems, local governance requires the concerted effort of multiple stakeholders (Loeffler, 2003).

The growing importance of trust in community governance

The argument in this chapter up to this point has suggested that a belief in multi-stakeholder working was thrust on both central and local government because of the underlying economic and political structural relationships in which they found themselves, which meant that they could more readily excuse their own failures by pointing to the deficiencies of other stakeholders. This growing pluralism could be seen as a response to the crisis of legitimacy of Western liberal democracies. It is important to stress, however, that there were also more positive forces at work which led to many senior staff – and even politicians – in central and local government voluntarily embracing a multi-stakeholder perspective. The public governance approach which emerged during the 1990s suggested that the deficiencies of multi-stakeholder working could be remedied and were already being tackled in many 'good practice' cases.

Loeffler (2003: 166) illustrates this with reference to community safety. She suggests that improvements in this sphere cannot be achieved by good government alone. Of course, it is indeed the case that, in order to reduce crime, the police service needs sufficient resources, to be efficiently managed, to behave in a fair and honest way and to avoid racial and gender discrimination. Without these prerequisites, crime levels could easily get out of hand in some areas and inappropriate police responses might well result in riots and an increase in lawlessness. However, it is probably fruitless to seek the long-term solution to the problem of crime simply by enhancing the power, effectiveness and governance of the police. At the root of the crime problem in specific areas may be insufficient integration of immigrants, a lack of job opportunities or inadequate availability of stimulating leisure opportunities for young people or simply a lack of hope in the community that any of its members face a positive future within current economic and social conditions. Loeffler suggests that, in this case, good local governance requires the cooperation of all relevant stakeholders in tackling the underlying problems, including not only the police but also schools, the NHS and local authorities. Moreover, it is also likely to require that people in local communities are prepared to be active in 'Neighbourhood Watch' activities, that community groups are prepared to launch initiatives to 'keep kids off the streets' and that local businesses are prepared to offer work opportunities to local people from disadvantaged and vulnerable groups, to counter their disillusion with the economic and social institutions which shape their lives.

However, this analysis throws up another critical issue. It seems probable in general that stakeholders will be more likely to be activated and to consent to work together intensively and positively if they trust each other. Thus, local people are unlikely to work together in a Neighbourhood Watch scheme if they suspect each other of potentially criminal behaviour. Trust conditions the degree to which joint working is likely to be undertaken as a serious and sustainable activity.

The importance of trust to joint working is likely to apply to both individuals within the general public who have a stake in specific services or issues, and also to organisational stakeholders, such as the different professions within organisations and the different sets of managers and professionals who need to work across organisations. Of course, as Putnam (2000: 137) argues, 'Trust in other people is logically quite different from trust in institutions and political authorities'. Berg (following Luhmann, 1999) suggests that, as modern societies are characterised by increasing complexity and risk, there is an growing importance of what she calls 'system trust'. Citing (Miztal, 1996: 74), she argues that:

> such abstract trust is a means to secure predictability in complex situations. In the modern world we are no longer placed in a fixed social setting and these new conditions of expanded choices, opportunities and dependencies require commitment and a sustained belief in the ability of systems to perform and maintain conditions, rather than personal trust. (Berg, 2003: 6)

The example we have cited above from Loeffler, in relation to community safety, can be replicated in relation to many other quality-of-life issues in local areas, where it has become clear that coordinated multi-stakeholder initiatives are more likely to be successful than the actions of any single government agency:

- Education – schools can only do so much. The influence of parents on a child's ability to read and their willingness to learn more generally is critical, but there is also great power to the old African saying: 'It takes a village to raise a child'.
- Environment – while the UK has highly efficient street cleaning services, it has very dirty streets. The only solution seems to be the reawakening of civic consciousness so that it is not socially acceptable to be seen dropping litter, as is the case in Germany, Switzerland and many other European countries.
- Social care – the role of Social Services Departments is honourable, but they account for only a small proportion of the hours of social care given to the needy each week. Far more is done by parents looking after

children with disabilities and by children and volunteers looking after elderly people in their own homes.

- Health – although clinicians like to believe that they play a major role in the health of the nation, their contribution is largely ineffective if people with, or in danger of developing, medical conditions are not encouraged by their families and friends to adopt healthier diets and life styles.

In all these examples, individuals and groups in the community have to use their influence to help others. For this to work, they must be trusted by those others as being motivated by public spiritedness rather than by pure self-interest.

Withering away of traditional trust relationships in communities?

Paradoxically, the growing awareness of the importance of trust in community governance has coincided with a period of intense breast-beating in the academic literature about the apparent withering away of trust relationships at community level. Many writers have pointed to the current lack of public trust in professionalised bureaucracies and representational politics in Western Europe and North America (Nye *et al.*, 1997; Bouckaert and van de Walle, 2003), and many of them have portrayed a situation in which trust was continuing to decline (Nye *et al.*, 1997; Pharr and Putnam, 2000; Citrin and Luks, 2001). A recent example is given by a survey of the general public in the UK which suggests that staff providing public services are in general trusted highly, but the public is less trusting of the organisations for which they work – and trust in these organisations is declining (Audit Commission, 2003).

The most prominent proponent of the view that trust is withering away at community level is Robert Putnam (1993, 2000), who places the argument in a context of the decline of social capital generally. He argues that 'Americans have been dropping out in droves, not merely from political life, but from organised community life more generally' (2000: 64).

However, there are alternative perspectives which contest this interpretation. Perhaps the best known is the communitarian perspective, which argues that many studies overlook the deep latent desire of people within communities to work together. Etzioni (1995, 1998, 2000) in particular has searched out myriad examples of where this tendency is still working and may even be growing.

More recently, the 'holistic governance' movement (Perri 6 *et al.*, 2002) has emphasised the need for joined-up working by the relevant agencies, including community groups, in order to ensure that all the needs of service users are taken into consideration and tackled systematically. From this perspective, the public service offer made to service users should be 'seamless', so that the individual identities of different public service providers are subsumed within an overall 'public service' identity. Clearly, such 'no logo' approaches are the antithesis of the brand marketing, which has characterised the 'contract culture' in parts of the public sector in the past 20 years. As with communitarianism, this movement has pointed to many examples of holistic governance and the successful building of trust relationships which must underpin it.

So how can we resolve these differences in opinion about whether trust in communities is declining or growing? Obviously, the argument is partly about interpretation of empirical data and has been made more problematic because interest in trust at community level is comparatively recent. As appropriate longitudinal data become available, the empirical debate may become clearer. However, it is likely that much of the divergence of views has stemmed from the different conceptual frameworks being used, so that comparisons have not been of like with like. It is therefore essential that the conceptual issues around trust are tackled directly, so that future research can be directed towards resolving clearly defined issues.

Trust as a coping mechanism in a climate of risk and uncertainty

We have emphasised that interest in the concept of trust in a community context has increased as actors have perceived a growing need to work together with other stakeholders. More generally, it has been suggested that trust is one coping mechanism by which actors can respond to risk and uncertainty in communities, at a time when the 'new climate of risk' (as characterised by Taylor-Goodby, 2000) was significantly increasing public sensitivity to the levels of risk and uncertainty which they faced. For example, Luhmann (1999) suggests that 'trust is seen as a means to cope with uncertainty in complex systems; trust serves to increase the potential of a system for complexity, and its function is the reduction of social complexity by increasing the tolerance of uncertainty' (Berg, 2003: 5).

This represents an important shift in the conceptual approaches to risk and uncertainty across the social sciences. As Taylor-Goodby (2000: 3) has argued:

> The way in which social scientists understand risk and the response to it has also changed. Economists have become more aware of the social and psychological factors that influence perceptions of risk as evidence accumulates to highlight the shortcomings of models that constitute people as predominantly rational actors, choosing self-consciously between alternatives on the basis of a deliberative calculus of benefits and disadvantages ... Psychologists have learnt to incorporate the methodological strengths of econometric approaches to the evaluation and comparison

of risks ... An increasing body of sociological work uses the resources of large longitudinal studies to assess risks faced in everyday life, and has developed middle range theories such as the notion of a 'coping strategy' to analyse patterns of behaviour.

This has meant that very different coping mechanisms are now being revealed and investigated. It has indicated the potential of trust-based relationships instead of constitutional rules or contract-based relationships to regulate behaviour of individuals and organisations or 'command-and-control' relationships to regulate behaviour within organisational hierarchies. As Bruno Frey (2000: 42) has argued:

> A different approach to constitutional economics puts faith in the citizen. ... Citizens are assumed to have in principle good will. While they dislike being exploited by others, they are considered to have a good measure of civic virtue. ... It has been concluded that in order to support the existing civic virtue, and to help to raise it further, the constitution should be benevolent towards the citizens. The constitution should put trust in the citizens (this is a different type of trust ... citizens [have] towards government and society). This trust is reflected by giving citizens many direct participation rights. Citizens should not only be given the right to elect their representatives, but also to participate directly by voting on issues.

Frey goes on to assert that 'There exists considerable empirical evidence that this view of human nature is realistic and not overly optimistic ... The assumption that a considerable amount of civic virtue exists amongst citizens and that it is crowded in by a constitution that puts faith in its citizens is ... warranted' (ibid.: 43). He concludes that a good constitution achieves a balance between faith in civic virtue and protecting citizens from the actions of those who would seek to exploit them.

Putnam does not reject Frey's basic thesis, but emphasises the need to distinguish between trust and trustworthiness: 'Generalised reciprocity is a community asset, but generalised gullibility is not. Trustworthiness, not simply trust, is the key ingredient [in trustful communities]' (Putnam, 2000: 136). This emphasises the mutuality of sustainable trust relationships.

However we judge the quality of the evidence which Frey cites, our interest here is in the dynamics of these relationships – what is it that is driving changes in trust – both positively and negatively, and how trust can be increased in those areas where it is necessary for improved community governance. Following Frey, we are interested in two-way or mutual trust – not only whether citizens trust government and its organisations, but whether government and its organisations are prepared to trust citizens.

The modes through which levels of trust can be changed

To explore the ways in which levels of trust can be changed, we need to recognise that actions can be altered by changes in cognition, affection or conation:

- Cognition – relating to knowledge, rational thought
- Affection – relating to emotional identification
- Conation – relation to volition, intent, purpose

Since these drivers of action can be anticipated, they are also likely to be the drivers of expectations about future action, and hence also of the levels of trust which actors have in each other's future actions. Clearly it is important to explore their workings.

These drivers of action and expectation are themselves influenced by other triggers which can arise from several underlying sources. These underlying triggers are based on different modes of sense making, or ways of gathering and interpreting empirical evidence. We shall highlight four major triggers here:

- *Tangibles* – where there is no previous track record of interaction available, action or expectations may be simply triggered by tangible signs which are interpreted as positive or negative (e.g. dress sense of an individual, condition of an organisation's premises).
- *Ideological* – where there is some knowledge of the belief system of an individual or an organisation, this may be enough to predispose other individuals or organisations towards it, favourably or negatively (e.g. knowledge of the religion to which an individual belongs; knowledge of which political party a local firm has supported through donations).
- *Experience* – previous interactions with the individual or organisation are likely to be major triggers to action or expectations.
- *Personal empathy* – where previous interactions with an individual have led one to believe that there are strong feelings of empathy on both sides, this is also likely to dispose one favourably towards that person.

In general, it is likely that, for most people, triggers for trust which derive from experience and personal empathy are more likely to be convincing than the purely tangible and ideological triggers.

What roles do these evidence-based triggers play in influencing the levels of trust between actors? Tables 8.1 and 8.2 suggest some of the possible patterns which are likely to characterise the emergence and sustainability of trust relationships.

In Table 8.1 we highlight some important differences between the likely triggers of trust as they affect people and organisations. For example, we suggest that organisations can benefit from ideological identification, but it is much less likely that people will trust other people simply on ideological grounds. On the other hand, people can be trusted because of the presence of personal empathy, but organisations are much less likely to benefit from this phenomenon. (However, the move over the last decade towards customer relations management demonstrates how organisations can attempt to improve the trust which people place in them by presenting their human face – thereby giving people an affective relationship with the organisation.)

Ann Marie Berg (2003) suggests that the strongest links in trust relations are likely to be trust between people. People will trust organisations rather less than other people, they will trust systems (such as 'health care') less still and they are likely to place least trust in the abstract notion of institutions (such as constitutions, 'codes of conduct', etc.). This is in line with the above analysis, which suggests that trust will be lower where personal experience is less possible (except, of course, where that personal experience is negative).

In Table 8.2, we suggest that organisations are unlikely to trust individuals on ideological grounds, although they may place trust in other organisations

Table 8.1 Influences on the levels of trust shown by individuals

	Individual–individual trust	Individual–organisation trust
Cognitive	Tangibles Experience	Tangibles Ideological Experience
Affective	Experience Personal empathy	Ideological Experience
Conative	Experience	Tangibles Ideological Experience

Table 8.2 Influences on the levels of trust shown by organisations

	Organisation–individual trust	Organisation–organisation trust
Cognitive	Tangibles Experience	Tangibles Ideological Experience
Affective	Experience Personal empathy	Ideological Experience
Conative	Tangibles Experience	Experience

which they believe to share similar ideological bases (depending on what these ideologies are, of course).

We also suggest that organisations may benefit from empathy relations developed by their staff in working with individuals in the community. They may be prepared to place some trust in people because of this (mutual) empathy. However, it is much less likely that one organisation will come to trust another just because some people in both organisations have developed affective relationships.

This analysis therefore leads us to the conclusion that changes in the level of trust between different parties depends on a number of factors:

- The *types of parties* concerned – it will be easier to increase trust between people than between people and organisations, and even harder to increase trust between people and systems or institutions. By the same token, however, trust can also be lost more quickly between people.
- The *types of organisation and the context of the sector* – where interactions are more likely to be frequent, intensive and personal, then trust relationships can more easily be built up (and damaged).
- The *type of relationship between the parties* – cognitive, affective or conative. It will be easier to change the level of the trust if the relationship moves towards an affective basis.
- The *evidence base* which is most used by the parties in determining how much trust to place in each other – tangibles, ideology, experience or empathy? The more the evidence base is rooted in personal experience or empathy, the easier it will be to change the level of trust in a relationship.

Paradox of controls in a 'trusting' regime

Many authors have argued that control is a substitute for trust in society and in organisations (e.g. in the New Public Management) (see also Kramer and Tyler, 1996; Power, 1997). Berg points out the paradox at the heart of modern managerialist approaches in the public sector:

> The present day regulatory regime is in principle a system based on trust by the fact that it emphasises deregulation, self-control, system control and decentralisation. At the same time, we see tendencies to withdrawal of the autonomy (decentralisation) and discretion (deregulation). Many of the reform initiatives imply the introduction of controls and procedures in order to satisfy the stated need for accountability and transparency. ... Trust is given and trust is won but the requirement of assurance is the expression of mistrust. (Berg, 2003: 7)

Part of the reason for this may lie in the sources of evidence on which trust is based. Luhmann (1999) has argued that we should distinguish between the concepts of faith, confidence and trust. However, in practice, the concept of trust is widely used to cover the commitments and expectations which arise through both faith and confidence. It is useful, therefore, to extend Luhmann's schema to suggest that *faith* is trust based on ideology, while *confidence* is trust based on cognitive evidence (e.g. through a risk-related assessment of likely behaviour and outcomes) and *personal trust* is based on affective relations.

This line of analysis throws up the hypothesis that control as a substitute for trust is most likely where either ideology or personal trust is lacking, i.e. in those instances where there is no relationship between the parties concerned or where any trust which exists is based largely on cognitive factors. By the same token, it suggests that there is a rationale for less reliance on controls where ideological or personal empathy is predominant.

Of course, people with other ideologies may need to be convinced that such trust is deserved. Similarly, outsiders not involved in an empathetic relationship between individuals may suspect that the empathetic relationship has gone too far and may even be leading to unfair preference, corruption or discrimination against excluded individuals. However, producing the level of proof needed to convince outsiders is likely to be less destructive to a trusting relationship than self-assessment based, apparently, on doubts in the mind of the other partner. This suggests the need to carefully distinguish between evaluations which are externally oriented and evaluations which are internally oriented. It may rarely be possible to combine them productively, as many of the proponents of performance measure have argued in the past. This point is very neatly illustrated by Rob Paton (2003: 74) in his analysis of three 'measurement leaders' in the non-profit sector in the UK and US.

Faith, confidence and affective trust in community public services

With this conceptual framework in place, we can return to the question posed earlier as to whether trust in communities is growing or declining. Given the triggers for changing levels of trust which we have outlined in the previous sections, we would expect to find a varied pattern, rather than monotonic trends.

Specifically, we would expect to find that the changing 'climate of risk', in Taylor-Goodby's phrase, has undermined the level of faith of many citizens in the innate 'goodness' of the public sector, so that trust based on ideological sympathy is now likely to be much weaker than before.

For illustrative purposes, let us look at the implications of the ageing society for levels of trust in society. The levels of confidence based in the public sector, its agencies and its staff, arising from cognitive evidence, are likely to be strongly affected by the personal experiences which citizens have had in relation to elderly services. On the one hand, far more elderly people are now in regular contact with the public sector than before and many of them have very positive experiences. On the other hand, the expectations of these people are growing, given that they have had greater levels of education and greater levels of choice in their own life styles than was the case with previous cohorts of elderly people (Taylor-Goodby, 2000: 9). It is to be expected that the trust placed by these people in the public sector is likely to vary quite widely depending on the experiences they have. Furthermore, the level of trust based on the personal empathy which they are able to build up with the paid carers they encounter is also likely to be variable – and all the more so as they become more demanding and heterogeneous in their requirements.

On the supply side of the equation, the public services are clearly increasingly stretched all over the developed world in dealing with the care consequences of an ageing society. Not only is public expenditure under pressure, but also the numbers of paid staff available (at least at conventional wage rates for this type of work) are now falling. In these circumstances, the level of personal experience and understanding of staff in relation to the everyday life experiences of their clients is falling. Furthermore, a greater distance in the relationships between paid carers and clients has been imposed, if accidentally, by the increasing regulation of personal contacts in care of the elderly services, designed to protect clients from abuse (e.g. by ensuring that staff do not handle the client's money or do not make any comments or carry out any tasks which could be construed as intruding upon family issues) and to protect staff from unreasonable risk (e.g. in relation to lifting elderly people from bed, bathing them, dealing with fits or spasms, etc.). This naturally undermines the level of empathy that is likely to be built up between carer and client. In consequence, the decreasing confidence in potential client behaviour and the lower levels of empathy achievable with clients are both likely to mean that public sector care services are now less able than before to place trust in their clients in the co-production of services.

Roles of local stakeholders in activating civil society

However, there is an alternative set of relationships which needs to be considered in relation to the care of the elderly in the community – the relationships between the elderly themselves and other members of civil society, including members of their family (who often act as the major carers for elderly people), friends, neighbours or local volunteers.

Here the picture is very different. The relationships are almost always personal rather than organisational. The scope for confidence based on personal experience and for trust based on empathy is therefore greater. Furthermore, the behaviour patterns are already in place in a large number of cases. And these behaviour patterns do not focus simply on the personal hygiene needs of the elderly, within carefully prescribed legal limits meant to limit the risks faced by both client and carer; they typically extend to days out together (e.g. trips to the local bingo hall and cinema), discussion of intimate personal issues, buying of gifts, etc.

What are the drawbacks to this alternative form of care which have meant that it is not more universally seen as the panacea to such growing social problems as the declining quality of life of the elderly? Clearly, there are risk assessment issues, as always, yet the number of cases of harm done in such relationships is very low relative to their occurrence, suggesting that current risk assessments in the public sector are absurdly pessimistic. Second, there are problems of exploitation of the carers, which are exacerbated because so many of the carers are female and therefore bear burdens of expectation in society that are grossly unfair. However, many of these burdens could be lessened if support systems were in place which allowed 'relief care' on a more frequent basis. Finally, there is the problem that these community-based care services may be less reliable, in that they depend on the personal decisions of individuals rather than the paid attendance of professionals. This latter point is quite central. If it turns out that community-based co-production of services is too unreliable, then the potential of community-based services is likely to be unexploited. However, the evidence on this is far from clear. Indeed, one of the main complaints about professional public sector care services is that they are quite unreliable, forcing family, friends and neighbours to step in on a frequent basis to help out.

This analysis leads to the conclusion that more provision for local services could be placed in the hands of citizens in the local community rather than in the public sector, and that the role of the public sector might be shifted significantly towards activating local stakeholders. At the same time, local stakeholders could themselves be encouraged to be more active in mobilising volunteers to help to improve the quality of life in local areas. For example, health charities can help to support carers and get 'expert carers' to advise others who are less experienced. Similarly, 'expert patients' can help people who have been recently diagnosed with serious conditions on how best to prepare for and recuperate from operations or chemotherapy, and how to improve their quality of life within the constraints of their illness.

Of course, the levels of activism in civil society differ widely from place to place within countries and across countries (Bovaird, Loeffler and Parrado Diez, 2002). Moreover, different types of 'activism' may have very different motives and effects – activism which is seen as partly self-seeking may often be ineffective and activism from political motives may create actual hostility. However, Bovaird *et al.* argue that the level of civil activism in most European countries could be significantly increased using mechanisms already available elsewhere in Europe. In each country, the approach which is most likely to be effective in activating civil society will depend on its existing characteristics, in which national cultural differences will play an important part, and should be based on the opportunities currently offered in the specific economic, social and political circumstances of that country. The alternative of simply seeking to reactivate trust in the public sector and its agencies is a high-risk strategy.

The implications for central government are also important. Just as local government needs to learn how to trust local civil society to a greater extent, while supporting it appropriately so that it can better carry out the functions which it is attempting to provide, so central government needs to learn how to trust local governance to look after itself. In a centralist country such as the UK there has been a marked temptation in the last two decades to believe that central government can impose methods of working at local level which will solve the 'wicked problems' facing communities. This approach has by and large failed, as outlined at the beginning of this chapter. Trusting in the potential of local governance is not, however, a counsel of *laissez faire*. Following Putnam, the watchword must be trustworthiness, not simply trust. However, a fixation on control, over-intervention and micro-management is likely to undermine the trust relationships between different levels of government and reduce their potential for fruitful joint action.

Conclusions

Crude indices of 'trust' cannot safely be used for practical decision-making on what to do to improve public services, public organisations, public service systems or public institutions. Measures of 'trust' must be contextualised with respect to which stakeholders are involved (in trusting and being trusted), the cognitive, affective and conative triggers of that trust and the type of evidence on which this trust is based (tangibles, ideological, experiential or empathetic).

Social capital is not just 'trust' and trust is a component of personal and organisational capital as well as 'social capital'. However, the importance of trust to social capital is central and ways of building greater trust in communities are essential if the potential for community action is to be exploited. In activating civil society, government can rely on money incentives, law (fear), pride and education as well as trust, but the efficacy of these other mechanisms is now much more uncertain, so that mechanisms based on trust may well need to play a more significant role in tackling 'wicked problems' than was the case in the past.

The extent of two-way interaction in trust relationships is unclear. Will people trust other people/organisations/systems or institutions which do not trust them – or do not appear to trust them? At the very least, it appears likely that trust relationships will be fostered more readily where both sides seem ready to place some level of trust in each other, but the level of trust required may be asymmetric. Further research is critical if governments are to move down the path of community-based initiatives.

There are grounds for believing that the leading roles in activating citizens for community governance should be context-specific. For example, in Germany and Spain there is likely to be significant scope for more action by higher levels of government, for example, by placing a legal obligation for local authorities to consult with citizens. In the UK, on the other hand, because of a long history of over-intervention from central government, it may be more important to have leadership from local government or from the voluntary sector within civil society itself. In each case, there is a need for more empirical research on the capacities and abilities of local stakeholders to activate civil society within specific regions and countries.

Finally, in seeking to make greater use of the potential unleashed by trust relationships between local stakeholders, there will be a parallel need to explore new modes of community governance which will be able to build up as well as to exploit the social capital within the local community.

References

Audit Commission (2003), 'Trust in Public Bodies Hinges on Service Quality and Honesty, Says New Research'. Press release, 10 June. London: Audit Commission.

Beck, U. (1992), *Risk Society*. London: Sage.

Berg, A. M. (2003), 'Creating Trust? A Critical Perspective on Intra- and Inter-organisational Reforms'. Paper to the European Group of Public Administration Annual Conference, Oeiras, Portugal, 3-6 September.

Bouckaert, G., Van de Walle, S., Maddens, B. and J. K. Kampen. (2002), *Identity vs. Performance: An Overview of Theories Explaining Trust in Government: Second Report 'Citizen Directed Governance: Quality and Trust in Government'*, Leuven: Public Management Institute.

Bouckaert, G. and van de Walle, S. (2003), 'Comparing Measures of Citizen Trust and User Satisfaction as Indicators of "Good Governance": Difficulties in Linking Trust and Satisfaction Indicators', *International Review of Administrative Sciences*, 69(3): 329–43.

Bovaird, T. (1986), 'Public and Private Partnerships for Financing Urban Programme', in E. A. Rose (ed.), *New Roles for Old Cities*, Aldershot: Gower Press.

Bovaird, T., Loeffler, E. and Diez, S. P. (2002), 'Finding a Bowling Partner: The Role of Stakeholders in Activating Civil Society in Germany, Spain and the United Kingdom', *Public Management Review*, 4(3): 1–21.

Citrin, J. S. and Luks, S. (2001), 'Political Trust Revisited: Déjà Vu All Over Again', in J. R. Hibbing and E. Theiss-Morse (eds.), *What is it About Government that Americans Dislike?* Cambridge: Cambridge University Press.

Etzioni, A. (1995), *The Spirit of Community: Rights, Responsibilities and the Communitarian Agenda*. London: Fontana Press.

—— (1998), *The New Golden Rule*. London: Profile Books.

—— (2000), *The Third Way to a Good Society*. London: Demos.

Frey, B. S. (2000), 'Motivation and Human Behavior', in P. Taylor-Goodby (ed.), *Risk, Trust and Welfare*. Basingstoke: Palgrave.

Kramer, R. M. and Tyler, T. R. (1996), *Trust in Organisations*. London: Sage.

Loeffler, E. (2003), 'Governance and Government – Networking with External Stakeholders', in T. Bovaird and E. Loeffler (eds.), *Public Management and Governance*. Routledge: London.

Luhmann, N. (1999), *Tillid-en mekanisme til reduktion af social kompleksitet*. Copenhagen: Hans Reitzels forlag; cited in A. M. Berg (2003) 'Creating Trust? A Critical Perspective on Intra- and Inter-organisational Reforms'. Paper to the European Group of Public Administration Annual Conference, Oeiras, Portugal, 3–6 September.

Martin, S. (2003), 'Engaging with Citizens and Other Stakeholders' in T. Bovaird and E. Loeffler (eds), *Public Management and Governance*, Routledge: London.

Miztal, B. A. (1996), *Trust in Modern Societies*, Cambridge: Polity Press.

Newman, J. (2002), 'The New Public Management, Modernization and Institutional Change: Disruptions, Disjunctures and Dilemmas', in K. McLaughlin, S. P. Osborne and E. Ferlie (eds.), *New Public Management: Current Trends and Future Prospects*, London: Routledge.

Nye, J. S., Zelikow, P. D. and Kings, D. C. (eds.), *Why People Don't Trust Government*, Cambridge, MA: Harvard University Press.

Paton, R. (2003), *Managing and Measuring Social Enterprises*, London: Sage.

Perri 6, Leat, D., Seltzer, K. and Stoker, G. (2002), *Towards Holistic Governance: The New Reform Agenda,*, Basingtoke: Palgrave Macmillan.

Pharr, S. and Putnam, R. (2000), *Disaffected Democracies: What's Troubling the Trilateral Countries?* Princeton, NJ: Princeton University Press.

Putnam, R. (1993), *Making Democracy Work: Civic Traditions in Modern Italy*, Princeton, NJ: Princeton University Press.

Putnam, R. (2000), *Bowling Alone: The Collapse and Revival of American Community*, New York, Simon & Schuster.

Rittel, H. W. J and Weber, M. M. (1973), 'Dilemmas in a General Theory of Planning', *Policy Sciences* 4: 155–69.

Schultze, C. (1968), *The Politics and Economics of Public Spending*, Washington, DC: Brookings Institution.

Shakespeare, T. (2000), 'The Social Relations of Care', in G. Lewis, S. Gerwitz and J. Clarke (eds.), *Rethinking Social Policy*, London: Sage.

Taylor-Goodby, P. (2000), 'Risk and Welfare', in P. Taylor-Goodby (ed.), *Risk, Trust and Welfare*, Basingstoke: Palgrave.

Part Three

Cultures of Risk: The Uncertainties of Trust

9

Reporting Risk: Science Journalism and the Prospect of Human Cloning

Stuart Allan, Alison Anderson and Alan Petersen

'THE LIVING NIGHTMARE: Sect first baby "clone"' declared the front page of Britain's *Daily Mirror* on 28 December 2002. The lead news item, featuring a photograph of 'Dr Boisselier', together with one ostensibly of 'the embryo of [the] first human clone' alongside it, reads as follows:

> A CULT'S claim to have produced the world's first human clone was branded a 'living nightmare' yesterday.
>
> The Geneva-based Raelian Movement, which believes mankind was created by aliens, said a 'healthy' 7lb cloned baby girl was born by caesarean section to US parents on Boxing Day.
>
> But British genetics expert Dr Patrick Dixon said if the claim was true it would prompt 'revulsion and disgust'.
>
> He said: 'This baby has been born into a living nightmare with a high risk of malformations, ill-health, early death and unimaginably severe emotional pressures.'
>
> 'We must not allow this terrible future.'
>
> Scientist Brigitte Boisselier, who heads a bio-research company set up by the Raelians, announced the alleged cloning at a Miami press conference.
>
> She produced no evidence of the child, known as Eve, but insisted she would back her claims with independent DNA proof.
>
> She said: 'I am creating life. But I do not want anyone to think that I am playing God.'
>
> Other experts scorned her announcement.
>
> Professor Robert Winston said: 'Nearly all scientists will regard this claim as ludicrous.' (Richard Wallace, *Daily Mirror*, 28 December 2002, p. 1)

Neatly encapsulated in this short item (the 'full story' appears on pages 4 and 5 of the same edition) are a number of issues which will be familiar to those interested in the debate about the prospect of human cloning. Of particular concern for this chapter's discussion, however, are the ways in which journalists determine whether a scientific claim is valid, let alone newsworthy. At stake, we shall argue, is a cultural politics of legitimacy whereby contending definitions of risk are narrativised in news accounts. This complex process of narrativisation, revolving as it does around questions regarding the negotiation of trust, expertise, evidence and uncertainty, necessarily has far-reaching implications for public deliberation and debate.

This chapter begins by considering the problem of 'risk' and its definition, from the vantage points of scientists and journalists, respectively. In seeking to render problematic several assumptions underpinning such definitions, our attention turns to the work of Ulrich Beck (1992a, 1992b, 1995, 1998, 2000). Of interest for our purposes is the need to situate the news media within the risk society in general, and with respect to the reporting of the possible risks associated with the prospect of human cloning in particular. Next, and following an overview of several pertinent studies of newspaper reporting, the chapter provides a brief case study of news of the Raelian cult's claim to have produced the world's first cloned baby. Deserving of careful scrutiny, as the analysis proceeds to show, are the ways in which newspapers contribute to the public framing of risk via certain preferred rhetorical strategies. The chapter concludes by examining several key imperatives shaping the interaction of scientists and journalists – posed as a series of questions – to highlight possible ways forward in improving the quality of science journalism, especially where the reporting of scientific uncertainty becomes controversial.

Media and risk

The problem of how best to define what counts as a 'risk' continues to be an awkward one. The subject of considerable debate both within and beyond scientific communities, what the term means often varies quite dramatically from one user to the next. In its technical sense, however, risk is usually defined as the calculated probability of an adverse consequence, such as a danger, harm or loss, arising because of a specific action or process. Adams (1999: 285) identifies three broad categories of risk:

- directly perceptible risks: e.g. traffic to and from landfill sites;
- risks perceptible with the help of science: e.g. cholera and toxins in landfill sites;
- virtual risks – scientists don't know or cannot agree: e.g. BSE/CJD (bovine spongiform encephalopathy or 'mad cow disease'/Creutzfeldt-Jakob disease) and suspected carcinogens.

Self-described 'risk managers' tend to focus on the first two of these three categories. The reason, Adams (1999: 285) argues, is that 'quantified risk assessments require that the probabilities associated with particular events be known or be capable of plausible estimation'. Scientists, as many of them are quick to acknowledge, tend to frame issues of risk in terms of probabilities which are little more than confident expressions of uncertainty. 'When scientists cannot agree on the odds,' writes Adams (1999: 285), 'or the underlying causal mechanisms, of illness, injury or environmental harm, people are liberated to argue from belief and conviction' (see also Collins and Pinch, 1998; Friedman *et al.*, 1999; Scanlon *et al.*, 1999; Select Committee on Science and Technology, House of Lords, 2000).

Scientists' perceptions of risk, one study after another suggests, can be at serious odds with those held by members of the public. Research commissioned on public perceptions of risk by Britain's Parliamentary Office of Science and Technology (POST, 1996), for example, provides a series of pertinent insights. In addition to the actual size of the risk, a variety of different factors are identified, which appear to influence public perceptions:

- *Control* – People are more willing to accept risks they impose upon themselves or they consider to be 'natural', than to have risks imposed on them.
- *Dread and scale of impact* – Fear is greatest where the consequences of a risk are likely to be catastrophic rather than spread over time.
- *Familiarity* – People appear more willing to accept risks that are familiar rather than new risks.
- *Timing* – Risks seem to be more acceptable if the consequences are immediate or short-term, rather than if they are delayed, especially if they might affect future generations.
- *Social amplification and attenuation* – Concern can be increased because of media coverage or graphic depiction of events, or reduced by economic hardship.
- *Trust* – A key factor is how far the public trusts regulators, policy-makers or industry. If these bodies are open and accountable – being honest, admitting mistakes and limitations and taking account of differing views without disregarding them as emotive or irrational – then the public is more likely to place credibility in them. (Parliamentary Office of Science and Technology, 1996)

These factors, taken together, contribute to a better understanding of why some risks are perceived as being more serious than others. At the same time, however, each also highlights, to varying degrees, the significance of the media in shaping these perceptions. That is to say, confronted by scientific uncertainty where risks are concerned, 'ordinary' or 'lay' members of the public are likely to turn to the news media in particular for a greater understanding of what is at stake. Journalists are charged with the responsibility of imposing meaning on uncertainties, that is, it is expected that they will render intelligible the underlying significance of uncertainties for their audiences' everyday experiences of modern life. More often than not, news accounts will offer the assurance that a potential risk will remain uncertain only until further research and scientific investigation are able to provide the expected clarity and certitude (see also Nelkin, 1995; Petersen, 1999, 2001, 2002; Adam, 2000; Allan *et al.*, 2000; Hilgartner 2000; Allan, 2002; Anderson, 2002; Hargreaves *et al.*, 2003; Kitzinger *et al.*, 2003).

Critical lines of enquiry, it follows, have to recognise the importance of accounting for the media's construction of risk as part of the lived politics of the everyday. In this context, the work of Ulrich Beck (1992a, 1995, 2000) has proved to be highly influential. Particularly consequential, for example, is his conception of the 'relations of definition' underpinning media discourses which condition what can and should be said about risks, threats and hazards by 'experts' and 'counter-experts', as well as by members of the 'lay public'. The analysis of risk, he argues, needs to account for the media's structuring significance in the formation of public opinions about risk. To clarify, Beck (1995) accords to the media a crucial role in the organisation and dissemination of knowledge about economic decision-making and political control vis-à-vis the uncertainties associated with risks:

> The system of institutionally heightened expectations forms the social background in front of which – under the close scrutiny of the mass media and the murmurs of the tensely attentive public – the institutions of industrial society present the dance of the veiling of hazards. The hazards, which are not merely projected onto the world stage, but really threaten, are illuminated under the mass media spotlight. (Beck, 1995: 101)

Important questions, therefore, arise as to who in the media controls this spotlight, under what circumstances and, moreover, where it is (and is not) directed and why. It follows that it is of the utmost significance how issues of proof, accountability and compensation are represented in and by media discourses. Risks, as Beck (1992a: 23) writes, can 'be changed, magnified, dramatized or minimized within knowledge, and to that extent they are particularly *open to social definition and construction*'. While Beck's work has stimulated considerable debate about these key questions, we still need more empirical analysis of how competing rationality claims about particular risks are represented across different media, since they are complexly differentiated and governed by different organisational, economic and political constraints (see Anderson, 1997; Cottle, 2000; Petts *et al.*, 2001; Murdock *et al.*, 2003). The ways in which journalists help to mediate the limits of risk, always in conjunction with and opposition to other institutions across society, consequently need to be carefully unravelled for purposes of analysis.

This process of mediation involves a series of procedures for knowing the world and, equally importantly, for not knowing that world as well. It is fraught with uncertainty, ambiguity and contradiction. As noted above, the preferred 'models' of the scientist, for example, do not 'translate' easily into the reportorial strategies of the journalist anxious to convey their meaning to the intended audience. 'Risk societies', writes Beck (1998: 19), 'are currently trapped in a vocabulary that lends itself to an interrogation of the risks and hazards through the relations of definition of simple, classic, first modernity.' As a result, he continues, this vocabulary is 'singularly inappropriate not only for modern catastrophes, but also for the challenges of manufactured uncertainties' (1998: 19). In the case of scientific perspectives, then, they must undergo a process of journalistic narrativisation before they are likely to 'make sense' to a public facing unknown and barely calculable risks. 'Dispassionate facts' must be marshalled into a 'balanced' news story, ideally one with a distinct beginning, middle and end, as well as with easily identifiable 'good' versus 'evil' conflicts. This struggle to narrativise the scientific world necessarily situates journalists at the point where, as Beck (1992b) observes, the antagonisms between those who produce risk definitions and those who consume them are at their most apparent. Daily newspaper reading, as he notes, becomes 'an exercise in technology critique'.

Media imagery of cloning

A key point of departure for this chapter's discussion, then, is this recognition that the taken-for-granted, seemingly commonsensical assumptions underpinning the media's preferred relations of definition are pivotal to the way we as members of the public understand, negotiate and challenge the uncertainties of today's risk society. Indeed, as Beck (2000: xiv) observes, this society 'can be grasped theoretically, empirically and politically only if one starts from the premise that it is always a knowledge, media and information society at the same time – or, often enough as well, a society of non-knowledge and disinformation'.

Several key aspects of Beck's theses regarding the risk society have been thrown into sharp relief by the emergent controversy surrounding the prospect of human cloning over recent years. Briefly, several of the key imperatives underpinning this controversy were set in motion; specifically, on 5 July 1996, the day when a rather unusual lamb was born in Scotland. Despite resembling any other newborn lamb, 'Dolly' was unique and destined to become the most famous lamb in history. As people living around the globe would soon discover to their astonishment on 24 February 1997, Dolly was a clone (the story had been broken the day before in *The Observer*). The worlds of science fiction and science fact had unexpectedly converged once again, and this time the implications – as voices on the front page of virtually every newspaper agreed – were particularly unsettling.

Cloning was one feat of genetic engineering too far in the eyes of many scientists, few of whom had believed it would be achieved in their lifetime. Even leading researchers in the field of mammalian genetics and embryology were shocked by the news, some wondering if it was a cruel hoax. Others made the immediate jump in thought to wonder if the same techniques might be applied to humans. They were not alone – as Pence (1998: 1) writes, 'thirty hours after the news of Dolly hit the streets, legislator John Marchi announced a bill to make human cloning illegal in New York State'. In the words of Silver, a biologist:

> Of course, it wasn't the cloning of a sheep that stirred the imagination of billions of people. It was the idea that humans could now be cloned as well in a manner akin to taking cuttings from a plant, and many people were terrified by the prospect. Ninety percent of Americans polled within the first week after the story broke felt that human cloning should be banned. And the opinions of many media pundits, ethicists, and policymakers, though not unanimous, seemed to follow those of the general public. The idea that humans might be cloned was called 'morally despicable', 'repugnant', 'totally inappropriate', as well as 'ethically wrong, socially misguided, and biologically mistaken'. (Silver, 1998: 108)

Around the world a diverse array of institutional stakeholders, each articulating their respective perceptions of science and technology, sought to define its significance for humankind. Imagery from science fiction was drawn on to tap into the public mood, frequently with great rhetorical effect.

Dolly was created using DNA from an adult sheep, something that had never been done successfully before. The researchers were led by Dr Ian Wilmut, an embryologist at the Roslin Institute near Edinburgh, working in collaboration with PPL Therapeutics. They took a mammary cell from a six-year-old sheep and altered its DNA to make it acceptable to another sheep's egg (that it was a mammary cell led to the wry choice of the name Dolly, after the country and western singer Dolly Parton). The egg's own genetic material was then removed and replaced by the DNA from the adult sheep by fusing the egg with the adult cell. The fused cells, carrying the adult DNA, grew and divided as they would in an egg fertilised in the ordinary way, eventually forming an embryo. This embryo was then implanted into another ewe, which gave birth to Dolly in July 1996. A startling example of asexual reproduction, one that reportedly took 277 such fusions to achieve, Dolly had in effect two mothers but no father. Interestingly, when Wilmut was asked by a reporter at the time of the announcement whether Dolly should be considered to be seven months old or six years old (the age of the cloned adult lamb), he was unable to say. 'I can't answer that,' he admitted. 'We just don't know' (cited in Pence, 1998: 18; see also Kolata, 1997).

If prior to Dolly's arrival animal cloning had been the subject of scientific conjecture, now it was suddenly real. In the eyes of many of the journalists charged with explaining these details to their audiences, this was science gone mad. From the outset Dolly was characterised by some as a 'genetic mutant', and as such surely the first seed being sown in what would inevitably lead to the destruction of humankind. The prospect of 'carbon-copy human reproduction' generated uproarious public debates (the mad scientist in such scenarios becoming a 'mad Xeroxer'), with some of the voices participating bordering on the hysterical. Efforts to point out that identical twins are clones, albeit 'naturally achieved' ones, and that cloning methods might have benefits for those involved in IVF, were difficult to hear in the media furore about human cloning. Wilmut acknowledged at the time of the initial announcement that a similar technique might make human cloning theoretically possible, but had insisted that he found the very idea abhorrent. Indeed, it could be safely dismissed as the subject of science fiction, in his view – a position echoed in a headline appearing in the *Guardian* that day: 'Scientists scorn sci-fi fears over sheep clone'. As Wilmut informed the press: 'We would find it ethically completely unacceptable and we would not do it.' Instead, he was convinced that the breakthrough might lead, in the long term, to the development of animals that could produce drugs to treat human diseases such as haemophilia more cheaply than current methods (the secrecy around the breakthrough was due to a corresponding patent application). Similarly held open was the possibility that cloned animals might be able to serve as models for human diseases such as cystic fibrosis, thereby allowing scientists to test new treatments.

Despite the reassurances of Wilmut and his colleagues that they would never attempt to clone humans, news coverage of the breakthrough over the next few weeks continued to focus on precisely this issue. The flurry of publicity surrounding the controversy opened up the discursive terrain for a multitude of positions to be rehearsed. Huxford (2000), in his study of the newspaper reporting in Britain and the US over the ensuing month, suggests that a headline in the *Daily Mail*, 'Monsters or a Miracle?', high-lighted an opposition which set the tone for the 'avalanche' of copy that followed. Journalists, he argues, turned to certain science fiction frames that emphasised anti-science themes, in part by 'establishing a series of narrative oppositions through which the coverage might be shaped: science versus religion, high culture versus low culture, the Romantic sense of the individual versus mass society' (2000: 187). Almost half (46 per cent) of the 204 articles surveyed made references to science fiction imagery, the vast majority in a negative manner by raising fears about the future use of cloning technology. 'British sheep clone raises spectre of Frankenstein' declared the Reuters news service (24 February 1997), while the main head-line in *The News and Observer* in Raleigh, North Carolina on 9 March 1997, demanded to know: 'Are we cloning a Brave New World?' Significantly, Huxford's (2000) findings suggest that in those news items with science fiction associations, Huxley's novel was the most frequently work cited by far, followed by Mary Shelley's *Frankenstein* – these two texts accounted for the bulk of the references, with 32 and 21 respectively. Next came *The Boys from Brazil* with 13, and then with four references the comedy film *Multiplicity* (its central character, played by Michael Keaton, is repeatedly cloned with each 'copy' being a progressively inferior version of the 'origi-nal', which had been screened in cinemas the previous year. 'The use of science fiction allusions in the newspapers,' Huxford's study suggests, 'had more to do with cueing certain cultural fears, as embodied in popular science fiction, than with providing an understanding of cloning' (2000: 192).

Further evidence to support this line of argument is found in Hornig Priest's (2001) analysis of 'elite' or 'agenda-setting' US newspaper coverage of the controversy, namely from 1994 to its aftermath in 1997. Focusing pri-marily on news items published by the *New York Times*, the *Washington Post*, the *Los Angeles Times* and the *Wall Street Journal*, she argues that the Dolly story dominated the US media in a way that perhaps no other science story had ever done before. Of particular interest for her study was the extent to which the story became one about disagreements over cloning's ethical implications. 'Both the norms of professional journalistic practice and a par-ticularly American cultural perspective contributed to the prominence of this story,' Hornig Priest (2001: 59) writes, 'creating a novel news "frame" in which the opinions of ethicists and occasionally of religious leaders acted as counterpoint to those of scientists'. Journalists, she points out, thrive on con-troversy. Cloning satisfied the needs of 'gee whiz' science reporting, but in her opinion the continuing salience of the issue had more to do with its role as a 'crystallizing symbol' for public concerns about biotechnology. That is to say, the controversy arose not over the technical facts or their interpretation *per se*, but rather over the ethics of making particular use of those facts. Ethicists' comments were regularly used by journalists to 'balance' scientific points of view, the effect of which – however unintentionally on the part of the reporters involved – was to contain the debate in highly circumscribed ways. The cloning controversy, Hornig Priest argues, 'was essentially harmless to the status quo arrangement whereby biotechnological development is driven primarily by narrow institutional economic interests rather than issues of broader social benefit' (2001: 67). As a result, she suggests, the pre-existing power relationships characteristic of the area were largely allowed to stand unchallenged. Indeed, when looking across the period under scrutiny, her study indicates that 'objections to genetic engineering for agricultural or pharmaceutical (rather than human reproductive) purposes on economic, environmental, or other grounds were nearly invisible' (2001: 67). The consequences for how the ensuing public debate was structured were thus far-reaching. (This conclusion strikes a resonance with Neresini's (2000) analysis of the Italian coverage.)

Clearly, then, as the issues surrounding biotechnology become evermore pressing, they are also becoming increasingly politicised in cultural terms. For some advocates of human cloning, the techniques involved the promise to bring the joys of parenthood to individuals otherwise denied the opportunity to have a genetically-related child. Much is made of how the public uproar over previous developments – blood transfusions, organ transplants and, of course, IVF – eventually subsided as the potential benefits became more widely recognised. This will be the case with cloning as well, they contend, but in the meantime they believe it is important that such work continues, not least to help secure a reliable source of embryonic stem cells. Some advocates, in contrast, seek to limit their support to therapeutic cloning – not surprisingly, given that reproductive cloning is illegal in many countries. In their view, there are exciting advances to be gained by therapeutic cloning, that is, where scientists create human embryos in the laboratory and then draw from them special cells for use in medical treatments. Typically cited in this context are beneficial possibilities for transplants as donated cells 'grown to order' are less likely to be rejected by a patient's immune system because they are recognised as the body's own. This type of cloning might make organ transplants standard treatment. It may also allow skin to be made for burns victims, or pancreatic cells to produce insulin for diabetics, and so forth. Advocates similarly point to potentially revolutionary treatments for treatment of leukaemia, Parkinson's and Alzheimer's disease, and other degenerative diseases.

For those holding diametrically opposed positions, however, this distinction between therapeutic and reproductive cloning is ultimately untenable. Indeed, many of them fear that it is the first step down a slippery slope towards 'designer children' and human clones being born *en masse*. Much of the criticism of human cloning techniques revolves around the scientists' use of human embryonic stem cells (parent cells for all tissues in body) which, as their name suggests, can be obtained only from embryos. Adult stem cells may be used in some circumstances, but are believed to lack the complete flexibility of embryonic cells. Various religious and anti-abortion groups have been particularly fierce in condemning the use of embryonic stem cells as an aberration of normality. Many of them argue that an embryo (including the small clump of cells being 'harvested', to use their word) is a unique human life and as such is sacrosanct. Fearful that scientists are seeking to 'play God' or 'defy nature', they have directed intense criticism at those conducting research on human cloning. Further lines of counter-argument are made on philosophical grounds, while others on the simple conviction that it is not safe. Cloning experiments, some maintain, will lead to babies suffering abnormalities, or dying soon after birth. Here they often point to studies of cloned mice, cows, pigs and goats for comparative evidence. The dream of 'disease-free super-children', in their view, is set to become a tragic nightmare.

The world's first human clone?

The story about the Raelian cult's claim to have produced the world's first cloned baby, reported in a number of UK newspapers between December 2002 and February 2003, illustrates how a particular framing of cloning, involving the merging of science fiction and science fact and a particular use of language, may contribute to the amplification of risk. A search of Newsbank and Lexis Nexis identified 37 news items (full news reports, news-in-brief, diary or feature items) during this period, with by far the greatest proportion appearing in *The Times* (18) and the *Guardian* (13). The coverage of this issue peaked in December 2002 and then rapidly declined after mid-February, with only one article appeared after this during the period, but it merely mentioned cloning and the Raelian cult in passing (*The Times*, 2 April 2003). An intense period of coverage and debate, with no subsequent disconfirmation of factual claims, is characteristic of many news articles on genetics, and may help to shape views by leaving a 'cultural residue' long after the decline of coverage of an issue (see Conrad, 1997).

A marked dystopian view of science and of 'maverick' scientists running amok was evident in news coverage, reflecting a theme identified in other newspaper reporting on human cloning attempts in the wake of Dolly (Petersen, 2002). The motives of the cult were portrayed as far from benign. A number of rhetorical devices was used to underline the lack of credibility of the claims. Clonaid is variously described as 'bizarre', 'lunatic', a 'weird sect', 'wacky', and a 'flying saucer cult'. The founder of the group, Vorilhan, is described as a 'weirdo', 'odd', eccentric' and 'spectacularly deluded'. He is portrayed as leading an austere lifestyle, avoiding coffee, alcohol and meat. Though there are few direct references to Frankenstein, Brigette Boisselier is described as a 'maverick scientist'. Frequent references are made to their appearance and attire in the newspaper coverage, helping to convey an image of the bizarre nature of the group. Both the *Guardian* and *The Times* describe Vorilhon as having a topknot and dressed in a white satin suit with 'elaborate' or 'Flash Gordon' shoulder pads (e.g. 15 February 2002, 17 August 2002). In one piece it is stated that 'his topknot [reportedly] enhances his annual telepathic conferences with his alien interlocutors, the Elohim' (*Guardian*, 15 February 2002). By contrast, the Raelian 'bishop', Brigette Boisselier, is described as dressed all in black (28 December 2002). The credibility of her claims is brought into question on a number of occasions. For example,

The Times reports that in a press conference announcing the birth of Eve: 'Her performance was not entirely convincing – she frequently broke into giggles and her scientific explanation merely likened the process to the existing cloning of sheep, "adapted to human cells"' (28 December 2002).

The opening sentences of the news of the claim that the first human cloning had taken place were as follows:

Cult scientists claim first human cloning: Calls for worldwide ban as anger at 'mavericks' grows
A cult which believes that humans were first created by aliens claimed yesterday that it had won the clandestine and increasingly bizarre race to produce a human clone. It said a baby girl was born on Thursday from an egg fertilised by a skin cell from her mother (*Guardian*, 28 December 2002)

Scientists doubt claim on difficult technique
CLONING experts condemn the Raelian cult's claims to have cloned a baby as fraudulent, and will continue to do so in the absence of clear proof.
   Their doubts are based on a lack of evidence that Clonaid, the cult's cloning wing, has any expertise in cloning or that – even if it had – it could achieve a live human baby. *(The Times,* 28 December 2002)

Cloning cult funded by US lawyer
AN American lawyer who wants to 'recreate' his dead son has emerged as one of the main financial backers of the **Raelian** cult, which claims to have produced the first human clone. (*The Sunday Times*, 29 December 2002)

A prominent theme in the coverage was the way in which the group set out to manipulate the media through a PR stunt, expertly timed to gain maximum coverage during a very slow news week in the run-up to Christmas. Mark Henderson, correspondent for *The Times* wrote:

The press conference ... was a perfect late Christmas present for duty editors. On one of the slowest news days of the year, here was a seasonal nativity tale with exotic protagonists, certain to spark ethical controversy. The only problem: the sect offered no evidence that baby Eve ever existed – let alone that she was a clone. (10 January 2003)

Many of the newspaper articles make reference to the sums of money that the Raelians hoped to make through selling their story. Such stories serve to reinforce the view of the disreputable nature of the cult. That is, commercial greed rather than public interest is seen as being the motivating factor. In particular, there is reference to the attempts made by Michael Guillen, a former science editor for ABC News, to sell exclusive coverage of the story to US TV channels and *The New York Times* for a substantial sum of money (e.g. *The Times*, 6 January 2003; *The Guardian*, 7 January 2003). Doubts are also raised about whether Michael Guillen was paid by Clonaid to mastermind the operation. The *Guardian* reported: 'Guillen said he was not being paid to coordinate the DNA tests on Eve, but speaking at a news conference last Friday, he failed to answer directly repeated questions about how he was selected' (31 December 2002).

Vorilhon, a former motor racing magazine journalist, is also described as a 'self-publicist'. In one article he is compared with David Icke, the former UK TV sports reporter, widely ridiculed in the media for his alternative religious beliefs (*Guardian*, 13 February 2003).

There is a number of references to the dilemma faced by journalists in covering a story with mass audience appeal and yet seemingly having no basis in fact. *The Times* in particular claims that it tried to distance itself from rivals such as the *Daily Telegraph, Guardian, Independent* and *Daily Mail* by giving it a lower profile. Thus it claimed that: '*The Times* took a different approach, choosing the front-page basement slot usually reserved for offbeat talking points rather than hard news' (10 January 2003) In this way, *The Times* tried to position itself as a more reputable, serious media outlet than newspapers or TV news bulletins that led with the story. To reinforce this, it gave space to the views of a select number of scientists on the media treatment of the story. The assistant editor is quoted as defending the decision to place the item lower down by stating: 'Since there was no evidence, and the organisation behind it was clearly lunatic, the story was a curiosity and therefore right for the basement slot' (10 January 2003).

Similarly interesting is the extent to which references to the views of experts in the articles are used to discredit further the claims of the cult. There are numerous comparisons made to the 'bizarre' views of the Raelians and the perspective of 'mainstream scientists'. *The Times* (28 December 2002) reported Dr David King of Human Genetics Alert as warning that the cult is irresponsible: 'Unless such claims are proven by independent DNA testing no one should accept them.' Experts such as Professor Winston and the American Society for Reproductive Medicine are quoted as dismissing the claims. An article in *The Sunday Times* quotes Winston as stating: 'I don't suppose there is a single qualified person with a background in reproductive medicine who believes they have done what they claim ... If Clonaid really has cloned a person, why didn't it put its research out in a scientific journal? Why didn't it want to take the credit for it in the proper way?' A former Cambridge University scientist, Steen Willadsen, is quoted as saying: 'It has got to be a publicity stunt, and these people have a track record of making false claims' (*Sunday Times*, 28 December 2002). Despite such comments casting doubts on the claims of the group, the Raelians were successful, at least for a period, in dominating the news headlines. In the aftermath, questions about the potential for human cloning continued to linger, as did doubts about whether errant scientists could be safely regulated.

Rethinking science journalism

Democracy requires a robust exchange of viewpoints, and journalism up to the challenge of giving them vigorous expression. New forms of dialogue about the prospect of human cloning need to be fostered, particularly where the absence of scientific certainty becomes controversial. In light of the analysis of the newspaper coverage presented in the previous section, it is vital that scientists be actively involved in the creation of consensus by experimentation and testing, but also with respect to sharing their assessments of the possible implications of a given risk for daily life. This is likely to mean that they will need to be far more proactive in the shaping of the very processes of science journalism. Knowledge of the imperatives underlying news production in general, and with respect to the reporting of risk and safety claims in particular, can help to close difficult gaps in mutual understanding.

To clarify, scientists agreeing to serve as sources for a given news story will – more likely than not – promptly find themselves caught up in the cacophony of claims and counter-claims. Of the myriad of concerns confronting them, several are particularly pertinent. Specifically, when interacting with a potential source, journalists will want to determine the answers to questions such as the following:

- Who is a credible, trustworthy and legitimate news source? Who is seen to possess sufficient expertise to interpret the possible threats, dangers or hazards associated with a risk in a reasonable manner? Whose scientific authority will anchor, in turn, the proclaimed impartiality of the news account?
- Wherein lies the news story? What will be of interest to my editor, fellow journalists and readership? Where is the sense of conflict, drama and timeliness, all of which heighten the news value of the story? Does the story have a clear narrative structure, a straightforward beginning, middle and end, which will allow facts to be communicated quickly and easily?
- Is it safe? An unfair question to be sure, but one that will be asked as a matter of routine. Given that responses which fall short of 'yes' or 'no' will be treated as inherently suspicious, what sort of risk vocabulary can be drawn on to communicate what is at stake in simple – but not simplistic – terms? How best to put a human face on scientific principles, let alone risk calculations?

- What happens when the experts disagree? Balanced reporting, by defini-tion, means that there are two sides to every story (the risk is either 'safe' or 'dangerous'). The greater the disagreement – and thus controversy – that can be engendered the better. What is an acceptable risk, who decides and by which criteria? If it eventually proves unacceptable, who will be blamed?
- What are the politics of risk? Who stands to benefit – and who will lose out – from the outcome of a particular risk decision? Who is going to be held accountable to resolve any ensuing risk crisis? How best to differentiate the public interest from what interests the public?

Expert sources, in contrast, may ask themselves questions such as:

- Why does this journalist want to talk to me? Where will I be made to fit in within the larger structure of the news item? That is to say, how will my views be aligned in relation to alternative views? How will the facts of the matter be contextualised? Can journalists be trusted to explain the story to the public in a manner that will avoid antagonising colleagues, let alone rivals?
- How to acknowledge that it is impossible to eliminate risk entirely, without at the same time calling into question the authority of the risk assessment itself? Wherein lies responsibility for how risk assessments inform the decisions – political, economic, industrial and scientific – of others? Do scientists have particular moral obligations as citizens in a democracy? Who is entitled to criticise science, and who is not?
- In the absence of guarantees, how best to manage public fears of risk? How to judge which risks to avoid altogether, which ones may be worth taking, and how to explain the difference? In the course of identifying gradations of risk, how best to make them meaningful for the layperson? How best to make layperson perceptions of risk meaningful for scientists?
- Where risk calculations are concerned, what sort of evidence will be judged by the non-scientist to be compelling proof to sustain a claim or sufficient grounds to challenge it? Who defines what counts as evidence, as well as the scientific consensus (where there is one) about its significance? Is it possible to separate out science from the attendant ethical implications of its use?
- How, and to what extent, are members of the public learning to live with the uncertainties associated with risk? Is risk an inevitable price to pay for scientific progress? Is risk aversion dangerous in itself?

It follows that responsibility for informing the public about possible risks associated with human cloning must be shared between scientists and jour-nalists, with the corresponding lines of accountability clarified. New ways need to be found to enhance the forms and practices of science journalism in a manner consistent with today's moral and ethical responsibilities for tomorrow.

To close, we wish to suggest that the identification of the framing strategies in media reporting needs to be simultaneously accompanied by a search for alternatives. In seeking to de-naturalise the ways in which the media process certain voices as being self-evidently 'expert' or 'authoritative' while simultaneously framing others as lacking 'credibility', we have sought to show that it is this very self-evidence which needs to be recognised as a terrain of discursive struggle. Nevertheless, searching questions remain about how best to improve the reporting of ongoing controversies around the prospect of human cloning. In light of our analysis, it is apparent how important it is to make the complexities of cloning understandable to members of the public while, at the same time, facilitating the means by which their perceptions of the attendant risks inform the basis of the science involved. 'Risks are not simply questions of abstract probabilities or theoretical reassurances,' as Richard Horton (1999), editor of *The Lancet* points out. 'What matters is what people believe about these risks and why they hold those beliefs.' It follows, then, that public trust is a prize to be won through open debate, and not something that can be assumed as a right by experts.

References

Adam, B. (2000). 'The Media Timescapes of BSE News', in S. Allan, B. Adam and C. Carter (eds.), *Environmental Risks and the Media*, London and New York: Routledge, pp. 117–29.

Adams, J. (1999) 'Cars, Cholera, Cows, and Contaminated Land: Virtual Risk and the Management of Uncertainty', in R. Bate (ed.), *What Risk? Science, Politics and Public Health*. Oxford: Butterworth Heinemann.

Allan, S. (2002), *Media, Risk and Science*, Buckingham and Philadelphia: Open University Press.

Allan, S., Adam, B. and Carter, C. (eds.) (2000), *Environmental Risks and the Media*, London and New York: Routledge.

Anderson, A. (2002), 'In Search of the Holy Grail: Media Discourse and the New Human Genetics', *New Genetics and Society* 21(3): 327–37.

Beck, U. (1992a), *Risk Society: Towards a New Modernity*, London: Sage.

—- (1992b), 'From Industrial Society to Risk Society: Questions of Survival, Social Structure and Ecological Enlightenment', *Theory, Culture and Society* 9: 97–123.

—- (1995), *Ecological Politics in an Age of Risk*. Cambridge: Polity.

—- (1998), 'Politics of Risk Society', in J. Franklin (ed.), *The Politics of Risk Society*, Cambridge: Polity.

—- (2000), 'Foreword', in S. Allan, B. Adam and C. Carter (eds.), *Environmental Risks and the Media*, London and New York: Routledge.

Collins, H. and Pinch, T. (1998) *The Golem at Large*, Cambridge: Cambridge University Press.

Conrad, P. (1997), 'Public Eyes and Private Genes: Historical Frames, News Constructions, and Social Problems', *Social Problems* 44(2): 139–54.

Cottle, S. (2000), 'TV News, Lay Voices and the Visualisation of Environmental Risks', in S. Allan, B. Adam, and C. Carter (eds.), *Environmental Risks and the Media*. London and New York: Routledge, pp. 29–44.

Friedman, S. M., Dunwoody, S. and Rogers, C. L. (eds.) (1999), *Communicating Uncertainty*, Mahwah, NJ: Lawrence Erlbaum Associates.

Hargreaves, I., Lewis, J. and Speers, T. (2003), *Towards a Better Map: Science, the Public and the Media*, Report prepared for the Economic and Social Research Council.

Hilgartner, S. (2000), *Science on Stage*, Stanford: Stanford University Press.

Hornig Priest, S. H. (2001), *A Grain of Truth: The Media, the Public and Biotechnology*, Oxford: Rowman and Littlefield.

Horton, R. (1999), 'Genetically Modified Foods: "Absurd" Concern or Welcome Dialogue? *Lancet* 354: 1312.

Huxford, J. (2000), 'Framing the Future: Science Fiction Frames and the Press Coverage of Cloning', *Continuum: Journal of Media and Cultural Studies* 14(2): 187–99.

Kitzinger, J., Henderson, L. Smart, A. and Eldridge, J. (2003), *Media Coverage of the Ethical and Social Implications of Human Genetic Research*. Final Report for the Wellcome Trust, February. Award no: GR058105MA.

Kolata, G. (1997), *Clone: the Road to Dolly and the Path Ahead*, London: Allen Lane.

Murdock, G., Petts, J. and Horlick-Jones, T. (2003), 'After Amplification: Rethinking the Role of Media in Risk Communication', in N. Pidgeon, R. E. Kasperson and P. Slovic (eds.), *The Social Amplification of Risk,* Cambridge: Cambridge University Press.

Nelkin, D. (1995), *Selling Science: How the Press Covers Science and Technology*, second edition, New York: W. H. Freeman.

Neresini, F. (2000), 'And Man Descended from the Sheep: The Public Debate on Cloning in the Italian Press', *Public Understanding of Science* 9(4): 359–82.

Parliamentary Office of Science and Technology (1996), *Safety in Numbers?* Report 81. London: House of Commons.

Pence, G. E. (1998), *Who's Afraid of Human Cloning?* Lanham: Rowman and Littlefield.

Petersen, A. (1999), 'The Portrayal of Research into Genetic-based Differences of Sex and Sexual Orientation: A Study of "Popular" Science Journals, 1980 to 1997', *Journal of Communication Inquiry* 23(2): 163–82.

—- (2001), 'Biofantasies: Genetics and Medicine in the Print News Media', *Social Science and Medicine* 52: 1255–68.

—- (2002), 'Replicating Our Bodies, Losing Our Selves: News Media Portrayals of Human Cloning in the Wake of Dolly', *Body & Society* 8(4): 71–90.

Petts, J., Horlick-Jones, T. and Murdock, G. (2001), *Social Amplification of Risk: The Media and the Public*, Contract Research Report, Health and Safety Executive.

Scanlon, E., Whitelegg, E. and S. Yates (eds.) (1999), *Communicating Science, Reader 2*, London: Routledge.

Select Committee on Science and Technology, House of Lords (2000), *Science and Society*. London: HMSO.

Silver, L. M. (1998), *Remaking Eden: Cloning and Beyond in a Brave New World*, London: Avon.

10
Transgressive Terrain: Risk, Otherness and 'New Age' Nomadism

Leah Wild

Nomadism has a history as old as the history of mankind. From the Hebrew bible to the contemporary road movie, life on the move has been allegorised, imagined and deciphered with a fantastical romanticism that has inspired both longing and contempt. Academic discourse is saturated with concepts of nomadism, mobility and displacement. At an everyday level our accounts of human social life constantly refer to metaphors of journey and escape. However, there is a profound ambivalence around mobility and mobile populations. Immigrants, guestworkers, refugees, the stateless, the homeless, hobos, freight-train riders, tramps and showmen – these diverse peoples have something particular in common: they arouse fear and suspicion, yet conversely fascination and longing among the sedentary populations they come into contact with. This ambivalence is particularly tangible in relation to Gypsies and other Travellers. Of course Gypsies, Travellers and other nomads comprise a large number of heterogeneous groups in terms of culture, language and history, however there is a common thread that runs through their miscellaneous histories – they are all attributed other status, an otherness that is in essence ambivalent and inextricably linked to notions of risk. Of course, 'there are no groups that are intrinsically other. Rather, such groups are constructed as other by the categories and concepts used to describe them' (Hetherington 2000: 10). 'New-Age Travellers, however, often actively create their own otherness. It is these constructs and their relationship to the various expressions of nomadism as a risk identity that can be either ascribed or elected that I examine throughout the course of this chapter. I argue that, unlike Gypsies, many first-generation 'New Age' Travellers claim that their otherness and their risk identities are structuring principles through which they formulate notions of 'self' and belonging. The adoption of a risk identity is, in part, an escape attempt that produces a certain amount of existential uncertainty – an uncertainty that many Travellers view in a positive light. Through the testimonies of 'New Age' Travellers I shall examine how and why individuals might choose to be other – to don the mantle of risk, to embrace uncertainty and place themselves at the margins.

Representations of nomadic others

Representations of 'traditional' Gypsies are usually characterised by simultaneous romanticism and disgust or fear, the Gypsy can thus be seen as the embodiment of the simultaneous 'pleasures and terrors' (Kearney, 2002: 13) of the other. The nomadic other in the form of the Gypsy is exotic, alluring and beguiling, yet concomitantly dangerous and deviant. These emblematic stereotypes of Gypsy Other can be found in countless literary, cinematic and artistic contexts, from Cervantes 'La Gitanella' to Alexander Pushkin's Gypsy poems; from the boat Gypsies in Lasse Hallström's 'Chocolat' to the 'Pikeys' in Guy Ritchie's 'Snatch'.

The ubiquity of suspicion and hatred of Gypsies and Travellers is often rationalised, in academic and popular discourse, by reference to their enduring disengagement from the settled world, its bureaucratic structures, practices, procedures and processes and the related official documentation and records that often act as an instrument of their surveillance. Nomads are seen as quintessentially elusive, they are 'shadow communities' who evade the watchful territorialising gaze of the state. Anti-Traveller discourses are often infused with notions of Travellers and Gypsies posing 'risks' or threats to the moral and social order of otherwise stable societies or communities and this aspect of nomad state relations seems to be something of an historical 'constant'.

Trumpener notes that Gypsies evoke 'a dream of historylessness' (in Lemon, 2000: 43) and an idealising envy of Gypsy life seemingly '*outside* of history and *beyond* the reach of the authorities' (ibid.). She highlights an all too common assumption that nomadic peoples are outside of or 'without history' (Yelka, 1912: 46). Those who are 'outside', 'beyond' or 'in-between', the unknown quantities, are central to the construction of risk. Liminal figures who occupy the space where 'lines do not hold' (Lupton, 1999: 135), create uncertainty and a sense of danger. Mossman's analysis of anxieties around homelessness in 1990s America is particularly useful in terms of the light it sheds on the status of those who are located betwixt material and symbolic boundaries:

> Homeless people tend to be placed conceptually in a category usually reserved for animals. This is because the distinction between 'nature' (or the animal world' and 'culture' (the human world) rests upon such differences as animals have no permanent homes, live outdoors, roam about, void their wastes outside, do not wash, smell offensive and have little control over their actions, while humans dwell in fixed residences, void their body wastes privately and indoors, bathe and use deodorant to avoid smelling badly and exert control over their action ... [T]he homeless are conceptualised as partly animalistic because although they are biologically human, they do not fit the distinctions between 'animal'

and 'human' ... [They] may be conceptualised as 'dirt', as matter out of place ... (Mossman, in Lupton, 1999: 135)

Nomads, like the homeless, fit this model of liminality and 'in-between-ness'. Perceptions of Nomad and Gypsy as 'outsider' are historically under-pinned by a taken-for-granted notion that 'they have been guided by instinct and not civilisation' (Pellegrino, 1994: 103). In this analysis mobil-ity and nomadism are somehow associated with a backward, almost animal intuitiveness as opposed to rational and civilised humanity. They are 'type-cast as rebellious wanderers, always at the borders of nations and centuries' (Lemon, 2000: 3), as parasites belonging nowhere, feeding voraciously off their reluctant hosts who are always represented as beleaguered victims. This image of a drifting and directionless nomadism has taken precedence over any representations that might be closer to the truth; and when the many-layered fabric of history is examined, the picture becomes infinitely more complex. The most reasonable conjecture is that the Gypsy diaspora was a very gradual and uneven dispersal taking place over many centuries and spanning many lands. One could hazard a guess that all the contemporary push/pull factors associated with migration have historically been at play in the ebb and flow of *all* nomadic peoples across the globe. Economic factors, military threats, environmental hazards and hardships, discrimination, persecution and geopolitical dynamics have no doubt at times had varying degrees of influence on the movements and motivations of Gypsies, Travellers and other nomads. Indeed, there is plentiful histori-cal evidence to confirm this. Nomadic mobility, a perceived risk in itself, is often driven by the kinds of extraneous risks I have outlined above.[1]

Myth, legend and literary and cinematic narratives are profoundly infused with notions of the nomad as other, with the idea that nomadism and mobility and sedentary existence are utterly incommensurable, that the nomad is destined to dwell in the margins. Mary Douglas claims that the anomalous and ambiguous other is intrinsically 'risky' (Douglas, in Lupton, 1999: 44) in the eyes of the dominant culture and that one way of dealing with the risk and uncertainty that the other poses is to manage it through ritual, poetry and mythology. This 'enrich[es] meaning [and] call[s] attention to other levels of existence' (ibid.). Figures of otherness occupy the frontier zone 'where reason falters and fantasies flourish' (Kearney, 2002: 3), fantasies that are the very stuff of ambiguity and uncer-tainty. Nomadic others, like many other out-groups, are often simultane-ously eroticised, romanticised and demonised. This is not a benign exoticisation. The erotic carries with it notions of risk, danger, pollution and bewitchment.[2]

Their women are ... revoltingly dirty. Amongst other glaring vices they are supposed to be addicted to incontinency; and they are reputed to sometimes band themselves together in search of men whom they compel by force to satisfy their lewd desires. (Dubois, [1906] 1992, on the Gypsies of Hindu India)

Cervantes' novella 'La Gitanella' (1613) is perhaps one of the earliest literary examples of these ambivalent representations. In Cervantes the Gypsy 'Rancho' is represented as a society in which animal pleasure is an organising principle. The central character, the 'Gypsy maiden' 'Preciosa'[3] is erotic, alluring and mysterious. Larceny and embezzlement are taken to be incontrovertible pursuits of the Gypsy community. Throughout 'La Gitanella' Cervantes vaguely asserts the moral equivalence of settled and nomadic society. However, the Gypsy is represented as having essential and particular negative attributes. The dishonesty and duplicity of the Gypsy is implicit throughout 'la Gitanella'. '[I]n the words of the story's narrator the only good Gypsy is a Gypsy in jail or on the gallows' (Presburg, 1998). The archetypes we find in Cervantes are replicated in literary and pictorial contexts across the globe.

'Social categories of stranger, pilgrim, outcast, vagabond, tent dweller and nomad also receive primordial formulation in the Hebrew bible' (Peters, in Naficy, 1999: 22). From the dual exile from the Garden of Eden and God's attendance, to the Jews' forty years of wandering, forced mobility, diaspora and exile were seen as a penalty for transgressions of one kind or another. History has been principally recorded by members of sedentary agricultural societies and these settled scribes have largely depicted nomads as 'people outside the gates, as a cruel barbarian tide without culture' (Pellegrino, 1994: 103). Perhaps it is here that nomad as an ascribed pariah identity and a marker of otherness has its origins. Gypsies and nomads have historically been linked to biblical wanderings and exile and cast as intrinsically wicked and malevolent, but enviably free. Sanderson observes that 'Gypsies have often been represented as the descendants of Cain, 'cursed and doomed to be fugitives and vagabonds' (Sanderson, 1970: 1195) for all eternity. It is interesting to note that an obscure legend claims that it was a 'Gypsy blacksmith who forged the nails for Christ's crucifixion and kept or stole the fourth nail' (ibid.), and that as Christ's bodyguards it was Gypsies in their drunkenness that failed to defend him: '[I]n punishment for these sins they have been condemned to wander the earth' (ibid.).

Representations that challenge the dominant images of the Gypsy as vagabond, thief and sexual predator only really emerged in the nineteenth century (Hunter and Hierl, 2001): 'In the 19th century a new stereotype evolved to accompany the earlier one, namely that of thief and vagabond, where the *romantic* life on the road (accompanied by seductive women and flashing gold earrings), was emulated by a number of writers, artists and aristocrats who took to hiking, camping and studying Gypsy folktales' (ibid.). Over a century later, 'Gypsiophiles' such as Charles Duff (1965) and Brian

Vesey-Fitzgerald (1973), although a great deal more sympathetic and sensitive to the lives of 'real' rather than 'imagined' or 'fantasized' Gypsies, were still prone to insensitive and deterministic accounts of the consanguine dishonesty and exoticism of many, if not most, Gypsies.

'Medieval brigands' and 'Giro Gypsies': representations of 'New Age' Travellers

The first generation of 'New Age' Travellers emerged in the late 1970s and early 1980s. They are a loose group or assemblage of individuals who variously chose a nomadic life in response to material deprivation, existential discontent or, in some cases, because it offered them a perceived freedom, autonomy and a more pleasure-filled existence than life in 'straight' society. Of course, there are many more motivations and attractions than I have suggested here, and I explore these elsewhere, but it is partly because this group have *chosen* nomadism that they are, in many ways, subject to a qualitatively different kind of negative stereotyping from Gypsies. Representations of these Travellers are far less ambiguous. However, we can find parallels between representations of Gypsies and 'New Age' Travellers, not least because 'the New Age [T]raveller way of life [is] associated with a romantic view of the nomadic lifestyle similar in some respect to that of other "nomads" such as [G]ypsies and [T]inkers' (Hetherington, 2000: 15).

'New Age' Travellers are associated, in the popular imagination, with a kind of freedom that provokes profound envy and resentment. Theirs is a liberty that creates antipathy and hostility, a form of elective sovereignty that has not been granted by birthright, as has that of traditional Gypsies. Rather, this freedom has been audaciously 'stolen', 'embezzled', a freedom taken by force or stealth through the act of 'dropping out' and rejecting the values and habits of so-called 'mainstream society'. Travellers are hyper-aware of the complex nature of this hatred:

> It doesn't matter what you say or do ... most of the time people are just getting rid of their frustrations to do with their life and their lifestyle out on you because they are of the opinion that you are totally freeloading and doing nothing ... Y' know you're conditioned to work in a job that you probably don't like and you don't get much satisfaction out of ... And you're just paying bills and mortgage or whatever and you're not really getting a lot out of your life and you see these people who, to you at least, are doing nothing, and they are taking ... and you are putting money in by paying your taxes and these people are not contributing anything ... when people start expressing themselves in a different way, that isn't regarded as the 'norm' people feel threatened, a lot of people just feel threatened by anything that isn't normal to them and it doesn't matter what it is. (Jed. Fieldwork interview, France, 2002)

Hatred, then, is partly engendered by an intense envy of a perceived autonomy and lack of responsibility. In the popular imagination, the 'New Age' Traveller enjoys a life free from the stifling fetters of tax-paying, bills and 9-5 employment. S/he enjoys private, arcane and perverse pleasures and freedoms and the more s/he is allowed to experience these, the less there is for the rest of society. This is a freedom that many dream of, but few are prepared to take:

> The hippies' army wanders through the West Country like the Golden Horde of Genghis Khan ... They want to live without the inconvenience of work ... The layabouts' army, dragging around with them pathetic children with no future, are thumbing their noses at hard-working people who pay for their idleness. How long are they going to get away with it? (*Sun*, 3 June 1986)

> They don't want to work ... unfettered, they are unlike the rest of us by the chores of time keeping, clock watching, paying bills and the tedium of jobs ... they are symptomatic of something so sick, so dangerous and potentially destructive in our society ... if we allow them to invade our sense and our land they will multiply ... They are predators who make the rest of us fear for our homes, our possessions, our land ... The instinct to protect our property is more primeval, more passionate even than self-preservation ... if something is not done immediately, this itinerant army will grow and grow and one day soon, in your village or mine, ordinary decent people will retaliate ... and there will be war. (*Daily Mail*, 4 June 1986)

There is also a fear and hatred that are profoundly embodied. The Traveller is positioned as excessively physical, almost animal, unable to control its bodily boundaries. Anti-Traveller discourse is often constructed around fears about toilet habits and personal hygiene. It is infused with notions that the 'grotesque'[4] Traveller body may seep outwards and contaminate those around it. These imaginary figures have almost lost their human qualities, they cease to be a collection of individuals, they are no longer someone's sons or daughters. They become a 'thing', a single, swollen, teeming, threatening 'mass', a shadow that threatens to engulf the community and defile public space. The risk of the Traveller other requires that they are removed in order to purify social and symbolic space and reduce the potential for uncertainty and fear.

Despite the relative absence of romantic images of this group, if you look hard enough they are to be found, in traces at least. Top-Shop's 1993 fashion campaign promoted the romantic allure of 'New Age' Traveller chic – delicate waifs in army surplus boots clothed in the flimsiest apparel, too insubstantial for the wear and tear of real Traveller life. *Today* newspaper claimed that Travellers were 'a not very wild bunch of gentle desperadoes' (*Today*, 5 June 1986). Deborah Lupton notes that '[A]ll cultural classifica-tion systems have anomalies, things that do not fit, and ambiguities, things that may fit in more than one category' (Lupton, 1999: 44). Notions of risk are a cultural response to ambiguity and the transgression of symbolic and material boundaries. Simon Clarke and Anthony Moran note the inherent ambiguity of all 'strangers' and others in their examination of the work of Georg Simmel:

> [The] stranger can be best described with one word – ambiguity. The stranger has a position that we find hard to put our finger on ... the uncertainty associated with the potential for wandering leaves us in an ambiguous state of mind: is s/he one of us or one of them? ... The stranger has the characteristics of an enemy, but unlike the enemy, is not kept at a safe distance ... [T]he stranger undermines order by straddling the boundary, causing confusion and anxiety, and as such, becomes a target of hatred. (Clarke and Moran, 2003: 166, 168)

The presence of the stranger triggers, for Julia Kristeva (1991: 4), comparable unease:

> [T]he face that is so Other bears the mark of a crossed threshold that irre-deemably imprints itself as peacefulness or anxiety. Whether perturbed or joyful, the foreigners appearance signals that he is 'in addition'.

The stranger constantly bears the loathing of others. S/he is perhaps what Mary Douglas would call 'Matter out of Place', something that needs to be removed in order to restore order. The stranger pollutes social space and transgresses boundaries, both symbolic and, through continuous acts of trespass and perceived intrusion, material. When the stranger as Gypsy, Traveller or nomad enters a strongly defined communal space s/he fractures the entrenched order that prevails within that community, s/he threatens disorder and thus becomes subject to ritual control. There is a paranoid fear of the danger of strangers that manifests itself in collective public hatred and fear fuelled by media moral panics. This paranoia and fear of the sinis-ter shadowy other in the form of the itinerant wanderer is typified in Patrick Suskind's novel *Perfume* (1987). In the French town of Grasse, the townsfolk, aghast at a recent spate of gruesome killings of local women, begin to level their suspicions at the Gypsies:

> People suspected the Gypsies. Gypsies were capable of anything. Gypsies were known to weave carpets out of old clothes and to stuff their pillows with human hair and to make dolls out of the skin and teeth of the hanged. Only Gypsies could be involved in such a perverse crime. There

were, however, no Gypsies around at the time, not a one near or far; Gypsies had last come through the area in December. (Suskind, 1987: 202)

This type of paranoia is not, however, an exclusively literary anecdote, it is, for most Gypsies and Travellers, a reality that they encounter on a day-to-day basis. For the 'New Age' Traveller public mistrust, anxiety, fantasy and paranoia are sometimes sources of amusement. They will often appropriate elements of these paranoid constructs, weaving them ironically and skilfully into self-deprecating witticisms that become 'in-jokes' or parodic caricatures that can be drawn upon as a means of resisting the negative impact that such labelling can have. Occasionally, fear and anxiety provoke anger or wearied exasperation. Often, it is so outrageous in its expression it is difficult to take seriously. Whatever reaction it does provoke, one can be sure that this paranoia continually compounds the Travellers' sense of otherness, the notion that he or she is stigmatised – a folk devil, an interloper to be scapegoated, suspected and accused.

Of course, those age-old myths of murderous nomads kidnapping local maidens, snatching babies from their cradles while their unsuspecting parents sleep, of Gypsies killing their own unwanted infants have reverberated through the generations. In ours, a supposedly enlightened and rationalistic milieu, unencumbered by such superstitions, the settled world still accords some credence to the chimerical Gypsy or Traveller of old, constructed around outlandish stereotypes and myths. 'New Age' Travellers complain frequently about outrageous allegations levelled at them by a hostile public:

It was bizarre! Someone's cat had been run over in the lane outside the site. We scraped it off the road and decided to bury it in the field next door. We thought nothing more of it and then the cops pulled on to site later on that afternoon with a carload of shovels and these weird white overalls on. Apparently they'd had a call from a local bloke saying that he'd seen the Travellers burying a dead baby in the field. They dug it up! I mean Christ! They dug the fuckin' cat up! I mean the guy who made the call must've been out with a pair of binoculars or something 'cos the nearest house was a fair distance away. Can you believe it? (Dennis. Notes from conversations, 2001)

It matters not that many allegations levelled at Travellers are unsubstantiated. Even when innocence is proved, the nomadic stranger's culpability is assumed to be a given, if not for the crime in question, then for infinite possible, other, as yet uncommitted deviant acts:

Excrement was smeared in a bus shelter earlier in the week. Many blamed the gypsies, but when ... a parish councillor and staunch supporter of the fair investigated, the man who cleans the toilets revealed he had seen the culprits at work – two local girls. Even so, the council had set up a hotline for people to report any similar incidents. (*Observer*, 15 May 1994)

'New Age' Travellers, risk and moral panic

I suggested above that 'New Age' Travellers are usually subject to ascribed identities and stereotypes that are often qualitatively different from those ascribed to 'traditional' Gypsies, who are seen as more 'authentic'. Both groups arouse hostility due to the perceived threat of mobility, trespass and the transgression of spatial boundaries. However the dichotomous stereotypes of 'rogue' and 'romantic' so common to representations of Gypsies feature less frequently in representations of 'New Age' Travellers. This group has been variously labelled as thieves, 'medieval brigands' (Douglas Hurd, Home Secretary, cited in *Daily Express*, 4 June 1986), beggars, scroungers, drug-takers, dissidents and deviants. They are seen as filthy, smelly, a source of pollution. This is resonant of racist rhetoric, but there is an added dimension. 'New Age' Travellers are in the main not 'foreigners' in terms of national origins (although some may be), and pivotal notions of 'race' and 'blood' are largely absent from this particular anti-Traveller discourse. Rather, it is often a perceived threat of dirt, alien values and dubious morals and a lack of civility that causes anxiety. Travellers are the enemy within, *moral strangers*, ambiguously neither 'us' nor 'them'; they have actively chosen the status of other by 'dropping out' of mainstream society. Like the Foucauldian transgressors in the Great Confinement, they represent the fearsome irrationality, untamed deviance and perversity that lurk behind the walls of the modern psyche, the potentiality within us all.

Kevin Hetherington (2000), drawing on the work of Stan Cohen (1973), links this notion of 'New Age' Travellers as an ascribed 'risk' identity to issues of panic. Psychometric research on risk perception has indicated that risks that are 'subject to a high level of media attention arouse greater concern than those that are not, even if they are relatively rare occurrences' (Lupton, 1999: 20). Cohen argues that the misrepresentation of a factual incident or phenomenon as it really is by the mass media is a central feature of a moral panic. He situates these kinds of distortions within the category of 'media inventory' and suggests that media 'over-reporting' is characterised by lurid headlines, melodramatic vocabulary and often shocking imagery. 'News' articles relating to Travellers and Travellers' sites are loaded with histrionic overtones, inflammatory rhetoric and (Travellers would argue) gross misrepresentation. During media coverage of moral panics, the mass media perpetuate these stereotypes or 'symbolisations'. In this analysis Gypsy and

Traveller sites are represented as potential sites of deviance, disorder and consequently 'risk'. Cohen (1973: 40) contends that:

> A word [in our case, Traveller or Gypsy] becomes symbolic of a certain status (delinquent or deviant); objects (hairstyle, clothing) [vehicle, caravan] symbolize the word; the objects themselves become symbolic of the status [and the emotions attached to the status].

'Gypsy' and 'Traveller' thus become general insults loaded with negative symbolic meanings. Indeed the words 'Gypo', 'Gippo' or 'Hippy' have become terms of abuse for individuals who are perceived as dirty, scruffy or simply different. Much of the media representation of 'New Age' Travellers in particular has focused on the drain on welfare, the threat to local youths posed by their deviant lifestyle, and the travesty of the freedom that this group experience while 'decent society' has to conform to the rigidities and rituals of 'civilised' life. Anti-'New Age' Traveller discourse in the media has, at its core, a fascination with emblematic 'objects' that ostensibly symbolise the 'riskiness' and danger of Travellers. Particular kinds of vehicles and tents (Tee-pees), clothing and hairstyles, even certain geographical locations (Stonehenge and Glastonbury)[5] are symbolically linked to the 'New Age' Traveller's risky status.

> [A] snaking convoy of old painted buses, rusty cars with blanked out windows, decrepit caravans driven by men with eerily white faces ... (*Daily Mail*, 4 June 1986)

> It resembled a giant scrapheap ... thousands of smelly misfits ... adults sported shaven heads with straggly ponytails and wore filthy jeans and jumpers. Children played in the dirt with mangy dogs and even policemen held their noses as they walked by. (*Daily Star*, 29 June 1992)

These objects in themselves trigger feelings of fear and horror, regardless of whether they are accompanied by the actual presence of Travellers. A whispered sighting of a Gypsy or Traveller vehicle in a far-flung locality can provoke a wave of panic responses. Farmers rush to shore up their fields, local residents remove the heads from the taps on standpipes so the Travellers cannot collect water, Neighbourhood Watch groups call emergency meetings to devise strategic responses to the possible 'invasion'.

This public fear has manifested itself variably in terms of palpable consequences. 'Vigilante' attacks on Gypsy and Traveller sites are not uncommon in the British Isles, particularly in the late 1980s and early 1990s when public furore and media panic around nomadism were at their most intense. 'New Age' Travellers tell of incidents where they have been shot at,[6] had their homes 'burned out', and of their brake pipes being cut while they slept.[7] However, as media interest in Travellers has subsided a little, so too have incidences of these kinds of violation. It must be noted though that while violent attacks have abated, a more general and often deliberate exclusion from key services such as health, welfare, education and the labour market has persisted. Pollution beliefs and notions of risk function to regulate the boundaries of the body politic in both a material and a symbolic sense.

Electing otherness and risk

As we have seen above, Gypsies and other Travellers can be seen as archetypical others, outsiders or strangers, the pariah *par excellence*. This analysis of otherness, as an ascribed negative identity, posing risks to the normative stability, imagined 'purity' and symbolic identity of a community, group or nation, is the account that one most frequently encounters in contemporary academic discourse. However, the testimonies of many 'New Age' Travellers indicate that otherness is a fundamental aspect of their identities. Otherness and risk can, in many ways, be seen as structuring principles through which they formulate a notion of individual and collective self. Of course, it is important to acknowledge that ascribed otherness as a category of exclusion is a means of reinforcing social boundaries, of removing the other, but a resonant theme throughout my fieldwork with 'New Age' Travellers is that they actively choose to be other, to place themselves at the margins. Perhaps, then, there is a basis for a re-conceptualisation of otherness as 'Janus-faced'. It can be viewed as category of exclusion, but conversely it also provides a framework for self-definition. Otherness in this context is a symbolic rejection of 'mainstream' values and an escape attempt; a striving for a degree of separatism that entails embracing a risk identity, with all the uncertainty that entails, in order to relinquish the perceived constraints of coercive, sedentary life.

Most of the research conducted on 'New Age' Travellers has furiously rejected the otherness of Travellers (see Sibley, 1995; Martin, 2002). It is certainly the case that hatred, fear, discrimination and exclusion are byproducts of complex notions of Travellers as other, and Travellers themselves are acutely aware of this. However there is, for many 'New Age' Travellers, a profound ambivalence around their other status. Otherness is experienced as simultaneously positive and negative; these positions are two sides of the same coin. Travellers do not merely passively receive an ascribed other status, they experience it in sometimes unexpected ways.

Understanding Travellers' experiences and perceptions of otherness is vital to an understanding of the motivations of individual Travellers and the emergence of the travelling phenomenon as a whole. Many Travellers acknowledge otherness in themselves, and it is often actively embraced and cultivated. Many recognise that they are 'foreigners', 'because they are already foreigner within' (Kristeva, 1991: 14). Furthermore, 'Hatred provides them with consistency, it makes them real, authentic so to speak, solid, or simply existing' (ibid.).

> Before [becoming a Traveller] I never felt like I fitted in anywhere. I suppose a lot of the people who live on site are disaffected, but they are disaffected for hundreds of different reasons ... you just have that common bond ... you're all doing this thing ... I'd always felt marginalised, and when I moved on to site I, all of a sudden, found loads of people who felt the same as I did. I felt like I fitted in for the first time, I felt secure, far more secure, living on site than I ever had done anywhere else ... I suppose that might be a bit weird, because of the thing with the police, and never really knowing where you are going or how long you're staying but, because of the people around, you belonged ... I always thought that I was on my own and I didn't have any security and ... [I] wasn't really that confident of what I was thinking ... because I didn't really have anyone else to back me up. On site you have loads of other people who feel the same, and I grew to really love living on site ... (Jed. Fieldwork interview, France, 2002)

> You know what [being a Traveller] feels like, don't you?[8] You feel special, you feel like you belong to something really big, like a special 'club' or secret society – you are one of the privileged few. Being an outsider is partly what attracted me [to travelling] it's a real buzz ... incredibly empowering ... even people's hatred is self-affirming ... and it makes them look smaller than you ... Some people get really evangelical about it y' know ... like we were on a mission and we would be the ones who could cope in the 'last days' [Armageddon] [laughs]. I know it sounds crazy ... but when you're cruising down the road in convoy and there's a roadblock ahead ... and the sun is shining and you're part of this throng ... it doesn't matter that you're hated ... you have each other. (Max. Fieldwork interview, Spain, 2003)

However, Travellers do recognise the duality of their otherness:

> A sense of otherness, of being something which is outside the norm is both a strength and a weakness. A sense of group identity and belonging provides many people on the travelling scene with an inner strength. However, this can also lead to a naïve sense of self-righteousness, which means that many Travellers are unable to function outside of their social scene. This in itself makes Travellers a vulnerable group of people who are seen by others as people to be hated. It also means that Travellers sometimes limit themselves in terms of their expectations of themselves and each other (Loz. Questionnaire respondent, 2001)

These Travellers are aware of the disadvantages that their other status can bring, but they take pleasure in celebrating it. Attempts to cast them as 'victims' are often met with objection, denial and defiance:

> It really made me feel different to the rest of society, like, I'm not a member of society, I am a Traveller, and it's just something else entirely. I certainly didn't feel like a victim. (Kela. Fieldwork interview, France, 2002)

> But you can use that being 'outsider' to your advantage because you end up having more self-reliance, self-confidence ... ability to survive basically. So that when you're confronted with something that someone in the 'straight' world might find difficult you know exactly how to deal with it. You've got this secret advantage ... (Lara. Fieldwork interview, France, 2002)

There is no attempt to be less other; in fact, otherness is often viewed as a marker of superiority, what Hetherington (2000) calls 'a communion of the elect'. Other status is subverted, it becomes a kind of naïve narcissism. This, I hasten to add, is by no means meant in a derogatory way. On the contrary, in the face of adversity this self-confidence is deeply empowering; it enables those who are deliberately excluded, to feel that they have choice. Otherness is not merely imposed, it is chosen and in a way it 'chooses you'. Many Travellers feel that they were marked out as different prior to their becoming Travellers. Otherness is self-determination, free will, it sets you apart from something you wish to have no part in. Exteriority is uniqueness, a form of escape, it is not merely a pejorative or deprecatory marker of inferiority. This is a robust otherness, potent, dynamic and life-affirming that undergoes a profound transformation in its transmission between 'purveyor' and 'beneficiary'. Julia Kristeva (1991: 6) remarks on the introspection of the foreigner around his or her ascribed status:

> Masochistic pleasure accounts for his or her submissiveness only in part. The latter in fact, strengthens the foreigner's mask – a second, impassive personality, an anesthetized skin he wraps himself in, providing a place where he enjoys scorning his tyrants hysterical weaknesses. Is this the dialectic of the master and slave?

If we are to understand the 'New Age' travelling phenomenon and nomadism more generally, it is vital that we question dominant social scientific approaches that have attempted to cast nomads as victims. Although they can be seen, in many instances, as oppressed minorities, victim status tends to rob them of their autonomy, to make quiet the voice that is already struggling to be heard. Travellers are not merely ill-fated underdogs, nor would they wish to be seen as such. Approaches that have emphatically rejected the otherness of Travellers have done little to help us understand them or to facilitate moves towards extending their rights and status.

Greg Martin provides an example of well-intentioned 'anti-otherness' in Traveller literature. Martin likens these Travellers to Zygmunt Bauman's 'vagabonds'. He sees them as nomads 'who are on the move because they have been pushed from behind, spiritually uprooted from the place that holds no promise' (Martin, 2002). Martin notes the profound influence that structural poverty, changes to the benefit system and tough legislation on squatting had on the explosion of the travelling scene in the late 1980s and early 1990s. He identifies 'the abrogation of social rights of citizenship, which were a direct consequence of Conservative policy' (Martin, 1998: 746), and claims that without the moves towards self-help that Travellers made, they might have ended up as 'economic refugees' (ibid.). While I do not dispute this – indeed, it is an account that many Travellers themselves favour – the picture is, perhaps, more complex than Martin's explanation suggests. It is likely that some of the misinterpretation of travelling identities stems from the kinds of accounts of travelling that Travellers give to 'outsider' or non-Traveller, researchers. Travellers have suggested that they often tend to tell 'stories' that they think are most suited to public consumption.

> Well! Y' just tell 'em what they want to hear, don't you. Y' know the 'poor Traveller' stories, where we're just innocent victims of the big bad state! (Rada. Fieldwork interview, Spain, 2003)

Martin asserts that 'we must be careful not to mystify and romanticise Travellers' lifestyle[s]' (Martin, 2002). However, I would argue that much of the sociological literature on 'New Age' Travellers does exactly that. In an attempt to provide positive representations of Travellers that counter the kinds of representations I have explored above, much of the existing research on 'New Age' Travellers presents them as either unfortunate victims or noble folk heroes. Neither of these stereotypes is particularly helpful in facilitating our understanding of their multiple identities. I would argue that the 'New Age' Travellers could just as easily be viewed as Bauman's 'tourist' who 'pay[s] for their freedom [and] the right to disregard native concerns and feelings, the right to spin their own web of meanings' (Bauman, 1993, in Urry, 2001), the tourist who relinquishes certain comforts, certainties and securities and renounces particular ways of life in order to enhance freedom, autonomy and sense of belonging. These Travellers are constantly in conflict with local residents, county council officials and the agents of law and order, this is the 'joy through disobedience' (Jed. Fieldwork interview, France, 2002) that some of my Traveller friends have spoken about and it is a central constituent of their elective risk identity. It is just unfortunate that this image of a semi-autonomous agent freely choosing, and clearly enjoying, his or her own risky status is not an acceptable one. Thus it must forever be denied, or at least framed in more palatable terms.

Moreover, despite conflict with the state apparatus, suggestions that there were any clear connections between a coherent revolutionary agenda and 'New Age' Travelling is also problematic. Contrary to popular opinion, many Travellers suggest that their motivations were not explicitly or intentionally political, nor were they in any way organised. Rather, there were emergent properties of this phenomenon that were contingent and incommensurate with the needs and demands of the state. One could argue that the adoption of an outsider identity is implicitly political in many ways and this is a question I discuss elsewhere in greater depth. However, the notes below from my fieldwork diaries indicate Travellers' ambivalence about the view that their lifestyle practices constitute a coherent mode of political resistance.

Notes from the valley

My conversation with Max revealed that he saw only weak connections between travelling and any clear political objectives. Hedonism was, he said, a large element of what galvanised him towards travelling. We discussed previous pieces of research that had attempted to downplay that aspect of travelling, as it didn't make a 'good story', and the underlying asceticism in Western, Judeo-Christian culture that rendered admissions of being motivated by pleasure alone tantamount to irredeemable immorality. Max highlighted the substantiality of travelling as a viable means of escaping the 'inevitability of a stifling future' that he felt was predetermined. Travelling, he said, provided a hitherto unforeseen opportunity to be, 'in the words of one of one of my fictional heroes, "A god of your own world", part of an elite, above the rest of society'. When I pointed out that this 'escape attempt' was far from apolitical, he begrudgingly conceded that perhaps he had made a political statement of sorts but that there were no political intentions behind it: 'I mean underneath it all we all wanted to be rock stars!' Max began to discuss a kids' movie, 'Antz', which he had seen quite recently:

> Woody Allen plays the vocal role as a completely insignificant Ant. At the start of the movie he's on the psychiatrist's couch, a bit like I am now! And he's going 'The thing is, I'm just so unimportant, so insignificant, I'm just one in a million!' ... the point of the movie is he becomes a star, which is what we all aspire to ... We all wanna be lifted out of that world of sameness, and I suppose that is a part of why

I chose to do what I did ... Because I didn't wanna stay in Manchester and in my heart, I didn't wanna be just another faceless engineer that had been through University and got a nice job and hopefully found a wife that was better looking than I was. I didn't want to follow the road that I was 'meant' to go down.

Max destested the idea of being a 'sheep ... part of the flock'; he had been filled with dread at the certainty of his future and claimed that his outsider status was an inevitable corollary of the lifestyle and not something he had deliberately planned. Being part of a community was deeply important to him, but he conceived of it as more of a 'pack ... or web of diverse individuals ... who couldn't agree on anything ... We all wanted different things but we still posed a common threat.'

Becoming other: the multiple trajectories of self-marginalisation

Perhaps the sometimes conflicting testimonies of Max and other Travellers necessitate a reinvention of the concept of the political, in which resistance is no longer conceptualised by an analysis of shared 'projects' or objectives. Rather, it is the imagination of alternative becomings, change and other possible futures that disrupts social order. Elizabeth Grosz notes 'the disconcerting notion of unpredictable, disordered, or incontrollable change – the idea of chance, of indeterminacy, of unforeseeability ... seems to unsettle ... political and cultural ideals of stability and control' (Grosz, 1999: 22). The open-endedness of Travellers' futurity has 'implications or consequences that cannot be known in advance ... [T]his is a most dangerous and disconcerting idea ... an anarchization of the future ... within a politics [that] seems to revel in the idea of progress, development, movement ... [but] if the revolution can carry no guarantee that it will improve the current situation or provide something preferable to what exists now, what makes it a sought-for ideal?' (ibid.: 17). Perhaps notions of risk also stem from questions and uncertainties around a multiplicity of possible futures for 'New Age' travelling. The management and control of risk, and the formulation of effective responses to it, are, to a large extent, dependent on prediction – prediction that is problematised in the context of a lack of shared aims, objectives or 'organisational purpose' among Travellers.

Thus 'New Age' travelling can be seen as the quintessential Deleuzian assemblage, a coming together of discrete parts, which is capable of producing any number of effects. The beauty of 'New Age' travelling lies in its lack of organisation and its ability to draw into its social body any number of disparate elements. Individuals within this assemblage are not held in place by the organisation of a unity. Rather, the process of becoming serves to account for the relationships between Travellers. In becoming, one piece of the assemblage is drawn into the territory of another, transforming its value as an element and bringing about a new unity that is forever shifting.

This is a many-sided, multifaceted nomadism. For this group of Travellers there are multiple planes of intentions, meanings, motivations and attractions. These planes intersect at variable, unpredictable and sometimes contradictory vertices; and they don't always 'hang together' neatly. This is a 'braided multiplicity' (Grosz, 1999) that none the less becomes an emergent singularity, despite its contradictions. Many Travellers reject Max's notions of contingency and political 'accidentalism'. Instead, they conceived of themselves as the antithesis of law and order; as 'outlaws'[9] or 'agents of disorder'. One Traveller notes:

> When I first came on the road, there was an attitude that we were an unstoppable force (for what no one really knew), but there was a purposeful feeling to take sites, put on festivals, travel, and ultimately to cause random 'trouble' around the UK. (Lara. Questionnaire respondent, 2001)

Another Traveller reflects on this antithetical posture:

> I enjoyed being part of 'the biggest gang' and fucking off society and the establishment. I had become sick of what was expected of me as a teenager and school-leaver. I wanted nothing to do with conformity. After all, we are the 'blank generation' and living as a Traveller suits that perfectly. (Baz. Questionnaire respondent, 2001)

This, at times omnipresent, ambience of belligerence is but one tiny strand in a complex web of self-definition. As I outlined above, other Travellers suggest that hedonism was a primary motivation:

> Well ... I just went to a festival and I never wanted to go home! (Kela. Fieldwork interview, France, 2002)

> I saw Cliff Richard's 'Summer Holiday' and I thought it looked like a great laugh so I bought a bus! (George. Notes from conversations, Spain, 2003)

Myriad stories, a fluid, variegated assemblage, a 'body without organs' (Deleuze and Guattari 1988), that is a 'plane of consistency which concretely ties together heterogeneous or disparate elements' (Deleuze and Guattari, 1988: 507). Otherness is part of this process, it has a powerful affective dimension that underpins the becoming of a social body. Choosing to be outside, embracing exteriority and a risk identity is part of a transformative, transgressive venting of life that consolidates heterogeneity.

'Beat' literature is perhaps one of the most faithful literary representations of self-marginalisation as self-affirmation and resistance. Jack
Kerouac, a devout Catholic, explained that by describing his generation as
'Beat' he was trying to capture the 'secret holiness of the downtrodden ...
"Beat" connoted hobos and exhausted proletarians' (Kerouac, in Arnold,
1972: 27), outsiders who had embraced their 'other' status. Indeed, the
term 'Beat Generation' came to describe anyone behaving rebelliously or
advocating a revolution in behaviour. Some authors have suggested that
the 'Beat' movement was perhaps the transatlantic antecedent of the
'Hippy convoy' in Britain, and that the inspiration for the development of
the 'New Age' travelling scene can be found between the pages of
Burroughs, Kesey, Mailer, Kerouac and Hunter S. Thompson, where themes
of drug-induced intemperance, rootlessness and otherness are strong.

In 'The White Negro'[10] Norman Mailer (1959) explores tensions that
belie the myths of America. He examines the outlooks of a white, largely
middle-class youth striving to reject the values of their own society. 'A
society which, Mailer suggests, is trying to make everyone over in its own
image' (Bird, 1957, in Mailer, 1959: 337). The processes of rebellion, rejection and discursive and symbolic negation of 'mainstream' culture and
values, which the 'White Negro' or 'Hipster' cleave to, separate him from
the 'general ignorance' (Mailer, 1959: 343) of the rest of society. The
'White Negro'; the 'Beat', is an outcast, a transgressor, a miscreant and,
most importantly, a *self*-marginalised man, who through 'the ineffable
frissons of mental becoming' (ibid.: 342), submits to an awareness of the
absurdities inherent in modern life. Relentlessly searching for existential
freedom, the 'Hipster' is 'to divorce himself from society, to exist without
roots' (ibid.: 349). In doing so, he takes an 'uncharted journey into the
rebellious imperatives of the self' (ibid.: 339). 'Whether the [Hipster] life
is criminal or not, the central decision is to encourage the psychopath in
oneself, to explore that domain of experience where security is boredom
and therefore sickness' (ibid.). Uncertainty, unpredictability and risk are
at the heart of this rebellious otherness.

The exterior landscape, the 'square cell' (ibid.), the 'totalitarian tissues of
American society' (ibid.) offer material security, but at a cost. The synthetic
dogmatism of society imprisons body and soul; it corrupts, poisons,
cramps, limits, prevents and obstructs. The 'unstated essence of hip, its psy-
chopathic brilliance' (ibid.), which is deeply embedded in the interior landscape, can truly be experienced and thus unleashed only when the exterior
is overcome, an exterior that is 'the prison air of other people's habits'
(ibid.). Overcoming the exterior landscape of mainstream society constitutes the unfettering of desire and the negation of an exterior life-world
that obstructs and limits that desire.

These themes are resonant throughout my fieldwork with 'New Age'
Travellers, who draw sharp distinctions between a 'free' Traveller and

an 'un-free' 'straight' world. One can also find echoes of Mailer's tensions between 'square' and 'hip' society in the Deleuzian paranoid, schizophrenic dichotomy (Deleuze and Guattari, 1988: 352–423). Deleuze and Guattari observe the tensions between the paranoid world, with its insistence on centralised power, rigid social organisation and authoritarian structure, a world that is fully Oedipalised, a rigid, stable 'reality', characterised by a preoccupation with coherence, structure, security; and the schizophrenic world, characterised by looser social organisations of smaller groups with no territorial limits or hierarchical structures. These are two very different models of society and socio-cultural-political space. Nomadic space is smooth and fluid, it stands in sharp contrast to state space, which is characterised by fixity, rigidity and hierarchy. Individuals in state space are organised on its grid-like system, fixed in defined roles in a rigid hierarchical structure. The state operates through the capture of movement and the partition of space. The nomad is a way of being in the middle, or between points, the nomad is movement and change:

> The nomad [too] has a territory ... [B]ut the question is what in nomad life is a principle and what is a consequence [the nomad's] path is always between two points, but the in-between has taken on all the consistency and enjoys both an autonomy and a direction of it's own. The life of the nomad is the intermezzo. (Deleuze and Guattari, 1988: 380)

Mailer's 'psychopaths' or 'Hipsters' are the primogenitors of Deleuze and Guattari's schizophrenics or nomads; his 'squares' the definitive paranoids. Mailer's hipster others 'are trying to create a new nervous system for themselves – to shrug off the inefficient and antiquated nervous circuits of the past which strangle our potentialities for responding to new possibilities' (Mailer, 1959: 345). God, for Mailer, is located in the 'senses of the body' (ibid.). God is 'energy, life, sex, force, the Yoga's *Prana*, The Reichian's Orgone, Lawrence's "blood"' – a paradise of limitless energy and perception' (ibid.: 343), an unrestrained libidinal force. For Deleuze and Guattari, desire is less explicitly libidinal, however it is also a productive, enabling energy, flowing through all living and non-living bodies.

Mailer's 'Beats' or 'Hipsters', like 'New Age' Travellers, arouse intense fear as they try to break out of the system. They blur the boundaries that separate, what for Mailer are reasonably discreet domains, the 'inside' and 'outside' of mainstream American society. Mailer advocates challenging hegemonic culture, through an emptying out of rational and undialectical life' (ibid.: 342) and an embracing of the 'incandescent consciousness and possibility which death opens up for them ... to move 'backwards into death' (ibid.), into existential deterritorialisation. For Deleuze and Guattari nomadic deterritorialisation is also articulated as a way of challenging hegemonic cultures, of marginalising the centre. The Deleuzian nomads are 'external to each state' (Deleuze and Guattari, 1986: 49-53), they exemplify deterritorialisation. Deleuzian nomadism, schizophrenia and deterritoriali-sation and Mailer's deterritorialisation, psychopathy and the liberation of the self from the super-ego of society, are the *modus operandi* of 'New Age' Travellers. This is a rhizomatic nomadism that is random, chaotic and at times lacking in a coherent programme. It develops organically and throws out shoots and tap-roots in multiple directions.

Finally, we must be mindful when examining 'New Age' Travelling as an attempt at a *permanent* 'escape' from state space. For many Travellers, this way of life is a temporary phase, or mode of existence, that we can perhaps conceive of as liminal in itself:

> More than ever I realise that the dispossessed position I was in as a 'New Age' Traveller was one I could have changed at any time. I could have stepped back in to the dominant culture, with my white skin and forgiving family, (Martin, 2002: 52)

However, one can never erase the imprint of nomadic existence and crossed thresholds. This is a place that one emerges from utterly trans-formed. Many Travellers who do 'return' console themselves with the pos-sibility that, in returning to the system they once rejected, they also change the shape of *that* place permanently:

> Our legacy is to have changed the cultural landscape forever. (Arthur. Fieldwork interview, Spain, 2003)

Conclusion

Through an analysis of representations of Gypsies and 'New Age' Travellers I have examined their ascribed identities of otherness that are inextricably linked to notions of risk. These notions are partly engendered by their con-tinual transgression of material and symbolic boundaries and uncertainties around the possible futures for 'New Age' travelling. 'New Age' Travellers are unique in that many have actively chosen other status. However, con-trary to popular opinion, they constitute a highly heterogeneous group or assemblage. It is their otherness and risky status that, in part, consolidate and bind them, providing them with strength and a shared identity. Media moral panics help to fuel notions of risk, presenting Travellers as a group with an explicit and coherent political agenda. This is a notion that many Travellers contest, suggesting instead that their desire for escape and their elected otherness are what positions them as so 'opposite' to the state. Their otherness is acknowledged as both a source of strength and a 'weak-ness' (Loz. Questionnaire respondent, 2001). Travellers' otherness is not passive acquiescence to the very real exclusion that they face, nor are they 'victims'. Rather, Travellers view their exteriority in quite positive terms. In the context of Travellers' experiences of otherness there is a basis for a reconceptualisation of otherness. This has only begun to be sketched out in this chapter. In attempting to undertake this task one must be mindful of the very real disadvantages that nomadic communities face. This chapter is not an attempt to deny the existence of those obstacles, nor is it an attempt to do away with otherness as a category of exclusion. Rather, it is an attempt to illustrate the ways in which labels can be subverted by those at the margins, and the way that elected otherness can be used to cross thresholds to reach those margins.

Notes

1 Elsewhere in my work I explore in greater detail the cultural and affective 'attractors' that characterise the self-organising, cellular distribution of nomadic communities.
2 Gypsy music, particularly pipes and violins, is inextricably linked, in myth and fable, to corrupting erotic power. Gypsy music is extensively portrayed as hypnotic, intoxicating and potentially dangerous. It is both revered and reviled for its sublime, sinister and almost transcendent unruliness. The wild abandonment and physical and mental raptures associated with the Bacchanalian Gypsy chorus are otherworldly, pseudo-erotic, depraved and wickedly decadent. The 'New Age' Travellers' festival has also often been the focus of discourse around the corrupting influence of music and dance. I discuss this in much greater detail elsewhere in my work.
3 'Preciosa', meaning both precious and beautiful, derives from the Latin *pretium* or 'price' and can be linked to the concept of pleasure.
4 For a more in-depth discussion of the 'grotesque body', see Stallybrass and White (1986).
5 Previous sites for Travellers' festivals.
6 Annie. Notes from conversations, August 1999. A reference to an incident at Wellsborne, near Stratford-upon-Avon, where her caravan was shot at by irate locals, the bullets narrowly missing her son's head as he slept.
7 Baz. Notes from conversations, October 2001. Referring to an incident in a lay-by in Woodchester, near Stroud, Gloucestershire, in 1993.
8 Max refers to my own past as a Traveller.
9 Mack. Fieldwork interview, France, 2001
10 Mailer popularised the term 'White Negro'. However, it does not owe its origins to him. The term was used for several centuries in the West Indies to refer to the white men who established intimate relationships with their black servants and concubines (see Carmichael, 1833; Tannenbaum, 1963).

References

Arnold, M. (1972), *The Story of Beat*, San Francisco: Melton Books.
Carmichael, A. C. (1833), *Domestic Manners of the West Indies*, London: Whitaker, Treacher & Co.
Charters, A. (1997), *The Portable Beat Reader*, New York: Penguin.

Clarke, S. and Moran, A. (2002), The uncanny stranger: haunting the Australian settler imagination. Free Associations (under review).

Cohen, S. (1973), *Folk Devils and Moral Panics: The Creation of Mods and Rockers*, London: Paladin.

Deleuze, G. and Guaratti, F. (1986), *Nomadology*, New York: Semiotext(e).

—— (1988), *A Thousand Plateaus: Capitalism and Schizophrenia*, London: Athlone Press.

Douglas, M. (2001), *Purity and Danger: An Analysis of Concepts of Pollution and Taboo*, London: Routledge.

Dubois, Abbé J. A. (1992), *Hindu Manners, Customs and Ceremonies*, New Delhi: Asian Educational Services.

Duff, C. (1965), *A Mysterious People*, London: Hamish Hamilton.

Grosz, E. (ed.) (1999), *Becomings: Explorations in Time, Memory and Futures*, New York: Cornell.

Hawes, D. and Perez, B. (1995) *The Gypsy and the State: The Ethnic Cleansing of British Society*, Bristol: Policy Press.

Hetherington, K. (2000), *New Age Travellers: Vanloads of Uproarious Humanity*, London: Cassell.

Hunter, K. and Hierl, S. (2001), *WESS Newsletter*, 25(1), Fall, Association of College and Research Libraries.

Kearney, R. (2002), *Strangers, Gods and Monsters*, London: Routledge.

Kristeva, J. (1991), *Strangers to Ourselves*, London: Harvester Wheatsheaf.

Lemon, A. (2000), *Between Two Fires: Gypsy Performance and Romani Memory. From Pushkin to Post-Socialism*, Durham, NC: Duke University Press.

Lupton, D. (1999), *Risk: Key Ideas*, London: Routledge.

Mailer, N. (1959), *Advertisements for Myself*, Cambridge, MA: Harvard University Press.

Martin, G. (1998), 'Generational differences amongst New Age Travellers', *Sociological Review*, 46(4).

—— (2002), 'New Age Travellers uproarious or uprooted', *Sociology: Journal of the British Sociological Association*, 36(3).

McKay, G. (1996), *Senseless Acts of Beauty: Cultures of Resistance since the Sixties*, London: Verso.

—— (1998), *DIY Culture: Party and Protest in Nineties Britain*, London: Verso.

Naficy, H. (ed.) (1999), *Home Exile, Homeland: Film, Media, and the Politics of Place*, London: Routledge.

Pellegrino, C. (1994), *Return to Sodom and Gomorrah: Bible Stories from Archeologists*, New York: Random House.

Presburg, C. D. (1983), 'Precious exchanges: the poetics of desire, power and reciprocity in Cervantes' *La gitanilla*', *Bulletin of the Cervantes Society of America*, 18(2), pp. 53–73.

Sanderson, S. (1970), 'Gypsies', *Man, Myth and Magic: An Illustrated Encyclopedia of the Supernatural*, Vol. 43.

Sibley, D. (1995), *Geographies of Exclusion*, London: Routledge.

Stalybrass, P. and White, A. (1986), *The Politics and Poetics of Transgression*, New York: Cornell.

Suskind, P. 91987), *Perfume*, London: Penguin.

Tannenbaum, F. (1963), *Slave and Citizen*, New York: n.p.

Urry, J. (2001), 'Mobile cultures' (draft), http://www.comp.lancs.ac.uk/sociology. Accessed 13 May 2002.

Yelka, R. (1912), *The Origins of the Gypsies*, London: Pearce & Price.

11
Trusting Aggression: The Siennese War Machine as Social Capital

Lita Crociani-Windland

Introduction

This chapter examines the unique civic structure of Siena, in the central Italian region of Tuscany. This structure evolved over centuries in connection with the horse race known as the *Palio*. The city is divided into 17 *'contrade'*, or wards, which function as independent city-states within the city. Each has its own administration and officials, territorial boundaries, social activities and rituals such as baptisms, weddings and funerals. Their existence is inextricably linked to the *Palio* race.

The extraordinary endurance of this system, whose origins can be traced back to the twelfth century and whose present form has changed little since 1729, merits wider sociological consideration. The focus of research for this chapter is the link between affective dynamics and the development of the present structure as a pivotal source of social capital. The study focuses on the relationship between affective dynamics and normative structures in their historical development using Deleuzian models to elucidate these dynamics. The ability of the system to adapt is also explored, as this is seen as a major contributor to its stability. The overall picture is one of a community that has achieved a balance between being and becoming, where identity and intensity can coexist. Social cohesion and social capital are enhanced, while aggression is contained without resorting to repression. The *Palio* is not just the race, but a way of life – in the words of the Siennese, *'Nel Palio ci sta sempre tutto'* ('Everything can always be contained in the *Palio*').

Siena's reality is inextricably linked to the *Palio*. Being at the race, of course, is the best way to appreciate its affective charge and vitality. However, for those unable to be there, the following account of the August 2000 race may go some way towards getting them acquainted with this extraordinary mixture of custom and event, ritual and affective impact, aggression and containment. Further information and historical analysis follow this section, so that the complexity and intensity of the *Palio* may

be understood in relation to the city's present structure, history and identity. The political and civic culture that has evolved around the *Palio* has
fostered a high level of social participation and cohesion. This can clearly
be viewed in terms of social capital generated by, and of great benefit to,
the Siennese population.

Two days at the race – August 2000

It is 15 August, the culminating date of the heat of summer. The crowd is
gathering in the late afternoon in the *Piazza del Campo* to watch the
general trial race (*prova generale*). The shell-shaped piazza gives a dramatic
setting at this time of day. Half the square is in the shade, while the other
half is bathed in the golden glow of late afternoon sun. The heat of the day
is held in the conch of beautiful medieval and Renaissance buildings lining
the square. Bodies give off heat in waves that are almost palpable. The
crowds of the *contradaioli* are colourful, the neck scarves displaying the
colours and emblems of their *contrada* are proudly worn and waved to
salute their own horse and jockey. Occasional chants break out, especially
between rival *contrade*. The melody is the same, based on a very simple
tune; the words are unique to each area, singing the worth of each. The
simple, unvarying tune is so embedded in people's ears that even as a relative outsider I can hear it in my head as I write. I can also hear childhood
memories of improvised wordings being chanted at a rival and responded
to by them – '*botta e risposta*' as they would say, which is hard to translate
with the same impact, literally hit and reply, accusation and counter-accu-
sation, but with far more cheek, immediacy and less self-consciousness, like
playground teasing. There is held tension. The racing of the horses today is
just to get them used to the circuit and the crowds, who for their part need
the occasion to demonstate their support and build up expectation and
hope. The race tomorrow morning will be even more restrained, as the
jockeys cannot run the risk of tiring or injuring their horses just before the
race proper. But the 15th is not over yet, as it is customary, after this dress
rehearsal, for the *contrade* to gather in strength for a common meal. My
English guests and I are lucky enough to find our way to eating in the *Onda*
(Wave) *contrada*, among hundreds of local diners. The street is festooned
with the *contrada* flags and fancy electric lights shaped in the dolphin
image, part of the Wave's emblem. About halfway down the street is a
podium decked in blue and white, the colours of the area, as well as flags
and microphones. From the podium, about halfway through the meal, the
dignitaries of the *contrada* give an amplified public speech. The main substance of the speech is to commemorate the efforts of the people in making
this August yet another opportunity for the area to be bathed in victory.
The relative strengths of horse and jockey are commented on, as well as
other more emotive reasons to see victory as a real possibility. The main

examples of these that I thought worthy of mention were the celebration of a child's drawing portraying the Wave's horse as winner, spontaneously (or so it was said) produced and presented to the *contrada*'s captain, and the presence of the *Palio* cloth painter for this race among the *contrada*'s guests. These events were taken as auspicious signs for the outcome of the next day's race. Following the speech is the singing of the area's anthem. A local family seated opposite us exemplify the sense of seriousness and belonging that surround the *Palio* for the Siennese. Three generations are gathered, from grandparents to baby; they all know the anthem and take great exception when some chatting is going on during the singing.

It is the *Palio* day at last; it's hot and the streets are crowded. Today we choose a position in the shady part of the square that has the best viewing point for filming. From where we stand we can see the downward slope between the bend known as *San Martino*, a treacherous bend lined with mattresses, and the entrance to the Council building where the horses, jockeys and race officials have their headquarters until the moment when each will find its position for the race itself. It is in the sunlit part of the square. The majority of the *contradaioli* groups prefer to have a view of the *mossa*, the 'move', or starting point of the race, as the starting order is considered most important in determining the outcome of the race. The beginning of events is signalled by the closing of the public gate, the clearing and sweeping of the circuit, followed by the ceremonial ingress of the historical pageant. It is a slow affair, highly ritualised, which lends *gravitas* to the proceedings and heightens the tension of expectation. The Council's musicians and the drummers of the *contrade* provide the musical element; overall it is a simple, yet atmospheric soundtrack. In spite of Siena's internationally renowned music academy, *Accademia Chigiana*, situated a few hundred metres away, the music of the *Palio* is based on simple rhythms and melodies, which do not require extraordinary musical prowess from their musicians, while giving a distinctly medieval and martial atmosphere. But all the pomp and ritual are discarded when it comes to the race itself. The explosion of a firecracker and beating of drums summon the horses to the starting point, the jockeys salute the authorities with the whips they are issued with as they leave the Council building's courtyard and proceed to the *mossa*.

From the moment the horses and jockeys appear, the tension really begins to build. The horses are nervous and there is jostling as the mayor announces the order of start, unknown till the last minute. Only now can the jockeys properly assess their chances and engage in the final alliances, negotiations and bribes to give themselves the best chance and their enemies the worst. Thus the jostling goes on as the horses line up between the ropes set at the starting point. One horse is always allowed to have a running start, its entry into the roped area will signal the start of the race, but it is the unenviable job of one man, known as *mossiere*, to declare the start valid or invalid. This is the highest moment of tension in the whole long build-up to the race. The alliances engaged in prior to the race can be activated at this point; the jockey behind the ropes can decide to take advantage of a badly positioned horse, to disadvantage a particularly strong horse or its own, or an allied *contrada*'s enemy, for instance. The jockeys are of necessity entrusted with having to judge how to use the situation to their best advantage. Trust, however, is lived as a contradictory reality in this case, as jockeys are known to be open to corruption. Thus 'the word of the jockey is sacred' is one saying; *'fantino, assassino'* (jockey, assassin) is another. This time there are only two false starts, but it can sometimes take a long time before a valid start. The race is fast – just over a minute and it is over. A very intense minute though – several jockeys are thrown, most at the infamous *San Martino* bend. The *contrada* of *Leocorno* (Unicorn), one of the smallest, is the winner. The *Leocorno contradaioli* immediately jump every barrier to claim the *Palio* cloth for themselves, surround and embrace the horse and jockey and lead them in triumph back to their headquarters.

As the action moves from the square following the winning *contrada*, people slowly file out. We decide to find a place to eat and are lucky enough to find seats in a restaurant on the border of the *Leocorno* territory. We are interrupted in our meal by the sound of drumming and singing as the winners celebrate and boast their victory by processing with the *Palio* cloth along the central streets and the square. This goes on late into the evening. For us the *Palio* is over; for them it is the start of celebrations culminating in a 'victory dinner' at which the victorious horse presides.

The next few days are filled with 'post-mortem' analysis of the events. One of the loveliest rationalisations for the unexpected victory of *Leocorno*, who had not been tipped as having either the best horse or jockey, was the sharing of information surrounding the personal lives of the winning jockey and the one with the best reputation in the square this time. The favourite jockey's wife, it transpires, had just left him for another, while the winning jockey is deeply in love and about to get married, and had dedicated his race to his future wife. Popular verdict: he had to win and it is not surprising that the other didn't.

The race in modern times

The race has changed little in the last 300 years. The fundamental rules for the modern *Palio* were determined in 1721 (Civai e Toti, 2000: 58). The horses run the circuit of the square three times at a furious pace. The horse wins with or without jockey. The jockeys ride bareback and use the whip indiscriminately against each other and each other's horses (*Regolamento per il Palio*, 1998, articles 42, 57, 84). Today's *Palio* is run by professional jockeys, mostly from outside the Siennese territory, who ride horses assigned to the *contrade* by drawing lots. At each race only ten *contrade* will be allowed to run; these are also selected by drawing lots. The seven remaining will run the next race by right, while there will be some lucky three, again drawn by lots, who will run twice in that year to make the numbers up to ten in both races.

On 29 June and 13 August a number of horses will be presented in the square to be selected for the race. As they will be assigned to the *contrade* by drawing lots, the main considerations will be to ensure the health and suitability of the horses to the race circuit and to select a relatively homogeneous group of ten horses. The next phase is the assignation of the horses selected to the *contrade*. The mayor presides over the drawing of the names of the horses and the *contrade*, which are held in separate urns and drawn by two children wearing page's costumes. The captains of the *contrade* and other officials concerned with the organisation of the race act as witnesses to the draw. The whole proceeding is eagerly followed by the waiting *contrade* members, whose *barbareschi* (grooms) immediately take charge of the assigned horse to escort it, along with *contrade* members, to 'the horse's house', as the *contrade*'s stables are often called.

Six trial races are run prior to the *Palio*. Their purpose is to assess the potential of horse and jockey, rather than being part of the competitive event. The order in which the horses are lined up is determined according to a fixed formula. This formula is based on the original order of extraction in the drawing of lots for *contrade* and horses, the original numbers assigned to the horses before these proceedings, and their inverted orders. This can be read as a sanctioning or an institutionalising of the role of chance, or luck, in the proceedings.

The structure of the city and its relation to the *Palio*

Since 1729 the city has been divided both territorially and in its civic constitution into 17 *contrade* (Civai e Toti, 2000: 59). These are 17 small states, 'most hated friends or most loved rivals amongst themselves' (Magi, 1996: 2). Each has defined territorial boundaries, its own population by birthright, its own elected governing body, its own headquarters and museum, recreational and welfare activities, which have in the past included educational activities, and above all, its own identity, tradition and history. Their relationship to the city council is strong and direct, founded on mutual consent and administered through a system of normative and administrative measures. These concern the organisation of *Palio* matters, as well as matters such as urban development and planning, cultural and social activities. The city council's administration is the recognised central authority in matters concerning the *Palio*, and in turn it recognises the *contrade* as fundamental entities for the urban community (*Regolamento del Palio*, 1998, Art. 9). This reciprocal relation is based on convention and lies outside the jurisdiction of Italian law (Magi, 1996: 12–14), as does the internal hierarchical structure of the *contrade*.

Each *contrada* elects its own dignitaries. The *Priore* is its highest officer. The appellation has a religious connotation. In fact, one of the *Priore*'s roles is to minister to the baptism of children born in that area in a ceremony which will officially sanction their group membership. He will also preside at weddings and funerals, deal with administration, represent the *contrada* in dealings with the city council and meet the other *Priori* to form what is known as the *Magistratura delle Contrade*. Its role is to coordinate all the *contrade*'s activities, to promote and safeguard the common interests, to settle any controversy and ultimately to be a reference point for the seventeen populations.

The territorial division of the *contrade* cuts across all social classes and differences. Membership of the group is able to override these possible sources of antagonism and jealousy within the *contrada* and unite the people round a common identity. Contributions of time and/or money are voluntary, yet members freely provide financial support, raising very substantial sums to secure every *contrada*'s dream: a win. Social activities are supported by voluntary contributions of work.

All my interviewees vouched for a social control function of the *contrade* in relation to moral codes and deviance. According to the deputy head of police, Siena has low levels of crime, mostly clustered round offences against property and, in spite of the aggression present in the system, serious crime against the person is rare.

The *contrade* and the celebrations preceding the race

Each *contrada* has its own symbol and colours, which appear on its flags and in the medieval costumes proudly worn at the time of the *Palio*. A solemn procession from the cathedral to the *Piazza del Campo* precedes the race, lasting about two hours and accompanied by the beating of drums and skilful flag displays. This is a ritual display of Siena's past and present, which has undergone various changes over the centuries. To some extent conscious intervention has always been dictated by the need to curb the ebullient and at times chaotic creativity of the population coexisting with a tendency to mirror in image form the reality of the time. The mid- to late 1800s saw the settling of the pageant as '*passeggiata storica*' (historic walk), as it is now known: a celebration of the history of the city, set in a mythical medieval reality, oriented towards 1400, a period of much social and political in-fighting. In 1928 the final touches were added, while regular renewal of the costumes is still an ongoing necessity, leading to gradual transformations in our time (Civai e Toti, 2000).

The ceremony of the *ceri* (candle offerings), dating back to 1200, has been incorporated into the *Palio* days' celebrations, with some simplifications. The order of procession associated with the original festivities of the

Virgin of the Assumption in mid-August has been absorbed and expanded to include later historical events. The strong presence of the past in this ritual parading clearly points to the importance of historical events in the formation of Siena's present social structure and identity.

A brief history of Siena and the Palio

The tradition of a horse race in the city of Siena is so long lived that it is hard to determine a precise moment for its inception. The first documentary sources refer to a linear race ending at the old cathedral of *San Bonifazio* and go back to the eleventh century (Falassi, 1998: 9). From 1200 the goal of the race was moved to the new cathedral and the *Palio* became the culmination of the imposing festivities of mid-August dedicated to Our Lady of the Assumption. On the eve of her festivities the residents of outlying areas under Siena's jurisdiction would be required to pay homage in the cathedral to the Virgin and to the leaders of the Siennese republic by bringing tributes of money and wax, according to their means. A proportion of this wax and that given by all institutions of Siena would be melted into one large ceremonial candle, while each citizen between 18 and 70 years of age also bore a candle (Civai e Toti, 2000). This religious and political rite was also an occasion for Siena to become an 'open city'. During the festivities trading in a wide variety of goods and itinerant services abounded, all manner of entertainers crowded the streets bedecked in flower garlands, festoons, tapestries and flags. Amnesty was granted to exiles and arrests suspended (Falassi, 1998: 9).

By 1200 Florence and Siena were the major powers in the region, vying for supremacy and engaging in alliances with other pretenders to local power. It is to be noted that Siena's prominence was disproportionate to its material and geographical resources and was largely based on its importance as a centre for financial activities. The hostility between the two cities came to a head in 1260, with the battle of Monteaperti. This battle endures in popular memory to this day. The Siennese forces were inferior to the Florentines, yet managed to defeat them in one of the bloodiest and most celebrated of medieval battles. It was on the eve of this event that the Siennese gathered *en masse* in the cathedral to beg the Virgin Mary for protection of Siena and its independence, symbolically offering her the keys of the city and electing her their queen (Bowsky, 1981). Already at this time there is a mention of local military companies headed by representatives of the *terzi*, or thirds of town, a geographical partitioning of the city around its three hills, once also important administratively. A contemporary chronicle records that as the people congregated on the roofs to follow events the night prior to the battle, a diffuse light spread over the Siennese side of the battlefield. This was interpreted as the mantle of Mary, as the Virgin watching over her people (Civai e Toti, 2000: 36).

It is from this moment that Siena's dedication and devotion to the Virgin, always portrayed enthroned with Child, becomes established in a tradition unbroken to this day. The coinage of this time bears the mark *'Sena Vetus Civitas Virginis'* (Siena Ancient City of the Virgin) and Siena's painters establish an enduring tradition in icon paintings to the point that Siena is second only to Rome for its collection of images of Mary (Civai e Toti, 2000: 37). This dedication is important and we shall return to it later.

Plague hit the city in 1348, decimating its population and bringing to an end the golden period of good government and political and social stability under the 'Government of the Nine', to which we shall return. The period that followed up to 1559 was troubled and culminated in the loss of Siena's independence. Five main political factions vied for power at one point, preferring the continual strife among the factions to the hegemony of one group. This dynamic is reflected in the *Palio* race to this day (Civai e Toti, 2000: 44). The only despot Siena has known also belongs to this period, though his reign was brief. The conflict with Florence forced the Siennese to seek foreign assistance around 1500 from Charles V of Spain. This resulted in the Pope's ire and an insufferable Spanish subjugation. In 1552, the Siennese rebelled by destroying the Spanish-built fortress and expelling their garrisons from the city. Spain responded by forming an alliance with Florence, while Siena allied itself with France. The war that ensued was very hard and ended with an eight-month siege of Siena. The city fell in deed, but not in spirit. Two hundred noblemen and their families with 400 citizens left to attempt to transfer the seat of the Republic of Siena to Montalcino. In spite of their successful reorganisation and some military success, in February 1559 Siena's fate was sealed by the foreign powers of France and Spain in the treaty of Chateau Chambresis, which assigned the Republic of Siena to Cosimo dei Medici, Duke and Lord of Florence (Civai e Toti, 2000: 45). Florence's reign lasted until the Risorgimento, in the 1800s (see also Falassi, 1998).

During the 1400s another form of festivity was added to the ones associated with the religious and political ceremonies of mid-August. On the day following these, hunting games, bullfights and the fighting game known as *pugna* would be organised by the now more distinguishable entities of the *contrade* in the *Piazza del Campo*. From this time come the first records of animal emblems being used to represent groups of citizens, who would build elaborate floats in the shape of animals, often depicting complex allegories. In Falassi's words 'Totem against ferocity, myth against reality' (Falassi, 1998: 13). These types of activities were not unique to Siena; there are records of them in Florence and other towns (Civai e Toti, 2000: 74; see also Falassi, 1998). The character of these additional events was secular and aggressive, leaning towards the carnivalesque.

The transition of the race from its traditional 'long' (*alla lunga*) or linear course to its present circuit of the main square followed an interesting displacement of celebrations of Mary and a gradual blending of sacred and secular traditions already in existence. In the mid-1500s the devotion to the small statue known as the *Madonna di Provenzano* overtook the mid-August Feast of the Assumption. The *Madonna di Provenzano* had been damaged by Spanish gunfire during the period of Spanish protection/oppression and had since then become a symbol of resistance against both Spain and, by inference, Florence, and also a refuge for the community's republican identity. A grandiose basilica to house the precious image was erected between 1594 and the next two decades. The *contrade*, while the church was still under construction, began to pay homage to the effigy on the feast of the visit of Mary to her cousin Saint Elizabeth, traditionally on 2 July. It is on this date that from this point on the activities organised by the *contrade* in *Piazza del Campo* will be focused. In addition to the fighting and hunting games, donkey, ox and horse races make their appearance in the square (Civai e Toti, 2000: 43, 54).

2 July 1656 is the date commonly accepted for the definitive structure and regular recurrence of the *Palio alla tonda* (meaning circular), which managed to combine popular passion and aristocratic tradition (Falassi, 2001: 72). The custom of covering the perimeter of the square in soil, to create a surface for the horses to race on, can be traced to this time. From 1671 the city's authorities began to involve themselves with the race. They formulated a series of regulations in terms of both its organisation and of much needed codes of behaviour for the *contrade*. The system of drawing lots to assign horses for the July race on the feast day of SS. Peter and Paul (29 June), for instance, was instituted then and remains unchanged. Over the course of the century more and more normative refinements were put in place and the social functions and autonomy of the *contrade* more clearly established (Civai e Toti, 2000: 54).

On 16 August 1701, by instigation of the *contrada* of *Oca* (goose), a second *Palio* race was run that year, though until 1802, when the city's authorities took financial responsibility for it, this *Palio* date depended on individual *contrade* initiatives and economic constraints (Civai e Toti, 2000: 56). (Falassi, 1998: 20, gives 1774 as the year the municipality ratified the two races.)

In spite of earlier normative measures, the litigious nature of Siena's citizens, as well as practical problems such as the presence of 17 horses in the square, demanded intervention. The figure that most stands out as an individual in the history of the *Palio* is Violante Beatrice di Baviera, a princess from the Medici household, herself in conflict with some members of the court of the Medici, a conscientious worker and good listener. The first governess of Siena, she took charge in 1717. In 1721 Violante's edict set out the structure that has guided the *Palio* to this day, and in 1729 another edict established the territorial boundaries of the *contrade* once and for all. Six *contrade* were suppressed. These are still represented in the historical pageant preceding the race.

Self/Other – subjugation/independence

From the historical outline given above several dynamics begin to emerge. What Freud called 'narcissism of minor differences' (Freud, 1973) is pervasive in the dynamics of the region. (See for confirmation the humorous book by Santini, 1998, *Toscani Contro Toscani* [*Tuscans against Tuscans*].) This phenomenon is common among adjacent social groups and is characterised by feuding and ridiculing of each other. (For instance, the British dislike the French; the Welsh dislike the English, and so on.) Difference becomes a useful tool for self-definition and social cohesion, while aggression is displaced outside the group onto an external enemy or rival (Crociani-Windland, 2003). This kind of relationship is endemic and enduring, especially in this region, though not exclusively. Umberto Eco's *Baudolino* (2000), whose protagonist comes from medieval northern Italy, imaginatively exploits this theme. Bergson refers to this phenomenon in relation to the war instinct as an innate predisposition, which endows us with an instinctive resistance to other social groups in inverse ratio to distance. He humorously sums up by stating that '*Homo homini deus* and *Homo homini lupus* are easily reconcilable. When we formulate the first, we are thinking of some fellow countryman. The other applies to foreigners' (Bergson [1935], 1986: 286). In the history of Siena, which we have had to limit to the period most relevant to the development of the *Palio* itself, we can see this continuous feuding with Florence in particular as an important part of the development of the city's identity and culture (Crociani-Windland, 2003).

   The threat from Florence was real, and Siena's most glorious period coincided with the victory of Monteaperti and the period of the 'Government of the Nine' (1287–1355), which was composed of three representatives from each *terza* of town. The 'Government of the Nine' introduces us to an important set of dynamics to be explored in this chapter, namely the role of normative rules in the development of the system to the present. The main characteristic of this government is its total commitment to the *civitas* and the common good. This is expressed in the way that all areas of culture are given support and encouragement, but always in subservience to the civic ideal of *bonum commune*. We owe to the 'Nine' the magnificent Council building and the *Piazza del Campo*, made up of nine segments (Bowsky, 1981). But, more germane for our present purposes, the main principle introduced by the 'Nine' is the supportive intervention of the authorities in all matters concerning the local community, to the point that it has been a matter of common agreement for some time that the Siena of today is in large measure the result of their politics and actions. The nine representatives were in office for only two months at a time, but participated in almost every area of civic activity, thereby acquiring accurate and constant information about the city's affairs and the population's views. There is a close relation between religious and political powers before and during this period as eloquently expressed in the August celebrations to the Madonna. However, the 'Nine' successfully challenged both the authority of the Church and that of the nobility, while strongly promoting the development of the already established university (Bowsky, 1981).

The plague that hit the area in 1348 caused great loss of life as well as administrative chaos in the region. In 1355 an uprising led by the wool workers (*lanaioli*) and butchers' guilds (*carnaioli*), who took the occasion of a visit to the city by the Emperor Charles V to air their discontents, led to the dissolution of the 'Government of the Nine' (Bowsky, 1981). This may be seen as one of the first examples where the influence of external authority led to a negative outcome in issues of litigation. A prolonged period of internal antagonisms and political instability followed. This created the need to seek again the help of higher power in dealing with the threat from Florence, which, as we have seen, led first to subjugation to Spain, then France and finally what was most feared became reality, subjugation to Florence. From this outline two different experiences of the intervention of authority in Siena's history come into view. In the case of the 'Nine' the intervention is experienced as enhancing the welfare of the community, while the following interventions ultimately damage and rob the city of its sovereignty and independence. Clearly the relation between Siennese and authorities would be an interesting issue from then on. In fact, this may explain the present relationships between local council administration and *contrade*, which are both formal and structured, yet lie outside national legislative powers.

In spite of having to bend to reality and accept outside rule, Siena's spirit of independence was never totally defeated. Thus, while the Florentine authorities establish the seat of power near the cathedral and dispossess the Siennese of their religious and political August celebrations by demanding their transfer to Florence's cathedral, a new symbol is found in the damaged Madonna di Provenzano, with its grand new site of worship. There is a spirit of ingenuity and creativity displayed in this ability to adapt to adverse circumstances, as well as a light-heartedness and playfulness. Siena's indomitable sense of identity endures thanks to its flexibility. The attitude is one of problem-solving, taking stock of what cannot be altered, while finding lateral solutions where loopholes can be found. This creative capacity speaks of an ability to transcend the limitations of reality and is also evident in the development of the race.

Issues of aggression, from both internal and external sources, and its containment appear as central to Siena's historical development, as well as a capacity to adapt creatively to circumstances. These are visible in the continuous risk of subjugation to outside powers and in the internal dynamics of the late fourteenth and fifteenth centuries, which is when the *contrade* appear in their more individualised guise. However, before going any further, let us introduce the theories that will offer us tools for further elaboration. In order to arrive at a theoretical understanding of Siena's affective dynamics and their relationship to *contrade* formation and their animal symbols we will draw mainly from the work of Deleuze and Guattari (1992).

War and state machine – identity and becoming

Deleuze and Guattari (1992: chs 12 and 13) speak of state and war machines. The war machine is of a 'rhizomic nature'. Weeds like ground elder, as well as some bulbs, are rhizomes. Hard to eradicate, they re-emerge as soon as your back is turned, and take over any derelict land, in an underground horizontal interconnectedness (Deleuze and Guattari, 1992: ch. 1). Their reproduction is asexual. Like liquids they are bound by gravity yet are able to flow and colonise any space available at the surface. The war machine thus is both a natural phenomenon and an irrepressible one. The state machine is of an arboreal nature; a central axis orders its vertical growth into ramifications both under- and above ground, yet its branches and roots are subordinated to a central stem and root. It relies on a central point of reference from which to depart and return.

Siena's dynamics of internal cohesion and external competition and aggression correspond to Bergson's description of a society close to the natural order (Bergson, 1986: 266). The systems of shifting alliances, the connectivity of state and religion described could appear as an early stage of development of intellectual activity over instinctual dynamics, or in other words the partial assimilation by the state of the war machine. The early celebrations to the Madonna of the Assumption contain all the ingredients that society is made of: the religious and political power as well as the military companies and population groups loosely identified round territorial denominations as precursors of later *contrade*. Ritual elements and public games in the form of horse races are part of the event. The connection between the military companies and the developing *contrade* has been a matter of great debate over time. The military companies came under the jurisdiction of the captain of the people (an officer of the medieval commune) for a good part of Siena's history (Bowsky, 1981: 38–42). These played a very important part in the life and defence of the city in medieval times and the *contrade* have been seen as a natural development issuing from them. The emblems of the companies present in their territories are to this day displayed on the *contrade* flags. However the *contrade*, which were originally territorial units of unequal size, as subdivisions of the administrative districts of the *terzi* (Bowsky, 1981: 12), do not automatically replace or displace the companies and, until the mid-1600s, the authorities address administrative and legislative measures relating to the safety and to the administration of territories indiscriminately to both (Civai e Toti, 2000: 51). For a time there appears thus to be a division and coexistence of two related war machines: the military companies assimilated by the state and acting on its behalf in defence of the city and in organising the population's clans, and the *contrade* organising themselves slowly in relation to territory and the development of public games (Bowsky, 1981). This development is fascinating as an example of what Deleuze and Guattari describe as the exteriority of the war machine to the state organisation. 'Collective bodies always have fringes or minorities that reconstitute equivalents of the war machine – in sometimes quite unforeseen forms – in specific assemblages such as building bridges or cathedrals or rendering judgements or making music or instituting a science, a technology' (Deleuze and Guattari, 1992: 366). Had they known Siena, no doubt they would have added instituting games. The relation of the *contrade* to the military companies is beautifully encapsulated in Barzanti's statement, 'the contrade are the party dress of the military companies' (Civai e Toti, 2000: 52). We come back to playfulness and ingenuity, but also to a deep relation between aggression and fluidity, resistance and opposition to centralised control and creativity. These are affective dynamics to which we shall turn in the following section. Affect, in Deleuze and Guattari's use of the word, 'is a prepersonal intensity corresponding to the passage from one experiential state of the body to another' (Deleuze and Guattari, 1992: xvi) and is fundamental to war machine dynamics. This intensity is indeed present in Siena in ample measure, presenting a challenge of containment of its negative potential.

Overall, it seems clear that the local state machine is able to impose an arboreal dimension on the city's structure for periods of time, yet fringes of affect are always present to re-territorialize the edges and lead to change. The wider state machine, the external authority pressing in on the city, appears either in the form of imperial rule or takeover from Florence, threatening Siena's own particular 'Enjoyment of the Thing' (Žižek, 1993). The war machine is fundamentally anti-state, it coexists and competes with the state machine in a perpetual field of interaction (Deleuze and Guattari, 1992: 360), it is suffused with a mercurial quality, which allows it to metamorphose and create new forms as alternatives to the established order at the edges of the state apparatuses of identity, bands, and kingdoms (Deleuze and Guattari, 1992: 361). The 'Nine' are defeated by the external and internal war machine in the form of rising violence in the whole region after the plague and a general rise in levels of internal unrest and violence. 'The onslaught of the Black Death in 1348 seems to mark a watershed. The plague struck Siena with exceptional severity, and the disorder and confusion that it left in its wake combined with a lack of available police to make the problem of police protection even more difficult and to strain the commune's every ability' (Bowsky, 1967: 15). Finally, popular insurrection, again a manifestation of the internal war machine, brings in the external state machine in the shape of Charles V, to defeat the 'Nine'. The internal vacuum of leadership allows war machine dynamics to invade government structures. Factions vying for power take the place of arboreal ordering. In the midst of conflict there is the brief, but none the less real, appearance of the only despot Siena has ever known, Pandolfo Petrucci, in the first years of 1500. This leads us to explore another aspect of the State and war machine, namely the dynamic vertical axis of interaction.

Becoming-animal, affective-infective dynamics, war and hunting

The dynamic of war machine or affect is peripheral, mostly unconscious, while the state is an apparatus of identity. Deleuze and Guattari's concept of becoming is hard to capture in words or in brief, yet it must be attempted. The emphasis in their work is to disengage thinking from structure in order to identify underlying processes of movement (movement is in this case to be understood in the Bergsonian sense of flow, rather than a plotting of distances between points), on both the horizontal plane of multiplicity and the vertical plane of becoming and transformation, while keeping an eye on differences of quantity and quality (Deleuze, 1991). This is what makes it possible to find similar dynamics in disparate manifestations of life, without losing focus on their individual particularities. What we have spoken of so far in terms of the relationships between state and war machines are relationships where each has maintained a degree of separateness in relating, causing alternations where the war machine has produced instability and forced change and the state has responded by reestablishing control. From a group relations perspective this could be likened to a catastrophic change dynamic where unconscious affect surfaces and disrupts conventions and assumptions, while offering an opportunity for new elements to be available for conscious transformation and inclusion. This is a condition of mutual exchange, a relatively actualised dynamic of symbiosis, where the movement between affective or unconscious levels of a social or individual entity and the intellectual or conscious faculties are only able to work together in a time frame of alternating movements. The dynamic is not dissimilar to Bion's (Bion, 1963; Eigen, 1993) interpretation of the passage between paranoid-schizoid and depressive positions as a recurrent mutual interaction, rather than applying specifically to particular stages in life or pathologies. In Siena when the war machine in its most basic biological aspect of infectious plague, combined with the human war machine of violence and dissent, the local state machine was overwhelmed. If through an effort of imagination we shift beyond 'sheer intellectualism confusing the thing itself with its expression or symbol' (Bergson, 1986: 269), and reconnect with its movements, dynamics of infection and symbiosis, becoming-animal, becoming-girl, becoming-child, disturbing or creative lines of flight (Deleuze and Guattari, 1992: ch. 10) suddenly become visible. Then Siena's next historical passage becomes more understandable.

After the fall of the Nine, Siena falls into internal disarray. The war machine has overpowered the internal state organs of structure and sought a new pairing with the external state machine, the emperor. However, this pairing does not address the fundamental internal conflicts, being too removed from local reality. And in fact this is the situation, factions engage in conflicting relations close to tribal warfare. Internal restructuring processes are hampered, instinctual aggression is preferred to structure. Clan segmentation processes take hold (Durkheim and Mauss, 1963). This phenomenon is indeed visible in Siena as part of the early formation of the *contrade*, which continues to be their tendency, also marked by continual territorial disputes, until 1729. This is a dynamic of infection by affect of internal organs of identity. Affect as multiplicity acts like a virus, affecting the social body. People relax into pack mentality, into becoming-animal (Deleuze and Guattari, 1992) and affective intensity (Massumi, 1996). The conditions are right for a pack leader to arise. It is not surprising that a Pandolfo Petrucci could suddenly turn up. In the aggressive dynamics we see a displacement of the affective realm, of un-actualised multiplicity (Deleuze and Guattari, 1987), the instinctual pole invading the realm of emotional differentiation. The concept of otherness has turned in on itself and can appear as a stimulus for division rather than cohesion, and overwhelm linking processes.

The development of the *contrade* has thus far been analysed as the war machine escaping appropriation by the state, creating a civilian clustering around hunting and fighting games, having a relation to the military companies. There appears to be a connection between the rising violence in the late period of the 'Nine' and the individuation process of the *contrade* and development of the games, and even more significant a coincidence between these dynamics and the *contrade*'s assuming of animal emblems or totems. The emblems could then be seen as symbols of the dynamic of affect infiltrating the human sphere or, in Deleuze and Guattari's terms, their becoming-animal (1992: 243). This phenomenon, which when I had approached it using more traditional theories of totemism left all sorts of questions unanswered and an unnecessary and unhelpful discrimination between primitive and modern states of being, is the more striking here in terms of a Western culture at a sophisticated stage of administrative and economic development.

The games reflect the same dynamic. What had been originally provided by the ruling classes as entertainment for the masses, the original linear *Palio* race, will eventually be re-established by the *contrade* as their own, but not without a detour. Games in fact initially reappear as bullfights or hunting games in the main square. They reflect the relation to the animal, man and animal in an interconnectedness of affect and competition. What is truly fascinating is that violent games of fist-fighting (*pugna*), wooden sword and lance fights (*elmora*) and stone-throwing battles (*battaglia de' sassi*), that had been practised throughout the region during most of medieval period, and some still later (Bowsky, 1981; Dundes and Falassi, 1994), gradually give way to games between men and animals, fought by far smaller groupings undergoing a process of identity formation.

There is something in this that speaks of the power of playing out the issues, as if the people can move beyond the process of infection by affect by giving expression to what is happening, acknowledging both the becoming-animal nature of the social dynamics of the time and the need for new apparatuses of identity. Without repudiating this passage of becoming, the dynamic of predator and prey is re-enacted. The *contrade* assume animal totems, yet move away from fully actualised aggression between humans. From the moment of the reappearance of the games in the main square, previously much feared by the 'Nine' as possible seeds of popular uprisings (Bowsky, 1981: 119), there is a gradual shift in the games from hunting to horse racing. While hunting portrays a becoming-animal, a conflictual, yet very close relation of human and animal nature, with man poised at the instinctual or affective pole of his own being, the passage back to horse race portrays the animal as selfless carrier of the human. The horse becomes the most trusted protagonist of the event, able to win on its own and having to be ridden 'naked' – no embellishments or riding tack are allowed. The horse is a symbol of body, of animal nature in man, carrying the human in movement and blessed in the *contrade* churches before the race.

The becoming-animal is now a line of flight, that is, a movement between different orders of reality (Deleuze and Guattari, 1992), in a vertical axis still capable of fluidity, connected with the animal, or we could say, the biological roots of existence, but able to transform itself further. In the fluidity are retained elements of virtuality (Massumi, 1996), or unactualised potential, and therefore of vitality and creativity. Aggression is diverted into a composite of ritual and game. This composite is creative enough to become a container for the various aspects of both state and war machines, as well as the religious element. The negotiated compromise between conflict and competition of the modern race (Crociani-Windland, 2003) reflects this ability to acknowledge conflictual dynamics, allowing them expression, while diverting them towards a third element of desire, namely the *Palio* banner dedicated to the Virgin.

Becoming-woman, becoming-child, play and creativity

As already mentioned, the origins of the modern *Palio* are associated with the new worship of the *Madonna di Provenzano* in July, after the

Florentines took over the August celebrations of the Madonna by trans-
ferring them to Florence. In the light of the previous analysis it should
clearly be no coincidence that it was the *contrade* that reintroduced the
horse race tradition from the grass roots (a significant term, in view of
the rhizomic nature of the war machine), and furthermore incorporating
new aspects, such as the extraordinary floats associated with their animal
identities and the extravagant costumes, which found a definite style relatively late. They also re-established the connection between the race
and worship. Looking at Siena's reality, it is impossible not to be struck
by the consistency of its devotion to the Madonna, which far exceeds
that found in other Italian cities. As we have seen, Mary has been the
queen of the city since 1260 and each race is dedicated to her. In Siena's
iconography the Madonna is always represented with child, enthroned
as majesty, sometimes in the act of nursing. The Siennese Madonna is
virgin, nourishing and regal. It was also the first Florentine governess of
Siena that was able to give the *contrade* and the *Palio* much needed legislation. These laws allow plenty of room for what would be considered
irregular elsewhere, yet hold sufficient order for things not to regress
into a becoming-animal.

Dundes and Falassi (1994) have analysed the *Palio* and Siena's connection to the Madonna from a psychoanalytical and anthropological stand-
point. Their analysis views the *Palio* as an initiation rite for young males.
The presentation of candles is seen as a symbol of phallic offering to the
Virgin, with whom the girls in turn can identify themselves. Their work is
thorough, detailed, backed by a huge wealth of observation and draws from
a Lacanian and Freudian tradition. Before obtaining a copy of their book I
had also considered similar ideas in relation to Siena. Yet I was struck at the
time by the concept of the desire of the woman as essential to the formulation of the Oedipus complex. This led me to question the aspect of virginity, so fundamental to the Catholic cult of Mary. Mary's virginity is in
seeming contradiction to the concept of the mother's desire and sexuality.
From an Oedipal perspective this aspect remains a mysterious peculiarity of
Catholic faith. However, viewed in the light of Deleuzian theory, a new
interpretation becomes available. If we think of the concept of rhizomic
asexual reproduction, all sorts of symbolism associated with the Madonna
take on a different connotation. The concept of virgin motherhood
becomes a symbol for rhizomic asexual reproduction and its close connection to the instinctual or war machine aspects of Siena's dynamics becomes
more transparent.

Deleuze and Guattari's work is well suited to capturing aspects of
becoming. For them every becoming is first and foremost a becoming-
woman. Becoming-woman has nothing to do with the literal being a
woman, but with a capacity for openness and transformation. For them
love is a becoming-woman of the man (Deleuze and Guattari, 1992:

275–7). This has to do with receptivity, with a permeability of boundaries, which is a molecular event. 'It means extracting ... the particles, the speeds and slownesses, the flows' (ibid.: 277), it means finding an ability to modulate oneself in response to otherness. 'The girl and the child do not become; it is becoming itself that is a girl or a child ... the girl is a becoming-woman of each sex, just as the child is the becoming-young of every age' (Deleuze and Guattari, 1992: 277), the Madonna and child as symbols of becoming.

In Siena the becoming-child is re-enacted in the *Palio* through various customs. The winning jockey is referred to as '*il cittino poppante*', 'the suckling child' (Dundes and Falassi, 1994). This gives relevance both to becoming-child and to the possibility of drawing nourishment from one's source. The winning *contrada* becomes the child of the city, its members parade after the victory carrying or sucking dummies, while the area that has waited longest for a win acquires the nickname of 'granny'. Thus a connection is made between youthfulness, nourishment, innocence, vitality and victory in the race. The whip the jockeys are issued with at the start of the race is made from the elongated penis of a suckling calf (Dundes and Falassi, 1994). Our animal nature, youthfulness, nourishment and sexuality are thus all paradoxically embodied simultaneously.

'*Nel Palio ci sta sempre tutto*', 'In the *Palio* everything can always be contained', as the old Siennese saying goes.

Conclusion: Social capital, trust, risk and uncertainty

Siena is a very particular example of Italian civic society. It is notable that the concept of social capital was first developed by Putnam (1993) from study of regional devolution processes in Italy, which clearly highlighted the importance of civic traditions to the success of democratic processes. From the concluding chapter of the book it is clear that 'social context and history profoundly condition the effectiveness of institutions' (1993: 182). Analysis of the historical development of Siena's civic structure fully supports their point and its corollary Tocquevillian view that 'democratic government is strengthened, not weakened, when it faces a vigorous civil society' (1993: 182). Civic society emerges from the analysis as founded on horizontal networks of association able to generate social capital. This, within the context of the Deleuzian theories used, can be viewed as the affective war machine aspect of society, whose potential excesses are moderated by an arboreal state machine. In Siena the *contrade* and their citizens form the vigorous civil society that strengthens government. Within this reality war and state machine approach one another with a double gesture of acceptance and challenge. Siena's citizens accept their dependence, but never uncritically. Local government accepts the *contrade's* independence, but also its responsibility to be arbiter among them for the overall common good. The importance of the reciprocal interaction and tension between civic society and institution, also highlighted in Putnam's last chapter, clearly emerges from the above analysis of Siena's dynamics. In a similar double gesture, trust and cooperation are developed among *contrade* members united by a common goal and identity. Mistrust and aggression are spared from the group by being projected onto its rival *contrade*.

Trust in Siena is a deep trust in the body and animal nature, powerfully symbolised by the revered figure of the horse, the only protagonist of the *Palio* deemed unequivocally selfless. There is a trust in attachment and dependency, symbolised by the Marian iconography. But the trust is not naïve, and is able to comprehend and contain the negative potential of these aspects, while enjoying their affective charge. This can be seen in the positive acceptance and inclusion of very real physical elements of risk to horse and jockey during the race and the psychological risk of injurious defeat for *contrade* members (the painful side of attachment), which are fundamental to the enjoyment of strong affective and emotional tension. The role of uncertainty in the *Palio* is also acknowledged, accepted and built into the system. The custom of drawing lots, as we have seen, is an integral part of the proceedings leading up to the race. While people will do anything, fair or foul, within their power to secure a win, it is accepted that ultimately Lady Luck will have her way.

The themes of trust, risk and uncertainty feature strongly in today's debates. The focus on one or other of these themes, however, tends to underplay their interconnectedness and common source. The common thread underlying them is 'not quite knowing' and the difference between them is fundamentally a difference in our appraisal of them. It is not knowing that fuels both the dread and the excitement associated with risk, while uncertainty is a weaker, but possibly more debilitating and hard to sustain aspect of not knowing. Trust could be seen as the antidote to the other two, abandoned in our time in favour of abstract systems supposed to be able to safeguard us from having to live with not-knowing. Present trust in systems is as naïve and uncritical, as would be absolute denial of negative human tendencies towards corruption and deceit. It also implies a sacrifice. We sacrifice affective intensity and social capital. Trust is eroded; risk is sought through the pursuit of danger sports. Gang warfare and ethnic conflict mar our cities. International conflict rears its ugly head. Uncertainty in economic markets is an ever-present aspect of life. Is it possible that the denial of the limit to which it is possible to control and know has not managed to provide us with a safer and more trustworthy society? Would it not be better to 'learn to embrace what we cannot grasp' (Campbell, 1999: 210) and by adopting a more trusting gesture, try to appreciate a little risk and uncertainty? Critically, of course.

A note on method

Data regarding Siena and the *Palio* have been obtained through a triangulation of data gathered through fieldwork, documents and interviews within a qualitative research design. Generally, I have given preference to referencing easily available documentary sources, when the same evidence has arisen from different areas of inquiry. Italian is my first language and birth, and family bonds in the area have greatly facilitated research. I have undertaken all translation, in the light of previous professional experience in this area. My thanks go to all who have shared with me their knowledge, time and passion for the *Palio* and Siena.

References

Bergson, H. ([1935] 1986), *The Two Sources of Morality and Religion,* Notre Dame, Indiana: University of Notre Dame Press.

Bion, W. R. (1963), *Elements of Psychoanalysis,* London: Heinemann.

Boundas, C. V. (1993), *The Deleuze Reader,* New York: Columbia University Press.

Bowsky, W. M. (1967), 'The Medieval Commune and Internal Violence: Police Power and Public Safety in Siena, 1287–1355', in *The American Historical Review,* LXXIII(1).

—— (1981), *Medieval Italian Commune: Siena under the Nine 1287–1355,* Berkeley: University of California Press

Campbell, T. A. (1999), *Getting to Know Waiwai,* London: Routledge.

Civai, M. and Toti, E. (2000), *Palio-La Corsa dell'Anima,* Siena: Edizioni Alsaba.

Coser, L. (1956), *The Functions of Social Conflict,* London: Routledge & Kegan Paul.

Crociani-Windland, L. (2003), 'What Can't be Cured, May be Enjoyed', *Organisational and Social Dynamics,* 3(1), London: Karnac Books.

Deleuze, G. (1991), *Bergsonism,* New York: Zone Books.

Deleuze, G. and Guattari, F. (1992), *A Thousand Plateaus: Capitalism and Schizophrenia,* Minneapolis: University of Minnesota Press

Dundes, A. and Falassi, A. (1994), *La Terra in Piazza,* Siena: Nuova Immagine Editrice.

Durkheim, E. ([1915] 1971), *The Elementary Forms of the Religious Life,* London: George Allen & Unwin.

Durkheim, E. and Mauss, M. (1963), *Primitive Classification,* London: Cohen and West.

Eco, U. (2000), *Baudolino,* Milano: Bompiani Editrice.

Eigen, M. (1993), *The Electrified Tightrope.* Northvale, NJ: Jason Aronson.

Falassi, A. (1998), *Palio – The Colours of Siena.* Siena: Comune di Siena.

—— (2001), in *L'Immagine del Palio* Siena: Monte dei Paschi di Siena.

Freud, S. (1973), *Civilisation and its Discontents,* in the Standard Edition of the Complete Psychological Works of Sigmund Freud, Vol. 21, London: Hogarth Press.

Gigli, S. (1996), *Il Palio di Siena,* Siena: Stefano Venturini Editore.

Grassi, V. (1973), *Le Contrade di Siena e le Loro Feste-Il Palio Attuale,* Vol. II, Italy: Edizioni U. Periccioli.

Lévi-Strauss, C. (1962), *Totemism,* London: Merlin Press.

Magi, P. (1996), *Il Palio Dentro e Fuor,* Firenze: Bonechi Ed.

Magrini, D. (1986), *Il Palio Verso Dove?* Italy: Ed. Periccioli.

Marchionni, R. (1992), *I Senesi a Monteaperti,* Italy: Roberto Meiattini Editore.

Marzucchi, M. (1998), *Le Contrade di Siena,* Pistoia: Industrie Grafiche Pistoiesi.

Massumi, B. (1996), *The Autonomy of Affect* in *Deleuze, a Critical Reader.* Oxford: Blackwell.

Monte dei Paschi di Siena, *Cenni storici.* Siena.

Putnam, R.D. (1993), *Making Democracy Work – Civic Traditions in Modern Italy,* Princeton, NJ: Princeton University Press.

Regolamento per il Pali (1998), Siena: Comune di Siena.

Santini, A. (1998), *Toscani contro Toscani,* Italy: Maria Pacini Fazi Editore.

Simmel, G. (1955), 'Conflict', in *Conflict and the Web of Group Affiliations,* New York: Free Press.

Storia e Costumi delle Diciassette Contrade di Siena (1980), Italy: S.E.A.B.

Watson, S. (1998), 'The Neurobiology of Sorcery: Deleuze and Guattari's Brain', *Body and Society,* 4(4), London: Sage, pp. 23–45.

Žižek, S. (1993), *Tarrying with the Negative,* Durham, NC: Duke University Press.

12
Trust and Uncertainty in a Settler Society: Relations between Settlers and Aborigines in Australia

Anthony Moran

Introduction

The recognition that 'trust' is a crucial feature of any well-functioning liberal democracy has been a staple of political theory since the early 1960s when books like Almond and Verba's *The Civic Culture* (1963) made their first impact. Long before that, 'trust' was at least implicitly important for political philosophers and social theorists concerned with concepts of social order, especially as society moved from tradition to modernity (Mitzal, 1996: ch. 1). The concern with 'trust' has had a dramatic revival in the work of Robert Putnam (1993, 1995, 2000), with his emphasis on the importance of widespread civic engagement for developing and sustaining trust among neighbours and in relation to the political system as a whole. Related work on the concept of 'civil society' as an important area of non-state interrelationships fundamental to the successful functioning of free democratic societies has been gaining ground in the last decade and a half (see Keane, 1998). Most of this literature is concerned with generalised trust within liberal democratic communities considered as cohesive, or poten-tially cohesive, societies of equal citizens (but see Varshney, 2001). This chapter is concerned with relationships of trust across Australia's racial divide, between settler and indigenous Australians.

For much of Australia's history, relations between the majority settler population and its indigenous peoples have been profoundly shaped by distrust and uncertainty. These cognitive and affective states, felt and expe-rienced on both sides of the colonial divide, have risen and fallen in inten-sity with changed circumstances. In this chapter I view the relationship between settler and indigenous peoples in Australia through the lens of a concern with trust and ongoing uncertainty. The issues are complex, as are the diverse forms of engagement (and disengagement) between indigenous and non-indigenous people, in both the past and in contemporary Australian society. Nevertheless, it is argued that the potential for distrust between settler and indigenous communities is the legacy of colonialism.

A brief history of trust between settler and indigenous Australians

Distrust and uncertainty were chronic features of early colonial society where two vastly different social realities were brought together through invasion (in 1788), and where conflict over use of land soon resulted in bloodshed, starvation, disease and defeat for Australia's indigenous peoples. While some contemporary eighteenth- century chroniclers (Tench [1789], 1996), and some historians (Clendinnen, 2003), provide evidence of examples of trust and friendship between early settlers and Aborigines around Sydney, these experiences were soon undermined by the harsh realities of colonisation. With the exception of certain remote areas, by the end of the nineteenth century settlers were in such a position of overwhelming power and control that questions of trust and uncertainty between settlers and Aborigines seemed distant memories. The land and its original peoples had been 'pacified'. Observation, rumour and scientific and racist speculation led many to believe that Aborigines were a 'dying race' for whom, if anything ought to be done, all that could be done was to 'smooth the dying pillow' (McGregor, 1997).

To the extent that 'trust' was a feature of social relations between settler and indigenous peoples – for example, through employment relations on the large pastoral properties upon which Australia's economic prosperity was built during the nineteenth and early twentieth centuries – this was shaped by the gross imbalance of power. Settler landowners and employers related to indigenous people on the basis of a 'morally indecent trust' (Mitzal, 1996: 146) rooted in their confidence in their superiority, and in their economic and coercive power. Though there were better and worse experiences on missions, stations and reserves, the same can be said of them. Trust was shaped by grossly disproportionate power relations, and this gave rise to physical and emotional abuses. There were, of course, decent authority figures at these places of Aboriginal containment, and strong relationships of trust, care, friendship and mutual respect were sometimes forged. For some Aborigines these places became refuges against the abuses of settler society, and strong feelings of home and belonging developed (Attwood *et al.*, 1994). At other places authorities were tyrannical, and Aborigines lived lives closer to penal incarceration. The limited trust of local Aborigines, based on the belief that government or the Crown had reserved for them certain lands in perpetuity, was undermined in the late nineteenth century, and even more spectacularly in the twentieth, as governments continued to play with Aboriginal lives in accordance with settler agendas far removed from Aboriginal desires or consent. Lands were sold off or reclaimed, missions and stations were closed or abandoned as government policies shifted (see Read, 1988; Brock, 1993; Goodall, 1996).

The twentieth century saw a gradual recuperation of the indigenous population. This changed the conditions of trust and uncertainty between settler and indigenous Australians, and raised important new issues and questions. From the 1960s there has been a rejuvenation of indigenous culture and a reassertion of indigenous identities. This has challenged settler Australians to rethink their relationship with indigenous Australians. To some extent, there has been an active attempt by governments, organisations and individuals to create new conditions of trust between non-indigenous and indigenous people. At the same time, some settler Australians express a profound distrust in the whole direction of indigenous politics since the shift away from assimilation.

Policies of assimilation gradually replaced policies of protection and segregation from about the 1940s onwards. The missions, stations and reserves that had emerged during the nineteenth century as a solution to the Aboriginal or 'native' problem gradually declined as repositories for desperate indigenous populations. Aborigines moved into cities and towns, or swelled the ranks of the fringe-dweller communities at the edges of towns, along riverbanks and railway sidings, and near rubbish tips. Assimilation was, in part, designed to find a solution to Aboriginal alienation from Australian society, and to raise the Aboriginal standard of living and level of participation in the wider society. Many features of assimilation policies have been rightfully condemned, but one should not lose sight of the more positive impulses that they engaged with and represented. Governments, for example, actively campaigned to encourage white communities to accept Aborigines into their midst as equal human beings and as citizens (Haebich, 2000: ch. 7; 2002). This was often paternalistic, and contained implicit or explicit negative assumptions about Aboriginal culture, communities and identities. On the other hand, assimilation drew upon humanitarian impulses and emphasised that Aborigines, too, deserved to reap the benefits of Australia's postwar affluence. Rather than being left in poverty and excluded from mainstream life – from education, employment, housing, services and social participation – on the fringes of Australia's towns and cities, Aborigines should be brought into the nation. Apart from managing growing Aboriginal communities, through assimilation governments were attempting to build trust between separated communities. On this level, one would have to conclude that government to some extent failed, and in some cases produced the opposite. Aborigines frequently point to the assimilation period as a time when governments believed that it was right to steal Aboriginal children from their parents, when their lives came under intense government surveillance, and where governments intensified their efforts to destroy Aboriginal identity once and for all.

To the extent that new forms of trust between settler and indigenous communities developed during the period from the 1930s to the 1960s, the churches, the many associations, leagues, committees and friendship societies devoted to Aboriginal causes – most, though not all, with mixed Aboriginal and non-Aboriginal leaderships and memberships – played a crucial role. These were the 'bridging' forums of social capital championed by theorists of civic engagement. As the 1960s gave way to the 1970s, some of the most important of these associations, such as the Federal Council for the Advancement of Aboriginal and Torres Strait Islanders (FCAATSI), fractured under the pressure of Aboriginal calls for greater communal autonomy, indigenous leadership and indigenous rights (Read, 1990). This development coincided with, and reflected, the emergence of a more militant, confident and creative indigenous political movement headed by astute and articulate indigenous political leaders. This movement has, since this time, fought for Aboriginal land rights, and other forms of indigenous cultural rights, for forms of autonomy, self-determination and self-government (Attwood, 2003).

Self-determination, land rights and trust

The precarious nature of trusting relations between settlers and Aborigines is apparent in the slow-burning settler resistance to the granting of Aboriginal land rights since the late 1960s. Aboriginal land rights have never been popular with settler Australians, and uncertainty about this development has sometimes spilled over into panic about what Aborigines might 'really' want and claim. Australia has two kinds of Aboriginal land rights. The first is the form legislated by governments at both state and federal levels since the late 1960s. The second is native title.

Legislated Aboriginal land rights were a response to Aboriginal protest and justice claims, and were linked to the winding back of government and religious Aboriginal missions, stations and reserves from the 1950s onwards. The most famous of these are the Pitjantjatjarra lands in South Australia, and the extensive (if economically insignificant) land given back to traditional owners in the Northern Territory under the Aboriginal Land Rights Act (Northern Territory) 1976. Though these were controversial for some political leaders (especially in the Northern Territory), commentators and mining interests, the remoteness and apparent economic insignificance of the areas meant that they did not become a major concern for most Australians. This changed, however, when the Hawke Labor government was elected in 1983 on a platform that included a plan to legislate nationally for Aboriginal land rights. The proposed national Aboriginal land rights legislation met resistance from mining and farming interests, the political interests of the states, and a fear in the community that 'backyards' were under threat from Aboriginal claims. Communal fears about threats to non-Aboriginal land title were enflamed by advertising campaigns by the mining industry, and by strong opposition and exaggerated claims from conservative political figures and commentators. In the face of public polling that suggested that Aboriginal land rights were unpopular with the public, and with strong resistance from a state Labor government in Western Australia, the Hawke government backed away, claiming the public was not ready for the proposed legislation (Libby, 1989).

Native title claims date from the Mabo judgment of 1992. The decision of the High Court in *Mabo* v. *the State of Queensland* (No. 2) on 3 June 1992 was a significant legal, moral and symbolic victory for Australia's indigenous peoples.[1] It changed the parameters of debate on Aboriginal land rights considerably. The country's highest court gave legitimacy to the concept of traditional indigenous rights in land. It refuted the claim that *terra nullius* applied to Australia, and made legal the concept of native title. This altered the ground from which land rights could be pursued by indigenous groups. Aboriginal plaintiffs now had a legal basis on which to pursue land claims in the courts. For settler-Australians the implications were also significant. An important narrative concerning the creation of the Australian nation throughout the continent was undermined (Attwood, 1996). The Mabo case had publicly focused attention on the ambiguous nature and legality of the settler possession of the country, and raised the possibility that the property rights of some of the original owners might still exist in accordance with the common law. The Native Title Act of 1993 (hereafter NTA), negotiated and carried through by the Keating Labor government, set up a National Native Title Tribunal to manage and adjudicate native title claims.

An intense political crisis, which drew a response from broad sections of Australian society, was provoked by the High Court's decision in *Wik Peoples* v. *State of Queensland and Others* of 23 December 1996. With four judges in favour and three against, the High Court ruled that, in principle, native title could coexist with pastoral leases, to the extent that the former did not interfere with the activities provided for as the conditions of the latter. The reaction from conservatives, including some federal and state political leaders, was immediate. Calls for legislative overturning of the decision quickly followed the ruling. Conservative anger at the High Court's handling of the issue was palpable. The four-to-three ruling seemed to add to the sense of uncertainty and to the anger of many conservatives. Some claimed that the ruling was unworkable and that the judges, in abdication of their duties, had handed the Australian population what they could not, themselves, satisfactorily resolve. Representatives of mining companies and pastoralists actively pressured the Howard government, elected in March 1996, to 'resolve uncertainty' by extinguishing native title on pastoral leases and by making other changes to the NTA.

In response, the Howard government released a Ten Point Plan setting out how they would deal with the 'uncertainties' raised by the Wik decision. Howard's Ten Point Plan included: more stringent testing of the right to make native title claims (the registration test); a sunset clause limiting all new native title claims; the removal of the right to negotiate over mining on pastoral leases, and a diminution of that right elsewhere; and the extinguishment of native title under certain pastoral leases, or possibly by stealth through the upgrading of certain activities on such leases, under the 'primary production' definition, which would interfere with many native title rights and activities not interfered with under the normal pastoral lease conditions. Some of these changes had been canvassed by the Howard government in 1996, under plans to amend the NTA, i.e. before the Wik decision had been handed down.

One of the more striking features of the public debate surrounding Wik was the call for certainty, and in a related way, for a simplification of the complexity of land title that Australians faced because of the history of colonisation. The call for certainty from pastoralists, miners and conservative leaders began almost immediately after the Wik ruling. The doubt over what Aboriginal native title would mean for settler Australians was experienced by some as an intolerable burden, resulting in the simplistic call for its wholesale removal from the national equation. At one point early in the negotiations over his Wik amendments, in April 1997, Prime Minister Howard grew tired of the difficulties involved in reaching a settlement between all affected parties, and threatened to extinguish native title completely on pastoral leases which, he argued, would be the simplest thing to do and would provide the most certainty for pastoralists and miners. The delicate question of the 'certainty' of Aboriginal claimants in relation to their lands was carefully avoided. Two months earlier Howard's deputy Tim Fischer called for legislation to overturn the High Court's decision and to extinguish native title on pastoral leases, a position both he and John Howard were forced to retreat from for legal and monetary reasons.[2]

Examining the Wik decision itself, it is less than apparent where the 'uncertainty' of pastoralists, let alone other settler-Australians, came from. The majority ruling clearly stated that while native title could coexist with pastoral leases, where the pastoral interest came into conflict with native title interests, the pastoral interest would prevail.[3] This was reiterated time and time again in the public domain by political figures, indigenous leaders, the legal profession, journalists, academics and other commentators; and yet the call for certainty became the driving ideological element of the debate. Though there were exceptions, many pastoralists and mining representatives displayed little trust in Aborigines to handle the issues fairly within the new post-Wik context.

The Wik amendments to the NTA passed in 1998 were widely perceived within indigenous communities as an example of governments overriding the small victory indigenous peoples had managed to achieve through their direct engagement with the 'white man's law'. They seemed to prove yet again that the law, parading as a neutral instrument, was there for the convenience of settler communities.

Both legislated and native title forms of Aboriginal-controlled land have been the subject of controversy, especially when governments and mining companies have wanted to exploit such land for its rich mineral deposits, or to develop the nation's infrastructure. Under each category of land rights the Crown retains ultimate sovereignty and has retained the right to negotiate with, and ultimately overrule, indigenous opinion and interests if these are deemed to conflict with the 'national interest'.

In addition to Aboriginal land rights, Australia has various forms of legislation covering Aboriginal heritage and sacred sites, and legal and political processes in place to deal with issues surrounding these as they arise. These forms of recognition of specific indigenous rights and concerns have always been controversial, with non-indigenous interests claiming that either the protections are unnecessary in 'modern' Australia, or casting doubt on the legitimacy or veracity of indigenous claims of sacredness or significance. From the 1970s onwards it has been a common complaint that indigenous people claim significance or sacredness for an area only if they can see the prospect of compensation or other income from mining companies, governments or developers. Such voiced doubts are, at least in part, symptomatic of a deep distrust of Aboriginal motives in an era that has seen a resurgence of Aboriginal culture and identity, and a drift away from the assumptions about the disappearance of Aboriginality through assimilation.

The era of Aboriginal land rights, native title and other forms of cultural recognition has brought the distrust and uncertainty rooted in Australia's unresolved colonial history to the surface, and serves to illustrate some of the ongoing impediments to the building of relations of trust between the majority settler and minority indigenous communities. The questions of legitimacy are far from settled. Unlike New Zealand, Canada or the US, Australia has never adopted treaty arrangements in its dealing with its indigenous peoples. Flawed as these regimes have proved to be in those other jurisdictions, they at least imply the legitimacy of indigenous clans, groups or tribes as political communities. There has been, of course, some form of recognition of political legitimacy involved in the legislative and native title responses to Aboriginal land rights, and in the setting up of land rights councils and representative bodies like the Aboriginal and Torres Strait Islander Commission (ATSIC). But this has been both piecemeal and tentative.

During the 1980s the Hawke Labor government opened debate on the signing of a treaty with Aborigines. Like the aborted national Aboriginal land rights initiative, the treaty was never really pursued by government. Though Hawke was initially a strong advocate for a treaty or 'compact', this also foundered amid doubts about its implications, including possible compensation. Some conservatives, including the future prime minister, John Howard, were strongly against the idea of a treaty, claiming that it was a nonsense and divisive to suggest that a nation should sign a treaty between its own people.

The period of assimilation called for forms of trust based on a shared humanity and shared national belonging. The post-1970s era of self-determination calls for a more complicated and uncertain form of trust between differentiated communities with different relationships to Australian history, lands, and the Australian state, and with different claims and potentially different aims. The language of nationalism has been reinvented by some in an attempt to accommodate these indigenous claims. By stressing new forms of unity and new understandings of common interests, this new nationalism attempts to maintain and enhance trust, and to inoculate the settler population against distrust of indigenous motives and claims. The search for new forms of national unity is one way of maintaining trust, through emphasising common interests even in the midst of differences. Discussion of indigenous rights, and notions of distinctiveness and separation, even for those who support such rights and notions, typically gravitates towards a kind of national framing. This calms and lessens the fear and suspicion that often attends relations between political communities like nations in the international arena. If Aborigines are Australians, even if Australians of a special kind, then it is assumed that all at least have their nationality in common and are fundamentally committed to the same national community. This is also why the concept of Aboriginal sovereignty is so difficult for settler Australians to accept. The same is true for self-determination which, when it is argued for by settler Australians, typically assumes that it is self-determination of a kind ultimately limited by the nation. These forms of limitation of sovereignty and self-determination are not accepted by some indigenous people, or by indigenous political organisations like the Aboriginal Provisional Government.

The state, trust and civic engagement

When thinking about the conditions of trust between non-indigenous and indigenous people in Australia today, one is faced with a conundrum. Writers on trust and civic engagement refer to the importance of thick networks of interrelationship between individuals, and between small and larger groups. Trust emerges out of such thick civic engagement. This realm of relationships is sometimes thought of as if it had a life of its own, independent of state or government (Skocpol, 1996). What then of relations between indigenous people and the rest of Australia? The anthropologist Jeremy Beckett (1989) has observed that, throughout Australia's history, its indigenous peoples have predominantly engaged with the rest of the society *through* the avenue of the state. In this case, the state is seen as a kind of conduit linking indigenous people with the (largely) settler nation that encloses them, but from which they maintain varying levels of social distance. In other words, indigenous people have never really moved out of a colonial relationship with the Australian nation-state. The level of trust for the rest of the society felt by indigenous people is tied to perceptions of the intentions and actions of government and its agencies. I am going to complicate this abstract political formulation later by stressing that indigenous people are at the same time and in many cases living *within* white society, and even within partly non-indigenous family relations. But the abstraction is a useful heuristic for understanding levels of separation and distinction that persist, and inform, trust relationships.

Aboriginal people, more than most, are alienated from mainstream civil society in Australia. This is reflected in ongoing forms of exclusion. Indigenous people have much higher unemployment and incarceration rates, and are in much poorer health. Aboriginal unemployment rates across Australia are at about 20 per cent compared to 6 or 7 per cent for non-indigenous Australians. When they are employed, they are much more likely than other Australians to be employed by government, and in lower-status jobs. Recent figures show that 18 per cent of Aborigines classified as employed were working full- or part-time in a Commonwealth Development Employment Projects (CDEP) scheme. This scheme allows Aboriginal communities to collect social security benefits as a lump sum and use the funds to provide employment for otherwise unemployed indigenous people. It is a kind of Aboriginal 'work for the dole' scheme which provides very low wages (Altman and Hunter, 2003).

Though they constitute only about 2 per cent of the Australian population, since the late 1990s indigenous people have constituted about 20 per cent of Australia's prison population. Aborigines live for about 20 years less than the rest of the population, and do much worse on most measures for health. Their housing is generally of a lower standard and is more crowded. Levels of poverty are much higher for Aborigines than they are for other Australians. Though there have been improvements in the last two decades, Aboriginal retention rates at secondary school are worse, with far fewer Aborigines completing the final year of schooling. As would be expected from school completion rates, Aborigines are under-represented in tertiary institutions. This also impacts adversely upon employment (Altman and Hunter, 2003; Human Rights and Equal Opportunity Commission, 2004).

The forums of 'bridging social capital' mentioned above have not translated into widespread everyday civic engagement between settler and indigenous Australians. For some settler Australians – especially those who understate the level of prejudice experienced by Aborigines – this claim will be controversial, but for many Aborigines it is accepted as a common-sense explanation of the current state of affairs. This is not to say that indigenous peoples are completely separated from mainstream society. As Australian citizens they do participate in the wider society, through everyday interactions, neighbourliness and work, through schools and higher education, through sporting and other associations and even through family relationships that mix indigenous and non-indigenous people. Some of this participation is, however, quite recent and plays against memories of exclusion of a profound degree. In the late 1960s, when Charles Perkins led the 'Freedom Rides' through rural New South Wales, local townspeople openly discriminated against Aboriginal people and kept them out of certain public spaces (Curthoys, 2002). These practices have continued in parts of Australia, despite being illegal. Some people I have interviewed for a recent project[4] spoke of the continuing separation of Aborigines from the white community in the rural towns of New South Wales, the Northern Territory and Queensland, where informal, and sometimes formal, segregation still occurs. Aboriginal people often speak of their wariness whenever they interact with mainstream society and with non-Aboriginal people. Trust of non-Aboriginal individuals is often achieved through hard work on both sides, and through the careful dismantling of initial suspicion.

The level of separation and alienation varies, of course, in many different locations across Australia. On the one hand there are small outback Aboriginal communities that arose from old government stations, missions and reserves, and from the outstation movement of the early 1970s. With the exception of non-Aboriginal service providers and professionals, and government and department officials, including police, with whom they are in more regular contact, and local and international tourists, these communities are isolated from mainstream society. In some remote communities, where Aborigines still speak traditional languages, English might be the second or even third language, adding another barrier to interaction with outsiders. This separation from mainstream Australia is not necessarily a bad thing from the perspective of indigenous people. Although it might mean that such groups are suspicious and distrusting of outsiders, and especially white Australians, they might at the same time experience strong bonds of trust within their own communities (Hunter, 2000). On the other hand, Aborigines living in more closely settled areas like towns and cities live in the same physical space as non-Aboriginal Australians, and experience varying levels of interaction with non-Aboriginal people. Intense, everyday experiences of living together in urban environments can help build trusting relationships. Mark Peel (2003), in a qualitative study of poor communities in three of Australia's capital cities – Mount Druitt in Sydney, Broadmeadows in Melbourne and Inala in Brisbane – has reflected on forms of everyday solidarity between indigenous people and others in the ethnically diverse communities of such places. Mount Druitt and Inala have large and long-standing Aboriginal communities, while Broadmeadows has a small Aboriginal community. In each of these disadvantaged suburbs, common local experiences sometimes overcome the racial divide. As one of Peel's Aboriginal respondents commented: 'When you're here, it's not being Aboriginal that matters all the time. It's where you are, you know, on the ladder. It's not just about being Black' (Peel, 2003: 92). Common experiences of poverty and negative experiences with government agencies make for levels of solidarity that reach beyond racial boundaries. Though people recognise differences, complain about the different levels of funding and service provision that ethnically defined groups receive, and partake of casual forms of racism, Peel argues that all of this goes on in the context of many far more positive everyday interactions. Expressions of intolerance were nearly always abstract, and contrasted with far more positive descriptions of concrete interactions with Aboriginal and migrant neighbors and friends (Peel, 2003: 152). In these diverse, struggling communities, Peel argues, multiculturalism and reconciliation between Aborigine and non-Aborigine is a creative lived experience.

Nevertheless, settler Australians from cities frequently comment that they have never met, or have hardly ever met, Aboriginal people. Andrew, a senior public servant who had had some past dealings with Aborigines when he lived and worked in a rural area, was asked about Aboriginal issues in a recent interview. He suggested that his life in Melbourne was now far removed from interaction with Aboriginal people:

> *How do you describe the relationship between Aborigines and the rest of Australian society at the moment?*
> Probably fairly dysfunctional. I don't know. Part of the reality is that there's just not that much interaction. There simply isn't much interaction outside what you perceive from the media. And there's a lot of negative stereotypes in the media. But if you say do I have much to do with Aboriginals, the simple answer is no.

As noted earlier, Aborigines represent only about 2 per cent of the Australian population (Australian Bureau of Statistics, 2003). While it is true that a third of Aborigines live in Australia's capital cities, the rest live in rural and regional towns (Birrell and Hirst, 2002). They are thus less urbanised than other Australians. Also, Aboriginal populations in cities tend to be concentrated in poorer areas, like those cited in Peel's (2003) study. These demographic characteristics help explain why people from cities, like Andrew, make such comments. Non-Aboriginal people in rural areas of Australia are more likely to come into contact with Aborigines in the course of their ordinary daily life. On the other hand, this does not mean that Aborigines are fully integrated into mainstream society in rural areas – social if not physical separation can also be a pervasive feature of such areas (Cowlishaw, 1988, 2004), and even in towns with relatively large Aboriginal populations non-Aboriginal people will frequently comment that they have little social contact with Aborigines, or that they have no Aboriginal friends.[5] Sandra, a librarian in a Victorian country town with a significant Aboriginal population, spoke of the processes of separation between local whites and Aborigines. A large part of the distrust and separation between the two groups she put down to government policies that she felt favoured Aborigines in certain ways, and to fears of Aboriginal crime and violence linked to the perception that Aborigines were treated much more leniently by the law. Sandra had grown up in the city but moved to the country as a young adult:

I guess that where you went to school probably didn't have any Aboriginal people?
None at all. And I guess here in town there's more than in a lot of places. But again I don't know many personally. A few that I'd be able to say hello to, but not many. And even my boys didn't have, oh Anthony had one Aboriginal friend, perhaps two. But yeah they tend to stick to their own.
So there is a kind of separation?
Oh, definitely.
A divided sort of society around here?
Yes. There certainly aren't any Aboriginal people in any of the women's groups I'm in or anything like that. There's certainly none in any of those sorts of groups.
So they're not involved in the National Council of Women?
No, no, certainly not. Not in any of those community groups. I mean if they were they'd be out at their own cultural centre. They'd be involved in those sorts of things. You see they've got their own basketball teams and football teams, and they're very much on their own. I remember when Anthony used to play basketball when he was younger, it was always a very rough game when you played the Aboriginal team. Very physical and very good athletes too. They're very good. There's no doubting that. But they're also very rough behind the play and you always come home with bruises and that sort of thing when you played the Aboriginal team. And I don't know that that's a good thing. I mean they obviously thrive on it I suppose and they wear their red, yellow and black uniforms, but again it puts them as separate, as different.

As Sandra suggests, there is at least a perception among settler Australians that Aborigines are treated differently by government, and that sometimes this amounts to preferential treatment. National survey research, both quantitative and qualitative, cites this perception as an issue of concern for settler Australians when they think about Aborigines, Aboriginal communities and the place of Aboriginal individuals and communities in Australian society (Irving Saulwick & Associates, 2000; Newspoll Market research, 2000). Speaking of the same town that Sandra lives in, another interviewee stressed what he believed was a link between forms of positive discrimination and racism towards Aborigines. Mick was a Vietnam veteran who had, like Sandra, moved from the city to the country:

There seems to be a hell of a lot of bad feeling towards Aborigines or the way they're portrayed. Again, I just listen. I've not heard anyone say a positive word about the way the Aborigine's looking after himself. You have Austudy, you have Abstudy.[6] And this in my opinion divides the country and a lot of other people. People in [nearby regional town], the people are so anti-Aborigine because they're better looked after and they feel the Aborigine can go to an ordinary school or an Aborigine school, but we can't go the other way. So therefore there's that split, they're better than us. Or hang on, they're given more than us. And whether it be right or wrong, people are feeling quite bitter about it. See we don't have, here there's very few Aborigines. I've been up to Queensland and people up there just despise them. Hate. You and I can say we like them, but we don't see them.

Mick told stories of seeing drunken Aborigines in places like Townsville in Queensland smashing bottles and engaging in other riotous behaviour. Once when camping he had been frightened of violence from a group of Aborigines camping nearby. Mick felt that Aborigines were allowed to get away with such behaviour, where he or other settler Australians would be penalised by the law. These and other examples of different treatment bred hatred:

And so what's happened is because that division's there, you're building up a hatred. In my opinion if they changed and educated people you could get rid of that hatred. Maybe had them go to the same school. Still have periods of Aborigine study. I say they've got to keep their culture but don't say in the outback where a person goes to a school, they get a plane home. The other person's got to pay. Automatically it splits them. And I think the government says alright, we're doing the right thing by the Aborigines, finish, and I don't think they listen. People I take to Vietnam from Queensland, they just call them coons. They're so disrespectful to them and I say that's not very nice. And then they say oh you don't live with them. And then they start. You think oh God, I didn't know that. And these are people that are good upstanding middle class. Not radicals. Got families ... So the government may think they're doing the right thing but I think they're creating a split. Something's got to be done about it. We don't want any racial tension. We don't want any more and we don't want a big buildup. So there should be, I don't know ... I don't disagree with giving them more money for example to go to university so they can come up and then they've got doctors and all that sort of thing. But when you've got ordinary schools and there's such a split. See [nearby regional town]'s a fairly poor area. You've got a lot of Muslims there, you've got all the different races and the Aborigines have got preference – so automatically! My niece is not really well off. She's fairly poor. She's bitter because they're living in a commission home. They see a house destroyed by Aborigines and they move into another one. If she destroys hers, they'll kick her out. So I think the government, I think they've got their head in the sand to be honest.

These comments from in-depth interviews are suggestive of poor relations between settler and indigenous Australians, and of low levels of social interaction across the racial divide. The qualitative nature of the research, however, prevents one from generalising. One way to explore interactions on a more general level is to examine data on social capital, but even here one encounters difficulties. Unlike the US where the data on social capital are now extensive, the data in Australia were, at least until very recently, scant (Goot, 2002: 32). Writers and researchers have been attending to this in the last few years, including efforts by the Australian Bureau of Statistics (2000) to gather relevant data. General data on Aboriginal civic engagement and relationships with the broader society are thin on the ground. One kind of evidence that some historians and demographers have recently attempted to use as proof of levels of Aboriginal integration into mainstream society are statistics on couples and the composition of households. Birrell and Hirst (2002), for example, make use of the 2001 Census to show that, in metropolitan areas, '87 per cent of metropolitan couples with an Aboriginal member are mixed'. The figure for couples living outside capital cities is lower, at 60 per cent. In the more remote areas, like the Northern Territory outside Darwin, the situation is reversed, with 87 per cent of such couples consisting of two self-identifying Aborigines. Taken as an Australia-wide figure, the 'intermixed couples made up 69 per cent of couples with an Aboriginal member'. Similar figures are produced for the percentage of non-Aboriginal/Aboriginal mixed households. Based on this evidence, Birrell and Hirst claim that Aborigines are thoroughly integrated into mainstream Australian society. In a separate article, Hirst (2001) has argued that this process of intermixing of 'races' will inevitably continue until there will no longer be a distinguishable Aboriginal population, but only a racially mixed people calling themselves Australians. Citing earlier claims of this kind, the anthropologist Gillian Cowlishaw has cautioned against the assumption that such statistics can be read in any obvious way. As she points out, based on her own and other anthropologists' ethnographic work, it is often the case that where a non-Aboriginal person becomes part of an Aboriginal household, they tend to be absorbed into Aboriginal communal relations, rather than the other way around (Cowlishaw, 1995: 57):

The fact that non-Aboriginal members of Aboriginal households have usually been forced to disassociate from their non-Aboriginal relatives and identify with the Aboriginal community shows how essential it is to understand the historical forces which have structured these relationships.

There has been one recent attempt to address the issue of Aboriginal social capital and levels of civic activity – voting, volunteering, participating in cultural events and festivals, and so on – by drawing on data from the Australian Bureau of Statistics' 1994 National Aboriginal and Torres Strait Islander Survey (see Hunter, 2000). Hunter emphasises the deleterious effect of high rates of unemployment on levels of indigenous community activity and its relation to 'proxies' for social capital like criminal arrests, drunkenness and long-term illnesses. Much of this evidence, however, relates to indigenous engagement in specifically indigenous events, organisations and activities, rather than with levels of engagement with wider society. However, if writers like Putnam (2000) are correct in claiming that lower levels of education and higher levels of unemployment correlate strongly with lowered levels of civic participation, then the overall statistics for Aborigines would in themselves suggest lower levels of participation in mainstream society, and as a concomitant of this, lower levels of trust in others. Compounding those effects, Aborigines have more specific reasons to be distrustful of mainstream Australian society, and to harbour a sense of grievance, based on historical and contemporary experiences.

Though quantitative data cannot be marshalled to prove it, many Aboriginal people claim that they feel quite separated and alienated from mainstream Australian society. Though some see such separation as a good thing, in the sense of maintaining their identity and attending to those whose needs are most important, such as kin, there is also a sense of exclusion from mainstream society, sometimes referred to as 'institutional racism'. The stories they tell to back up this feeling involve everyday experiences of prejudice such as being served last in shops or being overlooked, being turned away from hotels when they know that there are rooms available, and difficulties in renting houses from estate agents (see Bourke *et al.*, 1994). Non-indigenous people I have interviewed in rural areas have noted that local service industries will not employ Aborigines in positions that involve direct dealings with the public.

The evidence from at least some polling indicates that Australians recognise that there is a problem with the relationship between settler and Aboriginal Australians. In a survey carried out in the mid-1990s it was reported that 14 per cent of people believed relations between settler and indigenous Australia were 'very poor', 39 per cent felt they were 'quite poor', 43 per cent felt that they were 'fair' and only 2 per cent thought they were 'excellent' (Johnson *et al.*, 1996). In the many hearings and investigations over several years conducted for the Royal Commission into Aboriginal Deaths in Custody, it became apparent to the investigators that there was a serious problem of division between Aboriginal and settler Australia (Commonwealth of Australia, 1991). Other reports have documented extensive experiences of prejudice felt by Aborigines in their interactions in mainstream Australian society, and at least the perception that they have experienced widespread discrimination at both personal and institutional levels.

Building trust through the reconciliation process

For a number of reasons, including recognition that indigenous and settler Australians lived imaginatively and socially separated lives, during the 1990s Australians embarked on a process of reconciliation. This was both a government project, given institutional expression by the Council for Aboriginal Reconciliation, established at the beginning of the 1990s, and a broader public movement, expressed in organisations such as Australians for Native Title and Reconciliation (ANTaR), in local reconciliation groups, in events like the Sea of Hands, and the Journey of Healing, and in the mass marches for reconciliation in 2000–1. This public movement for reconciliation developed during the 1990s, partly in response to challenges thrown up by the Mabo and Wik decisions. Revelations about the 'stolen generation' of Aboriginal children, removed from their parents under state and federal laws, and policies in both the nineteenth and twentieth centuries, added further stimulus to this broader public movement. The idea of a 'stolen generation' had been around since the early 1980s (coined, for example, by Read, 1982), but it was not until 1997 that the federal government published its report on this issue and these policies, titled *Bringing Them Home* (Human Rights and Equal Opportunity Commission, 1997).

Bringing them Home comprehensively dealt with the long period of federal and state policies that resulted in the taking of indigenous children from their parents, and through the testimony of hundreds of indigenous witnesses, gave a strong indication of the devastating consequences of those policies, including maltreatment in the foster homes set up to take 'half-caste' children. The report made a number of allegations, including a carefully explained accusation that previous governments were guilty of acts of genocide in accordance with the accepted United Nations explanation of the concept as spelt out in the Convention on the Prevention and Punishment of the Crime of Genocide (Human Rights and Equal Opportunity Commission, 1997: Part 4). Among the recommendations was a request from indigenous people for governments to apologise to indigenous peoples for past policies and associated abuses, a recommendation of compensation for the living victims of those policies, and a recommendation that the government organise a national 'Sorry Day' in order to atone for past actions and to recognise indigenous suffering. The report provided graphic proof – at least in the eyes of indigenous people – that Aborigines were right to distrust the motives of governments, up to the recent past.

There was a passionate public response to *Bringing Them Home*, which included expressions of sympathy, sorrow, regret and shame, but also expressions of anger and claims that stories were fabricated or exaggerated.

The accusation of genocide was explosive, leading some non-Aboriginal commentators to dismiss the report outright. National Sorry Day became an annual event. During 1998 thousands of Australians signed and wrote comments in 'Sorry Books' made available in churches and public buildings all over Australia.

Some opposed such acts of contrition, arguing that, in taking children away, governments had generally acted with the best interests of indigenous people in mind. While Conservative Prime Minister John Howard made a form of personal apology at the Reconciliation Convention in Melbourne in 1997, he categorically refused on a number of occasions to apologise on behalf of the nation, in his capacity as prime minister, despite repeated requests from indigenous leaders and prominent non-indigenous leaders and public figures. In a response characteristic of his government's established position on the meaning of the *Bringing Them Home* report, Howard was quoted as saying: 'We did ... generations ago, treat our indigenous people appallingly and much remains to be done to achieve a complete reconciliation between various sections of the Australian community.'[7] The use of the qualifying 'generations ago' flew in the face of the report's documentation of very recent serious human rights abuses. In parliament Howard's response involved the same obfuscation, seeming to recognise the depth of abuses one moment then qualifying the character of those abuses the next – a flight from the meaning of national guilt or shame.

Various reasons were given by federal government representatives for refusing to apologise nationally. These included: the argument that it might lead to compensation; that it was not the responsibility of the government of the day to apologise for the actions of past governments, nor was it the responsibility of present generations to feel guilt or to say sorry for the actions of past generations; that the actions of past generations were possibly appropriate and definitely legal, in accordance with previous beliefs, mores and laws; that past generations had acted with good intentions in taking children away, and that, as Senator Herron (the Minister for Aboriginal and Torres Strait Islander Affairs) and other Coalition politicians argued, many Aborigines of today, including several prominent Aborigines, were beneficiaries of those past policies;[8] and that the government could not apologise on behalf of the 40 per cent of the population not born in Australia who, having come to Australia in the last 10–15 years, could have had no influence on these policies.[9]

Despite these rationalisations, many state parliaments, both Labor and Conservative-led, found their way to incorporate apologies via motions and resolutions, seemingly giving the lie to the Howard government's reasoning.[10] The behaviour in the parliament of Howard's Labor counterpart, Kim Beazley, was a stark contrast to Howard's defensive response. Responding to the *Bringing Them Home* report, Beazley openly wept as he read stories of the indigenous children who had been stolen from their parents. Howard chose not to take part in the debate, leaving the main points to be presented by other ministers; left the Chamber as the Opposition began to read out some of the terrible stories from the Report;[11] and then, as in the succeeding months, refused all requests to pass a resolution apologising for past government actions.

The virulent and dismissive response of some settler Australians, including some political leaders, to the Report and its claims revealed a profound distrust of Aboriginal motives and Aboriginal accounts of historical experiences. Some commentators referred to a 'false memory syndrome' which caused informants to the Report to reinvent their personal histories, swayed in part by a sense of grievance and by the encouragement of naïve or politically motivated sympathisers of Aboriginal causes (see Manne, 2001). Others, like the successful company owner Tjaart who we interviewed in 2002, suspected that there were more cynical political operators involved:

> I was at a function recently with Andrew Bolt [a conservative journalist] and I suspect that his politics are right. He gave us a big lecture on why there was no stolen generation. And after his lecture I thought, 'Yeah, that's probably right'. So I think that there are a lot of people who have investments in screwing the system to achieve their own goals, whatever those goals might be.

The 1990s call for 'reconciliation' was underpinned by the recognition that Aborigines remained thoroughly disadvantaged and mistreated in Australian society. It was inspired by the belief and assumption that, in order for the nation to 'move forward', new levels of trust and recognition had to be developed between settler and indigenous Australia. This included a strong emphasis on the need to educate the Australian public about the issues, about the impact of colonial history, and about the ongoing importance of indigenous identities and relationships with lands, waters and other natural resources. The Keating government championed reconciliation, but the high expectations and hopes of both the Council and the broader movement were dampened when Labor was defeated in 1996. The Conservative Howard government which succeeded it was critical of some of the ways that reconciliation discourse had developed, and instituted its own term, 'practical reconciliation'. By this was meant that government would be less concerned with symbolic issues and gestures, and more concerned with remedying Aboriginal disadvantages. In this regard, it is interesting to note that in the period of the Howard government's 'practical reconciliation' there have been no overall improvements in indigenous social indicators, and in some instances the indicators are worse than they were in the period of so-called 'symbolic' reconciliation (Altman and Hunter, 2003). Most recently, the Howard government has begun dismantling the Aboriginal and Torres Strait Islander Commission (ATSIC), an elected body

of indigenous leaders set up in the early 1990s by the federal Labor government. The Howard government has claimed that there needs to be main-
streaming of services to Aboriginal communities, and that the 'separatism'
of self-determination policies has largely failed. Some commentators see in
these developments a return to the assimilation era.

Conclusion

Clearly there is an ongoing problem of distrust between settler and indigenous communities. The extent to which the reconciliation process in the
1990s succeeded in building that trust is an open question. Some indigenous leaders never believed that such a process should be the main emphasis in the politics of settler/indigenous relations, and as the 1990s wore on,
important indigenous voices like Noel Pearson of Cape York argued that
the focus should progress from things like asking the prime minister to say
sorry, or even the broader symbolism of reconciliation. Instead, it should
be placed on dealing with the crisis in Aboriginal communities (drug and
alcohol abuse, physical and sexual violence, etc.), and in finding creative
ways for indigenous communities to raise their socioeconomic profile
through economic development (Pearson, 2004).

Distrust and uncertainty have shaped relations between settler Australians and indigenous people in the past, and continue to do so in the present. Suspicion of the other camp's motives, rooted in the ongoing colonial
relationship, simmers and sometimes boils over. Indigenous peoples have a
sense of grievance about unresolved issues arising from European invasion
and colonisation. While the settler population, and governments, have
engaged in attempts to address some of these issues, I have argued here
that this sense of grievance, among other factors, contributes to the alienation of indigenous people from mainstream society. This means that trust
between settler and indigenous communities, and individuals, is always a
difficult achievement that is threatened by larger historical forces.

Notes

1 The indigenous leader Noel Pearson (1994) argued that the Mabo decision was
   unique in that, unlike the various Land Rights Acts through which governments
   presumed to 'create' rights in land since the common law did not, after Mabo
   governments would have to accept that these rights were 'inherent' (ibid.: 180).
2 See John Short and Scott Emerson 'Wipe out Native Title, says Fischer', *The
   Australian*, 8 February 1997; John Short, 'Howard Toughens Stance on Wik', *The
   Australian*, 15 April 1997.
3 See *Wik Peoples* v. *State of Queensland* (1996) 141 ALR 129. For a very helpful
   overview of the implications of the decision for pastoralists, mining and other
   companies, and for settler/indigenous relations generally, see University of New
   South Wales (1997).

4 'Understanding a Changing Australia: Ordinary People's Politics' Australian Research Council Discovery Grant project (DP0343870203). This project involves over 400 hours of in-depth interviews with more than 80 people in South Eastern Australia. The people quoted later in this chapter are all drawn from this project, and were interviewed between 2002 and 2004.

5 I base this in part on my own observation, and on my research and interviews for the 'Understanding a Changing Australia' research project.

6 Abstudy is a form of government assistance to indigenous students. Austudy is student assistance for the general population.

7 See John Short, Colleen Egan and John Ellicott, '$56m Aboriginal Health Plan Expected to Overshadow Talks', *The Australian*, 12 December 1997.

8 See reports of Herron's comments in *The Weekend Australian*, 5–6 October 1996, pp. 1, 3; 'Herron Remark Draws Criticism', *The Age*, 7 October 1996, A2.

9 See James Woodford, 'Why PM Won't Say Australia Sorry', *Sydney Morning Herald*, 12 December 1997.

10 The parliaments of the Australian Capital Territory, Tasmania, New South Wales, South Australia, Victoria, and Western Australia all made formal apologies to the stolen generations around that time, while the Northern Territory and Queensland parliaments did not.

11 See Laura Tingle, 'Government's Week of Ignominy', *The Age*, 31 May 1997, p. A29.

References

Almond, G. A. and Verba, S. (1963), *The Civic Culture: Political Attitudes and Democracy in Five Nations*, Princeton, NJ: Princeton University Press.

Altman, J. and Hunter, B. (2003), 'Monitoring "Practical Reconciliation": Evidence from the Reconciliation Decade, 1991–2001', www.anu.edu.au/caepr (accessed 25 May 2004).

Attwood, B. (1996), 'Mabo, Australia and the End of History', in B. Attwood (ed.), *In the Age of Mabo*, St Leonards, NSW: Allen & Unwin, pp. 100–16.

—— (2003), *Rights for Aborigines*, Crows Nest, NSW: Allen & Unwin.

Attwood, B., Burrage, W., Burrage, A. and Stokie, E. (1994), *A Life Together, A Life Apart*, Melbourne: Melbourne University Press.

Australian Bureau of Statistics (2000), 'Measuring Social Capital: Current Collections and Future Directions', Discussion paper, www.abs.gov.au (accessed 25 May 2004).

—— (2003), *Year Book Australia 2003*, http://www.abs.gov.au (accessed 8 October 2003).

Beckett, J. (1989), 'Aboriginality in a Nation-State: The Australian Case', in Michael C. Howard (ed.), *Ethnicity and Nation-Building in the Pacific*, Tokyo: The United Nations University, pp. 118–35.

Birrell, R. and Hirst, J. (2002), 'Aboriginal Couples at the 2001 Census', *People and Place* 10(3): 23–8.

Bourke, E., Hollinsworth, D., Holt, L., Jull, P. and Sutherland, J. (1994), *Improving Relationships: Better Relationships between Indigenous Australians and the Wider Community*, Council for Aboriginal Reconciliation Key Issues Paer No 2, Canberra: Australian Government Publishing Service.

Brock, P. (1993), *Black Ghettos: A History of Aboriginal Institutionalisation and Survival*, Cambridge: Cambridge University Press.

Clendinnen, I. (2003), *Dancing With Strangers*, Melbourne: Text.

244   *Anthony Moran*

Commonwealth of Australia (1991), *Royal Commission into Aboriginal Deaths in Custody*, 5 volumes, Canberra: Government Publishing Service.
Cowlishaw, G. (1988), *Black, White or Brindle: Race in Rural Australia*, Sydney: Cambridge University Press.
—— (1995), 'Did the Earth Move For You? The anti-Mabo Debate', *The Australian Journal of Anthropology*, 6(1 & 2): 43–63.
—— (2004), *Black Fellas, White Fellas and the Hidden Injuries of Race*, Oxford: Blackwell.
Curthoys, A. (2002), *Freedom Ride: A Freedom Rider Remembers*, Crows Nest, NSW: Allen & Unwin.
Goodall, H. (1996), *Invasion to Embassy: Land in Aboriginal Politics in New South Wales, 1770–1972*, St Leonards, NSW: Allen & Unwin in association with Black Books.
Goot, M. (2002), 'Distrustful, Disenchanted and Disengaged? Public Opinion on Politics, Politicians and the Parties: An Historical Perspective', in D. Burchell and A. Leigh (eds.), *The Prince's New Clothes: Why Do Australians Dislike Their Politicians?*, Sydney: UNSW Press, Ch. 1.
Haebich, A. (2000), *Broken Circles: Fragmenting Indigenous Families 1800–2000*, Fremantle, WA: Fremantle Arts Centre Press.
—— (2002), 'Imagining Assimilation', *Australian Historical Studies*, 118: 61–70.
Hirst, J. (2001), 'Aborigines and Migrants: Diversity and Unity in Multicultural Australia', *Australian Book Review*, February/March: 30–5.
Human Rights and Equal Opportunity Commission (1997), *Bringing Them Home: Report of the National Inquiry into the Separation of Aboriginal and Torres Strait Islander Children from their Families*, (Commissioner: Sir Ronald Wilson), Canberra: Commonwealth of Australia.
—— (2004) 'A Statistical Overview of Aboriginal and Torres Strait Islander Peoples in Australia', www.hreoc.gov.au/social_justice/statistics/index.html (accessed 25 May 2004).
Hunter, B. (2000), 'Social Exclusion, Social Capital, and Indigenous Australians: Measuring the Social Costs of Unemployment', Discussion paper No. 204, Canberra, Centre for Aboriginal Economic Policy Research, www.anu.edu.au/caepr (accessed 25 May 2004).
Irving Saulwick & Associates (2000), *Research into Issues Related to a Document of Reconciliation: A Report Prepared for the Council for Aboriginal Reconciliation*, Canberra: Commonwealth of Australia.
Johnson, Sweeney & Associates (1996), *Unfinished Business: Australians and Reconciliation*, Prepared for the Council for Aboriginal Reconciliation, Canberra: Commonwealth of Australia.
Keane, J. (1998), *Civil Society: Old Images, New Visions*, Cambridge: Polity Press.
Libby, R. T. (1989), *Hawke's Law: the Politics of Mining and Aboriginal Land Rights in Australia*, Nedlands, WA, University of Western Australia Press.
Manne, R. (2001), 'In Denial: The Stolen Generations and the Right', *Quarterly Essay*, Issue 1, Melbourne: Schwartz Publishing.
McGregor, R. (1997), *Imagined Destinies: Aboriginal Australians and the Doomed Race Theory, 1880–1939*, Carlton: Melbourne University Press.
Mitzal, B. A. (1996), *Trust in Modern Societies: the Search for the Bases of Social Order*, Cambridge: Polity Press.
Newspoll Market Research (2000), *Quantitative Research into Issues Relating to a Document of Reconciliation: Summary of Findings*. Prepared for the Council for Aboriginal Reconciliation, Canberra: Commonwealth of Australia.

Pearson, N. (1994), 'From Remnant Title to Social Justice', in M. Goot and T. Rowse (eds), *Make a Better Offer: the Politics of Mabo*, Leichhardt: Pluto Press, pp. 179–84.

—— (2004), *Noel Pearson Priority Papers*, Cape York Partnerships, www.capeyorkpart-nerships.com/noelpearson/index.htm (accessed 30 June 2004).

Peel, M. (2003), *The Lowest Rung: Voices of Australian Poverty*, Cambridge: Cambridge University Press.

Putnam, R. (1993), *Making Democracy Work: Civic Traditions in Modern Italy*, Princeton, NJ: Princeton University Press.

—— (1995), 'Bowling Alone: America's Declining Social Capital', *Journal of Democracy* 6(1): 65–78.

—— (2000) *Bowling Alone: The Collapse and Revival of American Community*, New York: Simon & Schuster.

Read, P. (1982), *The Stolen Generations: The Removal of Aboriginal Children in New South Wales 1883 to 1969*, Sydney: New South Wales Ministry of Aboriginal Affairs, Occasional Paper No. 2.

—— (1988), *A Hundred Years War: the Wiradjuri People and the State*, Sydney: Australian University Press.

—— (1990), 'Cheeky, Insolent and anti-White: The Split in the Federal Council for the Advancement of Aboriginal and Torres Strait Islanders – Easter 1970', *Australian Journal of Politics and History* 36(1): 73–83.

Skocpol, T. (1996) 'Unravelling from Above', *The American Prospect*, 25, March-April: 20–5.

Tench, W. ([1789] 1996), *1788, Comprising A Narrative of the Expedition to Botany Bay and A Complete Account of the Settlement at Port Jackson*, edited and introduced by Tim Flannery, Melbourne: Text.

University of New South Wales (1997), *University of New South Wales Law Journal* 3(2).

Varshney, A. (2001) 'Ethnic Conflict and Civil Society: India and Beyond', *World Politics* 53(3), April: 362–98.

13
Pan's People? Pagan Magic, Uncertainty and Embodied Desire

Dave Green

Understanding that the erotic is energy opens up the potential for an erotic relationship with the earth. We can love nature, not just aesthetically, but carnally, with our meat, our bones. That sort of love threatens all the properties of estranged culture. Love that mirrors the wildness of nature can move us into the struggle to protect her, and can give us the deep strength we need ... To recognise that the erotic is energy is to restore eros to the whole body, to escape its limitations to a few narrow zones of pleasure. The whole body becomes an organ of delight, with it we can respond with pleasure to the vast beauty of the living world.

(Starhawk, 1990: 143)

Set against the threatened ecological backdrop of Ulrich Beck's *Risk Society* (1992), there has been a dramatic upsurge in numbers of self-proclaimed nature religions in the West (Albanese, 1990, 2002; Pearson *et al.*, 1998). These heterodox spiritual movements venerate nature as the locus of life, divinity and magic. Invoking Gaian sensibilities and attempting to transcend anthropocentrism, they seek to locate humanity within a sacred and interdependent, though endangered, global eco-system (for example, Pearson *et al.*, 1998). Contrary to theses of *radical de-traditionalisation* (see Heelas *et al.*, 1996: 3–7), the spiritual expression of these religions is marked by a return to the symbolism of pre-modern myth, often couched within the Dionysian practices of pre-modern indigenous earth spiritualities, and an emphasis on the sensual. Indeed, Catherine Albanese (1990) traces the roots of contemporary nature religions to the colonial meeting of Protestant settlers and indigenous cultures in North America and the settlers' attempts to make sense of these nature venerating cultures. She, therefore, sees two distinct strands within the Western experience of contemporary nature religiosity: First, indigenous peoples who wish to reclaim their indigenous animistic practices, in doing so politicising and universalising their struggles as critique of modern excess – indeed of late modernity's relationship to risk.

Second, New Agers who seek to make nature transcendental in their identifications with indigenous landscapes and spiritualities.

Contemporary Pagan movements are interesting in this respect as they liminally straddle the boundaries of these various indigenous and New Age identifications with nature. Some see the Pagan veneration of nature as akin to New Age transcendentalism (Hanegraaf, 1996: 77–93), while others view them as valid revivals of indigenous spiritual traditions, for example, Celticity (Hutton, 2003; also Bowman, 1996). The difficulty in placing Paganisms into a discrete religional category within nature religions partly rests on the fact that Paganisms tend to be *panentheistic*. That is, while they have sought to make nature a transcendent and divine signifier, they also see both nature and divinity as immanently located within the human body and psyche (Carpenter, 1996). Although this commitment to simultaneous immanence and transcendence is often viewed as a paradoxical and postmodern form of spiritual expression (for example, Griffin, 1990; Spretnak, 1991), it is, in fact, a uniquely modern artefact that is bound up with the exigencies and uncertainties of late modern life. Indeed, such paradoxes (immanence and transcendence, individualisation and the search for community, de- and re-traditionalisations), are directly analogous to the ways in which ambivalence and contradictions – social obligations and personal freedoms, hardware and software, the *solid* and the *liquid* – are said to characterise late modernity (Bauman, 2000).

While it is these very complexities that make Pagan magic sociologically interesting, they have also made it problematic for social theory. Magic was a central concern for the founding fathers of sociology, notably Durkheim, Weber and Mauss. Despite periodic efforts to resuscitate it as an object worthy of sociological study (for example, Truzzi, 1971; Tiryakian, 1972; O'Keefe, 1982; Stivers, 2001), magic has progressively been relegated to the position of a narrow specialism within the sociology of religion (itself increasingly marginalised within the sociological mainstream). Furthermore, as argued below, it has been constructed by the majority of sociologists in such a way that it is apprehended to be marginal – at best – to contemporary societal formations and trajectories.

With these points in mind, this chapter attempts to explore contemporary Paganisms through the lens of late modern theory – specifically the works of Ulrich Beck and Anthony Giddens – and particularly through their heuristics of risk, trust, reflexivity and intimacy. Specifically, the embodied desire encountered in sex magic will be used as a case study in order to understand the late modern underpinnings of Pagan esoteric practices, as well as providing a critique of some of its theoretical dogmas, especially its underlying Hegelianism. By doing this I wish to demonstrate that magic is once again worthy of urgent sociological attention.

Magic, modernity and sociology: From Hegel to Weber

A fundamental current in the work of Beck and Giddens is their commitment to social and ontological uncertainties while remaining within a
modern theoretical framework – albeit within new, radicalised forms of
modernity. Counter-intuitively, it is exactly within these radicalised social
formations that Pagan magical practices are flourishing. Indeed, there has
been a recent spate of books suggesting that mimetic magic is fundamental
to the social and technological imperatives of modernity (for example,
Davis, 1999; Stivers, 2001). 'Magic', in its broadest terms, is increasingly a
staple of global pop culture. In order to appreciate the extent to which the
current magical revival – following in the wake of *fin-de-siècle* occultism
and the Aquarian Age of the 1960s (for example, Lachman, 2001)[1] – is a fly
in the ointment of social theory, one must understand the dominant sociological construction of magic as being both primitive and moribund within
modern societies.

Pagan panentheism finds an important analogue in Hegel's works on the
philosophy of religion. His conception of *Geist* in *The Phenomenology of
Spirit* has referents to both the immanent and intangible human spirit and
the transcendent spirit of *der Heilige Geist* (Hegel, 1979). Developing this
notion in his *Lectures on the Philosophy of Religion* of 1827, Hegel postulates
that the study of religion is founded on the synthesis of object and subject,
the divine and the human believer (Hegel, 1988). In elucidating this, he
develops a religional dialectic in which a thesis of magical immanence is
synthesised with an anti-thesis of Judaic transcendent theism. This synthesis, for Hegel, produces modernist, ostensibly Christian, forms of panentheism, which in turn (re)produce modernity and the notional Hegelian state.

Thus, Hegel has a crucial, and often unacknowledged, role to play in the
formation of the dominant sociological discourse concerning magic. Hegel's
dialectical framework not only characterises Paganisms as purely immanen-
tist forms of spirituality, but also constructs them as pre-modern and retro-
gressive. Furthermore, his conception of panentheism is purely Christian,
thereby denying the possibility of a contemporary upsurge in Pagan panentheism. By viewing Christian panentheism as allied to both the Protestant
spirit of progress and processes of modernisation, he effectively orientialises
magical practices *tout court*.[2]

In these senses, Hegel is one of the first in a long line of theorists –
Hume being a potent philosophical precursor – to connote magical thinking purely with immanence and primitivism. Many others have followed
in using magic as an important denominator not only of the primitive
(versus the civilised), but variously of the pre-modern (versus the modern);
nature (versus culture); the irrational (versus the rational); for example,
Tylor, Frazer, Freud, and Levy-Bruhl (see Tambiah, 1991; Styers, 2004). Indeed, shorn of its teleological trimmings, Hegel's progressive and secular

unfolding of *Geist* has significant parallels with the rationalisation processes and *Entzauberung* of Weber.

Magic, uncertainty and late modern theory

Such an orientalisation of magic, however, is a double-edged sword for sociological theory. If it is to be argued that 'magic' – or more specifically, its absence – delineates what is modern, and that modern rationality is an indictment of the shortcomings of primitive magical mentalities, it conversely follows that 'magic' can be used as an evaluative instrument when interrogating theories of modernity. That is, if magic denotes that *which is* and that *which is not* modern, then it can be used as a heuristic device to critique the theorised modernities of Beck and Giddens. This interrogation will first look at the two major theoretical lacunae in their work – their almost teleological commitments to the reduction of ontological uncertainty; and their adherence to the radical de-traditionalisation thesis. These would appear to be problematic in the context of Pagan revivals. I will then explore, in the remainder of the chapter, how late modern theory can be used to understand Pagan magic.

In exploring the first lacuna, the following question needs to be posed: If modernity does indeed literally involve a Weberian 'removing the magic', then why the counter-intuitive revival of Pagan magico-religious practices at a time of increasing existential and environmental risk and ontological insecurity? The initial temptation would be to answer that individuals turn to magic at times of social and existential uncertainty. This is certainly witnessed by the upsurge in Paganism and the occult following the collapse of state socialism in the former Eastern Bloc (for example, Rosenthal, 1997; Shnirelman, 2002). While moral and existential crises are important heuristics in attempting to understand magical revivalism – particularly in the Giddensian sense that such revivals provide individuals with relevant existential frameworks in which to create ontological security and biographical coherence (see Giddens, 1991) – their use as a sole explanatory power is limited (and limiting). Viewing magic merely as an *aegis* against uncertainty not only smacks of those orientalising sociological discourses concerning magic, but, by virtue of the evaluative power of magic, it tends to reduce late modern living to a one-dimensional quest for existential certainty. In doing so, it dismisses the creative and pleasurable possibilities – indeed, the magical possibilities – of risk and uncertainty (Lupton, 1999: 148–72).

Pagans actively seek to ameliorate existential and ontological insecurity through spiritual practice. Counter-intuitively, however – as the example of sex magic below demonstrates – they do this through the use of uncertainty as a personally liberating, rather than an ontologically threatening, force. In particular, they use the uncertainties and instabilities inherent to the uncanniness of the label of 'witch' – and of 'druid', of 'shaman', of 'heathen', etc. – as a form of spiritual transformation. By adopting and interiorising these labels they are actively using uncertainty to change self and psyche (see Eilberg-Schwartz, 1989). Furthermore, the ambivalences and uncertainties of ritual and sacred spaces – Stonehenge being a prime example (Hetherington, 1996; Bender, 1998) – are actively used as conduits for existential transformation. In sum, these transformative uses of the uncertain stand in marked contrast to the foundational need for personal and societal ontological security mooted by Giddens (1990, 1991), and numerous theorists of magic (for example, Durkheim, 1915; Malinowski, 1935).

This procrustean view of uncertainty is not the only problem with late modern theory. The commitment of Beck and Giddens to the radical de-traditionalisation thesis is particularly problematic given the persistence of magical traditions in modernity, especially those Pagans dedicated to the reconstruction of pre-modern religious practices, whatever their authenticity (for example, Bowman, 1996; Kaplan, 1996).

Hermeticism, *eros* and modernity

Beck and Giddens construct their modernities on the shifting ontological sands provided by the absence of tradition. Giddens in particular creates a radical break between premodernity, dominated by traditional authority, and late modernity, dominated by its atomisation into a plurality of expert systems guiding personal existential choice. Indeed, Giddens (1991: 206–7) explicitly dismisses the viability of reconstructionism:

> Today, we see a definite tendency to seek to re-establish vanished traditions or even construct new ones … whether tradition can effectively be recreated in conditions of high modernity is seriously open to doubt. Tradition loses its rationale the more thoroughly reflexivity, coupled to expert systems, penetrates to the core of everyday life. The establishment of 'new traditions' is plainly a contradiction in terms. Yet, these things having been said, a return to sources of moral fixity in day-to-day life, in contrast to the 'always revisable' outlook of modern progressivism, is a phenomenon of some importance. Rather than constituting a regression towards a 'Romantic refusal' of modernity, it may mark an incipient move beyond a world dominated by internally referential systems. (ibid.: 206–7)

Not only does Giddens seriously misunderstand the dynamic nature of traditions (for example, Heelas *et al.*, 1996: 7–11), but he also – by emphasising the uniqueness of the reflexive self to the late modern world – underestimates the extent of self-reflexivity of other eras. To their credit, Beck and Giddens defend this claim by arguing that late modernity presents a more universal form of individualisation than earlier epochs (see, for example, Beck and Beck-Gernsheim, 1995: 8). It is significant, however, that self-reflexivity appears to have its modern roots in Renaissance esotericism (see Yates, 1964; Couliano, 1987).

The Renaissance of the fifteenth and sixteenth centuries is often held to be the golden age of magic. Not only was this an epoch of changing social and intellectual relations – particularly those seen to ease the birth pains of capitalism – but it was also an era when the social and cultural elite had a seemingly insatiable appetite for Hermetic magic and courtly sexual intrigue (Yates, 1964). Indeed, The Renaissance was the period when magic intimately became bound up with eroticism and desire. As I mention below, erotic motivations became an important factor in Renaissance high magical practices, but this was also the era of the witch-hunts where 'witches' – particular women deemed to be revelling in subversive forms of sexuality – were supposed to gain occult empowerment through diabolic sexual relations (see Roper, 1994). As a result, magic has become inextricably bound up with, and often theoretically reduced to, desire – particularly perverse sexual desire (Freud, 2001; also Roheim, 1955), and its regulation (see Styers, 2004; 165–217). Before looking at the role of desire in sex magical practices, it is important to understand the role that *eros* played in Renaissance magic, and its subsequent impact on the construction of occult bodies.

The importance of Hermetic magic, and its attendant Neoplatonic philosophy, within the Renaissance, while undoubted, remains ambiguous. The work of Frances Yates, for example, places the Hermetic thinking of mystics and magicians such as Marsilio Ficino, Pico della Mirandola and Giordano Bruno at the heart of the development of science and, by extension, the nascent modern project (see Yates, 1964, 1967). As Styers (2004: 152) explains:

> In the 1960s Frances Yates elaborated the argument that the Neoplatonic magic and hermetic occultism of the Renaissance played a significant role in the emergence of early modern science. While Yates acknowledged that there were important differences between hermetic magical thought and 'genuine science,' she argued that various strands of hermetic thought served to 'stimulate the will towards genuine science and its operations' by encouraging new attitudes towards the natural world.

Whilst Yates' ideas have many supporters (for example, Easlea, 1980) – as well as detractors (for example, Vickers, 1984) – her thoughts are significant in that the development of contemporary risk, via mechanical philosophical discourse, would seem to have its roots in the occult belief that nature could be manipulated through magical operations (see Cohen, 1994). Indeed, nature 'out there' could be operated on by human will through magical technologies, such as spells and ritual. These operations were revisable experimental procedures with their results recorded, and procedures changed as a result. In this sense, Hermetic magical practices, like the science it was to influence, was founded on self-reflexivity.

In addition to the rise of scientism and scientific expertise, which figure so centrally in the late modernities of Beck and Giddens, Renaissance esotericism also engendered two more strands which come together within Giddensian thought – notions of therapy and intimacy/love. Alchemy was a central component in Renaissance occultism. Jung's famous re-reading of alchemy sees it not as the forerunner of modern chemistry but as a sophisticated predecessor of analytic psychology and psychoanalysis. The exoteric quest to transmute base metals into gold is held to be a cover for the reflexive esoteric – and quasi-therapeutic – quest for individuation. Importantly, Renaissance esoteric thought produces a depth psychology of desire, *of eros*. As Couliano (1987) observes, such magical procedures were scientifically plausible attempts to manipulate not only nature, but also individuals and groups based on a knowledge of motivation, particularly erotic motivation. Indeed, Ficino himself makes the clear equation between eros and magic in his *De Amore* (1484):

> The whole power of Magic is founded on Eros. The way Magic works is to bring things together through their inherent similarity. The parts of this world, like the limbs of the same animal, all depend on Eros, which is one; they relate to each other because of their common nature. Similarly, in our body the brain, the lungs, the heart, liver, and other organs interact, favour each other, inter-communicate and feel reciprocal pain. From this relationship is born Eros, which is common to them all; from this Eros is born their mutual rapprochement, wherein resides true magic. (*De Amore*, VI, 10: 106)

Thus, an important notion within Renaissance magic is mediation (see Faivre, 1994: 10–15). The alchemic and Cabalistic quests ultimately concerned the unification of the microcosm with the macrocosm – the immanent individual spirit with the transcendent cosmic spirit, or Godhead. In order to do this, some form of mediation was required, be it ritual, Eros, or the material – as opposed to the spiritual – body. This tradition has continued into the practice of contemporary nature religions, especially Paganisms, where Renaissance magic is an important spiritual forebear (Hanegraaf, 1996).

Importantly, such forms of mediation act as existential anchors within Pagan practices, simultaneously permitting self-reflexive forms of embodied spiritual exploration – often with uncertain outcomes – while offering a carnal form of ontological security. Giddens in particular tends to stress the importance of psychic coherence at the expense of somatic practices and experimentation (for example, Giddens, 1991). The remainder of this chapter explores how the embodied spiritual practices of Pagans play with uncertainty – for example, by reclaiming and recasting traditional discourses attached to the body of the witch – while simultaneously conforming to late modern theoretical trajectories.

Indeed, having outlined two major theoretical lacunae within late modern theory – and Giddens' project in particular – it is now time to turn attention to the cases where late modern theory appears to have important things to say about modern magical movements.[3]

Intimacy and desire in late modernity

It is significant that both Beck and Giddens have placed desire and intimacy at the heart of their theoretical work, particularly in the wake of the familial breakdowns that striate late modern life (also Bauman, 2003: viii). Giddens (1992), for example, traces the ways in which intimacy has been transformed by modernity. He traces the shifts in which sexual relationships merely reproduced the economic sphere by being bound with production – through the sexual passion of the romantic love developed in the eighteenth century – to late modern forms of intimacy founded on confluence and contingency. The work of Beck and Beck-Gernsheim (1995) mirrors this history, adding that the contingencies of late modern relationships are made ever more fragile by the advent of sexual equality since the 1960s. Indeed, sexual permissiveness only serves to feed the contradictions of late modern relations. Given this, there are arguably two main features of late modern intimacy for Giddens: the advent of *plastic sexuality* and the *pure relationship*. Plastic sexuality 'is decentred sexuality, freed from the needs of reproduction' (Giddens, 1992: 2). The liberational potential of plastic sexuality, for Giddens, is, however, balanced by the frailty of human bonds in a world suffused with risk, uncertainty and contingency (Bauman, 2003). Indeed, human relatedness becomes so frail that the mutuality of romantic love is replaced by *pure relationships* founded on individualisation and marketisation – the ethic of 'we're in love' becomes replaced by an attitude that consistently poses the question 'What's in it for me?' As Giddens (1992: 58) states:

> A pure relationship ... refers to a situation where a social relation is entered into for its own sake, for what can be derived by each person from a sustained association with another; and which is continued only in so far as it is thought by both parties to deliver enough satisfactions for each individual to stay within it ... The pure relationship ... is part of a generic restructuring of intimacy.

A result of this is that it is the perceived quality of the relationship – especially the sexual act – which becomes the central component of intimate relatedness rather than the mutual affective security derived from romantic love. The act of love becomes akin to an act of worship in which the idols are overthrown and relationships terminated if satisfaction does not ensue (Beck and Beck-Gernsheim, 1995: 175). This newfound emphasis on the quality and efficacy of the sexual act – Bauman's 'pure sex' (Bauman, 2003: 50) – rather than the affective ties which bind individuals together post-coitus, is something which has always been central to sex magic practice.

While the sexual act is viewed as sacred and devotional by Pagans, it is discursively bound with carnal enjoyment – 'in the motions of hands, lips, tongue, genitals; in the thrust and arch of bodies' as the feminist witch Starhawk puts it (1990: 136). This is especially the case of Left-Hand magical paths such as Aleister Crowley's *Thelema* and neo-Satanism, which are founded on the reflexively quested divinity of the individual (see Sutcliffe, 1996).[4] In this sense, sexual ecstasy is used, almost shamanistically, as a way of entering the altered states of consciousness necessary for magical workings. That is, the sexual body becomes akin to the Jungian alchemic crucible and its synthesis of the magical elements required for individuation (see, for example, Crowley, 1998).

Before exploring the 'ins and outs' of sex magic, it is important to understand the centrality of the body and embodied practices, within contemporary Paganisms. The body is not only sexualised, but is the locus for ritual practices and central to Pagan forms of relatedness which are all built on *sexualised*, if not *sexual*, intimacy. In particular, one needs an understanding of how the magical body has been constructed within occult practices. Within the ritual context, bodily practices are viewed as magical Foucauldian *technologies of the self* which seek to acknowledge, and ultimately overcome, dualities – particularly polarities of gender; of self and other; of culture and nature, and, of microcosm and macrocosm (see Foucault, 1979, 1987, 1988; also, Smart, 2002: 108–17). Magical bodies become the locus through which ideas of transcendent and immanent spirit meet, melt and merge.

Occult bodies

Fittingly, the pagan eco-activist Adrian Harris (1996: 153) observes:

> In our rituals we reconnect with ourselves, healing the rift between body and mind through ecstatic dance, chanting and the drama of ritualised myth. We lose our ego-centred selves and achieve that somatic knowing of the unity of everything. It is in these moments of spiritual ecstasy that we know the wisdom of the body.

Such anti-Cartesian (as opposed to mind/body dualism) and spiritual views of the body within Paganisms are especially significant because, first, an avowed emphasis on immanent bodily practices is uncommon, if not unknown, within Western theological discourses; and second, throughout history, the dominant corporeal constructions have been occult, even magical. That is, bodies have ubiquitously been attributed with vital, occluded dimensions, normally accompanied by a radical separation between material physical bodies, and immaterial spiritual ones. The notion of The Fall is a central motif within occult constructions of bodies, often accompanied by a contrast between a prelapsarian self of physical and spiritual beauty, and the lapsed mortal and disenchanted body post original sin. As the occult historian B. J. Gibbons argues, Original Sin made humankind conscious of itself as composed of separate selves which is constructed only in opposition to others: the ashamed clothing of Adam and Eve's naked bodies attests to this. In an echo of Giddens, Beck's and Bauman's characterisations of late modern intimacy, 'Selfhood is thus constituted not by its freedom, but by its contingency' (Gibbons, 2001: 56). Thus, as Gibbons states:

> On the one hand, the body is a precondition of 'the category of the person', inextricably bound up with our sense of ourselves. Yet it is through the body that the otherness of the world invades our being. We experience the body both as an integral part of ourselves and as an object somehow 'out there'. (ibid.)

Indeed, it is this relation to alterity which is constitutive of all occult bodies, and Christian bodies, in particular. The Pauline notion of the body – a body constructed out of religious allegory – privileges spirit over the material body. The incorporeality of God was affirmed by Augustine, and this remained the dominant religious construction of the divine body until the Renaissance, when the later Neoplatonists and Spinozists began to conceive God as both constitutive of and coextensive with nature – as *pantheistic*, as opposed to *panentheistic*. By the time of the Renaissance, high magical practices, such as Hermeticism, offered the ritualistic means by which the microcosmic individual could reunite with macrocosmic divinity – methods still employed by contemporary ritual magicians. Thus, through these means the divine inscribed itself on humankind and human bodies. Gibbons (2001: 60), for example, notes how the body itself became a signifier of metaphysical reality.[5]

Despite these constructions of the body as alleged spiritual signifier, Western religious culture, betraying its Judaic roots, is often cited as a central protagonist in the cult of Cartesian bodily estrangement. The Reformation is theorised to be particularly significant in this process. The sociological theorists of the body, Philip Mellor and Chris Shilling, for example, contrast the richness and sensuality of bodily experience – if not corporeal practices – in Catholic countries with the rational, ascetic bodies of Protestant cultures. Centring on the Reformation, and placing these differing attitudes to religious bodies at the centre of the rise of modernity, Mellor and Shilling (1997) reveal how the baroque bodies of modernity are a response to the lack of sensual, corporeal experience. Such a perceived absence has also seen the rise of occult forms of embodied theory in more recent times. Examples which spring to mind are Deleuze and Guattari's 'body without organs' – which has roots in the vitalism of Aristotle, via Renaissance *magia naturalis*, to the vitalism of, for example, Bergson, Nietzsche, Dilthey and Reich – and Freudian readings of embodied selfhood, with its phantasmic roots in the Cabala (See Webb, 1976: 345–416; Gibbons, 2001: 103–11: also Greenwood, 2000: 125–8; Green, 2004).

The body of the witch

A fundamental Pagan antidote to Cartesian bodily estrangement is to construct 'magical' bodies as open to invasion by spirit and sexual and magical desire (Starhawk, 1990: Harris, 1996). Whereas the Cabalistic body was seen to bear a manifest imprint of divinity, the Pagan body is subject to sacred forms of *re-territorialisation*. As noted, the 'traditional' witch figure has become an increasingly important figure within Paganisms, particularly, feminist forms of witchcraft (for example, Salomonsen, 2002). In reclaiming the bodies and the associated somatic discourses of the premodern witch figure, the contemporary pagan witch has also tried to recapture some of the witch's dangerous sex appeal. Diane Purkiss, the author of a study concentrating on cultural constructions of the witch in history, for example, charts the way in which Romanticism sexualised the witch, literally removing the warts, but keeping some of the allure of the female who mythically dares to beg sexual favours from demons and the Devil:

> Meanwhile the Romantic poets had taken up the figure of the witch and transformed her into a muse, the object of a poetic quest fraught with danger and desire. The sexuality which came to be associated with the beautiful sorceress was still an object of fear, but also came to seem alluring because through access to the body of the woman, the poet gained access to not just to wild and untrammelled nature, but also to magical control over nature. (Purkiss, 1996: 35)

In reclaiming and romanticising this *other*, pagan bodies become akin to Deleuze and Guattari's notion of the body without organs – unbounded, rhizomatic, invasive and invaded (see Deleuze and Guattari, 1977, 1988; also Deleuze, 1990). Indeed, this reading of bodies has its counterpart in the witch persecutions – mostly targeted at women – of sixteenth- and seventeenth-century Europe. As Purkiss (1996: 119) states:

> The body in both elite and popular early modern thought was flowing with humours and liquids, resembling a bag full of potentially polluting substances. The idea of the body was shaped by fears that bodies may not be fully confined and kept separate from one another, resulting in problematic contacts and impingements. To the early modern ... one way to understand those impingements was witchcraft.

For Carolyn Merchant, this equation of the female body with chaos and disorder discursively underpinned the witch-hunts, paralleling postmodern feminist perspectives concerning the female sexual body. One can, for example, detect the influence of Cixous and Irigaray in Elisabeth Grosz as she states:

> Can it be in the West ... the female body has been constructed not only as a lack or absence, but with more complexity, as a leaking, uncontrollable, seeping liquid; as formless flow; as viscosity, entrapping, secreting; as lacking not so much or simply the phallus but self-containment – not a cracked or porous vessel, like a leaking ship, but a formlessness that engulfs all form, a disorder that threatens all order? (Grosz, 1994: 203)

Merchant argues for an historical tendency to contrast this rhizomatic somatic disorder of the female body with the ordered regularity of masculine culture. In doing so, she argues that the early moderns began to equate women, and particularly the fecundity of their bodies, with nature. Such equations of the female form with the natural landscape – rightly held by critics as a negative form of essentialism – is a recurring eco-feminist motif which runs through Paganisms and is particularly emphasised within Goddess feminisms (for example, Starhawk, 1989, 1990: 143). Much goddess feminism rests on the myth of matriarchy, the idea that there once existed an era of pre-historic, pre-patriarchal goddess worship expounded by figures as diverse as the Lithuanian archaeologist Marija Gimbutas, J. J. Bachofen, Robert Graves and Aleister Crowley. While this myth is subject to academic contention, its fictive message has proved to be empowering for women wishing to reclaim their selves and their bodies in an era they perceived to be dominated by patriarchy and body fascism (see, for example, Starhawk, 1990). The equation of women and nature is, therefore, central to conceptions of the earth-mother and the crone – Pagan and New Age reconstructions of the positive attributes of female expressivism, and the corporeal wisdom and aesthetics of elderly female bodies, respectively. Within these discourses, it is a short step away from seeing the body as natural – rather than purely as a discursive construct – to perceiving it as sexual (see Harris, 1996).

Sex, magic and paganisms

Although sex and desire within Paganisms are inextricably bound up with dominant occidental perceptions of the early modern witch figure, sex magic has literally intimate links with colonialism and orientalism (Said, 1978). It was through colonial contact that the West first encountered the spiritual, sexual practices of the Tantric *Vama Marga*. In essence, this 'Left Hand Path' is built on five basic principles: 1), that human consciousness can be transformed into divine consciousness through participation in erotic rites; 2), that these rites, particularly those involving sexual congress, exalt the sacred and sexual feminine principle of *Shakti*; 3), that initiates into the *Vama Marga* become adepts through the deliberate violation of social, personal, and sexual taboos; 4), that the path is one of individuation and individualisation, as opposed to the collective rites of orthodox religion; finally, 5) that spiritual liberation is rooted in an appreciation of the material realm with an emphasis on personal and sexual awakening in the here-and-now (see Shreck and Shreck, 2002: 19–22). While these currents, which run through many branches of Hinduism and Buddhism, found occidental counterparts in the notion of sacred prostitution – a current still to be found within Paganisms (Hopman and Bond, 1996: 139–51; Nightingale, 2002: 226) – it was not until the mid-nineteenth century that the West came to understand the spiritual nature of Tantra. The idiosyncratic pornographic writings of Edward Sellon struck a chord with occultists such as P. B. Randolph, who sought to rebel against the restrictions of Victorian sexual norms (Randolph, 1998). Sex magic, particularly some sort of sexual initiation into magical groups and orders, became common currency in the *fin-de-siècle* occult revival. Indeed, its influence can be seen as central components in the ideas of many mystics of that period, for example, Gurdjieff, Rasputin, Maria de Naglowska,[6] through to Aleister Crowley and Gerald Gardner, the father of contemporary Pagan witchcraft (see Shreck and Shreck, 2002: 173–277).

Just as the great mages of the Renaissance synthesised Hermeticism, Neoplatonism and Cabalism, Crowley set about systematising and modernising magic under the auspices of *Thelema* – Crowley's own neo-Nietzschean magical religion, based on the primacy of individual will. Crowley brought occultism further into line with the social, cultural and intellectual imperatives of the early twentieth century by his incorporation of psychology, scientific thought – especially reflexivity and the experimental method – notions of democracy and, in particular, sex and eroticism (and increasingly homosexual sex) into Thelemic magic (for example, Crowley, 1973). This centrality of sex magic to Thelema, particularly its transgressive and antinomian nature – was demonstrated to me recently while attending a symposium on Thelemic magic in London. The following is an extract of my research notes reporting on a sex magic ritual which was enacted in front of several hundred conference participants:

Following the lunch break there was a talk in the main hall by Dr Tuppy Owens from the Sexual Freedom Coalition, discussing the activities of the SFC and the importance of sexual blossoming in what she perceived to be a sexually repressed society. The talk was accompanied by an explicit slide-show. First of all there were pictures of erect penises in extreme close-up, with a particular focus on Mapplethorpe's homoerotic photography. There were also slides depicting fellatio, old erotic engravings depicting sex acts and scenes of sadomasochism. Following the talk, a large, attractive woman with gothic make-up wearing a PVC basque and miniskirt and fishnet stockings mounted the stage and asked for a volunteer from the audience for a demonstration – the nature of which was left undisclosed, but clearly involved some sort of BDSM practice. There was silence, and no one appeared willing to volunteer until someone rose from the front row of the hall. It was a man called G. I had met G. once before at a conference on Paganism hosted by the Pagan Federation. I understand him to be well known on the London Pagan and occult scenes and someone involved in Satanism. My previous acquaintance with him, included him setting his large mutton chop sideburns alight with a disposable lighter – which he then hastily doused with his pint of beer – and so I concluded that he was no stranger to masochism. The self-styled dominatrix explained that she was a Pagan and a witch, who had her own pantheon of 'bitch god-desses'. She explained the role that sadomasochism can have in producing altered states of consciousness, with pain being a common method within shamanic cultures of shifting consciousness into those required for magical efficacy. After leading G. around the stage on a studded collar and lead, she got him to beg for his punishment and then made him bend over the hall's lectern to receive his beating. She bared his buttocks and then he was whipped for about 10 minutes with a variety of implements – a whip, cat o' nine tails, and a cane. It often made for uncomfortable viewing. All the while the dominatrix paced around a flinching, prostrate G. explaining the effect she was after, trying to produce a particular redness and pattern of striations on the buttocks which demonstrated that endorphin production was at its peak. From the grimace of physical pain and sexual ecstasy etched on G's face, he certainly seemed to be enjoying the proceedings.

The Pagan eco-activist Adrian Harris has observed that the wisdom and empowerment gained through the naturalisation of the body is predominantly a form of sexual liberation providing a healing of 'the Aristotelian self/other split which locks us in isolation' (Harris, 1996: 153). For Harris, sexual liberation is intertwined with spiritual liberation, just as orgasmic bliss parallels divine intoxication. Certainly, such healing is often the focus for

Pagan ritualism and the spiritual dimension of sex is obvious within the symbolism and corporeal enactments of pagan ritual.

The sexual imagery of the inter-penetration of grail and lance or cauldron and spear is commonly employed in Wiccan ritual. Sexual rites – usually symbolic, but sometimes involving *coitus* – are common within the initiation rituals of some Pagan traditions, particularly Gardnerian Wicca. Such intimate initiations often represent a Jungian reading of the initiation process with the meeting of heterosexual lovers symbolising the erotic interiorisation of god and goddess, *animus* and *anima*. Similarly, as outlined above, sex magic – the ritualistic spiritual alchemy of two lovers – is common in ceremonial magic traditions, with orgasmic ecstasy used as a method of altering ordinary consciousness. Indeed, there are a plethora of parallels with the alchemic process: The efficacy of heterosexual sex magic is built around the creative tensions of sexual polarity, with the earthing of this tension notionally allowing connection with the divine through the act of sexual communion (see Voigt, 1992: 86). The mingling of alchemic elements is termed the *hieros gamos*, or sacred marriage, and is often depicted in alchemic texts as either the erotic meeting of male (solar) and female (lunar) energies, accompanied by illustrations of heterosexual lovers, or by the figure of the *androgyne* representing the sexual and cosmic harmony of male and female elements. Importantly, the intimate relatedness of sex magic is fragile as it is built on mutual reflexive monitoring of the magical efficacy of the sexual act. If that efficacy is lost – the sexual chemistry is no longer working (Voigt, 1992: 87) – then other partners, or other forms of sex magic, are sought by practitioners.

Given these elemental readings of Pagan ritual sensuality coupled with its status as a nature religion, it is perhaps unsurprising that Pagan sexuality is bound with Dionysian celebration of natural rhythms and seasonal cycles – 'a feeling of unity with the Earth that we have in our gut' (Harris, 1996: 153). Indeed, Pagan sensuality is commonly constructed by practitioners as *chthonic*. That is, as both subterranean and transformative, with the 'earthiness' of such ritualism causing practitioners to cast aside their mundane identities – to die symbolically, to be reborn as sensual beings within a sacred cosmos (Harris, 1996). This notion becomes a powerful rationale for *skyclad* – that is naked – ritual workings prevalent within Gardnerian witchcraft, as the literal shedding of clothes parallels the adoption of magical forms of identity, which consciously transgress roles and norms of everyday existence. An analogy sometimes used in tandem with such transformations is the idea of *ferality*; with the once domesticated returning to the wild – perhaps a return to White's *Wild Man* or Pinkola Estes' *women who run with the wolves* (see White, 1978; Pinkola Estes, 1992).[7] Very much in the spirit of Bataille, the eroticism associated with Pagan ritual is a simultaneous affirmation of life and a recognition of death (Bataille, 1957).

Perfect love and perfect trust

Given these transgressive juxtapositions of, for example, self and other, masculine and feminine, the material and the sacral, and life and death within ritual practice, the bodies of magicians are themselves anomalous, composed of, and often governed by, otherness. Such paradoxes delineate Paganisms, just as they shape wider late modern social formations. Indeed, just as late moderns concurrently quest for individuality and community, a simultaneous search for individual spiritual expression is certainly at the heart of Paganisms.

Any notion of Pagan 'community' requires further qualification. In an important sense, the wider Pagan community is, like Benedict Anderson's national identities, *imagined* (Anderson, 1983). Second, the 'community' itself is a contested sociological construction. On the one hand, community is seen as a traditional and significant form of social solidarity; on the other, it is seen as a repressive remnant of premodernity. Helen Berger (1999: 67) rightly states that in late modernity:

> Both positions have some validity. On the one hand, the growth of expert systems has intruded on the autonomy of individuals and encroached upon small-town life. On the other hand, urbanization has opened up possibilities for individual choice ... communities in traditional societies are a two-edged sword: they are sites of caring as well as pettiness, power struggles, and control of individual behaviour, particularly for those who are different – including homosexuals or members of unorthodox religions, such as Witches.

Importantly, late modern communities do not imply conformity, but rather election. Berger invokes the work of Shane Phelan on lesbian communities as applicable to Pagan communities. Phelan argues that although the lesbian community, like the Pagan community, is diverse, it participates in four major processes which give it the internal consistency of a community (see Phelan, 1995: 87–8):

> First, it provides a place that lesbians can be insulated from hostility to their sexual orientation. Second, it furnishes an escape for lesbians from invisibility in the larger community. Third, it supplies models for creating a lesbian persona, helping entrants interpret (or reinterpret) their lives. Fourth, it furnishes an avenue for political activity. (Berger, 1999: 68)

Thus, for Berger, late modern forms of community furnish collective forms of identification without denying either the agencies or the identities of the individuals involved. In Paganisms these mechanisms are catalysed by ritualism and bound with issues of reflexivity and trust linked to the sensuality of ritual.

Just as ritual sex magic is premised on the notion of pure relatedness, Pagan groups operate on the same reflexively fragile basis, with an ever-present potential for conflict and schism (Reid, 2000). Due to the real dis-crimination some Pagans still face, coupled with the sensual nature of ritual, many Pagans choose to disclose their spiritual identity only within the confines of the magical group. Thus, magical communities are suffused with risks and uncertainties concerning disclosure, as well as spiritual possi-bility. Trust – and the intimacy which accompanies secrecy – becomes an important by-product of the sensuality of Pagan ritual. Indeed, the trust engendered through such sensuality acts as a powerful integrative force within magical groups as it forces members into bonds of mutual trust con-cerning the non-disclosure of sensitive information, especially concerning skyclad working or rituals of a sexual nature, outside of the context of the group.

Conclusions: rabbits out of hats

Late modern theory is undoubtedly an important way of exploring, con-figuring and understanding contemporary magical movements. Notions of risk, trust, reflexivity and intimacy structure Pagan practices, bodily con-structions and relations in fundamental ways. Conversely, as argued above, the roles that uncertainty and radical de-traditionalisation play in the work of Beck and Giddens are important theoretical lacunae when it comes to understanding the sociological significance of the current magical revival. This is because their treatment of uncertainty and tradition rests on a new Hegelianism. I demonstrated how Hegel's religional dialectic constructs magic as marginal. In a similar way, embodied magical selves sit uncom-fortably with the late modern *telos* of ontologically secure selfhood. To explain, I wish to begin with Giddens' perverse perspective on religious tra-ditions in his post-traditional society.[8]

Giddens claims that late modernity is a perfect vehicle for religious tradi-tions as they provide ontological security in an uncertain world – they provide, to paraphrase Peter Berger, *sacred canopies* (Berger, 1967). This appears paradoxical when set against Giddens' simultaneous claims about the death of tradition. Indeed, for Beckford (1996), this paradox is under-pinned by Giddens' use of untestable claims about the existential needs of late modern individuals. That is, Beckford is critical of Giddens' underly-ing functionalism concerning the perceived unmet moral and existential needs of individuals.[9] Beckford observes that:

> the repressed morality asserts itself. This 'volcanic' or emergent vision of moral agency is inadequate insofar as it runs the risk of implying that

the real moral agent is pre-or even non-social. It is difficult to avoid the suspicion that the 'return of the repressed' is a rabbit pulled out of a hat when all other tricks have failed to make sense of the persistence of religion at a time when, according to the theory of high [late] modernity, religion's chances of survival are extremely slim. (Beckford, 1996: 36–7)

Furthermore, Giddens in particular weds notions of ontological security to psychic integrity. The Giddensian self reflexively monitors its world and seeks holism. Thus, the Giddensian self is a therapeutic self, part of a 'therapy culture' obsessed with problems of individual need and difference but increasingly blind to the imperatives of social structure (Furedi, 2003). In this profound sense, late modern theory is *unsociological*. This raises two further related problems.

First, for all of Giddens' discussions of new forms of individual agency in post-traditional society, late modern selves only appear to have an illusory form of agency within his late modernity.[10] While the absence of tradition proliferates existential choice for Giddens, these choices are dictated by his meta-narrative of self-consistency. That is, the radicalisation of modernity by Beck and Giddens rests firmly on a reworked Hegelianism. Their *telos* is disembedded from the social structure and re-embedded within the individual sphere. That is, the *telos* of late modernity is not concerned with utopianism, but rather with the integrity of the self. The risks and uncertainties of de-traditionalisation are thought to threaten individual integrity. That is, 'tradition' and 'uncertainty' – both reified by Giddens, in particular – become 'bads' within late modernity, which must be overcome for the 'good' of the self. Paganisms demonstrate the perversity of this claim. As outlined above, through magical ritual, Paganisms point to ways in which uncertainty and tradition become modes of individual liberation.

Second, just as social structure appears to be squeezed from late modernity, the body is also excluded from the late modern self, to the extent that it appears almost disembodied. Lash and Urry, for example, contend that late modern theory has a tendency to exclude the aesthetic and habitual dimensions of existence to the extent that 'the subject is an entity that reflexively controls bodies rather than something which itself is bodily' (Lash and Urry, 1994: 32). Sex magic practices within Paganisms not only demonstrate the aesthetic and habitual dimensions of embodied ritual practice, but also the existential importance of somatic knowledge (see Harris, 1996). Given this, late modern theory needs to revise its Cartesian, reductionist approach to the self. It needs to begin to accommodate cognitions and bodily practices which are rhizomatic – akin to the body of the witch–as opposed to cognitions and affective states which strive for coherence and consistency.

Clearly, embodied magical selfhood – invaded by alterity and uncertainty and shaped by spiritual traditions – is not congruent with the procrustean

selves of Beck and Giddens. In other respects, however, their *oeuvre* possesses
a heuristic power which illuminates Paganisms: risk, reflexivity, trust and
the fragility of intimacy are all powerful ways through which one can begin
to comprehend Pagan practices. In particular, one begins to grasp the ritualistic centrality of the body, sensuality and 'sex' (in its broadest meaning).
Indeed, the heuristic and evaluative power of contemporary magic demonstrates that, while late modern theory captures the ambivalent nature of
contemporary life with profane elegance – its joys, freedoms and beauties, as
well as its risks, uncertainties and crises – late modern theory requires fundamental revision to accommodate the transformative possibilities of the
sacred. Sociologists can accomplish this only by rethinking its underlying
Hegelianism.

Notes

1   Throughout this chapter I will be using the term 'occult' as a general term to
refer to knowledge that has been somehow occluded from dominant discourses
of modern knowledge. Such occult knowledge may be arcane, such as Goethean
science, but is not necessarily magical, in the sense that it cannot be used for
purposes of immediate spiritual transformation. Occultism, on the other hand,
is used specifically to refer to a constellation of magical practices in which occult
knowledge has been subjected to modernist re-interpretations for the purposes
of effecting spiritual transformation. Aleister Crowley's *Thelema* is a prime
example of an occultist movement which incorporates science and psychology
into its magical portfolio.
2   Contemporary Pagan magic is still subject to orientalist attitudes despite being
occidental and modernist in orientation. I will argue that Beck and Giddens
both contain an underlying Hegelianism which is problematic when trying to
understand contemporary selfhood, especially the embodied magical self.
3   I shall return to these lacunae in the concluding section.
4   Left Hand Path magic is based on a spiritual neo-Nietzscheanism where magical
practices – often highly sexualised as in Tantra – reveal the inner divinity of the
individual, often by the realisation of a divine self – for example, *Thelema's Holy
Guardian Angel*.
5   This was particularly true of the Cabala, the Ancient Jewish spiritual road-map of
ascension to and unison with the Godhead based on the symbolism of the tree of
life and the ten spheres, or sephirah, of creation, insight and affect. Indeed, an early
Cabalist work, *The Bahir*, argues that the ten fingers are a corporeal representation of the sephirah. The body as a whole is also said to be a representation of the
Torah with the 248 positive commandments of the Pentateuch reflected in the
248 members of humanity, and the 365 negative commandments in the body's
365 major blood vessels (see, for example, Gibbons, 2001: 60; Atzmon, 2003).
6   Interestingly, de Naglowska was said to be a key influence on the surreal sociology of Georges Bataille, and on the Traditionalist political philosophy of Julius
Evola, who was also a lover of de Naglowska (see Bataille, 1957; Evola, 1983,
1992).
7   There is an important analogue here with Deleuze and Guattari's notion of
becoming-animal (Deleuze and Guattari, 1988).

8   While my critique of late modernity rests on an evaluation of Giddens, Elliott (2002) has made a number of parallel criticisms of Beck.

9   This neo-Durkheimianism was to become a central plank of Giddens' Third Way and points to the problems with Giddens' late modernity, particularly his dogmatic stances on uncertainty and tradition (for example, Giddens, 2000; also, Levitas, 1998).

10 Giddens' *oeuvre* rests on an idea of *structuration*. This is Giddens' laudable aim to create a sociology that pays simultaneous attention to micro- and macro-levels of social reality, particularly the ways in which these interact to produce social formations. His conception of late modern life, however, appears to fall between the stools of agency and structure. Instead, he produces a sociology where social structure is as absent as the traditions that once defined it; and an agency which is, on one hand, without limit and, on the other, always limited by the needy self.

References

Albanese, C.L. (1990), *Nature Religion in America*, Chicago: Chicago University Press.
—— (2002), *Reconsidering Nature Religion*, New York: Continuum.
Anderson, B. (1983), *Imagined Communities*, London: Verso.
Atzmon, L. (2003), 'A Visual Analysis of Anthropomorphism in the Kabbalah: Dissecting the Hebrew Alphabet and Sephirotic Diagram', *Visual Communication*. 2(1): 97–114.
Bataille, G. (1957), *Eroticism*, London: Marion Boyars.
Bauman, Z. (2000), *Liquid Modernity*, Cambridge: Polity Press.
—— (2003), *Liquid Love*, Cambridge: Polity Press.
Beck, U. ([1986] 1992), *Risk Society: Towards a New Modernity*, London: Sage.
Beck, U. and Beck-Gernsheim, E. (1995), *The Normal Chaos of Love*, Cambridge: Polity Press.
Beckford, J. A. (1996), 'Postmodernity, High Modernity and New Modernity: Three Concepts in Search of Religion', in K. Flanagan and P. Jupp (eds.), *Postmodernity, Sociology and Religion*, London: Macmillan, pp. 30–47.
Bender, B. (1998), *Stonehenge: Making Space*, Oxford: Berg.
Berger, H. A. (1999), *A Community of Witches*. Columbia, SC: University of South Carolina Press.
Berger, P. L. (1967), *The Sacred Canopy: Elements of a Sociological Theory of Religion*, New York: Doubleday.
Bowman, M. (1996), 'Cardiac Celts: Images of the Celts in Paganism', in G. Harvey and C. Hardman (eds.), *Paganism Today*, London: Thorsons, pp. 242–51.
Carpenter, D. D. (1996), 'Emergent Nature Spirituality: An Examination of the Major Spiritual Contours of the Contemporary Pagan Worldview', in J. R. Lewis (ed.), *Magical Religion and Modern Witchcraft*, Albany, NY: SUNY Press, pp. 35–72.
Cohen, H. F. (1994), *The Scientific Revolution: A Historiographic Inquiry*, Chicago: Chicago University Press.
Couliano, I. P. (1987), *Eros and Magic in the Renaissance*, Chicago: Chicago University Press.
Crowley, A. (1973), *Magick*, ed. J. Symonds and K. Grant, London: Routledge & Kegan Paul.
Crowley, V. (1998), *Jungian Spirituality*, London: Thorsons.
Davis, E (1999), *Techgnosis: Myth, Magic and Mysticism in the Age of Information*, London: Serpent's Tail.

Deleuze, G. ([1969] 1990), *The Logic of Sense*, London: Athlone.
Deleuze, G. and Guattari, F. ([1972] 1977), *Anti-Oedipus: Capitalism and Schizophrenia*, Minneapolis: Minnesota University Press.
—— ([1980] 1988), *A Thousand Plateaus: Capitalism and Schizophrenia*, London: Athlone.
Durkheim, E. (1915), *The Elementary Forms of the Religious Life*, London: Allen & Unwin.
Easlea, B. (1980), *Witch-Hunting, Magic and The New Philosophy*, Brighton: The Harvester Press.
Eilberg-Schwartz, H. (1989), 'Witches of the West: Neopaganism and Goddess Worship as Enlightenment Religions', *Journal of Feminist Studies in Religion* 5(1): 77–95.
Elliott, A. (2002), 'Beck's Sociology of Risk', *Sociology* 36(2): 293–316.
Evola, J. (1983), *The Metaphysics of Sex*, New York: Inner Traditions.
—— (1992), *The Yoga of Power*. Rochester, VT: Inner Traditions International.
Faivre, A. (1994), *Access to Western Esotericism*, Albany, NY: SUNY Press.
Ficino, M. (1484), *De Amore*.
Foucault, M. (1979), *The History of Sexuality, Vol. 1: An Introduction*, London: Penguin.
—— (1987) *The History of Sexuality, Vol. 2: The Use of Pleasure*, London: Penguin.
—— (1988) *The History of Sexuality, Vol. 3: The Care of the Self*, London: Penguin.
Freud, S. (2001), *Totemism and Taboo*, London: Routledge.
Furedi, F. (2003), *Therapy Culture*, London: Routledge.
Gibbons, B. J. (2001), *Spirituality and the Occult: From the Renaissance to the Modern Age*, London: Routledge.
Giddens, A. (1990), *The Consequences of Modernity*, Cambridge: Polity Press.
—— (1991), *Modernity and Self-Identity*, Cambridge: Polity Press.
—— (1992), *The Transformation of Intimacy*, Cambridge: Polity Press.
—— (2000), *The Third Way and its Critics*. Cambridge: Polity Press.
Green, D. A. (2004), 'Wishful Thinking? Notes towards a Psychoanalytic Sociology of Pagan Magic', *Journal for the Academic Study of Magic*, 2: 48–78.
Greenwood, S. (2000), *Magic, Witchcraft and the Otherworld: An Anthropology*, London: Berg.
Griffin, D. R. (1990), 'Introduction: Sacred Interconnections', in D. R. Griffin (ed.), *Sacred Interconnections*. Albany, NY: SUNY Press.
Grosz, E. (1994), *Volatile Bodies: Toward a Corporeal Feminism*, Bloomington: Indiana University Press.
Hanegraaf, W. (1996), *New Age and Western Culture*, Leiden: Brill.
Harris, A. (1996), 'Sacred Ecology', in G. Harvey and C. Hardman (eds.), *Paganism Today*, London: Thorsons, pp. 149–56.
Heelas, P. (1996), 'Introduction: Detraditionalization and its Rivals', in P. Heelas, S. Lash and P. Morris (eds.), *Detraditionalization*. Oxford: Blackwell, pp. 1–20.
Hegel, G. W. F. (1979), *The Phenomenology of Spirit*. Oxford: Oxford University Press.
—— (1988) *Lectures on the Philosophy of Religion: The Lectures of 1827*. Berkeley: University of California Press.
Hetherington, K. (1996), 'Identity Formation, Space and Social Centrality', *Theory, Culture & Society*, 13(4): 33–52.
Hopman, E. E. and Bond, L. (1996), *People of the Earth: The New Pagans Speak Out*, Rochester, VT: Destiny.
Hutton, R. (2003), *Witches, Druids and King Arthur*, London: Hambledon and London.

Kaplan, J. (1996), 'The Reconstruction of the Asatru and Odinist Traditions', in J. R. Lewis (ed.), *Magical Religion and Modern Witchcraft*. Albany, NY: SUNY Press, pp. 193–236.

Lachman, G. V. (2001), *Turn off Your Mind*. London: Sidgwick and Jackson.

Lash, S. and Urry, J. (1994), *Economies of Signs and Space*, London: Sage.

Levitas, R. (1998), *The Inclusive Society?* Basingstoke: Palgrave Macmillan.

Lupton, D. (1999), *Risk*, London: Routledge.

Malinowski, B. (1935), *Coral Gardens and their Magic*, London: George Allen & Unwin.

Mellor, P. A. and Shilling, C. (1997), *Re-forming the Body: Religion, Community and Modernity*, London: Sage.

Nightingale, M. (2002), 'Ritual, Sex, and Neo-Paganism', in S. Rabinovitch and J. Lewis (eds.), *The Encyclopedia of Modern Witchcraft and Neo-Paganism*, New York: The Citadel Press, pp. 224–8.

O'Keefe, D. L. (1982), *Stolen Lightning: The Social Theory of Magic*, New York: Continuum.

Pearson, J., Roberts, R. H. and Samuel, G. (eds.), *Nature Religion Today: Paganism in the Modern World*, Edinburgh: Edinburgh University Press, pp. 45–56.

Phelan, S. (1995), *Getting Specific: Postmodern Lesbian Politics*, St. Paul, MN: University of Minnesota Press.

Pinkola Estes, C. (1992), *Women Who Run with the Wolves*, London: Rider.

Purkiss, D. (1996), *The Witch in History*, London: Routledge.

Randolph, P. B. (1988) *Sexual Magic*, New York: Magical Childe.

Reid, S. (2000), 'Witch Wars: Factors Contributing to Conflict in Pagan Communities', www.uscolo.edu/natrel/pom/backisues.html.

Roheim, G. (1955), *Magic and Schizophrenia*, New York: International Universities Press.

Roper, L. (1994), *Oedipus and the Devil*, London: Routledge.

Rosenthal, B. G. (ed.) (1997), *The Occult in Russian and Soviet Culture*. Ithaca, NY: Cornell University Press.

Said, E. (1978), *Orientalism*, Harmondsworth: Penguin.

Salomonsen, J. (2002), *Enchanted Feminism: the Reclaiming Witches of San Francisco*, London: Routledge.

Shnirelman, V. A. (2002), '"Christians! Go Home": A Revival of Neo-Paganism between the Baltic Sea and Transcaucasia (an Overview)', *Journal of Contemporary Religion* 17(2): 197–211.

Shreck, N. and Shreck, S. (2002), *Demons of the Flesh*, New York: Creation Books.

Smart, B. (2002), *Michel Foucault*, London: Routledge.

Spretnak, C. (1991), *States of Grace: The Recovery of Meaning in the Postmodern Age*, San Francisco: HarperCollins.

Starhawk (1989), *The Spiral Dance*. San Francisco: Harper.

—— (1990), *Dreaming the Dark: Magic, Sex and Politics*, Boston: Beacon.

Stivers, R. (2001), *Technology as Magic: The Triumph of the Irrational*, New York: Continuum.

Styers, R. (2004), *Making Magic*, Oxford: Oxford University Press.

Sutcliffe, R. (1996), 'Left-Hand Path Ritual Magick: an Historical and Philosophical Overview', in G. Harvey and C. Hardman (eds.), *Paganism Today*, London: Thorsons, pp. 109–37.

Tambiah, S. J. (1991), *Magic, Science, Religion and the Scope of Rationality*, Cambridge: Cambridge University Press.

Tiryakian, E. A. (1972) 'Toward the Sociology of Esoteric Culture', *American Journal of Sociology*, 78: 491–512.

Truzzi, M. (1971), 'Definition and Dimensions of the Occult: Towards a Sociological Perspective', *Journal of Popular Culture*, 5(3): 635–46.

Vickers, B. (ed.) (1984), *Occult and Scientific Mentalities in the Renaissance*, Cambridge: Cambridge University Press.

Voigt, V. (1992), 'Sex Magic', in C. S. Clifton (ed.), *Witchcraft Today, Book One: The Modern Craft Movement*, St. Paul, MN: Llewellyn Publications, pp. 85–108.

Webb, J. (1976), *The Occult Establishment*. La Salle, Ill.: Open Court Publishing Company.

White, H. (1978), *Tropics of Discourse: Essays in Cultural Criticism*, Baltimore: Johns Hopkins University Press.

Yates, F. (1964), *Giordano Bruno and the Hermetic Tradition*, London: Routledge & Kegan Paul.

—— (1967), 'The Hermetic Tradition in Renaissance Science', in C. S. Singleton (ed.), *Art, Science and History and the Renaissance*, Baltimore: Johns Hopkins University Press, pp. 255–74.

Index